THE

ELECTRA

OF

SOPHOCLES

THE

ELECTRA

OF

SOPHOCLES

WITH A COMMENTARY
ABRIDGED FROM THE LARGER EDITION

OF

Sir RICHARD C. JEBB, Litt.D.

BY

GILBERT A. DAVIES, M.A.

CAMBRIDGE
AT THE UNIVERSITY PRESS
1967

CAMBRIDGE
UNIVERSITY PRESS

University Printing House, Cambridge CB2 8BS, United Kingdom

Cambridge University Press is part of the University of Cambridge.

It furthers the University's mission by disseminating knowledge in the pursuit of education, learning and research at the highest international levels of excellence.

www.cambridge.org
Information on this title: www.cambridge.org/9781107429154

© Cambridge University Press 1908

First edition 1908
First published 1908
Reprinted 1930, 1939, 1952, 1960, 1967
First paperback edition 2014

A catalogue record for this publication is available from the British Library

ISBN 978-1-107-42915-4 Paperback

PREFACE

THIS abridgment follows the same lines as its predecessors in the same series. I have made it my aim to omit nothing which contributed directly to the elucidation of the play. In a very few cases I have made small alterations and additions with the view of making particular points clearer.

G. A. D.

September, 1908.

CONTENTS

INTRODUCTION

§ 1. THE story of Orestes the avenger was complete in every essential particular before it came to the earliest of those three Attic dramatists, each of whom has stamped it so strongly with the impress of his own mind.

In the *Iliad* there is no hint that the house of Pelops lay under a curse which entailed a series of crimes. The sceptre made by Hephaestus for Zeus, and brought by Hermes to Pelops, is peacefully inherited by Atreus, Thyestes and Agamemnon. Yet the *Iliad* makes at least one contribution to the material which Aeschylus found ready to his hand. It is the figure of Agamemnon himself, with eyes and head like those of Zeus, in girth like Ares, in breast like Poseidon. This is the royal Agamemnon, ὁ παντόσεμνος, who lives in the Aeschylean drama, and whose image reappears in later poetry. For the rest, the *Iliad* gives us just one far-off glimpse of the king's home beyond the Aegaean, where Orestes is a child in the fortress-palace at Mycenae, with three sisters, Chrysothemis, Laodicè, and Iphianassa, children of that Clytaemnestra to whom, in the opinion of her lord at Troy, the damsel Chryseïs was 'in no wise inferior, in beauty or in stature, in wit or in skill.'

The *Odyssey* tells the story as follows. Agamemnon, before going to Troy, charged a certain minstrel (ἀοιδός) to watch over Clytaemnestra at Mycenae. The precaution implies a sense of possible danger, but not necessarily distrust of Clytaemnestra. Presently a tempter came to the lonely wife in the person of her husband's first-cousin, Aegisthus, son of Thyestes, who, while his kinsmen were fighting at Troy, dwelt 'at peace, in

the heart of Argos.' For some time Clytaemnestra 'refused
the shameful deed; for she had a good understanding.'
Meanwhile the gods themselves, by their messenger Hermes,
warned Aegisthus against the course of crime upon which he
was entering. But Hermes spoke in vain. Aegisthus removed
the minstrel to a desert island, and there left him, a prey to
dogs and birds. He then took the 'willing' Clytaemnestra to
his home; while he sought to propitiate the gods by burnt-
offerings on their altars, and by hanging up in their temples
'many gifts of embroidery and gold.'

Agamemnon, after a stormy voyage from Troy, landed on
the coast of Argolis at a point not far from the dwelling of
Aegisthus; who, apprised by a watcher, came in his chariot,
and invited the king to a banquet; after which he slew him,
'as a man slays an ox at the manger.'

In this narrative (given by Menelaüs to Telemachus)
Clytaemnestra is not even named; though Menelaüs had
previously spoken of her 'guile' as aiding the crime. It is
only in a part of the *Odyssey* which is of later origin than the
'Telemachy' in books I—IV,—viz., the Νέκυια in the eleventh
book,—that Clytaemnestra appears as actively sharing in the
horrors of the banquet, where she slays Cassandra with her
own hand. And, even there, it is by the sword of Aegisthus
alone that Agamemnon is slain.

The young Orestes fled, or was conveyed, to Athens. For
seven years Aegisthus and Clytaemnestra reigned at Mycenae.
In the eighth, Orestes returned, and slew Aegisthus. Clytaemnestra died at the same time, but how, we are not told;
and Orestes 'made a funeral feast,' for both of them, 'to the
Argives.'

Two points distinguish this Homeric legend from later
versions. First, Aegisthus is the principal criminal[1]. Clytaem-

---

[1] The *conception* of the murder (no less than the execution) is always
attributed to him in the *Odyssey* (3. 194 Αἴγισθος ἐμήσατο: 4. 529
Αἴγ. δολίην ἐφράσσατο τέχνην: 11. 409 Αἴγ. τεύξας θάνατόν τε μόρον τε).

nestra's part is altogether subordinate to that of her paramour. Secondly, the vengeance of Orestes is regarded as a simple act of retributive justice. It is not said that he slew his mother; the conjecture is left open that she may have died by her own hand. Nothing comes into the Epic view which can throw a shadow upon the merit of the avenger.

§ 2. In the interval between the *Odyssey* and the Lyric age, legends connected with the house of Pelops were further developed in some of the Cyclic epics[1]. The *Cypria*, ascribed to Stasínus of Cyprus (*circ.* 776 B.C.), related the immolation of Iphigeneia at Aulis,—a story unknown to Homer,—and distinguished her from the Iphianassa of the *Iliad* (9. 145). A new source of poetical interest was thus created, since it could now be asked (as Pindar asks[2]) how far Clytaemnestra was actuated by resentment for the sacrifice of her daughter. In another epic, the *Nostoi* (by Agias of Troezen, *circ.* 750 B.C.), Clytaemnestra aided Aegisthus in the murder, though probably in a subordinate capacity. Further, Pylades was associated with Orestes. And the name of Pylades at once points to Delphi,—the agency by which the primitive legend of Orestes was ultimately transformed.

§ 3. The influence of the Delphic priesthood rose and spread with the power of the Dorians. It did so, not merely because that power was an apt instrument for its propagation, but also because in Hellas at large the time was favourable. The religion of

Cyclic epics.

Influence of Delphi.

---

[1] The Epic Cycle ('Επικὸς κύκλος) was a body of epic poems by various hands, arranged in the chronological order of the subjects, so as to form a continuous history of the mythical world. One part of this Cycle consisted of poems concerning the Trojan war. A grammarian named Proclus (*circ.* 140 A.D.?), in his Χρηστομάθεια, or 'Manual of Literature,' gave short prose summaries of the poems in the Trojan part of the Cycle. The Manual itself is lost, but fragments have been preserved by the patriarch Photius (9th century) in his *Bibliotheca*.

[2] *Pyth.* : 1. 22. See below, § 5.

Apollo, as his Pythian interpreters set it forth, was suited to an age which had begun to reflect, but which retained a vivid faith in the older mythology. Here we are concerned with only one aspect of the Apolline cult, that which relates to blood-guiltiness. The Homeric man who has killed another may either pay a fine to the kinsfolk, or go into exile; but in Homer there is no idea that he can be purified by a ritual. In other words, there is the notion of a debt in this respect, but hardly of a sin; of quittance, but not of absolution. It was a somewhat later stage when men began more distinctly to recognise that in cases of homicide there are kinds and degrees of moral guilt which cannot be expressed in the terms of human debtor and creditor. Clearly a man ought to do what the gods command. But what if a god tells a man to do something which most men think wrong? If the man obeys, and if his conduct is to be judged aright, the tribunal, like the instigation, must be divine. Nor is this so only when the opinion offended is that of men. A god may command a mortal to do an act by which some other god, or supernatural being, will be incensed. Suppose, for instance, that a man receives a divine mandate to slay a guilty kinsman; if he obeys, nothing can save him from angering the Erinyes, who resent every injury to kinsfolk.

For questions such as these the Pythian creed provided

Purification from blood-guilt. an answer, or at least a mystic compromise. Apollo, the god of light, is the all-seeing arbiter of purity. A man who commits homicide displeases Apollo, who abhors every stain of blood. But Apollo can estimate the degree of guilt. And he has empowered his servants to administer rites by which, under certain conditions, a defiled person may be freed from the stain. In later days the critics of Apollo could object that he had encouraged crime by thus far alleviating its consequences. But in the age when the doctrine was first put forth, it must have been, on the whole, beneficent. It tempered the fear of capricious or vindictive deities by trust in a god who, as his priests taught, never swerved from equity, and who was always capable of clemency. At the same time it laid the unabsolved offender under a ban worse than mere outlawry, for it cut him off from the worship of the temple and of the nearth, and, indeed, from all intercourse with god-fearing men. It made his hope depend on submission to a religion representing the highest spiritual influence which ever became widely operative among the people of pagan Hellas.

The ritual of Apollo the Purifier had already a place in the Cyclic epic called the *Aethiopis*, said to have been composed by Arctînus of Miletus, about 776 B.C. More than a century elapsed after that date before Lyric poetry was matured ; and meanwhile the worship of the Pythian Apollo, with its ritual·of purification from blood, was diffused throughout the Greek world. It was to be expected, therefore, that, when the story of Orestes began to receive lyric treatment, the influence of Delphi should be apparent. If, in avenging his father, Orestes killed Clytaemnestra as well as Aegisthus, the Pythian priesthood had a text than which they could desire none more impressive. For, according to the immemorial and general belief of Hellenes, Orestes did well to avenge Agamemnon. If, however, he slew his mother, the Erinyes were necessarily called into activity. Who, then, was to vindicate the avenger? Who was to assert, even against the Erinyes, that his deed was righteous? Who but Apollo, the supreme judge of purity? And then it was only another step to represent Apollo himself as having prescribed the vengeance.

§ 4. Stesichorus, of Himera in Sicily, flourished towards the close of the seventh, and in the earlier part of the sixth, century B.C. The Choral Lyric, which Alcman had already cultivated under the Dorian inspirations of Sparta, received a new development from Stesichorus. He applied it to those heroic legends which had hitherto been the peculiar domain of Epos. One of his most celebrated poems was that in which he told the story of

The *Oresteia* of Stesichorus.

Orestes ('Ορέστεια). It was of large compass, being divided into at least two books or cantos. The direct sources of information concerning it are meagre, consisting only of a few small fragments (less than twelve lines altogether), gleaned from the passing allusions of later writers. But archaeology comes to the aid of literature. The supplementary evidence of Greek art makes it possible to reconstruct, if not with certainty, at least with high probability, a partial outline of the once famous poem. This has been done by Carl Robert, in an essay on 'The death of Aegisthus,'—one of the series of essays, entitled *Bild und Lied*, in which he brings archaeological illustration to bear upon the heroic myths[1].

A combination of literary with artistic evidence leads to the hypothesis that the *Oresteia* of Stesichorus was planned somewhat as follows. Clytaemnestra slew her husband by striking him on the head with an axe. The nurse Laodameia saved the young Orestes, and entrusted him to his father's faithful herald Talthybius, who carried him away,—probably to Phocis. After some years, Clytaemnestra has the alarming dream, and sends Electra (accompanied by the nurse) with gifts to Agamemnon's tomb. Orestes arrives there with Talthybius, and is recognised by his sister. He then enters the house, while Talthybius keeps watch near the doors[2]. Clytaemnestra, hearing the shriek of the dying Aegisthus, rushes to his aid with an axe; a cry from Electra warns Orestes of the peril; but Talthybius has already seized Clytaemnestra; who is presently slain by her son. The Erinyes then appear to Orestes, who defends himself with the bow and arrows given by Apollo[3].

---

[1] *Bila und Lied: Archaeologische Beiträge zur Geschichte der griechischen Heldensage* (Berlin, 1881). The fifth essay is 'Der Tod des Aigisthos,' pp. 149—191.

[2] As the Paedagogus does in Sophocles (*El.* 1331 f.).

[3] There is no clue to the manner in which Stesichorus managed the sequel. He may have followed the local Peloponnesian legend, which assigned a refuge to Orestes at the Arcadian town of Orestheion (Thuc. 5. 64) in Parrhasia, the primitive home of the Orestes-myth. Robert (*Bild und Lied*, p. 181, n. 30) finds a possible trace of this in Eur. *Or.* 1643 ff.

It would appear that Aeschylus followed the general outlines of Stesichorus pretty closely; while Sophocles, who did not do so, has retained at least
one Stesichorean trait, the part of the old man.
Aeschylus did not need him, since *his* Clytaemnestra herself sent Orestes to Strophius; on the other
hand, he retains the part of the nurse, which for Sophocles was
superfluous. That fragment of the Stesichorean poem which
describes Clytaemnestra's dream proves that Stesichorus conceived her in a manner which was much nearer to the
Aeschylean than to the Homeric. And this change—whether
first made by him or not—was connected with another of still
larger scope. Stesichorus related in the *Oresteia* that Tyn-
dareus had incurred the anger of Aphroditè, who doomed his
daughters, Helen and Clytaemnestra, to evil careers[1]. Here is
the tendency—wholly absent from the *Iliad*—to bring crimes
into the house of Pelops. The Dorian conquerors of Peloponnesus envied the renown which the old local lore, worked
up by Ionian art in the *Iliad*, had shed around their Achaean
predecessors, the ancient masters of Mycenae and Sparta.
Under Dorian influences, the story of the Pelopidae was inter-
woven with those dark threads which appear in Attic Tragedy,
while brighter traits were given to the legends of Heracles and
the Heracleidae.

§ 5. Between Stesichorus and Aeschylus, the only poet
who illustrates the story of Orestes is Pindar.
In the eleventh Pythian ode (478 B.C.), he describes a victory in the Pythian games as won 'in the rich
corn-lands of Pylades, host of Laconian Orestes; whom, when
his sire was murdered, the nurse Arsinoè rescued from the
violent hands of Clytaemnestra and from her deadly guile.'
That 'pitiless woman' slew Agamemnon and Cassandra. What,
asks Pindar, was her motive? Was it 'the slaying of Iphigeneia

---

[1] Frag. 35.

at the Euripus'? Or was it an adulterous passion? 'Meanwhile, Orestes, a young child, became the guest of the aged Strophius, who dwelt at the foot of Parnassus. But in time, with the help of Ares, he slew his mother, and laid Aegisthus in blood[1].'

Three points in this sketch are noteworthy. (1) Pindar makes Orestes 'a Laconian'; following the tradition, adopted also by Stesichorus and Simonides that Amyclae in Lacedaemon was the place where Agamemnon was slain. (2) The house of Strophius, 'at the foot of Parnassus,' is the refuge of Orestes; and Pylades is his friend. Probably the *Nostoi (circ.* 750 B.C.), in which Pylades figured, gave this account; but Pindar is the earliest extant source of it. (3) Clytaemnestra, not Aegisthus, is in the foreground; and the speculation as to her *motive* reminds us that the myth had now grown into a shape which was ready for dramatic handling. Twenty years after this ode was written, Aeschylus produced his *Oresteia*.

§ 6. A poet imbued with the ideas of Aeschylus could

Aeschylus.

never have accepted the view presented in the *Odyssey*; that the vengeance of Orestes was a simply righteous retribution, by which the troubles of the house were closed. To the mind of Aeschylus the version which Stesichorus had followed would naturally commend itself: Orestes, the slayer of a mother, could be saved from the Erinyes only by divine aid. And the trilogy, the distinctively Aeschylean form of work, was a framework perfectly suited to such a conception. Clytaemnestra's crime is the subject of the *Agamemnon*; the vengeance of Orestes fills the *Choephori*; and the judgment upon him is given in the *Eumenides*.

The *Agamemnon* is pervaded from first to last by the thought of the hereditary curse upon the house: Clytaemnestra, indeed, identifies herself with this 'ancient, bitter Alastor'; and the Argive Elders recognise that this dread

---

[1] Pind. *Pyth.* 11. 15—37.

power, though it does not excuse her, has presumably helped her. She is the principal agent in the crime. Her dominant motive is not love of her paramour, but hatred of the husband who slew Iphigeneia. Aegisthus is a dastard, 'the wolf mated with the lioness'; at the close he blusters, and threatens the Elders, while the strong woman treats them with a cold scorn. The shadow of the vengeance is cast before. Cassandra predicts the return of the exiled heir; 'for the gods have sworn a great oath.' And the Chorus reply to the menaces of Aegisthus by reminding him that Orestes lives.

The *Choephori* begins with a scene at Agamemnon's grave, near the palace. Orestes, who has just arrived from Phocis, enters with Pylades, and lays a lock of his own hair on the tomb. A train of women, dressed in mourning, approaches. These are fifteen Trojan captives, now domestics of the palace, who form the Chorus. They escort Electra. Orestes thinks that he recognises his sister, and draws aside, with Pylades, to observe the procession.

Analysis of the *Choephori*.

The Chorus chant the parodos, and we learn that they have come with libations to the tomb. 'The impious woman' has been alarmed by a dream; and the sooth-sayers declare that the dead king is wroth. But such offerings, the Chorus add, cannot atone for her deed.

Electra asks the Chorus what prayer she is to utter in pouring the libations. Can she ask the dead to receive these gifts from the murderess? Or shall she present them in silence? Guided by the counsel of her attendants, she prays to Hermes, and to her father's spirit,—with a special petition that Orestes may return.

In pouring the drink-offerings on the tomb, she finds the lock of hair, and turns in excitement to the Chorus. It resembles her own, and she surmises that it is the hair of Orestes,—not brought by him, of course, but sent. Presently she notices footmarks, which have a resemblance to her own.

Orestes now steps forward, and, after a short dialogue, reveals himself. She at first fears an imposture, but is afterwards convinced.

Orestes then declares the oracle of Apollo, commanding him, under terrible penalties, to avenge his father.

Then comes one of the most characteristic and magnificent passages of the play,—a prolonged lyric chant or dirge (kommos), in which the Chorus, Orestes, and Electra take part by turns. It is a solemn litany, addressed to the divine powers who are to aid the vengeance, and to the spirit of the dead.

Then Orestes asks why his mother had sent gifts to the tomb? She dreamed—the Chorus reply—that she gave birth to a serpent, and was suckling it, when it drew blood from her breast. Orestes accepts the omen: the part of the serpent shall be his own.

He announces his plan. Electra is to enter the house. He and Pylades will arrive at the outer gate, wearing the garb of travellers, and imitating the Phocian accent. Electra now goes within, while Orestes and Pylades withdraw to prepare for their enterprise.

The Chorus, left alone, comment on the power of passion over women.

Orestes and Pylades are courteously received by Clytaemnestra. He describes himself as a Phocian from Daulis. With his companion, he was on his way to Argos, when a Phocian named Strophius—a stranger—asked him to carry the news that Orestes was dead, in case the youth's friends should wish to fetch the ashes home.—Clytaemnestra speaks, or rather declaims, as the afflicted mother, and then has the two visitors ushered into the guest chambers, saying that she will break the sad news to 'the master of the house.'

A short choral ode follows.

An old slave-woman, who had been the nurse of Orestes, then comes forth, having been sent by Clytaemnestra to summon Aegisthus. She mourns for Orestes,—recalling, with quaint pathos, all the trouble that the child had given her.— It seems that the queen has ordered Aegisthus to come *with armed attendants*. The Chorus prevail on the nurse not to give this part of the message, but to summon Aegisthus alone.

In the second stasimon the Chorus invoke Zeus, Apollo and Hermes. Next they apostrophise Orestes as though he were present.

Aegisthus enters. The report that Orestes is dead seems to him doubtful. Women are credulous. He must see the messenger, who will not impose on *him*. And so he enters the house.

A moment of suspense is marked by the short third stasimon.

The shriek of the dying Aegisthus is heard within. A slave runs out, crying that his master is slain, and summons Clytaemnestra. She knows that she is lost; but her spirit never quails; she calls for a battle-axe. But, before she can obtain a weapon, Orestes comes forth:—''Tis for thee that I am looking; with *him*, 'tis well enough.' She appeals to her son by the breasts that suckled him. For one instant he falters, and asks Pylades what to do. Pylades (who speaks only here) briefly reminds him of Apollo's command. Orestes wavers no more. In vain Clytaemnestra pleads. He drives her into the house, to slay her where Aegisthus fell.

The Chorus exult in the retribution and the deliverance.

Then the spectators are shown the corpses of Clytaemnestra and Aegisthus, with Orestes standing beside them. He is prepared to seek the protection of Apollo. He denounces the crime of the murderers who have been slain, and displays the robe which Clytaemnestra cast over Agamemnon, 'like a net,' when she slew him in the bath. But, as he proceeds, a strange vehemence and a strange anguish begin to trouble his speech. He is going mad, and in terrible words he says that he knows it. Now he cries out that he sees forms clad in dusky robes, with snaky locks,—the avengers of his mother. 'Ye cannot see them,' he exclaims to the Chorus, 'but I see them...They drive me forth':—and so he rushes from the scene. The Chorus pray that Apollo may protect him.

§ 7. The leading characteristic of the *Choephori* is the tremendous importance of those invisible and supernatural allies who assist the vengeance. Zeus, Apollo, Hermes, Hades, the spirit of Agamemnon, are felt throughout as if they were present with the human agents. This is the significance of the prolonged scene at the tomb, which forms more than one half of the play. It is not properly a suspension of action, but rather a dramatic prelude, emphasising the greatness of the issues involved in the action to come. It brings out the heinousness of the crime which calls for retribution, the appalling nature of the divine mandate to Orestes, and the supreme need of arousing and marshalling those superhuman forces which alone can secure the victory. The human strategy, as subsequently developed, is not especially skilful. The story told to Clytaemnestra by the pretended Phocian, who mentions the death of Orestes as a bare fact casually learned from a stranger, was not well fitted to find ready credence with the astute woman whose fears had just been quickened, as the conspirators knew, by a warning dream,—even if they assumed that she had missed the meaning which her dream at once conveyed to Orestes. And that Clytaemnestra did, in fact, suspect the 'Phocian's' story appears from her wish that Aegisthus should bring his body-guards. But then again the old nurse of Orestes was hardly the safest person to whom a message of such critical moment could be entrusted. The gods indeed justify the maxim of Pylades ; they are the worst enemies of the guilty.

From the moment when the two 'Phocians' enter the house, the swiftness of the concentrated action is unchecked, save by that brief pause in which the tragic interest culminates,—the dialogue between Clytaemnestra and her son. She holds the same place in the retribution which she held in the crime. Her

(marginal note: Supernatural agency.)

(marginal note: Clytaemnestra.)

death is the climax; it is by her Erinyes that Orestes is driven forth to seek refuge with Apollo. The fate of Aegisthus is a subordinate incident. Though Clytaemnestra's longest speech is limited to twelve lines, and her whole part to forty-six, Aeschylus has been marvellously successful in continuing that sense of horror, hard to describe or to define, which she produces in the *Agamemnon*.

The attitude of the Aeschylean Orestes is illustrated by
Orestes. the nature of the command which he obeys. In the play of Sophocles the oracle briefly directs that he shall take the just vengeance without the aid of an armed force. But in the *Choephori* he speaks of reiterated admonitions from the god, full of explicit threats as to the penalties which await him if he *refuses* to act. Spectral terrors shall haunt him in the night; leprous ulcers shall rise upon his flesh; his whole body shall be shrivelled and blasted with torturing disease; he shall be an outcast, under a ban cutting him off from human fellowship and from the altars of the gods. Oracles of such a tenor plainly intimate that the task prescribed was one from which even a brave man might recoil. Apollo's purpose is to make Orestes feel that disobedience is the greater of two evils. It is dreadful to shed a mother's blood, but worse to leave a father unavenged. In the *Choephori* Orestes is indeed resolute; not, however, because the duty before him is simple, but because the god's messages have braced him to perform it. Once—at the moment when a mother's claim to pity is presented in the most pathetic form—he does hesitate;—Πυλάδη, τί δράσω; μητέρ' αἰδεσθῶ κτανεῖν; But Pylades reminds him of the god's word. It will presently be seen how marked is the contrast here between Aeschylus and Sophocles.

The Electra of Aeschylus appears to have no sister living.
Electra. She performs the errand which Sophocles assigns to Chrysothemis, by carrying her mother's gifts to the tomb; she could not refuse, for she is virtually a slave.

Turning to the real slaves, her companions, she appeals to the common hatred which unites them, and asks what prayer she is to make. The Sophoclean Electra would hardly have sought advice on that point; yet the question is in place here, since her action, if contrary to the queen's orders, might compromise her unhappy escort. The heroic fortitude and bold initiative of the Sophoclean Electra are qualities which Aeschylus, with his different plan, has not desired to portray; but he has done full justice to her steadfast and affectionate loyalty. And with regard to the actual mechanism of the plot, she is, in one sense, even more important with Aeschylus than with Sophocles. It rests with her alone to decide whether the young stranger is her brother, and, if she is convinced, to aid his plan within the house. The latter service is assigned by Sophocles to the old man, who could also have established the identity of Orestes, if there had been need. When the 'recognition' has been effected, and the prayers at the tomb are over, the Aeschylean Electra can be dismissed from the scene.

The part of Aegisthus is notably brief, even allowing for the indifference with which his fate is treated. He merely passes across the scene; fourteen verses are all that he has to speak. The part of the Nurse is a masterpiece in its kind. And we note the happy inspiration by which Pylades is made to break silence once—at the supreme moment—as the voice of Apollo.

Minor persons.

Nearly a third of the play is lyric. The Chorus have their share in the action; at the outset they are the counsellors of Electra; they persuade the Nurse to help the plan; and they send Aegisthus forward to his doom. But their function is, above all, to interpret the sense of reliance upon divine aid. 'Justice may delay, but it will come,' is the burden of the choral song; 'the sinner shall suffer' ($\delta\rho\acute{a}\sigma a\nu\tau\iota \pi a\theta\epsilon\hat{\iota}\nu$); 'even now, Destiny is preparing the sword.' And when, at the close, a dark cloud gathers over Orestes, it is with unwavering faith that the Chorus commend

The Chorus.

him to Apollo, though no human eye can pierce the gloom which rests upon the future.

§ 8. Sophocles reverts to the epic view that the deed of Orestes is simply laudable, and therefore final. It suited this aim to concentrate the sympathies of the spectators against Clytaemnestra as well as Aegisthus. And nothing could be more effective for that purpose than to show how their long oppression had failed to break down the heroic constancy of Electra.

The *Electra* of Sophocles.

We will now trace the plot of Sophocles.

The scene is laid before the palace of the Pelopidae at Mycenae. Three persons enter,—on the left of the spectator, for they are travellers from a distant place. These are, Orestes, who is about twenty years of age; his Phocian friend Pylades (son of Strophius, king of Crisa near Delphi—from whose home they come); and an old man, a faithful retainer of Agamemnon, who had been the paedagogus of Orestes, and had secretly carried him, as a child, away from Mycenae to Crisa, at the time when Agamemnon was slain.

Analysis of the play.
I. Prologue: 1—120.

The old man points out to Orestes the chief features in the landscape before them, and then exhorts the two youths to concert their plan of action without delay; already it is the hour of dawn, and the morning-song of the birds is beginning.

Orestes, in reply, states the purport of the oracle given to him at Delphi. Apollo commanded him to 'snatch his righteous vengeance by stealth,' without the aid of an armed force. He then sets forth his plan. The old man is to enter the palace in the guise of a messenger sent by Phanoteus, a Phocian prince friendly to Clytaemnestra and Aegisthus. He is to announce that Orestes has been killed in a chariot-race at the Pythian games. Meanwhile Orestes and Pylades will make offerings at the tomb of Agamemnon near the palace. They will then present themselves in the house, bearing a funeral urn. They, like the old man, will pretend to be Phocians, who have brought the ashes of Orestes to Mycenae.

A female voice of lament is now heard in the house (v. 77). Orestes asks if it can be Electra's, and proposes to wait and listen; but the old man dissuades him. All three now leave the scene (v. 85).

Electra comes out of the house; she is alone, for the Chorus have not yet appeared. Greeting the 'pure sunlight and the air,' to which her sorrow has so often been uttered at dawn, she speaks of the grief which ceases not, day or night, for her father, whom the wicked pair struck down, 'as woodmen fell an oak.' She invokes the Powers of the nether world to avenge him,— and to send her brother; for her own strength is well-nigh spent.

(θρῆνος ἀπὸ σκηνῆς: 86—120.)

The Chorus, composed of fifteen Mycenaean women, had entered as Electra's lament was closing. They sympathise with her; and they do not conceal their abhorrence of the deed which she mourns. But they remind her that grief cannot restore the dead to life: they urge her to be calm, trusting in the gods, and hoping for the return of Orestes. She must not aggravate her lot by waging a fruitless strife with the rulers.

Parodos: 121—250.

Electra replies that to abandon her grief would be disloyalty. If her father is not to be avenged, there will be an end to reverence for gods or men.

The Chorus say that they spoke only for her good; she knows best, and she shall be their guide. Electra then justifies her conduct by describing what she has to see and suffer daily in the house;—Aegisthus in her father's place; her mother living with Aegisthus, and keeping the death-day of Agamemnon as a festival. Hardship and insult are her own portion continually. The Chorus cautiously inquire if Aegisthus is at home; and, on learning that he is absent in the country, ask Electra whether she

II. First episode: 251—471.

thinks that Orestes will return. 'He promises,' she answers, 'but does not keep his promise.' 'Courage,' they reply: 'he is too noble to fail his friends.'

At this moment Chrysothemis approaches, bearing funeral offerings. She begins by sharply chiding her sister for this 'vain indulgence of idle wrath,'—in public, too, at the palace-gates. But she admits that she herself feels anger against the tyrants; were she strong enough, she would let them know it. Electra has right upon her side: only, if one is to live in freedom, one must yield to the stronger.

Electra tells her that the choice is between loyalty to the dead and worldly prudence. 'Canst thou, the daughter of Agamemnon, wish to be only the daughter of Clytaemnestra?' The Chorus timidly deprecate a quarrel. Chrysothemis says that she is used to Electra's vehemence. She would not have spoken, but that she had to convey a warning. As soon as Aegisthus returns, Electra is to be imprisoned in a dungeon, at a distance from Mycenae—unless she becomes more docile. Electra declares that she would welcome such a doom;—'that I may escape,' she says, 'far from *you*,'—thus identifying her sister with the oppressors.

Chrysothemis, finding her counsels repelled, is about to proceed on her errand, when Electra asks her whither she is taking those offerings. 'Our mother sends me,' is the answer, 'with libations to our father's grave.' It then appears that Clytaemnestra has been terrified by a dream. Agamemnon returned to life; he planted his sceptre at the hearth; a branch blossomed from it, and overshadowed the land.

Electra feels a sudden joy. This dream, she believes, has been sent by the gods below, and by the spirit of the dead. 'Dear sister,' she cries, 'cast those impious offerings away; take, instead of them, such gifts as *we* can give,—and pray at the tomb that our father's spirit may come to help us, and that Orestes may live to conquer.'

Chrysothemis is touched and subdued. She agrees to do

as her sister bids; only Electra and the Chorus must keep the secret; she dreads her mother's anger.

The Chorus, encouraged by Clytaemnestra's dream, predict the vengeance. Agamemnon's spirit is not forgetful. The Erinys, now lurking in ambush, will come. The curse upon the house of Pelops claims yet more victims.

First stasimon: 472—515.

Clytaemnestra enters, followed by a handmaid bearing offerings of various fruits for Apollo Lykeios, whose altar stands in front of the house. 'At large once more, it seems!' is her greeting to Electra;—'since Aegisthus is not here to restrain thee.' She defends her murder of Agamemnon. 'Justice slew him, and not I alone.' Had he not slain her daughter, Iphigeneia, in the cause of his brother Menelaüs?

III. Second episode: 516—1057. (1) 1st scene: 516—659.

Electra replies that her father acted therein under constraint from the goddess Artemis; but that, even if he had been a free agent, Clytaemnestra's plea would not avail. Then, passing from argument to reproach and defiance, Electra avows her wish that Orestes might come as an avenger; though she also shows the anguish which she feels at the attitude towards a mother which is forced upon her.

An angry dialogue ends by Clytaemnestra enjoining silence, in order that she may make her offerings to Apollo. She prays that the god will rule the issues of the vision for her good, and for the discomfiture of her foes. Other wishes, too, she has, but will not utter them; the god can divine them...

Here the Paedagogus enters, disguised as a Phocian messenger from Phanoteus. He relates how the young Orestes, after wonderful feats at the Pythian games, was killed in the chariot-race. Other Phocians are on their way to Mycenae with his ashes.

(2) 2nd scene: 660—803.

Clytaemnestra hears the news with feelings in which joy is crossed by at least a touch of natural grief; but the joy quickly prevails, and she openly recognises that the news is good. At

last she will be safe from Orestes—and from Electra, who has
been even a worse foe.

Electra invokes Nemesis to avenge her brother; while Clytaemnestra cruelly taunts her, and then conducts the Phocian
messenger into the house.

Left alone with the Chorus, Electra gives free vent to her
anguish and despair. She will enter that house
no more, but cast herself down at the gates, and
await death—which cannot come too soon.

(3) 3rd
scene: 804—
870.

In the lyric dialogue which follows, the women of Mycenae
gently endeavour to suggest comfort. Was not
the seer Amphiaraüs betrayed to death by a false
wife? And is not his spirit now great beneath
the earth? Alas, Electra answers, there was a son to avenge
him, and to slay the murderess; but Agamemnon can have no
such avenger. Orestes has perished, in a foreign land, without
receiving the last offices of sisterly love.

Kommos:
823—870.

Chrysothemis enters hurriedly, in a flutter of joyful excitement. On reaching the tomb, with her sister's
gifts and her own, she found that unknown
hands had just been honouring it. Libations
of milk had been poured there; the mound was wreathed with
flowers; and on the edge of it lay a lock of hair. These gifts
can be from no one but Orestes !

(4) 4th
scene: 871—
1057.

With pitying sorrow, Electra breaks to her the news which
has come from Phocis. Probably the gifts at the tomb were
brought by some one in memory of the dead youth. And now,
as the delusive hope vanishes from her sister's mind, Electra
seeks to replace it by a heroic resolve. Will Chrysothemis aid
her in the purpose which she has formed—to slay the two
murderers with her own hand? Electra reminds her of the joyless
lot which otherwise awaits both Chrysothemis and herself; and
pictures the noble renown which such a deed would achieve.

To Chrysothemis this is sheer madness. She foresees only
certain failure and a terrible death. In vain she seeks to

dissuade Electra, who declares that she will make the attempt unaided. With a parting word of compassionate warning, Chrysothemis enters the house. Electra remains outside.

The Chorus lament the weaker sister's failure in that Second natural piety which the very birds of the air stasimon: teach us. A sorrowful message for Agamemnon 1058—1097. in the shades will be this quarrel between his daughters. How noble is Electra,—all alone, yet unshaken, in her loyalty! May she yet win the reward which she has deserved!

Orestes enters, with Pylades, followed by two attendants, one of whom carries the funeral urn (v. 1123). IV. Third He asks for the house of Aegisthus, and, on episode: 1098—1383. learning that he has reached it, requests that (1) The recog-nition: 1098— their arrival may be announced. The Chorus 1287. suggest that Electra should do this. A dialogue ensues between Electra and the disguised Orestes. She learns that the strangers come from Strophius, king of Crisa, with her brother's ashes; and she is allowed to take the urn into her hands. She then utters a most touching lament, recalling the memories of her brother's childhood,—the close affection which bound them to each other,—her care for him, and her bright hopes, which have thus ended. 'Therefore take me to this thy home, me, who am as nothing, to thy nothingness... When thou wast on earth, we shared alike; and now I fain would die, that I may not be parted from thee in the grave.'

The disguised Orestes finds it hard to restrain himself. In the dialogue which follows, he gradually prepares her mind for the discovery,—leading her through surprise, conjecture, and hope, to conviction. The scene is one of exquisite art and beauty (vv. 1176—1226).

In lyrics, Electra now utters her joy,—which reaches the μέλος ἀπὸ height, when Orestes tells her that he has been σκηνῆς: 1232— sent by Apollo. He endeavours to check her 1287. transports (though he is loth to do so), lest she should be overheard.

At length he succeeds in recalling her to their scheme of
action, and warns her against allowing Clytaemnestra to perceive her happiness. She promises
obedience in all things. The old Paedagogus

*The plan of
action: 1288—
1383.*

now comes out, and scolds them both for their imprudence.
When Electra learns that the faithful servant is before her, she
greets him warmly, as the preserver of their house. Then, by
his advice, Orestes and Pylades enter the palace, after saluting
the ancestral gods in the porch; and the old man follows them.
Electra addresses a brief prayer to Apollo Lykeios, and then
she also enters.

The Chorus, now alone, sing a short ode. The Erinyes
have passed beneath the roof; the Avenger is
being led by Hermes, in secrecy, to his goal.
Electra rushes forth to tell the Chorus that
Orestes and Pylades are about to do the deed.
Clytaemnestra is dressing the funeral urn for
burial, while the two youths stand beside her.

*Third
stasimon:
1384—1397.*

*V. Exodos:
1398—1510.
Kommos:
1398—1441.*

In another moment her dying shrieks are heard. Orestes, with
Pylades, then comes out; and, in answer to his sister's question,
says: '*All is well in the house, if Apollo's oracle spake well.*'

Aegisthus is seen approaching, and the youths quickly re-
enter the house. He is exultant, for he has heard the report
that Orestes is dead. Electra confirms it, adding that the body
has been brought to Mycenae; Aegisthus can satisfy his own
eyes. The tyrant orders the palace-doors to be thrown wide,
in order that his subjects may see the corpse, and know that all
hope from that quarter is over.

The doors are opened; a corpse, hidden by a veil, lies on
a bier; close to it stand the two Phocians who are supposed
to have brought it. Aegisthus lifts the veil—and sees the dead
Clytaemnestra. He knows that he is doomed, and that Orestes
stands before him. Nor is he suffered to plead at length:
though some bitter words pass his lips, before Orestes drives
him in, to slay him in the hall where Agamemnon was slain.

The Chorus rejoice that the house of Atreus has at last found peace.

§ 9.   When this play is compared with the *Choephori*, the first difference which appears is broader than any that could arise from divergent views of the particular story. It concerns the whole stamp of the drama, and illustrates the difference, in bent of genius, between the two poets. Aeschylus exhibits in grand outline the working of an eternal law, full of mystery and terror. Justice, Destiny, the Erinys, are the paramount agencies. The human agents are drawn, indeed, with a master's hand, but by a few powerful strokes rather than with subtle touches or fine shading. Nor is much care shown for probability in minor details of the plot. With Sophocles the interest depends primarily on the portraiture of human character. The opportunities for this are contrived by a series of ingenious situations, fruitful in contrasts and dramatic effects. We have seen that the Greek art of the sixth century B.C. knew a version of this legend in which Talthybius, the herald of Agamemnon, saved the young Orestes from murder,—receiving him, doubtless, from the hands of the nurse—and in due time conducted the heir home again ; a version which Stesichorus had probably popularised. It suited Aeschylus to leave out Talthybius, while keeping the part of the nurse. Sophocles revives the old herald in the person of the trusty Paedagogus, who received the child, not from a nurse, but from Electra herself, and carried him to Crisa. This change is a source of large advantage to the plot. It is a weak point in the *Choephori* that the story told by Orestes was not likely to impose upon Clytaemnestra, and does not, in fact, disarm her suspicion. The Sophoclean stratagem is of a different order. When the old man, as an envoy from Phanoteus, gives Clytaemnestra his circumstantial account of her son's death, he plays his part to perfection. He evinces some natural feeling for the tragic death of a brilliant youth, but at the same time

(Marginal note:) General comparison with the *Choephori*.

shows that he is disappointed when the queen hesitates whether to rejoice or to mourn. 'Then it seems that I have come in vain,' he says, half aggrieved; and she hastens to re-assure him. A little later the two 'Phocians' arrive with the urn, as envoys from Strophius, the old ally of Agamemnon. This device of two independent missions, each from an appropriate quarter, was really fitted to win belief. It also provides a keen interest for the spectator, who is in the secret. The Aeschylean Electra is from the outset the accomplice of the avengers. But here she is herself deceived by them. And from the belief that her brother is dead springs the resolve which shows her spirit at the highest—to execute the vengeance without aid. In the *Choephori*, again, Electra is still trembling between hope and doubt, when Orestes steps forward, and almost at once reveals himself. Here, she is convinced that his ashes are in the urn which the young Phocian permits her to handle; the irresistible pathos of her lament over it compels him to shorten her probation; and then comes the dialogue, so characteristic of Sophocles, which gently leads up to the recognition.

Like the poet of the *Odyssey*, Sophocles regards the vengeance as a deed of unalloyed merit, which brings the troubles of the house to an end. Clytaemnestra's part is much larger than in the *Choephori*; but it is the death of Aegisthus which forms the climax. Sophocles reverses the Aeschylean plan. Here it is Clytaemnestra whose dying shriek is heard; it is Aegisthus whose doom is preceded by a dialogue with Orestes.

§ 10. Throughout the play, there is not a hint that a son who slays his mother is liable to the Erinyes. This silence cannot be explained by the plea that Sophocles was concerned only with the vengeance itself. For, although the pursuit of Orestes by the Erinyes was not to be included in the plot, still the play shows him both when he was meditating the deed, and after he has done it. Yet he neither shrinks from it in prospect, nor feels

The stain of matricide is ignored.

the slightest uneasiness when it has been accomplished. From
first to last, his confidence is as cheerful as the morning sun-
shine in which the action commences. When he comes forth
with dripping sword, this is his comment; 'All is well in the
house, if Apollo's oracle spake well.' How could an Athenian
poet of the fifth century B.C. venture thus to treat the subject
before an Athenian audience, whose general sentiment would
assuredly be that of the *Choephori*, and in the forefront of
which sat priestly exponents of the religious view which was
so signally ignored? Euripides is here, at least, at one with
Aeschylus. True, Sophocles has been careful to remind us,
again and again, how completely Clytaemnestra had forfeited
all *moral* claim to a son's loyalty. The question here is, however, not moral but religious; a matter, not of conduct, but of
kinship. It may also be granted that the Sophoclean oracle of
Apollo differs from that in the *Choephori*. It is a brief command to do a righteous deed; it threatens no penalties, and so
implies no reason for reluctance. Still, that does not alter the
fact of the matricidal stain upon Orestes. I do not know any
adequate solution of this difficulty, which seems greater than
has generally been recognised: I can only suggest one con-
sideration which may help to explain it. The Homeric colour-
ing in the *Electra* is strongly marked; thus the *Odyssey* is
followed in the version of Agamemnon's murder as perpetrated
at the banquet,—there are even verbal echoes of it[1]; the
chariot-race in the *Iliad* (book XXIII) has furnished several
traits to the narrative of the disaster at the Pythian games[2].
Sophocles seems to say to his audience, 'I give you, modified
for drama, the story that Homer tells; put yourselves at the
Homeric stand-point; regard the act of Orestes under the light
in which the *Odyssey* presents it.' The Homeric Athena
declares that Orestes has won universal praise by slaying the
villainous Aegisthus. The final scene of Sophocles is designed

[1] See commentary on v. 95, and on vv. 193—196.
[2] See on vv. 712, 721 f., 748.

to leave a similar impression; the tyrant is exhibited in all his baseness,—insolent and heartless; he is driven in to meet his just doom; Orestes points the moral; and the Chorus welcome the retribution. Having resolved to limit his view by the epic horizon, Sophocles has executed the plan with great skill. But his plot 'labours under a disadvantage which no skill could quite overcome. He could not, like his Homeric original, dispense with Apollo: the Apolline thread had long ago become so essential a part of the texture that he could not get rid of it. But, the moment that Apollo is introduced, the thought of the stain upon Orestes becomes importunate, since the very purpose for which Apollo first came into the story was that of showing how the supreme arbiter of purity could defend his emissary against the claim of the Erinyes. Stesichorus and Aeschylus had deeply impressed this on the Greek mind; and it would have been hard for Athenians, familiar with the lyric and the dramatic *Oresteia*, to feel that the story, as told by Sophocles, reached a true conclusion. His Chorus might, indeed, close the play by describing the house of Atreus as

$$\tau\hat{\eta} \; \nu\hat{\upsilon}\nu \; \acute{o}\rho\mu\hat{\eta} \; \tau\epsilon\lambda\epsilon\omega\theta\acute{\epsilon}\nu.$$

But would not many spectators have ringing in their ears the last words of the *Choephori*?

$$\pi o\hat{\iota} \; \delta\hat{\eta}\tau a \; \kappa\rho a\nu\epsilon\hat{\iota}, \; \pi o\hat{\iota} \; \kappa a\tau a\lambda\acute{\eta}\xi\epsilon\iota$$
$$\mu\epsilon\tau a\kappa o\iota\mu\iota\sigma\theta\grave{\epsilon}\nu \; \mu\acute{\epsilon}\nu o\varsigma \; \acute{a}\tau\eta\varsigma \;;$$

§ 11. The Sophoclean Electra resembles Antigone in heroism and in loyalty to the dead, but the modes in which their characters are manifested differ as widely as the situations. Antigone is suddenly required to choose between omitting a sacred duty and incurring death; within a day she has chosen, and died. The ordeal of Electra is that of maintaining a solitary protest through years of suffering. Her timid sister's sympathy is only secret; the tyrants ill-treat her, and she witnesses their insults

Character of Electra.

to her father's memory. Meanwhile there is only one feeble ray of light for her, the hope that Orestes may return; but it becomes fainter as time goes on. One of the finest traits in the delineation of Electra by Sophocles is the manner in which he suggests that inward life of the imagination into which she has shrunk back from the world around her. To her, the dead father is an ally ever watchful to aid the retribution; when she hears of Clytaemnestra's dream, it at once occurs to her that *he* has helped to send it[1]. The youthful Orestes, as her brooding fancy pictures him, is already invested with the heroic might of an avenger[2]. There are moments when she can almost forget her misery in visions of his triumph[3]. Like Antigone, she is contrasted with a weaker, though amiable, sister. Chrysothemis is of the same type as Ismene; her instincts are right, and respond to the appeal of Electra, whom she loves; only she is not heroic. The stronger nature, when brought into conflict with the feebler, almost inevitably assumes, at certain moments, an aspect of harshness[4]: yet the union in Electra of tenderness with strength can be felt throughout, and finds expression in more than one passage of exquisite beauty[5]. When she believes that Orestes is dead, and that it rests with her alone to avenge Agamemnon, she calls upon Chrysothemis to co-operate, who reproves her as forgetting that she is a woman[6]. But when Orestes is restored to her, she submits herself in all things to his wishes[7]. Hers is the part which Aeschylus gives to the Chorus, of speaking with Aegisthus on his way to the house. She is present almost from the beginning to the end of the play, and the series of her emotions is the thread which gives unity to the whole.

---

[1] Vv. 459, 460.

[2] Vv. 1220 f.

[3] See on v. 814.

[4] Vv. 391; 1027 ff.

[5] See especially the kommos, 823—870; and her lament, 1126—1170.

[6] 997 γυνὴ μὲν οὐδ᾽ ἀνὴρ ἔφυς.   [7] 1301 ff.

§ 12. The cause which she holds sacred is elaborately arraigned and defended in the scene with Clytaemnestra. Sophocles portrays the queen in a manner very distinct from that of Aeschylus; a difference due not merely to the general tendencies of the poets, but also to the dramatic setting. Aeschylus created his Clytaemnestra in the *Agamemnon*, where she is seen just before and just after the murder. There is a fascination in her dreadful presence of mind; what an adamantine purpose can be felt under the fluent eloquence with which she welcomes her husband! How fearful, again, is her exultation in the deed, when she tells the Argive elders that she rejoices in the blood upon her robe 'as a cornfield in the dews of spring,' or when she imagines Iphigeneia advancing to greet Agamemnon in the shades, and kissing him! Sophocles had to show Clytaemnestra, not at a crisis of action, but as she lived and felt in the years which followed her crime. Electra's fortitude was to be illustrated by withstanding and denouncing her. The Clytaemnestra of Aeschylus was ill-suited to such a situation. If she had been confronted with a daughter who impugned her deed, scorn and hatred would have flashed from her; but she would not have argued her case in detail, and then listened to a reply. The almost superhuman force of that dark soul would have been fatal to the dramatic effect of any woman opposed to her. In the *Choephori* Aeschylus has taken care that Electra shall have no dialogue with Clytaemnestra. Sophocles clearly felt this. The Clytaemnestra whom he draws is strong and wicked, but her temperament is not one which separates her from ordinary humanity. She feels at least a pang of maternal grief when she first hears that Orestes is dead[1], even though a little later she can address heartless taunts to Electra. She has not the Aeschylean queen's cynical contempt for public opinion; thus she complains that Electra misrepresents her, and seeks

[1] *El.* 766 ff. Contrast her hypocritical rhetoric at the corresponding moment in Aesch. *Cho.* 691 ff.

to justify herself[1]. Sophocles has thus avoided investing Clytaemnestra with a tragic interest which would have required
that her punishment, rather than her paramour's, should form
the climax.

The function of the Chorus is naturally to some extent

The Chorus. the same as in the *Choephori*,—viz., to sympathise with Electra and to assert the moral
law: but there is a difference. The Trojan slave-women
of the Aeschylean Chorus hate the tyrants and are friendly
to Electra's cause, but have no further interest in the vengeance. The Sophoclean Chorus consists of freeborn women,
belonging to Mycenae, but external to the palace. They represent a patriotic sentiment in the realm at large, favourable to
the son of Agamemnon, and hostile to the usurper. The city
is sympathetic with the family[2].

§ 13. While the strictly human interest predominates in the

Supernatural agency. *Electra*, we must not undervalue the dramatic
importance which Sophocles has given to the
supernatural agency, or the skill with which it is
carried through the texture of the play. In the opening scene
we hear the oracle which Apollo has given to Orestes. The
enterprise is presently placed under the protection of the
Chthonian powers by those ceremonies at the tomb which,
as the old man urges, must precede everything else. Then
Electra comes forth, and invokes the deities of the underworld.
A little later it appears that Clytaemnestra has had an ominous
dream; Electra sees in it an answer to her prayer, and the
Chorus express the same conviction. Next, the queen makes
her offerings and half-secret prayers to Apollo; the very god,
though she knows it not, who has already sent Orestes home.
With a similar unconsciousness, in her joy at the news from

---

[1] *El.* 520 ff.

[2] Cp. the words of the Chorus in v. 1413, ὦ πόλις, ὦ γενεὰ κ.τ.λ. In
v. 1227 Electra addresses them as πολίτιδες. Their feeling towards Orestes
as the heir is seen in 160 ff.: cp. too 251 ff. (n.).

Phocis, she declares that Nemesis has heard those who deserved to be heard, and has ordained aright. The last act of Orestes and Pylades before entering the house is to salute the images of the gods; while Electra makes a short prayer to Apollo. Lastly, in the moments of suspense before the deed, the choral song reminds us that the Erinyes have passed beneath the roof, and that Hermes is guiding the avenger to the goal.

Thus the whole drama is pervaded by an under-current of divine co-operation; the gods are silently at work; step by step the irresistible allies advance; the very effort of Clytaemnestra to bespeak Apollo's favour is a new impiety, which only makes his wrath more certain.

§ 14. Let us now see how the subject is treated by Euripides.

The Electra of Euripides. The scene is laid before the cottage of a husbandman, or small farmer (αὐτουργός), who lives in Argolis, but near the borders, and far from the city of Argos. The time is dawn.

The play is opened by a speech of the farmer. Aegisthus and Clytaemnestra have given him Electra in marriage ; fearing that, if she wedded a richer spouse, he or his offspring might avenge Agamemnon. The worthy man adds that respect for the family has forbidden him to regard the union as more than formal.

Electra comes out of the cottage, poorly clad, with her hair cut short (in sign of mourning), and bearing a water-jar upon her head. She is not forced, she says, to do these menial tasks, but she wishes to show the insolence of Aegisthus to the gods. The farmer deprecates such work for her, and she expresses her grateful esteem for him. Then she goes on her way to the spring, and he to his plough.

Orestes enters, with Pylades (who is a mute person through-out). An oracle of Apollo (he says) has sent him. He does not dare to go within the walls of the city. But in the night he has secretly sacrificed at Agamemnon's tomb, and has placed a lock of hair upon it. He has now come to find Electra, of whose marriage he has heard, and to seek her co-operation. —He now sees a woman, apparently a slave, approaching, and proposes to seek information from her. This is Electra, returning with her water-jar from the spring. In a lyric lament she speaks of Agamemnon's fate and her brother's exile. Orestes, listening, soon learns who she is, for she introduces her own name.

The Chorus enters. It consists of fifteen maidens from the neighbourhood, who hold a lyric dialogue with Electra.

Electra now perceives that two armed strangers are near her cottage, and is disquieted. Orestes does not reveal himself, but says that he has come to bring her news of her brother. Having heard his tidings, she speaks of her own fortunes.

The farmer now reappears, and is somewhat disconcerted at first, but quickly recovers himself, and gracefully offers hospitality to the strangers. Orestes accepts the invitation. The two guests having gone in, Electra reproves her husband for having invited them, when he knew the poverty of the household. He must now go, she says, and look for a certain old man in the neighbourhood, who is capable of bringing some better fare for the visitors. This old man, it seems, had been an attendant of Agamemnon when the latter was a boy. The farmer obeys, and goes forth—to be seen no more.

The old retainer of Agamemnon, for whom the farmer went, now arrives, bringing lamb, cheeses, and some good wine for the guests.

On his way he has visited Agamemnon's tomb, and has been surprised by finding recent offerings there. One of these, a lock of hair, he brings with him, and suggests that, since it is like Electra's, it may be from the head of Orestes. She ridicules his surmise; and here follows the well-known satire on the other signs used by Aeschylus for the 'recognition.'

Orestes and Pylades come out of the cottage. Electra

introduces the old man to the strangers as one who formerly saved her brother's life. The old man recognises Orestes by a scar over one eyebrow.

Orestes now consults the old man as to a scheme of vengeance. It would be impossible (says the old man) for Orestes to enter the guarded stronghold of the usurpers (615 ff.). But Aegisthus is now in the country, about to sacrifice to the Nymphs. He has no guards with him,—only servants. Orestes must present himself at the sacrifice, and take his chance of being asked to assist. Clytaemnestra is at Argos. But Electra undertakes to send her a message which will bring her to the cottage.

The old man promises to take this message. He will also guide Orestes to Aegisthus. Electra then enters the house, while Orestes sets forth with his guide.

A messenger tells Electra how Orestes has slain Aegisthus. The Chorus and Electra express their joy. Orestes enters with a ghastly trophy—the body of Aegisthus, carried by attendants. Electra expresses her hatred in a long speech over the corpse.

Clytaemnestra now approaches from Mycenae, in a chariot, with a retinue. Orestes is seized with shuddering at the thought of slaying his mother. Electra nerves him; reminds him of his duty to his father, and of Apollo's oracle. He enters the cottage—resolved to do the deed, and yet shrinking from it.

The Chorus briefly greet Clytaemnestra with pretended reverence. Then follows a dispute between mother and daughter as to the fate of Iphigeneia and of Agamemnon. But the queen is presently touched by Electra's misery, and expresses regret for the past. Electra, however, is not softened. Then Clytaemnestra enters the house, to perform the rite on behalf of the (supposed) child. Electra presently follows her in.

The Chorus recall the death of Agamemnon, and foretell

the vengeance. In the midst of their chant, Clytaemnestra's dying shriek is heard from within.

Orestes and Electra are now shown (by the eccyclema) standing by the corpse of Clytaemnestra; that of Aegisthus lies near.

Orestes is full of anguish and despair. He describes how he drew his cloak over his eyes as he slew his mother. Electra, on the contrary, is in this scene almost a Lady Macbeth. She tells how she urged her brother on, and even guided his sword when he covered his eyes. Then she throws a covering over her mother's body.

At this moment the Chorus greet the apparition of two bright forms in the air. These are the Dioscuri. Clytaemnestra, they say, has been justly slain, and yet Orestes is defiled. Apollo gave him *an unwise oracle*; though, as that god is their superior, they will say no more. Electra is to marry Pylades, and go to Phocis—taking with her the good farmer, who is to receive a large estate (v. 1287). Orestes is to go to Athens, where, under the presidency of Pallas, he will be tried and acquitted; he will then settle in Arcadia.

The play ends with a most curious dialogue in anapaests between the Dioscuri and the other persons. The Chorus bluntly ask the demigods why they did not avert murder from their sister Clytaemnestra? Well, they reply, the blame rests on Fate, and on *the unwise utterances of Phoebus*[1]. Electra then asks why she—to whom no oracle had been given—was involved in the guilt of matricide? The only answer which occurs to them is that she suffers through the hereditary curse upon the whole house of Pelops. Orestes changes the awkward subject by taking leave of Electra, whom he is not to see again. The Dioscuri have words of comfort for each. And then they warn Orestes to hasten away; already dark forms can be seen approaching, with snaky arms.

---

[1] 1302 Φοίβου τ' ἄσοφοι γλώσσης ἐνοπαί.

§ 15. It is in this closing scene, where the Dioscuri are cross-examined, that the drift of Euripides is most patent. The dialogue is equivalent to an epilogue by the dramatist, who, in effect, addresses the audience as follows:—'I have now told you this story in my own way—adhering to the main lines of the tradition, but reconciling it, as far as possible, with reason. And now, having done my best with it, I feel bound to add that it remains a damning indictment against Apollo, and a scandal to the moral sense of mankind.'

Drift of Euripides— adverse to Apollo.

Euripides could not relieve Orestes from the guilt of matricide; tradition forbad; but he has sought to modify that guilt. He has divided the responsibility between Orestes and Electra in such a manner as to make the sister appear the more cold-blooded of the two. It is she who plans the snare into which her mother falls. While Orestes wavers and falters, Electra never hesitates for a moment. She unflinchingly bears her part in the murder, when her brother is fain to cover his eyes while he strikes. Yet (as is brought out in the dialogue with the Dioscuri) she had not his excuse. No oracle had been given to *her*. Her ruling motive appears as an inflexible hatred of her mother. The Electra of the two other dramatists has indeed that feeling, but the noble and gentle side of her character is far more prominent. The general result, then, is this:—Euripides gives up Apollo, who told Orestes to commit matricide, as indefensible; while, by a skilful contrast with a more odious person, he contrives to increase our commiseration for Orestes, the hapless instrument of the god.

His Orestes and Electra.

§ 16. It has hitherto been generally held that the *Electra* of Sophocles belongs to an earlier date than its Euripidean namesake. A contrary view is however maintained by v. Wilamowitz, who further thinks that the *Electra* of Euripides was the stimulus which moved Sophocles to treat the subject[1]. Certain

Did his play precede and influence the *Electra* of Sophocles?

---

[1] *Hermes*, vol. XVIII. pp. 214—263: *Die beiden Elektren.*

relations (the able critic contends) exist between the two plays which show that one of them was influenced by the other, and a closer scrutiny proves that the play of Euripides was the original.

The critic points out that there is a striking resemblance between the openings of the two dramas. In each Orestes appears in the prologue; then there is a monody for Electra; and she is presently joined by the Chorus. And there is internal evidence that Euripides was the model, since he had a clear motive for making Orestes appear early and for composing his Chorus of persons external to the palace, and he provides the Chorus with a reason for their arrival, whereas this is not the case with Sophocles. But, in the first place, the likeness between the two plays in these particular points is immeasurably less striking than the general contrast. And even if imitation could be proved, it does not follow that Sophocles was the imitator. Is it strange that Orestes and his companions should reconnoitre the ground on which they will soon have to act, or that the old man should point out the chief features of the scene? The poet's invention of the double embassy from Phocis was a novelty, and he wished to give the spectator a clue to it at the outset. And when Sophocles, like Euripides, composes his Chorus of persons external to the house, a desire to vary from Aeschylus would account for this as easily as a desire to copy Euripides; but why should not the poet's motive have been independent of both? The free-born women of Mycenae are exponents of the public goodwill towards the rightful heir. But how, we are asked, had they become friends of Electra? Chrysothemis and Clytaemnestra tell us, it may be answered, that Electra frequently passed beyond the doors. Lastly, it is objected that the Chorus come to Electra without a definite reason. Is there not reason enough in their purpose of consoling and counselling her,— the purpose which she gratefully acknowledges?

Again, both Sophocles and Euripides bring Electra into controversy with Clytaemnestra. In the play of Euripides, the

tenor of this controversy is such as to mitigate the odiousness
of Clytaemnestra, and to emphasise the hardness of Electra.
This was what Euripides meant to do. The aim of Sophocles
was the opposite, to concentrate our sympathy upon Electra.
But, says Prof. v. Wilamowitz, Sophocles has involuntarily
given the advantage in dignity and self-command to Clytaemnestra; and this shows that he has (unskilfully) imitated
Euripides. Is it true that the Clytaemnestra of Sophocles
appears to more advantage than his Electra? Every reader
must judge for himself; I should not have said so, nor, indeed,
do I find it easy to understand how any one could receive that
impression. Moreover the controversies in the two plays
respectively differ both in topics and in style.

Finally, let us consider the more general ground upon
which it is argued that Sophocles was stimulated
to write his *Electra* by the work of Euripides.
The Euripidean *Electra* is certainly a play which
Sophocles would have viewed with repugnance. He would
have thought that both the divine and the human persons
were degraded. The whole treatment is a negation of that
ideal art to which Sophocles had devoted his life. It is perfectly conceivable that such a piece should have roused him to
make a protest,—to show how the theme could once more be
nobly treated, as Aeschylus long ago had treated it, and yet
without raising the moral and religious problem of the *Choephori*. But is such a hypothesis *more* probable than the
converse? Suppose that the Sophoclean *Electra* was the
earlier of the two. Is it not equally conceivable that Euripides
should have been stirred to protest against the calm condona-
tion of matricide? Might he not have wished to show how
the subject could be handled without ignoring, as Sophocles
does, this aspect of the vengeance, and also without refraining
from criticism on the solution propounded by Aeschylus? This,
in my belief, is what Euripides actually did wish to do.

I cannot, then, see any valid reason for supposing that

Argument from general probability.

Euripides preceded Sophocles in treating this subject. On the other hand, the new line taken by Euripides is the more intelligible if he had before him the pieces of both the elder dramatists.

§ 17. There are, however, strong grounds of internal coincidence for believing that the *Electra* is among the later plays of Sophocles. It cannot, on any view, be placed more than a few years before the Euripidean *Electra*, of which the probable date is 413 B.C. The traits which warrant this conclusion are the following. (1) The frequency of ἀντιλαβή, *i.e.* the partition of an iambic trimeter between two speakers. The ordinary form of such partition is when each person speaks once, so that the trimeter falls into two parts (*a, b*). Taking the two latest plays, we find 22 such examples in the *Philoctetes*, and 52 in the *Oedipus Coloneus*. The *Electra* ranks between them, with 25. Next comes the *Oedipus Tyrannus*, with only 10. Further, verse 1502 of *Electra* is so divided between two persons that it falls into three parts (*a, b, a*). The other Sophoclean instances of this are confined to the *Philoctetes* (810, 814, 816), and the *Oedipus Coloneus* (832).

(2) Anapaestic verses (1160—1162) are inserted in a series of iambic trimeters. The only parallel for this occurs in the *Trachiniae* (v. 1081, vv. 1085 f.), a piece which may be placed somewhere between 420 and 410 B.C. In the earlier practice, a series of iambic trimeters could be broken only by shorter iambic measures, or by mere interjections.

(3) The 'free' or 'melic' anapaests in *El.* 86—120 are of a type which can be strictly matched only in plays of a date later than *circ.* 420 B.C., such as the *Troades*, the *Ion*, and the *Iphigeneia in Tauris*.

(4) The actors have a notably large share in the lyric element of the play. (*a*) Thus the anapaests just mentioned are delivered by Electra as a μονῳδία. Such a monody can be paralleled only from the later plays of Euripides. It is

characteristic of the new music—satirised by Aristophanes in the *Frogs*—which came into vogue *circ.* 420 B.C. (*b*) Again, the Parodos of the *Electra* is in the form of a lyric dialogue (κομμός) between the heroine and the Chorus. Here, too, it is only in the latest plays that we find parallels. A 'kommatic' parodos occurs also in the *Oedipus Coloneus*. That of the *Philoctetes* has something of the same general character, although there Neoptolemus replies to the Chorus only in anapaests. (*c*) Another illustration of the same tendency is the lyric duet between Electra and the coryphaeus in vv. 823—870, which may be compared with similar duets in the *Philoctetes* (*e.g.* 1170 ff.), and the *Oedipus Coloneus* (178 ff., 1677 ff.). (*d*) In the μέλος ἀπὸ σκηνῆς between Electra and Orestes (1232—1287), the Chorus take no part. On the other hand, the songs given to the Chorus alone are of relatively small compass (472—515; 1058—1097; 1384—1397).

(5) The Parodos shows different classes of metre (the γένος ἴσον and the γένος διπλάσιον) combined within the same strophe; and, at the close, the epode re-echoes them all. This πολυμετρία is a further sign of a late period.

When all these indications are considered, there seems to be at least a very strong probability that the *Electra* was written not earlier than 420 B.C. There is only one point that might seem to favour an earlier date. The long syllables of the trimeter are here resolved more rarely than in any other of the seven extant plays. But, though a very great *frequency* of such resolution (as in the *Philoctetes*) has a clear significance, a *negative* application of the test would be, as the statistics show, most unsafe; and, in this instance, all the other internal evidence is on the opposite side. Those, then, who hold (as I do) that the play was produced before the *Electra* of Euripides (413 B.C.), will conclude that the years 420 and 414 B.C. mark the limits of the period to which it may be referred.

MANUSCRIPTS, EDITIONS, ETC.

§ 1. THE *Electra* was one of the most popular plays in Byzantine as in older times, and ranks second only to the *Ajax* in respect to number of MSS. This popularity bears upon another fact which is illustrated by the scholia (see below, § 3),—viz., the frequency of variants indicating a text, or texts, inferior to that represented by the better codices. On the other hand, though the great mass of the later MSS. are of no independent value, and teem with errors due to carelessness or to feeble conjecture, yet it happens now and again that some one among them preserves or confirms a true reading, offers a noteworthy variant, or presents some other point of interest.

The most important of the MSS. referred to in the critical notes are L = cod. Laur. 32. 9 (first half of 11th century), and A = cod. 2712 in the National Library of Paris. Next to these comes Γ = cod. Laur. 2725 at Florence, a vellum codex written in 1282 A.D. L is by far the best but not the sole source of the existing MSS.

S denotes the first reviser and scholiast whose corrections are found in L: corrections by later hands are signified by L^c.

r denotes one or more of the MSS. other than L.

§ 2. In common with the later MSS., L exhibits the interpolation αὐδᾶς δέ ποῖον (856), first deleted by Triclinius. It shares also the interpolation πατέρων after γενναίων (128), first removed by Monk (*Mus. Crit.* I. p. 69, ann. 1814). But the general superiority of L is not less apparent in this play than in the rest. Thus in v. 174, where, like the other MSS., it now has the corrupt ἔστι, it originally had the genuine reading, ἔτι. In 192 most MSS. have lost ἀμφίσταμαι, but L has at least ἀφίσταμαι, while the majority have ἐφίσταμαι.

Verses 584—586, accidentally omitted from the text of L, have been supplied in the margin by the first hand. It is the first hand also which has inserted verse 993 in the text. But the addition of verse 1007 in the margin is due to the first corrector (S). A comparison of v. 993 with 1007 is instructive in regard to the difference between the two handwritings, which is often less clear than in this example. The addition of verses 1485—6 in the margin may also be attributed to the first corrector.

§ 3. The scholium in L on v. 272 preserves αὐτοίντην, changed in the MSS. to αὐτοφόντην. The scholium on 446 confirms (by the words τῇ ἑαυτῶν κεφαλῇ) the true reading κάρᾳ in 445, lost in almost all MSS. At v. 1281 the lemma of the scholium in L preserves ἁν, corrupted in the text of L, as in most MSS., to ἁν. Several of the variants recorded in the scholia are curious for the free indulgence in feeble guess-work which they suggest. A typical example occurs in the schol. on 1019, where οὐδὲν ἧσσον figures as a *v. l.* for αὐτόχειρι.

§ 4. There are some gaps in the text. A trimeter has certainly been lost after v. 1264. In 1283 something has fallen out before ἔσχον. In 1432 the latter part of the trimeter is wanting.

In many instances lacunae have been suspected by various critics : in several cases it has been suggested that transposition is required to restore the original order : and no less than 110 verses have been regarded by one or more commentators as interpolations. In a vast majority of these instances, the suspicion or rejection appears wholly unwarrantable, and, so far as I am able to see, verse 691 is the only one in this play which affords reasonable ground for strong suspicion.

Conjectural emendation (as the notes will show) has not left much to glean,—for those, at any rate, who conceive that the proper use of that resource is restorative, not creative ; but, to mention two examples of small points, no one seems to have suggested that in 1380 προπίτνω ought to be προπίπτω, or that the halting verse, 1264, τότ' εἶδες ὅτε θεοί μ' ἐπώτρυναν μολεῖν, might be healed by the mere change of ὅτε to εὖτε.

§ 5. Besides the various complete editions of Sophocles
Editions.
    I have consulted F. A. Paley's commentary, in his volume containing the *Philoctetes, Electra, Trachiniae,* and *Ajax* (London, 1880); the 3rd edition of G. Wolff's *Electra,* revised by L. Bellermann (1880) ; and, above all, the 3rd edition of Otto Jahn's *Electra,* as revised and enlarged by Professor Michaelis, a work of the highest value for textual criticism, which contains also a well-digested selection both of the ancient materials for interpretation of the play, and of modern conjectures.

J. E.   4

METRICAL ANALYSIS

THE lyric metres of the *Electra* are the following. (1) Logaoedic, based on the choree (or 'trochee'), $-\smile$, and the cyclic dactyl $-\smile\smile$, which is metrically equivalent to the choree. (2) Choreic, based on the choree (trochee). (3) Dactylic. (4) Dochmiac, $\smile : --\smile | -\wedge$.

(5) Anapaestic dimeters, with anacrusis, are used in the Parodos (third Strophe, and Epode); and, without anacrusis, in the first Kommos, second Strophe, 850 ff. Like the anapaests of Electra's θρῆνος preceding the Parodos (vv. 86—120), these belong to the class which may be described as 'free' or 'melic' anapaests, in contradistinction to the march-anapaest.

(6) The 'paeon quartus,' $\smile\smile\smile-$, is appropriately introduced in the first verse of the third Stasimon—that short ode which marks the moment of suspense, just after the avengers have entered the house. In v. 1388, the paeon is replaced, and as it were balanced, by a kindred measure, the bacchius, $--\smile$, often employed to denote perplexity or surprise.

The lyrics of the *Electra* have a special interest in regard to the question concerning the period to which the play belongs. Down to about 420 B.C. it is somewhat rare in tragic lyrics to find different classes of metre combined within the same strophe. One class is the γένος ἴσον, in which the time-value of the thesis is equal to that of the arsis, as it is in the dactyl, the spondee, and the anapaest. The other class, the γένος διπλάσιον or ἄνισον, includes the trochee and iambus, with the measures based upon them. In plays of the earlier period, the same strophe seldom represents both these classes. But in the Parodos of the *Electra* a single strophe combines dactyls or anapaests with choreic or logaoedic verses; and the Epode unites all four kinds. Such πολυμετρία was associated with the new tendencies in music which began to prevail shortly before the Sicilian Expedition.

In the third Stasimon (1384—1397) we have an example of dochmiacs in combination with other elements, the paeon, bacchius, and iambic. Another feature worthy of notice is presented by the μέλος ἀπὸ σκηνῆς in 1232—1287, viz., the use made of the iambic trimeter in connection with dochmiacs. Iambic trimeters, when thus interposed in a melic passage, were not spoken, as in ordinary dialogue, but given in recitative with musical accompaniment (παρακαταλογή).

In the subjoined metrical schemes, the sign ‿ denotes that the ordinary time-value of a long syllable, commonly marked −, is increased by one half, so that it becomes equal to −◡ or ◡◡◡: the sign ⏖ denotes that such time-value is doubled, and becomes equal to −− or −◡◡. The sign ≳ means that an 'irrational' long syllable (συλλαβὴ ἄλογος) is substituted for a short. The letter ω, written over two short syllables, indicates that they have the time-value of one short only.

At the end of a verse, ∧ marks a pause equal to ◡, ‾∧ a pause equal to −. The *anacrusis* of a verse (the part preliminary to the regular metre) is marked off by three dots placed vertically, ⋮ .

The end of a rhythmical unit, or 'sentence,' is marked by ‖. The end of a rhythmical 'period' (a combination of two or more such sentences, corresponding with each other), is marked by]].

If a rhythmical sentence introduces a rhythmical period without belonging to it, it is called a προῳδός, or prelude (marked as πρ.): or, if it closes it, an ἐπῳδός, epode, or postlude. Similarly a period may be grouped round an isolated rhythmical sentence, which is then called the μεσῳδός, mesode, or interlude.

I. Parodos, vv. 121—250.

FIRST STROPHE.—The measures of the several periods are as follows:—
I. dactylic: II. dactylic: III. choreic (or 'trochaic'): IV. dactylic: V. logaoedic : VI. choreic.

I.   1.   −− | −− | −◡◡ | − ‾∧ ‖
     2.   −− | −− | −◡◡ | ⌣ ‖ −− | −◡◡ | −◡ | −− | − ‾∧]]
                                                                  ἐπ.

II. 1.   −◡◡ | −◡◡ | −◡◡ | −◡◡ ‖
     2.   −◡◡ | −◡◡ | −◡◡ | −◡◡]]

III. 1.   ◡⋮−◡ | ⏝◡ | ϖ◡ | −◡ | ◡◡◡ | − ∧
     2.   ◡⋮⌐ | ⌐ | −◡ | −◡ | ⌐ | − ∧]]

IV. 1.   −◡◡ | −− | ⌣ | − ‾∧ ‖   πρ.
     2.   −◡◡ | −◡◡ | −◡◡ | −◡◡ ‖
     3.   −◡◡ | −◡◡ | −◡◡ | −◡◡ ‖
     4.   −◡◡ | −◡◡ | −◡◡ | −◡◡ ‖
     5.   −◡◡ | −◡◡ | −◡◡ | −◡◡]]

V.   ⌒ː⌞│⌞│⌞│ – ∞ ‖ ⌣⌣ │ ⌣⌣ │ – ⌣ │ – ⋀ ⟧
VI. 1. ⌒ː – ⌣ │ – ⌣ │ ⌞ │ – ⋀ ‖
    2. ⌞ │ – ⌣ │ ⌞ │ – ⋀ ⟧

SECOND STROPHE.—Choreic in periods I., II., and IV.; dactylic in III.

I.   > ː⌞│⌞│⌞│⌞‖⌣⌣⌣│⌣⌣⌣│ – ⌣ │ – ⋀ ⟧
II. 1. ⌒ː⌣⌣⌣ │⌞│ – ⌣ │ – ⌣ │⌞│ – ⋀ ‖
    2. > ː⌣⌣⌣ │⌞│ – ⌣ │ – ⌣ │⌞│ – ⋀ ‖
    3. –> │ – ⌒∞ │ – ⌣> │ – ∞> │ – ∞ │ – ⌒> ‖
    4. ⌒ː – ⌣ │ – ⌣ │⌞│ – ⋀ ‖
    5. > ː⌣⌣⌣ │⌞│⌞│ – ⋀ ‖
    6. > ː⌣⌣⌣ │⌞│⌞│ – ⋀ ‖
    7. – ∞ │ – ∞ │ – ∞ │ – ∞ ‖
    8. > ː⌣⌣⌣ │⌣⌣⌣⌣⌣ │ – ⌣ │ ⌣⌣⌣⌣⌣ │⌞│ – ⋀ ‖
    9. > ː⌣⌣⌣ │⌣⌣⌣ │⌣⌣⌣⌣⌣ │ – ⌣ │⌞│ – ⋀ ‖
    10. ⌣ː⌣⌣⌣⌣ │⌞│ – ⌣ │ – ⌣ │⌞│ – ⋀ ⟧
III. 1. – ⌣ ⌣ │ – ⌣ ⌣ │ – ⌣ ⌣ │ – ⌣ ⌣ ‖
    2. – ⌣ ⌣ │ – ⌣ ⌣ │ – ⌣ ⌣ │ – ⌣ ⌣ ‖
    3. – ⌣ ⌣ │ – ⌣ ⌣ │ – ⌣ ⌣ │ – ⌣ ⌣ ‖
    4. – ⌣ ⌣ │ – ⌣ ⌣ │ – ⌣ ⌣ │ – ⌣ ⌣ ⟧
IV. 1. ⌣ː⌞│⌞│ – ⌣ │ – ⋀ ‖
    2. ⌣ː –> │ – ⌣ │ – ⌣ │ –> ⟧

THIRD STROPHE.—Periods I., II., and III. consist of anapaestic dimeters, with anacrusis. In I., the spondees give a slow and solemn movement, suited to the theme; in II., where the subject changes from the crime to the passion which prompted it, the rhythm is lightened and accelerated by dactyls. Period IV. shows a blending of different measures, characteristic of the πολυμετρία to which reference was made above. The 1st and 4th verses are still anapaestic dimeters; but v. 2 is a choreic tripody, and v. 3 a logaoedic tripody, of the form known as a 'first Pherecratic.' In period V. we have choreic tetrapodies.

I. 1. – ː – – │ – – │ ⌣⌣ │ – ⋀̄ ‖
   2. – ː – – │ – – │ – – │ – ⋀̄ ‖
   3. ⌣ ⌣ ː – – │ – – │ – – │ – ⋀̄ ‖
   4. ⌣⌣ ː – – │ – – │ ⌣⌣ │ – ⋀̄ ⟧

II. 1. ⏑ ⏑ ⋮ – ⏑ ⏑ | – ⏑ ⏑ | – – | – Λ̄ ‖
2. – ⋮ – – | – ⏖ | – – | – Λ̄ ‖
3. – ⋮ – ⏕ | – ⏑ ⏑ | – ⏑ ⏑ | – Λ̄ ‖
4. ⌞ ⏑ | ⌞ ⏑ | ⊔ | – Λ̄ ⟧ ἐπ.

III. 1. – ⋮ – – | – – | ⏖ – | ⏖ Λ̄ ‖
2. – ⋮ – – | – – | ⊔ | – Λ̄ ⟧

IV. 1. – ⋮ – – | – – | – – | – Λ̄ ‖
2. > ⋮ ⌞ | ⌞ | – Λ ‖
3. ⁓ ⏑ | ⏑ ⏑ ⏑ | – Λ ‖
4. ⏑ ⏑ ⋮ – ⏕ | – ⏑ ⏑ | – ⏕ | – Λ̄ ⟧

V. 1. > ⋮ ⏑ ⏑ ⏑ | ⌞ | – ⏑ | – Λ ‖
2. ⏑ ⏑ ⏑ | – ⏑ | – ⏑ | – Λ ‖
3. ⏑> ⋮ ⏑ ⏑ ⏑ | ⏑ ⏑ ⏑ | – ⏑ | – Λ ‖
4. ⏑> ⋮ ⏑ ⏑ ⏑ | ⏑ ⏑ ⏑ | – ⏑ | – Λ ‖
5. – ω | – ω | – ω | – ω ‖
6. ⏑> ⋮ ⏑ ⏑ ⏑ | – ⏑ | ⌞ | – Λ ⟧

Epode.—I. Anapaestic dimeters (spondaic, as in period I. of the third Strophe), with anacrusis. These afford a soothing effect, after the passionate imprecation which closed the third Antistrophe. Then, in II., the dactylic tetrapodies once more express Electra's vehement grief. Period III. consists of anapaestic dimeters, with a logaoedic tripody. In IV., logaoedic and choreic tripodies are combined; and V. is choreic. Thus the measures used in the preceding part of the Parodos are repeated at the close.

I. 1. – ⋮ – – | – – | ⊔ | – Λ̄ ‖
2. – ⋮ – – | – – | ⊔ | – Λ̄ ‖
3. – ⋮ – – | – – | ⊔ | – Λ̄ ⟧

II. 1. – ⏑ ⏑ | – ⏑ ⏑ | – ⏑ ⏑ | – ⏑ ⏑ ‖
2. – ⏑ ⏑ | – ⏑ ⏑ | – ⏑ ⏑ | – ⏑ ⏑ ‖
3. – ⏑ ⏑ | – – | – – | – – ⟧

III. 1. – ⋮ – – | – – | – – | – Λ̄ ‖
2. – ⋮ – – | – – | – – | – Λ̄ ‖
3. – ⋮ – – | – – | – ⏑ ⏑ | – Λ̄ ‖
4. – ⋮ – – | – – | – ⏑ ⏑ | – Λ̄ ‖
5. ⁓ ⏑ | – ⏑ | – Λ ⟧

IV. 1. ⌣⌣ | – ⌣ | ⌞ ‖ ⌣⌣ | – ⌣ | – ∧ ‖
   2. – ⌣ | – ⌣ | ⌞ ‖ – ⌣ | – ⌣ | – ∧ ⟧
V. 1. – > | ⌣⌣ | – ⌣ | – ∧ ‖
   2. > ⋮ – ⌣ | ⌞ | – ⌣ | – > ‖ – ⌣ | – ⌣ | ⌞ | – ∧ ⟧

II. First Stasimon, vv. 472—515.

STROPHE.—I. Logaoedic. II., III., and IV., Choreic.

I. 1. – > | ⌣⌣ | ⌞ | ⌣⌣ | – ∧ ‖   πρ.
   2. > ⋮ – > | ⌣⌣ | – ⌣ | ⌞ ‖ – ⌣ | – ⌣ | ⌞ | – ∧ ⟧
II. 1. ⌣ ⋮ – ⌣ | – ⌣ | ⌣⌣⌣ | – ⌣ | – ⌣ | – ∧ ‖
   2. ⌣ ⋮ – ⌣ | ⌞ | – ⌣ | – ⌣ | – ⌣ | – ∧ ⟧
III. 1. ⌣ ⋮ – ⌣ | – ⌣ | – ∧ ‖
   2. > ⋮ – ⌣ | – ⌣ | – ⌣ ‖
   3. – ⌣ | – ⌣ | – ⌣ | – ∧ ⟧   ἐπ.
IV. 1. > ⋮ – ⌣ | – > | – ⌣ | – > ‖ ⌞ | ⌞ | – ⌣ | – ∧ ‖
   2. > ⋮ – ⌣ | – > | – ⌣ | – ⌇ ‖ ⌞ | ⌞ | – ⌣ | – ∧ ‖
   3. > ⋮ ⌣⌣ | – ⌣ | – ⌇ | – ⌣ | – > | – ∧ ⟧   ἐπ.

EPODE.—Choreic, in verses of four feet, varied by two hexapodies.

   1. > ⋮ ⌣⌣⌣ | ⌞ | ⌞ | – ⌣ | ⌣⌣⌣ | ⌞ | ⌞ | – ∧ ‖
   2. > ⋮ ⌣⌣⌣ | ⌞ | ⌞ | ⌞ | – ⌣ | – ∧ ‖
   3. > ⋮ ⌣⌣⌣ | ⌞ | ⌞ | – > ‖ ⌣⌣⌣ | ⌞ | ⌞ | – ∧ ‖
   4. > ⋮ – ⌣ | ⌞ | ⌞ | – > ‖ – > | ⌞ | ⌞ | – ∧ ‖
   5. > ⋮ – ⌣ | ⌞ | ⌞ | ⌞ | – ⌣ | – ∧ ‖
   6. ⌣ ⋮ – ⌣ | ⌞ | – > ‖ – ⌣ | ⌣⌣⌣ | ⌞ | ⌞ | – ∧ ⟧

III. First Kommos, vv. 823—870.

FIRST STROPHE.—Logaoedic.

I. 1. > ⋮ ⌣⌣⌣ | ⌞ | ⌣⌣ | ⌞ | ⌣⌣ | – ∧ ‖
   2. ⌣⌣ | ⌞ | ⌣⌣ | ⌞ ‖ – > | ⌣⌣ | ⌞ | – ∧ ‖
        – – – –
      [ε ε α ι α ι
      ε ε ι ω]

3. ⌞ | ⏖ | ⌞ | ⌞ ∧ ||
4. – > | ⏖ | ⌞ | ⏖ | ⌞ | – ∧]]

II. 1. > ⁝ ⏖ | ⌞ | ⏖ | – ∧ ||
2. ⏖ | ⌞ | ⏖ | ⌞ || ⏖ | ⌞ | ⏖ | – ∧ ||
3. ⏖ | ⌞ | ⌞ | – ∧]]

SECOND STROPHE.—I. Anapaestic dimeters, with a trochaic pentapody as prelude. II. and III., Logaoedic and Choreic verses. Thus here, again, as in the Parodos, the γένος ἴσον and the γένος διπλάσιον are combined.

I. 1. – ⏑ | ⌞ | – ⏑ | – ⏑ | – ∧ || πρ.
2. – ⁝ – – | – – | ⏑ ⏑ – | – ∧ ||
3. – ⁝ – – | – – | – – | – ∧̄ ||
4. – ⁝ – – | – – | ⊔ | – ∧̄]]

II. 1. ⏖ | ⌞ | ⌞ | – ∧ ||
2. – ⏑ | ⌞ | – ⏑ | – ∧ ||
3. ⏑ ⏑ ⏑ | – ⏑ | – ⏑ | – ∧]]

III. 1. ⏑ ⁝ – ⏑ | – ⏑ | – ⏑ | – ∧ ||
2. ⏖ | – ∧ ||
3. ⏖ | – ⏑ | ⌞ | – ∧]]

IV. Second Stasimon, vv. 1058—1097.

FIRST STROPHE.—Logaoedic. A verse of six feet forms the prelude to a series of tetrapodies, which are chiefly first Glyconics, varied, however, by second Glyconics in I. 5, II. 1, 2, 3.

I. 1. ⏑ ⁝ – ⏑ | ⌞ | ⏖ | – ⏑ | – ⏑ | ⌞ || πρ.
2. ⏖ | – ⏑ | – ⏑ | ⌞ ||
3. ⏖ | – ⏑ | – ⏑ | ⌞ ||
4. ⏖ | – ⏑ | – ⏑ | ⌞ ||
5. ⏖ | ⏖ | – ⏑ | – ⏑]]

II. 1. – > | ⏖ | – ⏑ | – ∧ ||
2. – ⏑̲> | ⏖ | – ⏑ | – ∧ ||
3. – ⏑> | ⏖ | ⌞ | – ∧]] ἐπ.

III. 1. ⏑⏑ | –⏑ | –⏑ | ⌣ ‖
    2. ⏑⏑ | –⏑ | –⏑ | ⌣ ‖
    3. ⏑⏑ | –⏑ | –⏑ | ⌣ ‖
    4. ⏑⏑ | ⏑⏑ | –⏑ | –>]

SECOND STROPHE.—I. Logaoedic. II. Choreic.

I. 1. –> | ⏑⏑ | ⌣ | – ∧ ‖
    2. –⏑ | –> | –⏑ | –> | –⏑ | – ∧ ‖
    3. ⏑⏑ | ⌣ | ⌣ | – ∧]

II. 1. ⏒ ⋮ –⏑ | ⌣ | –⏑ | ⌣ ‖ –⏑ | –⏑ | ⌣ | – ∧ ‖
    2. ⏑ ⋮ –⏑ | ⪥ ⏑ | –⏑ | –⏑ | ⏑⏑⏑ | –⏑ | ⏑⏑⏑ | – ∧ ‖
    3. ⏑ ⋮ –⏑ | ⌣ | –⏑ | –⏑ | ⌣ | – ∧]   ἐπ.

V. Lyrics for actors (μέλος ἀπὸ σκηνῆς), vv. 1232—1286.

STROPHE.—I. and II., Dochmiac. III. Choreic. IV. Logaoedic.

I. 1. ⏑ ⋮ ⊔ ⏑ | – ∧ ‖
    2. ⏑ ⋮ ––⏑ | –⏑ ‖ ––⏑ | – ∧ ‖
    3. ⏑ ⋮ ⏑⏑––⏑ | – ∧]

[Here follow two iambic trimeters, vv. 1235, 1236, corresponding with vv. 1256, 1257 in the antistrophe.]

     ⏑ ⋮ ⌣ | – ∧ ‖
     τί δ' ἔστιν   (*Extra metrum.*)
     τί δρῶσα

[Here follows a second pair of trimeters, vv. 1238, 1239, corresponding with vv. 1259, 1260 in the antistrophe.]

II.   ⏑ ⋮ ⏑⏑–⏑ | –⏑ ‖ ––⏑ | – ∧]
III. 1. ⏑ ⋮ –⏑ | –⏑ | ⌣ | – ∧ ‖
     2. ⏑ ⋮ ⌣ | –⏑ | ⌣ | – ∧]

[Here follows a third pair of trimeters, vv. 1243, 1244, corresponding with v. 1264 in the antistrophe, after which a trimeter has been lost.]

IV. 1. ⏑ ⋮ ⏑⏑⏑ | –⏑ | – ∧ ‖
    2. ⏒ ⋮ ⏑⏑⏑ | ⏑⏑⏑ | – ∧ ‖

3. > ⋮ ∪ ∪ ∪ | ∪ ∪ ∪ | − ∧ ‖
4. > ⋮ ∪ ∪ ∪ | ⌣ ∪ | − ∧ ‖
5. > ⋮ ∪ ∪ ∪ | ⌣ ∪ | − ∪ | − ∧]]   *ἐπ.*

[Here follows a fourth pair of trimeters, vv. 1251, 1252, corresponding with vv. 1271, 1272 in the antistrophe.]

EPODE.—Choreic, in verses of six, four, or two feet.

I.   1.   ∪ ⋮ − ∪ | ⌐ | − ∪ | − ∧ ‖
     2.   ∪ ∪ ∪ | − ∪ | ⌐ | ⌐ ‖ − ∪ | − ∪ | ⌐ | − ∧ ‖
     3.   > ⋮ ∪ ∪ ∪ | ∪ ∪ ∪ | − ∪ | − ∧]]
II. 1.   ∪ ⋮ − ∪ | − > | − ∪ | − ∪ | ⌐ | − ∧ ‖
     2.   > ⋮ − ∪ | − > | − ∪ | − ∪ | ⌐ | − ∧]]

          [Here follows an iambic trimeter, v. 1279.]

III. 1.   ∪ ⋮ ⌐ | − ∧ ‖
     2.   ∪ ⋮ ⌐ | − ∧]]
IV. 1.   ⌣ ∪ | ⌣ ∪ | − ∪ | − ∧ ‖
     2.   − ∪ | − ∪ | ⌐ | − ∧ ‖
     3.   − ∪ | − ∪ | ⌐ | − ∧ ‖
     4.   ∪ ⋮ − ∪ | − ∪ | − ∪ | − ∪ | ⌐ | − ∧]]   *ἐπ.*
V.   1.   ∪ ⋮ − ∪ | − ∪ | − ∪ | − ∪ | ⌐ | − ∧ ‖
     2.   − ∪ | − ∪ | − ∪ | − ∪ ‖
     3.   − ∪ | − ∪ | − ∪ | − ∪ | ⌐ | − ∧]]

VI.   Third Stasimon, vv. 1384—1397.

The Strophe of this short ode is noteworthy for the different elements combined in it. Verse 1 contains two paeons, of the form known as the *paeon quartus*, ∪ ∪ ∪ −. Verses 2 and 3 are dochmiac dimeters. In verse 4, instead of again using paeons, the poet employs a kindred measure, the bacchius, − − ∪.

     1.   ∪ ∪ ∪ − | ∪ ∪ ∪ − ‖
     2.   ∪ ⋮ ∪ ∪ − ∪ | − ∪ ‖ − − ∪ | − ∧ ‖

[Here follows a trimeter, v. 1386, corresponding with v. 1393 in the antistr.]

     3.   ∪ ⋮ ∪ ∪ − ∪ | − ∪ ‖ − − ∪ | − ∧ ‖
     4.   ∪ ⋮ − − ∪ | − ⌐∧]]

[Here follows an iambic dimeter, v. 1389, corresponding with v 1396 in the antistrophe. Then an iambic trimeter, v. 1390, corresponding with v. 1397.]

VII. Second Kommos, vv. 1398—1441.

The lyric verses which are in strophic correspondence are not all con-secutive, as is shown by the numbering below. But the series constitutes a strophe and an antistrophe, in which each of the three groups of verses forms a rhythmical period. The first and third periods are choreic; the second is logaoedic.

I.   Verses 1407, 1428
        $>\,\vdots\,-\,\smile\;|\;\bigsqcup\;|\;-\,\smile\;|\;\bigsqcup\;\|\;-\,\smile\;|\;-\,\smile\;|\;\bigsqcup\;|\;-\,\wedge\,\|$

II. 1.   1413, 1433
        $\frown\,\smile\;|\;\frown\,\smile\;|\;-\,\smile\;|\;-\,\smile\;|\;-\,\overset{\smile}{>}\,\|$

   2.   1414, 1434
        $\frown\,\smile\;|\;\frown\,\smile\;|\;-\,\smile\;|\;-\,\smile\;|\;-\,\wedge\,]\!]$

III. 1.   1419, 1439
        $\smile\,\vdots\,-\,\smile\;|\;\bigsqcup\;|\;-\,\smile\;|\;\bigsqcup\;\|\;-\,\smile\;|\;\bigsqcup\;|\;-\,\smile\;|\;-\,\wedge\,\|$

   2.   1420, 1440
        $\smile\,\vdots\,-\,\smile\;|\;-\,\smile\;|\;-\,\smile\;|\;-\,\overset{\smile}{>}\,\|\;-\,\smile\;|\;-\,\smile\;|\;\bigsqcup\;|\;-\,\wedge\,\|$

   3.   1421, 1441
        $-\,\smile\;|\;-\,\smile\;|\;\bigsqcup\;|\;-\,\wedge\,]\!]$ ἐπ.

ΤΑ ΤΟΥ ΔΡΑΜΑΤΟΣ ΠΡΟΣΩΠΑ.

ΠΑΙΔΑΓΩΓΟΣ.   ΧΡΥΣΟΘΕΜΙΣ.
ΟΡΕΣΤΗΣ.   ΚΛΥΤΑΙΜΝΗΣΤΡΑ
ΗΛΕΚΤΡΑ.   ΑΙΓΙΣΘΟΣ.
ΧΟΡΟΣ.

The parts would be cast as follows ;—

1. *Protagonist.* Electra.

2. *Deuteragonist.* Orestes, Clytaemnestra.

3. *Tritagonist.* Paedagogus, Chrysothemis, Aegisthus.

Fifteen women of Mycenae (πολίτιδες, 1227) form the Chorus. The mute persons noticed in the text are, Pylades; a handmaid of Clytaemnestra (634); and the πρόσπολοι of Orestes (1123).

STRUCTURE OF THE PLAY.

1. πρόλογος, verses 1—120, including a θρῆνος ἀπὸ σκηνῆς, 86—120.

2. πάροδος, in the form of a κομμός, 121—250.

---

3. ἐπεισόδιον πρῶτον, 251—471.

4. στάσιμον πρῶτον, 472—515.

---

5. ἐπεισόδιον δεύτερον, 516—1057, including a κομμός, 823—870.

6. στάσιμον δεύτερον, 1058—1097.

---

7. ἐπεισόδιον τρίτον, 1098—1383, including a μέλος ἀπὸ σκηνῆς, 1232—1286.

8. στάσιμον τρίτον, 1384—1397.

---

9. ἔξοδος, 1398—1510, including a κυμμός, 1398—1441.

ΗΛΕΚΤΡΑ.

ΤΑ ΤΟΥ ΔΡΑΜΑΤΟΣ ΠΡΟΣΩΠΑ.

ΠΑΙΔΑΓΩΓΟΣ.
ΟΡΕΣΤΗΣ.
ΗΛΕΚΤΡΑ.
ΧΟΡΟΣ.
ΧΡΥΣΟΘΕΜΙΣ.
ΚΛΥΤΑΙΜΝΗΣΤΡΑ.
ΑΙΓΙΣΘΟΣ.

ΗΛΕΚΤΡΑ.

ΠΑΙΔΑΓΩΓΟΣ.

Ὦ ΤΟΥ στρατηγήσαντος ἐν Τροίᾳ ποτὲ
Ἀγαμέμνονος παῖ, νῦν ἐκεῖν' ἔξεστί σοι
παρόντι λεύσσειν, ὧν πρόθυμος ἦσθ' ἀεί.
τὸ γὰρ παλαιὸν Ἄργος οὐπόθεις τόδε,
τῆς οἰστροπλῆγος ἄλσος Ἰνάχου κόρης·   5
αὕτη δ', Ὀρέστα, τοῦ λυκοκτόνου θεοῦ
ἀγορὰ Λύκειος· οὐξ ἀριστερᾶς δ' ὅδε
Ἥρας ὁ κλεινὸς ναός· οἷ δ' ἱκάνομεν,
φάσκειν Μυκήνας τὰς πολυχρύσους ὁρᾶν,
πολύφθορόν τε δῶμα Πελοπιδῶν τόδε,   10
ὅθεν σε πατρὸς ἐκ φόνων ἐγώ ποτε
πρὸς σῆς ὁμαίμου καὶ κασιγνήτης λαβὼν
ἤνεγκα κἀξέσωσα κἀξεθρεψάμην
τοσόνδ' ἐς ἥβης, πατρὶ τιμωρὸν φόνου.
νῦν οὖν, Ὀρέστα, καὶ σὺ φίλτατε ξένων   15
Πυλάδη, τί χρὴ δρᾶν ἐν τάχει βουλευτέον·
ὡς ἡμὶν ἤδη λαμπρὸν ἡλίου σέλας
ἑῷα κινεῖ φθέγματ' ὀρνίθων σαφῆ,
μέλαινά τ' ἄστρων ἐκλέλοιπεν εὐφρόνη.
πρὶν οὖν τιν' ἀνδρῶν ἐξοδοιπορεῖν στέγης,   20

4 ΣΟΦΟΚΛΕΟΥΣ

ξυνάπτετον λόγοισιν· ὡς ἐνταῦθ' ἐμὲν
ἵν' οὐκέτ' ὀκνεῖν καιρός, ἀλλ' ἔργων ἀκμή.

ΟΡΕΣΤΗΣ.

ὦ φίλτατ' ἀνδρῶν προσπόλων, ὥς μοι σαφῆ
σημεῖα φαίνεις ἐσθλὸς εἰς ἡμᾶς γεγώς.
ὥσπερ γὰρ ἵππος εὐγενής, κἂν ᾖ γέρων,   25
ἐν τοῖσι δεινοῖς θυμὸν οὐκ ἀπώλεσεν,
ἀλλ' ὀρθὸν οὖς ἵστησιν, ὡσαύτως δὲ σὺ
ἡμᾶς τ' ὀτρύνεις καὐτὸς ἐν πρώτοις ἔπει.
τοιγὰρ τὰ μὲν δόξαντα δηλώσω, σὺ δὲ
ὀξεῖαν ἀκοὴν τοῖς ἐμοῖς λόγοις διδούς,   30
εἰ μή τι καιροῦ τυγχάνω, μεθάρμοσον.
ἐγὼ γὰρ ἡνίχ' ἱκόμην τὸ Πυθικὸν
μαντεῖον, ὡς μάθοιμ' ὅτῳ τρόπῳ πατρὶ
δίκας ἀροίμην τῶν φονευσάντων πάρα,
χρῇ μοι τοιαῦθ' ὁ Φοῖβος ὧν πεύσει τάχα·   35
ἄσκευον αὐτὸν ἀσπίδων τε καὶ στρατοῦ
δόλοισι κλέψαι χειρὸς ἐνδίκους σφαγάς.
ὅτ' οὖν τοιόνδε χρησμὸν εἰσηκούσαμεν,
σὺ μὲν μολών, ὅταν σε καιρὸς εἰσάγῃ,
δόμων ἔσω τῶνδ', ἴσθι πᾶν τὸ δρώμενον,   40
ὅπως ἂν εἰδὼς ἡμὶν ἀγγείλῃς σαφῆ.
οὐ γάρ σε μὴ γήρᾳ τε καὶ χρόνῳ μακρῷ
γνῶσ', οὐδ' ὑποπτεύσουσιν ὧδ' ἠνθισμένον.
λόγῳ δὲ χρῶ τοιῷδ', ὅτι ξένος μὲν εἶ
Φωκεύς, παρ' ἀνδρὸς Φανοτέως ἥκων· ὁ γὰρ   45
μέγιστος αὐτοῖς τυγχάνει δορυξένων.
ἄγγελλε δ' ὅρκον προστιθεὶς ὁθούνεκα
τέθνηκ' Ὀρέστης ἐξ ἀναγκαίας τύχης,
ἄθλοισι Πυθικοῖσιν ἐκ τροχηλάτων

21 f. ὡς ἐνταῦθ' ἵνα | οὐκ ἔστ' ἔτ' ὀκνεῖν καιρός conj. Hotchkis (but with ἔστιν instead of ἔστ' ἔτ').   47 ὅρκῳ MSS.: corr. Reiske.

δίφρων κυλισθείς· ὧδ' ὁ μῦθος ἑστάτω.　　50
ἡμεῖς δὲ πατρὸς τύμβον, ὡς ἐφίετο,
λοιβαῖσι πρῶτον καὶ καρατόμοις χλιδαῖς
στέψαντες, εἶτ' ἄψορρον ἥξομεν πάλιν,
τύπωμα χαλκόπλευρον ἠρμένοι χεροῖν,
ὃ καὶ σὺ θάμνοις οἶσθά που κεκρυμμένον,　　55
ὅπως λόγῳ κλέπτοντες ἡδεῖαν φάτιν
φέρωμεν αὐτοῖς, τοὐμὸν ὡς ἔρρει δέμας
φλογιστὸν ἤδη καὶ κατηνθρακωμένον.
τί γάρ με λυπεῖ τοῦθ', ὅταν λόγῳ θανὼν
ἔργοισι σωθῶ κἀξενέγκωμαι κλέος;　　60
δοκῶ μέν, οὐδὲν ῥῆμα σὺν κέρδει κακόν.
ἤδη γὰρ εἶδον πολλάκις καὶ τοὺς σοφοὺς
λόγῳ μάτην θνῄσκοντας· εἶθ' ὅταν δόμους
ἔλθωσιν αὖθις, ἐκτετίμηνται πλέον·
ὡς κἄμ' ἐπαυχῶ τῆσδε τῆς φήμης ἄπο　　65
δεδορκότ' ἐχθροῖς ἄστρον ὣς λάμψειν ἔτι.
ἀλλ', ὦ πατρῷα γῆ θεοί τ' ἐγχώριοι,
δέξασθέ μ' εὐτυχοῦντα ταῖσδε ταῖς ὁδοῖς,
σύ τ', ὦ πατρῷον δῶμα· σοῦ γὰρ ἔρχομαι
δίκῃ καθαρτὴς πρὸς θεῶν ὡρμημένος·　　70
καὶ μή μ' ἄτιμον τῆσδ' ἀποστείλητε γῆς,
ἀλλ' ἀρχέπλουτον καὶ καταστάτην δόμων.
εἴρηκα μέν νυν ταῦτα· σοὶ δ' ἤδη, γέρον,
τὸ σὸν μελέσθω βάντι φρουρῆσαι χρέος.
νὼ δ' ἔξιμεν· καιρὸς γάρ, ὅσπερ ἀνδράσιν　　75
μέγιστος ἔργου παντός ἐστ' ἐπιστάτης.

ΗΛΕΚΤΡΑ.

ἰώ μοί μοι δύστηνος.

ΠΑ. καὶ μὴν θυρῶν ἔδοξα προσπόλων τινὸς
ὑποστενούσης ἔνδον αἰσθέσθαι, τέκνον.

52 λοιβαῖσι L: λοιβαῖς τε r.　　57 φέρωμεν Γ: φέροιμεν L, vulg.
J. E.　　　　　　　　　　　　　　　　　　　　　　5

6 ΣΟΦΟΚΛΕΟΥΣ

ΟΡ. ἆρ' ἐστὶν ἡ δύστηνος Ἠλέκτρα; θέλεις   80
μείνωμεν αὐτοῦ κἀπακούσωμεν γόων;
ΠΑ. ἥκιστα· μηδὲν πρόσθεν ἢ τὰ Λοξίου
πειρώμεθ' ἔρδειν κἀπὸ τῶνδ' ἀρχηγετεῖν,
πατρὸς χέοντες λουτρά· ταῦτα γὰρ φέρει
νίκην τ' ἐφ' ἡμῖν καὶ κράτος τῶν δρωμένων.   85

στρ. ΗΛ. ὦ φάος ἁγνὸν
καὶ γῆς ἰσόμοιρ' ἀήρ, ὥς μοι
πολλὰς μὲν θρήνων ᾠδάς,
πολλὰς δ' ἀντήρεις ᾔσθου
στέρνων πληγὰς αἱμασσομένων,   90
ὁπόταν δνοφερὰ νὺξ ὑπολειφθῇ·
τὰ δὲ παννυχίδων ἤδη στυγεραὶ
ξυνίσασ' εὐναὶ μογερῶν οἴκων,
ὅσα τὸν δύστηνον ἐμὸν θρηνῶ
πατέρ', ὃν κατὰ μὲν βάρβαρον αἶαν   95
φοίνιος Ἄρης οὐκ ἐξένισεν,
μήτηρ δ' ἡμὴ χὠ κοινολεχὴς
Αἴγισθος, ὅπως δρῦν ὑλοτόμοι,
σχίζουσι κάρα φονίῳ πελέκει·
κοὐδεὶς τούτων οἶκτος ἀπ' ἄλλης   100
ἢ 'μοῦ φέρεται, σοῦ, πάτερ, οὕτως
αἰκῶς οἰκτρῶς τε θανόντος.

ἀντιστρ. ἀλλ' οὐ μὲν δὴ
λήξω θρήνων στυγερῶν τε γόων,
ἔστ' ἂν παμφεγγεῖς ἄστρων   105
ῥιπάς, λεύσσω δὲ τόδ' ἦμαρ,
μὴ οὐ τεκνολέτειρ' ὥς τις ἀηδὼν
ἐπὶ κωκυτῷ τῶνδε πατρῴων

81 κἀπακούσωμεν Nauck: κἀνακούσωμεν MSS.   87 ἰσόμοιρος
MSS.: corr. Porson.   105 f. The MSS. have λεύσσω twice, after
ἔστ' ἂν and after ῥιπάς: Hermann deleted it in the former place.

πρὸ θυρῶν ἠχὼ πᾶσι προφωνεῖν.
ὦ δῶμ' Ἀΐδου καὶ Περσεφόνης, 110
ὦ χθόνι' Ἑρμῆ καὶ πότνι' Ἀρά,
σεμναί τε θεῶν παῖδες Ἐρινύες,
αἳ τοὺς ἀδίκως θνήσκοντας ὁρᾶθ',
αἳ τοὺς εὐνὰς ὑποκλεπτομένους,
ἔλθετ', ἀρήξατε, τείσασθε πατρὸς 115
φόνον ἡμετέρου,
καί μοι τὸν ἐμὸν πέμψατ' ἀδελφόν·
μούνη γὰρ ἄγειν οὐκέτι σωκῶ
λύπης ἀντίρροπον ἄχθος. 120

ΧΟΡΟΣ.

στρ. ά. ὦ παῖ, παῖ δυστανοτάτας
2 Ἠλέκτρα ματρός, τίν' ἀεὶ τάκεις ὧδ' ἀκόρεστον
οἰμωγὰν
3 τὸν πάλαι ἐκ δολερᾶς ἀθεώτατα
4 ματρὸς ἁλόντ' ἀπάταις Ἀγαμέμνονα 125
5 κακᾷ τε χειρὶ πρόδοτον; ὡς ὁ τάδε πορὼν
6 ὄλοιτ', εἴ μοι θέμις τάδ' αὐδᾶν.

ΗΛ. 7 ὦ γενέθλα γενναίων,
8 ἥκετ' ἐμῶν καμάτων παραμύθιον. 130
9 οἶδά τε καὶ ξυνίημι τάδ', οὔ τί με
10 φυγγάνει· οὐδ' ἐθέλω προλιπεῖν τόδε,
11 μὴ οὐ τὸν ἐμὸν στενάχειν πατέρ' ἄθλιον.
12 ἀλλ' ὦ παντοίας φιλότητος ἀμειβόμεναι χάριν,
13 ἐᾶτέ μ' ὧδ' ἀλύειν, 135
14 αἰαῖ, ἱκνοῦμαι.

---

113 f. ὁρᾶθ', | αἳ τοὺς Dobree: ὁρᾶτε, | τοὺς MSS. 124 ἀθεωτάτας
MSS.: corr. Erfurdt, Porson. 129 After γενναίων the MSS. add
πατέρων (or τοκέων r): del. Monk, Hermann.

8 ΣΟΦΟΚΛΕΟΥΣ

ἀντ. ά. **ΧΟ.** ἀλλ' οὔτοι τόν γ' ἐξ Ἄϊδα
2 παγκοίνου λίμνας πατέρ' ἀνστάσεις οὔτε γόοις
οὔτε λιταῖσιν·
3 ἀλλ' ἀπὸ τῶν μετρίων ἐπ' ἀμήχανον   140
4 ἄλγος ἀεὶ στενάχουσα διόλλυσαι,
5 ἐν οἷς ἀνάλυσίς ἐστιν οὐδεμία κακῶν.
6 τί μοι τῶν δυσφόρων ἐφίει;
ΗΛ. 7 νήπιος ὃς τῶν οἰκτρῶς   145
8 οἰχομένων γονέων ἐπιλάθεται.
9 ἀλλ' ἐμέ γ' ἁ στονόεσσ' ἄραρεν φρένας,
10 ἁ Ἴτυν, αἰὲν Ἴτυν ὀλοφύρεται,
11 ὄρνις ἀτυζομένα, Διὸς ἄγγελος.
12 ἰὼ παντλάμων Νιόβα, σὲ δ' ἔγωγε νέμω θεόν,   150
13 ἅτ' ἐν τάφῳ πετραίῳ
14 αἰεὶ δακρύεις.

στρ. β'. **ΧΟ.** οὔτοι σοὶ μούνᾳ, τέκνον, ἄχος ἐφάνη βροτῶν,
2 πρὸς ὅ τι σὺ τῶν ἔνδον εἶ περισσά,   155
3 οἷς ὁμόθεν εἶ καὶ γονᾷ ξύναιμος,
4 οἵα Χρυσόθεμις ζώει καὶ Ἰφιάνασσα,
5 κρυπτᾷ τ' ἀχέων ἐν ἥβᾳ,
6 ὄλβιος, ὃν ἁ κλεινὰ   160
7 γᾶ ποτε Μυκηναίων
8 δέξεται εὐπατρίδαν, Διὸς εὔφρονι
9 βήματι μολόντα τάνδε γᾶν Ὀρέσταν.
ΗΛ. 10 ὅν γ' ἐγὼ ἀκάματα προσμένουσ', ἄτεκνος,
11 τάλαιν' ἀνύμφευτος αἰὲν οἰχνῶ,   165
12 δάκρυσι μυδαλέα, τὸν ἀνήνυτον
13 οἶτον ἔχουσα κακῶν· ὁ δὲ λάθεται
14 ὧν τ' ἔπαθ' ὧν τ' ἐδάη. τί γὰρ οὐκ ἐμοὶ

139 οὔτε γόοις οὔτε λιταῖσιν L, vulg. (λιταῖς r): οὔτε γόοισιν οὔτ' εὐχαῖς
conj. Erfurdt (οὔτε γόοισιν οὔτ' ἄνταις Hermann). 160—163 The
MSS. and older edd. give these four vv. to Electra: corr. Tyrwhitt, Reiske.
164 ὅν γ' ἐγὼ Hermann: ὃν ἔγωγ' MSS.

15 ἔρχεται ἀγγελίας ἀπατώμενον;   170
16 ἀεὶ μὲν γὰρ ποθεῖ,
17 ποθῶν δ' οὐκ ἀξιοῖ φανῆναι.

ἀντ. β'.   ΧΟ. θάρσει μοι, θάρσει, τέκνον· ἔτι μέγας οὐρανῷ
2 Ζεύς, ὃς ἐφορᾷ πάντα καὶ κρατύνει·   175
3 ᾧ τὸν ὑπεραλγῆ χόλον νέμουσα
4 μήθ' οἷς ἐχθαίρεις ὑπεράχθεο μήτ' ἐπιλάθου.
5 χρόνος γὰρ εὐμαρὴς θεός.
6 οὔτε γὰρ ὁ τὰν Κρῖσαν   180
7 βούνομον ἔχων ἀκτὰν
8 παῖς Ἀγαμεμνονίδας ἀπερίτροπος,
9 οὔθ' ὁ παρὰ τὸν Ἀχέροντα θεὸς ἀνάσσων.

ΗΛ. 10 ἀλλ' ἐμὲ μὲν ὁ πολὺς ἀπολέλοιπεν ἤδη   185
11 βίοτος ἀνέλπιστος, οὐδ' ἔτ' ἀρκῶ·
12 ἅτις ἄνευ τεκέων κατατάκομαι,
13 ᾇς φίλος οὔτις ἀνὴρ ὑπερίσταται,
14 ἀλλ' ἀπερεί τις ἔποικος ἀναξία
15 οἰκονομῶ θαλάμους πατρός, ὧδε μὲν   190
16 ἀεικεῖ σὺν στολᾷ,
17 κεναῖς δ' ἀμφίσταμαι τραπέζαις.

στρ. γ'.   ΧΟ. οἰκτρὰ μὲν νόστοις αὐδά,
2 οἰκτρὰ δ' ἐν κοίταις πατρῴαις
3 ὅτε οἱ παγχάλκων ἀνταία   195
4 γενύων ὡρμάθη πλαγά.
5 δόλος ἦν ὁ φράσας, ἔρος ὁ κτείνας,
6 δεινὰν δεινῶς προφυτεύσαντες
7 μορφάν, εἴτ' οὖν θεὸς εἴτε βροτῶν

174 ἔτι L¹: ἔστι Lᶜ, A, vulg.—μέγας ἐν οὐρανῷ MSS.: ἐν del. Heath.
180 Κρῖσαν r: Κρίσαν L, vulg.   181 βούνομον L¹: βουνόμον Lᶜ, A.
187 τεκέων Meineke (a conjecture found also in a Vienna MS., cod. Vindob.
281, of the 14th or 15th cent.): τοκέων MSS.   192 ἀμφίσταμαι r: ἀφίσταμαι L¹: ἐφίσταμαι Lᶜ, A, vulg.   195 ὅτε σοι MSS.: corr. Hermann.

8 ἦν ὁ ταῦτα πράσσων. 200

ΗΛ. 9 ὦ πασᾶν κεῖνα πλέον ἀμέρα
10 ἐλθοῦσ᾽ ἐχθίστα δή μοι·
11 ὦ νύξ, ὦ δείπνων ἀρρήτων
12 ἔκπαγλ᾽ ἄχθη,
13 τοὺς ἐμὸς ἴδε πατὴρ 205
14 θανάτους αἰκεῖς διδύμαιν χειροῖν,
15 αἳ τὸν ἐμὸν εἷλον βίον
16 πρόδοτον, αἵ μ᾽ ἀπώλεσαν·
17 οἷς θεὸς ὁ μέγας Ὀλύμπιος
18 ποίνιμα πάθεα παθεῖν πόροι, 210
19 μηδέ ποτ᾽ ἀγλαΐας ἀποναίατο
20 τοιάδ᾽ ἀνύσαντες ἔργα.

ἀντ. γ΄. ΧΟ. φράζου μὴ πόρσω φωνεῖν.
2 οὐ γνώμαν ἴσχεις ἐξ οἵων
3 τὰ παρόντ᾽ οἰκείας εἰς ἄτας 215
4 ἐμπίπτεις οὕτως αἰκῶς;
5 πολὺ γάρ τι κακῶν ὑπερεκτήσω,
6 σᾷ δυσθύμῳ τίκτουσ᾽ ἀεὶ
7 ψυχᾷ πολέμους· τὰ δὲ τοῖς δυνατοῖς
8 οὐκ ἐριστὰ πλάθειν. 220

ΗΛ. 9 δεινοῖς ἠναγκάσθην, δεινοῖς·
10 ἔξοιδ᾽, οὐ λάθει μ᾽ ὀργά.
11 ἀλλ᾽ ἐν γὰρ δεινοῖς οὐ σχήσω
12 ταύτας ἄτας,
13 ὄφρα με βίος ἔχῃ. 225
14 τίνι γάρ ποτ᾽ ἄν, ὦ φιλία γενέθλα,
15 πρόσφορον ἀκούσαιμ᾽ ἔπος,
16 τίνι φρονοῦντι καίρια;
17 ἄνετέ μ᾽, ἄνετε, παράγοροι·
18 τάδε γὰρ ἄλυτα κεκλήσεται, 230

221 ἐν δεινοῖς...ἐν δεινοῖς MSS.: corr. Brunck.

19 οὐδέ ποτ᾽ ἐκ καμάτων ἀποπαύσομαι
20 ἀνάριθμος ὧδε θρήνων.

ἐπ. ΧΟ. ἀλλ᾽ οὖν εὐνοίᾳ γ᾽ αὐδῶ,
μάτηρ ὡσεί τις πιστά,
μὴ τίκτειν σ᾽ ἄταν ἄταις.   235

ΗΛ. καὶ τί μέτρον κακότατος ἔφυ; φέρε,
πῶς ἐπὶ τοῖς φθιμένοις ἀμελεῖν καλόν;
ἐν τίνι τοῦτ᾽ ἔβλαστ᾽ ἀνθρώπων;
μήτ᾽ εἴην ἔντιμος τούτοις,
μήτ᾽, εἴ τῳ πρόσκειμαι χρηστῷ,   240
ξυνναίοιμ᾽ εὔκηλος, γονέων
ἐκτίμους ἴσχουσα πτέρυγας
ὀξυτόνων γόων.
εἰ γὰρ ὁ μὲν θανὼν γᾶ τε καὶ οὐδὲν ὢν
κείσεται τάλας, οἱ δὲ μὴ πάλιν   245
δώσουσ᾽ ἀντιφόνους δίκας,
ἔρροι τ᾽ ἂν αἰδὼς ἁπάντων τ᾽ εὐσέβεια θνατῶν. 250

ΧΟ. ἐγὼ μέν, ὦ παῖ, καὶ τὸ σὸν σπεύδουσ᾽ ἅμα
καὶ τοὐμὸν αὐτῆς ἦλθον· εἰ δὲ μὴ καλῶς
λέγω, σὺ νίκα· σοὶ γὰρ ἑψόμεσθ᾽ ἅμα.

ΗΛ. αἰσχύνομαι μέν, ὦ γυναῖκες, εἰ δοκῶ
πολλοῖσι θρήνοις δυσφορεῖν ὑμῖν ἄγαν·   255
ἀλλ᾽ ἡ βία γὰρ ταῦτ᾽ ἀναγκάζει με δρᾶν,
σύγγνωτε. πῶς γάρ, ἥτις εὐγενὴς γυνή,
πατρῷ᾽ ὁρῶσα πήματ᾽ οὐ δρῴη τάδ᾽ ἄν,
ἁγὼ κατ᾽ ἦμαρ καὶ κατ᾽ εὐφρόνην ἀεὶ
θάλλοντα μᾶλλον ἢ καταφθίνονθ᾽ ὁρῶ;   260
ᾗ πρῶτα μὲν τὰ μητρὸς ἥ μ᾽ ἐγείνατο
ἔχθιστα συμβέβηκεν· εἶτα δώμασιν
ἐν τοῖς ἐμαυτῆς τοῖς φονεῦσι τοῦ πατρὸς
ξύνειμι, κἀκ τῶνδ᾽ ἄρχομαι, κἀκ τῶνδέ μοι

244 γᾶ L, vulg.: γᾷ A.

λαβεῖν θ᾽ ὁμοίως καὶ τὸ τητᾶσθαι πέλει.   265
ἔπειτα ποίας ἡμέρας δοκεῖς μ᾽ ἄγειν,
ὅταν θρόνοις Αἴγισθον ἐνθακοῦντ᾽ ἴδω
τοῖσιν πατρῴοις, εἰσίδω δ᾽ ἐσθήματα
φοροῦντ᾽ ἐκείνῳ ταὐτά, καὶ παρεστίους
σπένδοντα λοιβὰς ἔνθ᾽ ἐκεῖνον ὤλεσεν,   270
ἴδω δὲ τούτων τὴν τελευταίαν ὕβριν,
τὸν αὐτοέντην ἡμὶν ἐν κοίτῃ πατρὸς
ξὺν τῇ ταλαίνῃ μητρί, μητέρ᾽ εἰ χρεὼν
ταύτην προσαυδᾶν τῷδε συγκοιμωμένην·
ἡ δ᾽ ὧδε τλήμων ὥστε τῷ μιάστορι   275
ξύνεστ᾽, Ἐρινὺν οὔτιν᾽ ἐκφοβουμένη·
ἀλλ᾽ ὥσπερ ἐγγελῶσα τοῖς ποιουμένοις,
εὑροῦσ᾽ ἐκείνην ἡμέραν ἐν ᾗ τότε
πατέρα τὸν ἀμὸν ἐκ δόλου κατέκτανεν,
ταύτῃ χοροὺς ἵστησι καὶ μηλοσφαγεῖ   280
θεοῖσιν ἔμμην᾽ ἱερὰ τοῖς σωτηρίοις.
ἐγὼ δ᾽ ὁρῶσ᾽ ἡ δύσμορος κατὰ στέγας
κλαίω, τέτηκα, κἀπικωκύω πατρὸς
τὴν δυστάλαιναν δαῖτ᾽ ἐπωνομασμένην
αὐτὴ πρὸς αὑτήν· οὐδὲ γὰρ κλαῦσαι πάρα   285
τοσόνδ᾽ ὅσον μοι θυμὸς ἡδονὴν φέρει.
αὕτη γὰρ ἡ λόγοισι γενναία γυνὴ
φωνοῦσα τοιάδ᾽ ἐξονειδίζει κακά·
ὦ δύσθεον μίσημα, σοὶ μόνῃ πατὴρ
τέθνηκεν; ἄλλος δ᾽ οὔτις ἐν πένθει βροτῶν;   290
κακῶς ὄλοιο, μηδέ σ᾽ ἐκ γόων ποτὲ
τῶν νῦν ἀπαλλάξειαν οἱ κάτω θεοί.
τάδ᾽ ἐξυβρίζει· πλὴν ὅταν κλύῃ τινὸς
ἥξοντ᾽ Ὀρέστην· τηνικαῦτα δ᾽ ἐμμανὴς
βοᾷ παραστᾶσ᾽, οὐ σύ μοι τῶνδ᾽ αἰτία;   295
οὐ σὸν τόδ᾽ ἐστὶ τοὔργον, ἥτις ἐκ χερῶν

272 γρ. αὐτοέντην schol. in L: αὐτοφόντην MSS.

κλέψασ' Ὀρέστην τῶν ἐμῶν ὑπεξέθου;
ἀλλ' ἴσθι τοι τείσουσά γ' ἀξίαν δίκην.
τοιαῦθ' ὑλακτεῖ, σὺν δ' ἐποτρύνει πέλας
ὁ κλεινὸς αὐτῇ ταὐτὰ νυμφίος παρών,   300
ὁ πάντ' ἄναλκις οὗτος, ἡ πᾶσα βλάβη,
ὁ σὺν γυναιξὶ τὰς μάχας ποιούμενος.
ἐγὼ δ' Ὀρέστην τῶνδε προσμένουσ' ἀεὶ
παυστῆρ' ἐφήξειν ἡ τάλαιν' ἀπόλλυμαι.
μέλλων γὰρ ἀεὶ δρᾶν τι τὰς οὔσας τέ μου   305
καὶ τὰς ἀπούσας ἐλπίδας διέφθορεν.
ἐν οὖν τοιούτοις οὔτε σωφρονεῖν, φίλαι,
οὔτ' εὐσεβεῖν πάρεστιν, ἀλλ' ἔν τοι κακοῖς
πολλή 'στ' ἀνάγκη κἀπιτηδεύειν κακά.

ΧΟ.   φέρ' εἰπέ, πότερον ὄντος Αἰγίσθου πέλας   310
λέγεις τάδ' ἡμῖν, ἢ βεβῶτος ἐκ δόμων;

ΗΛ.   ἦ κάρτα· μὴ δόκει μ' ἄν, εἴπερ ἦν πέλας,
θυραῖον οἰχνεῖν· νῦν δ' ἀγροῖσι τυγχάνει.

ΧΟ.   ἦ κἂν ἐγὼ θαρσοῦσα μᾶλλον ἐς λόγους
τοὺς σοὺς ἱκοίμην, εἴπερ ὧδε ταῦτ' ἔχει;   315

ΗΛ.   ὡς νῦν ἀπόντος ἱστόρει· τί σοι φίλον;

ΧΟ.   καὶ δή σ' ἐρωτῶ, τοῦ κασιγνήτου τί φής,
ἥξοντος, ἢ μέλλοντος; εἰδέναι θέλω.

ΗΛ.   φησίν γε· φάσκων δ' οὐδὲν ὧν λέγει ποεῖ.

ΧΟ.   φιλεῖ γὰρ ὀκνεῖν πρᾶγμ' ἀνὴρ πράσσων μέγα.   320

ΗΛ.   καὶ μὴν ἔγωγ' ἔσωσ' ἐκεῖνον οὐκ ὄκνῳ.

ΧΟ.   θάρσει· πέφυκεν ἐσθλός, ὥστ' ἀρκεῖν φίλοις.

ΗΛ.   πέποιθ', ἐπεί τἂν οὐ μακρὰν ἔζων ἐγώ.

ΧΟ.   μὴ νῦν ἔτ' εἴπῃς μηδέν· ὡς δόμων ὁρῶ
τὴν σὴν ὅμαιμον, ἐκ πατρὸς ταὐτοῦ φύσιν,   325
Χρυσόθεμιν, ἔκ τε μητρός, ἐντάφια χεροῖν
φέρουσαν, οἷα τοῖς κάτω νομίζεται.

300 ταῦτα MSS.: corr. Blomfield.   309 πολλῆστ' L: πολλή γ' r.
314 ἦ δ' ἂν L¹, vulg. (ἦ δᾶν r): ἦ κἂν L⁰, A.

ΧΡΥΣΟΘΕΜΙΣ.

τίν' αὖ σὺ τήνδε πρὸς θυρῶνος ἐξόδοις
ἐλθοῦσα φωνεῖς, ὦ κασιγνήτη, φάτιν,
κοὐδ' ἐν χρόνῳ μακρῷ διδαχθῆναι θέλεις   330
θυμῷ ματαίῳ μὴ χαρίζεσθαι κενά;
καίτοι τοσοῦτόν γ' οἶδα κἀμαυτήν, ὅτι
ἀλγῶ 'πὶ τοῖς παροῦσιν· ὥστ' ἄν, εἰ σθένος
λάβοιμι, δηλώσαιμ' ἂν οἷ' αὐτοῖς φρονῶ.
νῦν δ' ἐν κακοῖς μοι πλεῖν ὑφειμένῃ δοκεῖ,   335
καὶ μὴ δοκεῖν μὲν δρᾶν τι, πημαίνειν δὲ μή.
τοιαῦτα δ' ἄλλα καὶ σὲ βούλομαι ποεῖν.
καίτοι τὸ μὲν δίκαιον οὐχ ᾗ 'γὼ λέγω,
ἀλλ' ᾗ σὺ κρίνεις· εἰ δ' ἐλευθέραν με δεῖ
ζῆν, τῶν κρατούντων ἐστὶ πάντ' ἀκουστέα.   340
ΗΛ. δεινόν γέ σ' οὖσαν πατρὸς οὗ σὺ παῖς ἔφυς
κείνου λελῆσθαι, τῆς δὲ τικτούσης μέλειν.
ἅπαντα γάρ σοι τἀμὰ νουθετήματα
κείνης διδακτά, κοὐδὲν ἐκ σαυτῆς λέγεις.
ἔπειθ' ἑλοῦ γε θάτερ', ἢ φρονεῖν κακῶς,   345
ἢ τῶν φίλων φρονοῦσα μὴ μνήμην ἔχειν·
ἥτις λέγεις μὲν ἀρτίως ὡς, εἰ λάβοις
σθένος, τὸ τούτων μῖσος ἐκδείξειας ἄν·
ἐμοῦ δὲ πατρὶ πάντα τιμωρουμένης
οὔτε ξυνέρδεις τήν τε δρῶσαν ἐκτρέπεις.   350
οὐ ταῦτα πρὸς κακοῖσι δειλίαν ἔχει;
ἐπεὶ δίδαξον, ἢ μάθ' ἐξ ἐμοῦ, τί μοι
κέρδος γένοιτ' ἂν τῶνδε ληξάσῃ γόων;
οὐ ζῶ; κακῶς μέν, οἶδ', ἐπαρκούντως δ' ἐμοί.
λυπῶ δὲ τούτους, ὥστε τῷ τεθνηκότι   355
τιμὰς προσάπτειν, εἴ τις ἔστ' ἐκεῖ χάρις.
σὺ δ' ἡμὶν ἡ μισοῦσα μισεῖς μὲν λόγῳ,

ἔργῳ δὲ τοῖς φονεῦσι τοῦ πατρὸς ξύνει.
ἐγὼ μὲν οὖν οὐκ ἄν ποτ', οὐδ' εἴ μοι τὰ σὰ
μέλλοι τις οἴσειν δῶρ', ἐφ' οἷσι νῦν χλιδᾷς,   360
τούτοις ὑπεικάθοιμι· σοὶ δὲ πλουσία
τράπεζα κείσθω καὶ περιρρείτω βίος.
ἐμοὶ γὰρ ἔστω τοὐμὲ μὴ λυπεῖν μόνον
βόσκημα· τῆς σῆς δ' οὐκ ἐρῶ τιμῆς τυχεῖν.
οὐδ' ἂν σύ, σώφρων γ' οὖσα. νῦν δ' ἐξὸν πατρὸς 365
πάντων ἀρίστου παῖδα κεκλῆσθαι, καλοῦ
τῆς μητρός· οὕτω γὰρ φανεῖ πλείστοις κακή,
θανόντα πατέρα καὶ φίλους προδοῦσα σούς.
ΧΟ. μηδὲν πρὸς ὀργὴν πρὸς θεῶν· ὡς τοῖς λόγοις
ἔνεστιν ἀμφοῖν κέρδος, εἰ σὺ μὲν μάθοις   370
τοῖς τῆσδε χρῆσθαι, τοῖς δὲ σοῖς αὕτη πάλιν.
ΧΡ. ἐγὼ μέν, ὦ γυναῖκες, ἠθάς εἰμί πως
τῶν τῆσδε μύθων· οὐδ' ἂν ἐμνήσθην ποτέ,
εἰ μὴ κακὸν μέγιστον εἰς αὐτὴν ἰὸν
ἤκουσ', ὃ ταύτην τῶν μακρῶν σχήσει γόων.   375
ΗΛ. φέρ' εἰπὲ δὴ τὸ δεινόν· εἰ γὰρ τῶνδέ μοι
μεῖζόν τι λέξεις, οὐκ ἂν ἀντείποιμ' ἔτι.
ΧΡ. ἀλλ' ἐξερῶ σοι πᾶν ὅσον κάτοιδ' ἐγώ.
μέλλουσι γάρ σ', εἰ τῶνδε μὴ λήξεις γόων,
ἐνταῦθα πέμψειν ἔνθα μή ποθ' ἡλίου   380
φέγγος προσόψει, ζῶσα δ' ἐν κατηρεφεῖ
στέγῃ χθονὸς τῆσδ' ἐκτὸς ὑμνήσεις κακά.
πρὸς ταῦτα φράζου, καί με μή ποθ' ὕστερον
παθοῦσα μέμψῃ· νῦν γὰρ ἐν καλῷ φρονεῖν.
ΗΛ. ἦ ταῦτα δή με καὶ βεβούλευνται ποεῖν;   385
ΧΡ. μάλισθ'· ὅταν περ οἴκαδ' Αἴγισθος μόλῃ.
ΗΛ. ἀλλ' ἐξίκοιτο τοῦδέ γ' οὕνεκ' ἐν τάχει.
ΧΡ. τίν', ὦ τάλαινα, τόνδ' ἐπηράσω λόγον;
ΗΛ ἐλθεῖν ἐκεῖνον, εἴ τι τῶνδε δρᾶν νοεῖ.

378 ἐξερῶ σοι L: ἐξερῶ τοι r.

16   ΣΟΦΟΚΛΕΟΥΣ

ΧΡ.   ὅπως πάθῃς τί χρῆμα; ποῦ ποτ' εἶ φρενῶν: 390
ΗΛ.   ὅπως ἀφ' ὑμῶν ὡς προσώτατ' ἐκφύγω.
ΧΡ.   βίου δὲ τοῦ παρόντος οὐ μνείαν ἔχεις;
ΗΛ.   καλὸς γὰρ οὑμὸς βίοτος ὥστε θαυμάσαι.
ΧΡ.   ἀλλ' ἦν ἄν, εἰ σύ γ' εὖ φρονεῖν ἠπίστασο.
ΗΛ.   μή μ' ἐκδίδασκε τοῖς φίλοις εἶναι κακήν.   395
ΧΡ.   ἀλλ' οὐ διδάσκω· τοῖς κρατοῦσι δ' εἰκαθεῖν.
ΗΛ.   σὺ ταῦτα θώπευ'· οὐκ ἐμοὺς τρόπους λέγεις.
ΧΡ.   καλόν γε μέντοι μὴ 'ξ ἀβουλίας πεσεῖν.
ΗΛ.   πεσούμεθ', εἰ χρή, πατρὶ τιμωρούμενοι.
ΧΡ.   πατὴρ δὲ τούτων, οἶδα, συγγνώμην ἔχει.   400
ΗΛ.   ταῦτ' ἐστὶ τἄπη πρὸς κακῶν ἐπαινέσαι.
ΧΡ.   σὺ δ' οὐχὶ πείσει καὶ συναινέσεις ἐμοί;
ΗΛ.   οὐ δῆτα· μή πω νοῦ τοσόνδ' εἴην κενή.
ΧΡ.   χωρήσομαί τἄρ' οἶπερ ἐστάλην ὁδοῦ.
ΗΛ.   ποῖ δ' ἐμπορεύει; τῷ φέρεις τάδ' ἔμπυρα;   405
ΧΡ.   μήτηρ με πέμπει πατρὶ τυμβεῦσαι χοάς.
ΗΛ.   πῶς εἶπας; ἦ τῷ δυσμενεστάτῳ βροτῶν;
ΧΡ.   ὃν ἔκταν' αὐτή· τοῦτο γὰρ λέξαι θέλεις.
ΗΛ.   ἐκ τοῦ φίλων πεισθεῖσα; τῷ τοῦτ' ἤρεσεν;
ΧΡ.   ἐκ δείματός του νυκτέρου, δοκεῖν ἐμοί.   410
ΗΛ.   ὦ θεοὶ πατρῷοι, συγγένεσθέ γ' ἀλλὰ νῦν.
ΧΡ.   ἔχεις τι θάρσος τοῦδε τοῦ τάρβους πέρι;
ΗΛ.   εἴ μοι λέγοις τὴν ὄψιν, εἴποιμ' ἂν τότε.
ΧΡ.   ἀλλ' οὐ κάτοιδα πλὴν ἐπὶ σμικρὸν φράσαι.
ΗΛ.   λέγ' ἀλλὰ τοῦτο· πολλά τοι σμικροὶ λόγοι   415
      ἔσφηλαν ἤδη καὶ κατώρθωσαν βροτούς.
ΧΡ.   λόγος τις αὐτήν ἐστιν εἰσιδεῖν πατρὸς
      τοῦ σοῦ τε κἀμοῦ δευτέραν ὁμιλίαν
      ἐλθόντος εἰς φῶς· εἶτα τόνδ' ἐφέστιον
      πῆξαι λαβόντα σκῆπτρον, οὑφόρει ποτὲ   420

─────────
413 λέγοις Triclinius: λέγεις L, vulg.
414 σμικρὸν Lᶜ, Γ: σμικροῦ (or -ῷι) L¹: σμικρῶν r.

αὐτός, τανῦν δ' Αἴγισθος· ἔκ τε τοῦδ' ἄνω
βλαστεῖν βρύοντα θαλλόν, ᾧ κατάσκιον
πᾶσαν γενέσθαι τὴν Μυκηναίων χθόνα.
τοιαῦτά του παρόντος, ἡνίχ' Ἡλίῳ
δείκνυσι τοὔναρ, ἔκλυον ἐξηγουμένου.   425
πλείω δὲ τούτων οὐ κάτοιδα, πλὴν ὅτι
πέμπει με κείνη τοῦδε τοῦ φόβου χάριν.
πρός νυν θεῶν σε λίσσομαι τῶν ἐγγενῶν
ἐμοὶ πιθέσθαι μηδ' ἀβουλίᾳ πεσεῖν·
εἰ γάρ μ' ἀπώσει, σὺν κακῷ μέτει πάλιν.   430
ΗΛ. ἀλλ', ὦ φίλη, τούτων μὲν ὧν ἔχεις χεροῖν
τύμβῳ προσάψῃς μηδέν· οὐ γάρ σοι θέμις
οὐδ' ὅσιον ἐχθρᾶς ἀπὸ γυναικὸς ἱστάναι
κτερίσματ' οὐδὲ λουτρὰ προσφέρειν πατρί·
ἀλλ' ἢ πνοαῖσιν ἢ βαθυσκαφεῖ κόνει   435
κρύψον νιν, ἔνθα μή ποτ' εἰς εὐνὴν πατρὸς
τούτων πρόσεισι μηδέν· ἀλλ' ὅταν θάνῃ,
κειμήλι' αὐτῇ ταῦτα σῳζέσθω κάτω.
ἀρχὴν δ' ἄν, εἰ μὴ τλημονεστάτη γυνὴ
πασῶν ἔβλαστε, τάσδε δυσμενεῖς χοὰς   440
οὐκ ἄν ποθ', ὅν γ' ἔκτεινε, τῷδ' ἐπέστεφε.
σκέψαι γὰρ εἴ σοι προσφιλῶς αὐτῇ δοκεῖ
γέρα τάδ' οὖν τάφοισι δέξεσθαι νέκυς,
ὑφ' ἧς θανὼν ἄτιμος ὥστε δυσμενὴς
ἐμασχαλίσθη, κἀπὶ λουτροῖσιν κάρᾳ   445
κηλῖδας ἐξέμαξεν. ἆρα μὴ δοκεῖς
λυτήρι' αὐτῇ ταῦτα τοῦ φόνου φέρειν;
οὐκ ἔστιν. ἀλλὰ ταῦτα μὲν μέθες· σὺ δὲ
τεμοῦσα κρατὸς βοστρύχων ἄκρας φόβας
κἀμοῦ ταλαίνης, σμικρὰ μὲν τάδ', ἀλλ' ὅμως   450
ἄχω, δὸς αὐτῷ, τήνδ' ἀλιπαρῆ τρίχα

433 ἀπό om. L¹, add. Lᶜ (above the line): it is wanting in some of the
later MSS. (as Γ), but present in A, E, and others.   443 δέξεσθαι
Heath : δέξασθαι MSS.   451 τήνδε γ' (τ' J.) ἀλίπαρον conj. Hartung.

καὶ ζῶμα τοὐμὸν οὐ χλιδαῖς ἠσκημένον.
αἰτοῦ δὲ προσπίτνουσα γῆθεν εὐμενῆ
ἡμῖν ἀρωγὸν αὐτὸν εἰς ἐχθροὺς μολεῖν,
καὶ παῖδ᾽ Ὀρέστην ἐξ ὑπερτέρας χερὸς   455
ἐχθροῖσιν αὐτοῦ ζῶντ᾽ ἐπεμβῆναι ποδί,
ὅπως τὸ λοιπὸν αὐτὸν ἀφνεωτέραις
χερσὶ στέφωμεν ἢ τανῦν δωρούμεθα.
οἶμαι μὲν οὖν, οἶμαί τι κἀκείνῳ μέλον
πέμψαι τάδ᾽ αὐτῇ δυσπρόσοπτ᾽ ὀνείρατα·   460
ὅμως δ᾽, ἀδελφή, σοί θ᾽ ὑπούργησον τάδε
ἐμοί τ᾽ ἀρωγά, τῷ τε φιλτάτῳ βροτῶν
πάντων, ἐν Ἅιδου κειμένῳ κοινῷ πατρί.
ΧΟ. πρὸς εὐσέβειαν ἡ κόρη λέγει· σὺ δέ,
εἰ σωφρονήσεις, ὦ φίλη, δράσεις τάδε.   465
ΧΡ. δράσω· τὸ γὰρ δίκαιον οὐκ ἔχει λόγον
δυοῖν ἐρίζειν, ἀλλ᾽ ἐπισπεύδειν τὸ δρᾶν.
πειρωμένη δὲ τῶνδε τῶν ἔργων ἐμοὶ
σιγὴ παρ᾽ ὑμῶν πρὸς θεῶν ἔστω, φίλαι·
ὡς εἰ τάδ᾽ ἡ τεκοῦσα πεύσεται, πικρὰν   470
δοκῶ με πεῖραν τήνδε τολμήσειν ἔτι.

στρ. ΧΟ. εἰ μὴ 'γὼ παράφρων μάντις ἔφυν
2 καὶ γνώμας λειπομένα σοφᾶς, εἰσιν ἁ πρόμαντις 475
3 Δίκα, δίκαια φερομένα χεροῖν κράτη·
4 μέτεισιν, ὦ τέκνον, οὐ μακροῦ χρόνου.
5 ὕπεστί μοι θάρσος, ἁδυπνόων κλύουσαν   480
6 ἀρτίως ὀνειράτων·
7 οὐ γάρ ποτ᾽ ἀμναστεῖ γ᾽ ὁ φύσας σ᾽ Ἑλλάνων ἄναξ,
8 οὐδ᾽ ἁ παλαιὰ χαλκόπλακτος ἀμφάκης γένυς,   485
9 ἅ νιν κατέπεφνεν αἰσχίσταις ἐν αἰκίαις.

479 θάρσος L (made by an early hand, perh. the first, from θράσος),
A, vulg. : θράσος r.   480 κλύουσαν L: κλυούσῃ (or -ᾳ) r.   482 ὁ
φύσας σ᾽] σ᾽ om. MSS., add. Fröhlich.

ἀντ. ἥξει καὶ πολύπους καὶ πολύχειρ
2 ἁ δεινοῖς κρυπτομένα λόχοις χαλκόπους Ἐρινύς.
3 ἄλεκτρ᾽ ἄνυμφα γὰρ ἐπέβα μιαιφόνων   491
4 γάμων ἀμιλλήμαθ᾽ οἷσιν οὐ θέμις.
5 πρὸ τῶνδέ τοί μ᾽ ἔχει μή ποτε μή ποθ᾽ ἡμῖν 495
6 ἀψεγὲς πελᾶν τέρας
7 τοῖς δρῶσι καὶ συνδρῶσιν. ἦ τοι μαντεῖαι βροτῶν
8 οὐκ εἰσὶν ἐν δεινοῖς ὀνείροις οὐδ᾽ ἐν θεσφάτοις, 500
9 εἰ μὴ τόδε φάσμα νυκτὸς εὖ κατασχήσει.

ἐπ. ὦ Πέλοπος ἁ πρόσθεν πολύπονος ἱππεία,   505
ὡς ἔμολες αἰανὴς τᾷδε γᾷ.
εὖτε γὰρ ὁ ποντισθεὶς Μυρτίλος ἐκοιμάθη,
παγχρυσέων δίφρων δυστάνοις αἰκίαις   510
πρόρριζος ἐκριφθείς, οὔ τί πω
ἔλειπεν ἐκ τοῦδ᾽ οἴκου πολύπονος αἰκία.   515

ΚΛΥΤΑΙΜΝΗΣΤΡΑ.

ἀνειμένη μέν, ὡς ἔοικας, αὖ στρέφει·
οὐ γὰρ πάρεστ᾽ Αἴγισθος, ὅς σ᾽ ἐπεῖχ᾽ ἀεὶ
μή τοι θυραίαν γ᾽ οὖσαν αἰσχύνειν φίλους·
νῦν δ᾽ ὡς ἄπεστ᾽ ἐκεῖνος, οὐδὲν ἐντρέπει
ἐμοῦ γε· καίτοι πολλὰ πρὸς πολλούς με δὴ   520
ἐξεῖπας ὡς θρασεῖα καὶ πέρα δίκης
ἄρχω, καθυβρίζουσα καὶ σὲ καὶ τὰ σά.
ἐγὼ δ᾽ ὕβριν μὲν οὐκ ἔχω, κακῶς δέ σε
λέγω, κακῶς κλύουσα πρὸς σέθεν θαμά.
πατὴρ γάρ, οὐδὲν ἄλλο, σοὶ πρόσχημ᾽ ἀεὶ   525

495 f. πρὸ τῶνδε...ἡμῖν] So A and most MSS. The second μή ποτε is
absent from L, Γ, and a few others. After ἔχει, Γ, Aug. c, and Pal. add
θάρσος. A possible reading is, πρὸ τῶνδέ τοι θάρσος ἴσχει με, μή ποθ᾽ ἡμῖν.
506 αἰανὴς L¹: αἰανὴ Lᶜ, vulg.   510 παγχρύσων MSS.: corr.
Hermann.   513 οὔ τίς πω MSS.: corr. Hermann.   514 ἔλειπεν
L, A, vulg.: ἔλιπεν Γ.—οἴκου L (but with traces of an erased σ), vulg.:
οἴκους Triclinius: οἶκον conj. Dobree.

ὡς ἐξ ἐμοῦ τέθνηκεν. ἐξ ἐμοῦ· καλῶς
ἔξοιδα· τῶνδ' ἄρνησις οὐκ ἔνεστί μοι·
ἡ γὰρ Δίκη νιν εἷλεν, οὐκ ἐγὼ μόνη,
ᾗ χρῆν σ' ἀρήγειν, εἰ φρονοῦσ' ἐτύγχανες.
ἐπεὶ πατὴρ οὗτος σός, ὃν θρηνεῖς ἀεί,   530
τὴν σὴν ὅμαιμον μοῦνος Ἑλλήνων ἔτλη
θῦσαι θεοῖσιν, οὐκ ἴσον καμὼν ἐμοὶ
λύπης, ὅτ' ἔσπειρ', ὥσπερ ἡ τίκτουσ' ἐγώ.
εἶεν, δίδαξον δή με, τοῦ χάριν, τίνων
ἔθυσεν αὐτήν; πότερον Ἀργείων ἐρεῖς;   535
ἀλλ' οὐ μετῆν αὐτοῖσι τήν γ' ἐμὴν κτανεῖν.
ἀλλ' ἀντ' ἀδελφοῦ δῆτα Μενέλεω κτανὼν
τἄμ' οὐκ ἔμελλε τῶνδέ μοι δώσειν δίκην;
πότερον ἐκείνῳ παῖδες οὐκ ἦσαν διπλοῖ,
οὓς τῆσδε μᾶλλον εἰκὸς ἦν θνῄσκειν, πατρὸς   540
καὶ μητρὸς ὄντας, ἧς ὁ πλοῦς ὅδ' ἦν χάριν;
ἢ τῶν ἐμῶν Ἅιδης τιν' ἵμερον τέκνων
ἢ τῶν ἐκείνης ἔσχε δαίσασθαι πλέον;
ἢ τῷ πανώλει πατρὶ τῶν μὲν ἐξ ἐμοῦ
παίδων πόθος παρεῖτο, Μενέλεω δ' ἐνῆν;   545
οὐ ταῦτ' ἀβούλου καὶ κακοῦ γνώμην πατρός;
δοκῶ μέν, εἰ καὶ σῆς δίχα γνώμης λέγω.
φαίη δ' ἂν ἡ θανοῦσά γ', εἰ φωνὴν λάβοι.
ἐγὼ μὲν οὖν οὐκ εἰμὶ τοῖς πεπραγμένοις
δύσθυμος· εἰ δὲ σοὶ δοκῶ φρονεῖν κακῶς,   550
γνώμην δικαίαν σχοῦσα τοὺς πέλας ψέγε.
ΗΛ ἐρεῖς μὲν οὐχὶ νῦν γέ μ' ὡς ἄρξασά τι
λυπηρόν, εἶτα σοῦ τάδ' ἐξήκουσ' ὕπο·
ἀλλ' ἢν ἐφῇς μοι, τοῦ τεθνηκότος θ' ὕπερ
λέξαιμ' ἂν ὀρθῶς τῆς κασιγνήτης θ' ὁμοῦ.   555
ΚΛ. καὶ μὴν ἐφίημ'· εἰ δέ μ' ὧδ' ἀεὶ λόγους
ἐξῆρχες, οὐκ ἂν ἦσθα λυπηρὰ κλύειν.

τίνων r: τίνος L, A, vulg.   556 λόγους L¹: λόγοις Lᶜ, A, vulg.

ΗΛ. καὶ δὴ λέγω σοι. πατέρα φῂς κτεῖναι. τίς ἂν
τούτου λόγος γένοιτ' ἂν αἰσχίων ἔτι,
εἴτ' οὖν δικαίως εἴτε μή; λέξω δέ σοι,   560
ὡς οὐ δίκῃ γ' ἔκτεινας, ἀλλά σ' ἔσπασεν
πειθὼ κακοῦ πρὸς ἀνδρός, ᾧ τανῦν ξύνει.
ἐροῦ δὲ τὴν κυναγὸν Ἄρτεμιν, τίνος
ποινὰς τὰ πολλὰ πνεύματ' ἔσχ' ἐν Αὐλίδι·
ἢ 'γὼ φράσω· κείνης γὰρ οὐ θέμις μαθεῖν.   565
πατήρ ποθ' οὑμός, ὡς ἐγὼ κλύω, θεᾶς
παίζων κατ' ἄλσος ἐξεκίνησεν ποδοῖν
στικτὸν κεράστην ἔλαφον, οὗ κατὰ σφαγὰς
ἐκκομπάσας ἔπος τι τυγχάνει βαλών.
κἀκ τοῦδε μηνίσασα Λητῴα κόρη   570
κατεῖχ' Ἀχαιούς, ὡς πατὴρ ἀντίσταθμον
τοῦ θηρὸς ἐκθύσειε τὴν αὑτοῦ κόρην.
ὧδ' ἦν τὰ κείνης θύματ'· οὐ γὰρ ἦν λύσις
ἄλλη στρατῷ πρὸς οἶκον οὐδ' εἰς Ἴλιον.
ἀνθ' ὧν βιασθεὶς πολλὰ κἀντιβὰς μόλις   575
ἔθυσεν αὐτήν, οὐχὶ Μενέλεω χάριν.
εἰ δ' οὖν, ἐρῶ γὰρ καὶ τὸ σόν, κεῖνον θέλων
ἐπωφελῆσαι ταῦτ' ἔδρα, τούτου θανεῖν
χρῆν αὐτὸν οὕνεκ' ἐκ σέθεν; ποίῳ νόμῳ;
ὅρα τιθεῖσα τόνδε τὸν νόμον βροτοῖς   580
μὴ πῆμα σαυτῇ καὶ μετάγνοιαν τιθῇς.
εἰ γὰρ κτενοῦμεν ἄλλον ἀντ' ἄλλου, σύ τοι
πρώτη θάνοις ἄν, εἰ δίκης γε τυγχάνοις.
ἀλλ' εἰσόρα μὴ σκῆψιν οὐκ οὖσαν τίθης.
εἰ γὰρ θέλεις, δίδαξον ἀνθ' ὅτου τανῦν   585
αἴσχιστα πάντων ἔργα δρῶσα τυγχάνεις,
ἥτις ξυνεύδεις τῷ παλαμναίῳ, μεθ' οὗ
πατέρα τὸν ἀμὸν πρόσθεν ἐξαπώλεσας,

564 ἔσχ' ἐν L, vulg.: ἔσχεν r.   581 τίθηις L: τίθης A, vulg.
J. E.   584 τίθης L, vulg.: τιθῆς r.   6

καὶ παιδοποιεῖς· τοὺς δὲ πρόσθεν εὐσεβεῖς
κἀξ εὐσεβῶν βλαστόντας ἐκβαλοῦσ' ἔχεις.   590
πῶς ταῦτ' ἐπαινέσαιμ' ἄν; ἢ καὶ ταῦτ' ἐρεῖς
ὡς τῆς θυγατρὸς ἀντίποινα λαμβάνεις;
αἰσχρῶς δ', ἐάν περ καὶ λέγῃς· οὐ γὰρ καλὸν
ἐχθροῖς γαμεῖσθαι τῆς θυγατρὸς οὕνεκα.
ἀλλ' οὐ γὰρ οὐδὲ νουθετεῖν ἔξεστί σε,   595
ἣ πᾶσαν ἵης γλῶσσαν ὡς τὴν μητέρα
κακοστομοῦμεν. καί σ' ἔγωγε δεσπότιν
ἢ μητέρ' οὐκ ἔλασσον εἰς ἡμᾶς νέμω,
ἣ ζῶ βίον μοχθηρόν, ἔκ τε σοῦ κακοῖς
πολλοῖς ἀεὶ ξυνοῦσα τοῦ τε συννόμου.   600
ὁ δ' ἄλλος ἔξω, χεῖρα σὴν μόλις φυγών,
τλήμων Ὀρέστης δυστυχῆ τρίβει βίον·
ὃν πολλὰ δή με σοὶ τρέφειν μιάστορα
ἐπῃτιάσω· καὶ τόδ', εἴπερ ἔσθενον,
ἔδρων ἄν, εὖ τοῦτ' ἴσθι. τοῦδέ γ' οὕνεκα   605
κήρυσσέ μ' εἰς ἅπαντας, εἴτε χρῇς κακὴν
εἴτε στόμαργον εἴτ' ἀναιδείας πλέαν.
εἰ γὰρ πέφυκα τῶνδε τῶν ἔργων ἴδρις,
σχεδόν τι τὴν σὴν οὐ καταισχύνω φύσιν.

ΧΟ.   ὁρῶ μένος πνέουσαν· εἰ δὲ σὺν δίκῃ   610
       ξύνεστι, τοῦδε φροντίδ' οὐκέτ' εἰσορῶ.

ΚΛ.   ποίας δ' ἐμοὶ δεῖ πρός γε τήνδε φροντίδος,
       ἥτις τοιαῦτα τὴν τεκοῦσαν ὕβρισεν,
       καὶ ταῦτα τηλικοῦτος; ἆρά σοι δοκεῖ
       χωρεῖν ἂν εἰς πᾶν ἔργον αἰσχύνης ἄτερ;   615

ΗΛ.   εὖ νυν ἐπίστω τῶνδέ μ' αἰσχύνην ἔχειν,
       κεἰ μὴ δοκῶ σοι· μανθάνω δ' ὁθούνεκα
       ἔξωρα πράσσω κοὐκ ἐμοὶ προσεικότα.
       ἀλλ' ἡ γὰρ ἐκ σοῦ δυσμένεια καὶ τὰ σὰ

ἔργ' ἐξαναγκάζει με ταῦτα δρᾶν βίᾳ· 620
αἰσχροῖς γὰρ αἰσχρὰ πράγματ' ἐκδιδάσκεται.
ΚΛ. ὦ θρέμμ' ἀναιδές, ἦ σ' ἐγὼ καὶ τἄμ' ἔπη
καὶ τἄργα τἀμὰ πόλλ' ἄγαν λέγειν ποεῖ.
ΗΛ. σύ τοι λέγεις νιν, οὐκ ἐγώ· σὺ γὰρ ποεῖς
τοὔργον· τὰ δ' ἔργα τοὺς λόγους εὑρίσκεται. 625
ΚΛ. ἀλλ' οὐ μὰ τὴν δέσποιναν Ἄρτεμιν θράσους
τοῦδ' οὐκ ἀλύξεις, εὖτ' ἂν Αἴγισθος μόλῃ.
ΗΛ. ὁρᾷς; πρὸς ὀργὴν ἐκφέρει, μεθεῖσά μοι
λέγειν ἃ χρῄζοιμ', οὐδ' ἐπίστασαι κλύειν.
ΚΛ. οὔκουν ἐάσεις οὐδ' ὑπ' εὐφήμου βοῆς 630
θῦσαί μ', ἐπειδὴ σοί γ' ἐφῆκα πᾶν λέγειν;
ΗΛ. ἐῶ, κελεύω, θῦε· μηδ' ἐπαιτιῶ
τοὐμὸν στόμ', ὡς οὐκ ἂν πέρα λέξαιμ' ἔτι.
ΚΛ. ἔπαιρε δὴ σὺ θύμαθ' ἡ παροῦσά μοι
πάγκαρπ', ἄνακτι τῷδ' ὅπως λυτηρίους 635
εὐχὰς ἀνάσχω δειμάτων ἃ νῦν ἔχω.
κλύοις ἂν ἤδη, Φοῖβε προστατήριε,
κεκρυμμένην μου βάξιν· οὐ γὰρ ἐν φίλοις
ὁ μῦθος, οὐδὲ πᾶν ἀναπτύξαι πρέπει
πρὸς φῶς παρούσης τῆσδε πλησίας ἐμοί, 640
μὴ σὺν φθόνῳ τε καὶ πολυγλώσσῳ βοῇ
σπείρῃ ματαίαν βάξιν εἰς πᾶσαν πόλιν.
ἀλλ' ὧδ' ἄκουε· τῇδε γὰρ κἀγὼ φράσω.
ἃ γὰρ προσεῖδον νυκτὶ τῇδε φάσματα
δισσῶν ὀνείρων, ταῦτά μοι, Λύκει' ἄναξ, 645
εἰ μὲν πέφηνεν ἐσθλά, δὸς τελεσφόρα,
εἰ δ' ἐχθρά, τοῖς ἐχθροῖσιν ἔμπαλιν μέθες·
καὶ μή με πλούτου τοῦ παρόντος εἴ τινες
δόλοισι βουλεύουσιν ἐκβαλεῖν, ἐφῇς,
ἀλλ' ὧδέ μ' ἀεὶ ζῶσαν ἀβλαβεῖ βίῳ 650
δόμους Ἀτρειδῶν σκῆπτρά τ' ἀμφέπειν τάδε,
φίλοισί τε ξυνοῦσαν οἷς ξύνειμι νῦν

24 ΣΟΦΟΚΛΕΟΥΣ

εὐημεροῦσαν καὶ τέκνων ὅσων ἐμοὶ
δύσνοια μὴ πρόσεστιν ἢ λύπη πικρά.
ταῦτ᾽, ὦ Λύκει᾽ Ἄπολλον, ἵλεως κλύων   655
δὸς πᾶσιν ἡμῖν ὥσπερ ἐξαιτούμεθα.
τὰ δ᾽ ἄλλα πάντα καὶ σιωπώσης ἐμοῦ
ἐπαξιῶ σε δαίμον᾽ ὄντ᾽ ἐξειδέναι·
τοὺς ἐκ Διὸς γὰρ εἰκός ἐστι πάνθ᾽ ὁρᾶν.

ΠΑΙΔΑΓΩΓΟΣ.

ξέναι γυναῖκες, πῶς ἂν εἰδείην σαφῶς   66ο
εἰ τοῦ τυράννου δώματ᾽ Αἰγίσθου τάδε;
ΧΟ. τάδ᾽ ἐστίν, ὦ ξέν᾽· αὐτὸς ἤκασας καλῶς.
ΠΑ. ἦ καὶ δάμαρτα τήνδ᾽ ἐπεικάζων κυρῶ
κείνου; πρέπει γὰρ ὡς τύραννος εἰσορᾶν.
ΧΟ. μάλιστα πάντων· ἥδε σοι κείνη πάρα.   665
ΠΑ. ὦ χαῖρ᾽, ἄνασσα· σοὶ φέρων ἥκω λόγους
ἡδεῖς φίλου παρ᾽ ἀνδρὸς Αἰγίσθῳ θ᾽ ὁμοῦ.
ΚΛ. ἐδεξάμην τὸ ῥηθέν· εἰδέναι δέ σου
πρώτιστα χρήζω, τίς σ᾽ ἀπέστειλεν βροτῶν.
ΠΑ. Φανοτεὺς ὁ Φωκεύς, πρᾶγμα πορσύνων μέγα.   670
ΚΛ. τὸ ποῖον, ὦ ξέν᾽; εἰπέ· παρὰ φίλου γὰρ ὢν
ἀνδρός, σάφ᾽ οἶδα, προσφιλεῖς λέξεις λόγους.
ΠΑ. τέθνηκ᾽ Ὀρέστης· ἐν βραχεῖ ξυνθεὶς λέγω.
ΗΛ. οἲ ᾽γὼ τάλαιν᾽, ὄλωλα τῇδ᾽ ἐν ἡμέρᾳ.
ΚΛ. τί φής, τί φής, ὦ ξεῖνε; μὴ ταύτης κλύε.   675
ΠΑ. θανόντ᾽ Ὀρέστην νῦν τε καὶ πάλαι λέγω.
ΗΛ. ἀπωλόμην δύστηνος, οὐδέν εἰμ᾽ ἔτι.
ΚΛ. σὺ μὲν τὰ σαυτῆς πρᾶσσ᾽, ἐμοὶ δὲ σύ, ξένε,
τἀληθὲς εἰπέ, τῷ τρόπῳ διόλλυται;
ΠΑ. κἀπεμπόμην πρὸς ταῦτα καὶ τὸ πᾶν φράσω.   680
κεῖνος γὰρ ἐλθὼν εἰς τὸ κλεινὸν Ἑλλάδος
πρόσχημ᾽ ἀγῶνος Δελφικῶν ἄθλων χάριν,

676 πάλαι λέγω L, vulg.: τότ᾽ ἐννέπω A (a v. l. noted by schol. in L).

ὅτ' ἤσθετ' ἀνδρὸς ὀρθίων κηρυγμάτων
δρόμον προκηρύξαντος, οὗ πρώτη κρίσις,
εἰσῆλθε λαμπρός, πᾶσι τοῖς ἐκεῖ σέβας· 685
δρόμου δ' ἰσώσας τάφεσει τὰ τέρματα
νίκης ἔχων ἐξῆλθε πάντιμον γέρας.
χὤπως μὲν ἐν πολλοῖσι παῦρά σοι λέγω,
οὐκ οἶδα τοιοῦδ' ἀνδρὸς ἔργα καὶ κράτη.
ἓν δ' ἴσθ'· ὅσων γὰρ εἰσεκήρυξαν βραβῆς 690
[δρόμων διαύλων πένταθλ' ἃ νομίζεται,]
τούτων ἐνεγκὼν πάντα τἀπινίκια
ὠλβίζετ', Ἀργεῖος μὲν ἀνακαλούμενος,
ὄνομα δ' Ὀρέστης, τοῦ τὸ κλεινὸν Ἑλλάδος
Ἀγαμέμνονος στράτευμ' ἀγείραντός ποτε. 695
καὶ ταῦτα μὲν τοιαῦθ'· ὅταν δέ τις θεῶν
βλάπτῃ, δύναιτ' ἂν οὐδ' ἂν ἰσχύων φυγεῖν.
κεῖνος γὰρ ἄλλης ἡμέρας, ὅθ' ἱππικῶν
ἦν ἡλίου τέλλοντος ὠκύπους ἀγών,
εἰσῆλθε πολλῶν ἀρματηλατῶν μέτα. 700
εἷς ἦν Ἀχαιός, εἷς ἀπὸ Σπάρτης, δύο
Λίβυες ζυγωτῶν ἀρμάτων ἐπιστάται·
κἀκεῖνος ἐν τούτοισι Θεσσαλὰς ἔχων
ἵππους, ὁ πέμπτος· ἕκτος ἐξ Αἰτωλίας
ξανθαῖσι πώλοις· ἕβδομος Μάγνης ἀνήρ· 705
ὁ δ' ὄγδοος λεύκιππος, Αἰνιὰν γένος·
ἔνατος Ἀθηνῶν τῶν θεοδμήτων ἄπο·
Βοιωτὸς ἄλλος, δέκατον ἐκπληρῶν ὄχον.
στάντες δ' ὅθ' αὐτοὺς οἱ τεταγμένοι βραβῆς
κλήρους ἔπηλαν καὶ κατέστησαν δίφρους, 710
χαλκῆς ὑπαὶ σάλπιγγος ᾖξαν· οἱ δ' ἅμα

686 τάφεσει Musgrave: τῇ φύσει MSS.   691 Michaelis, Tournier
and J. would reject this v., and read ἄθλων instead of τούτων in 692.
709 ὅθ' αὐτοὺς L, vulg. (ὅτ' αὐτοὺς Γ): ἵν' αὐτοὺς Nauck.   710 κλήροις
MSS.: corr. Wunder.

ἵπποις ὁμοκλήσαντες ἡνίας χεροῖν
ἔσεισαν· ἐν δὲ πᾶς ἐμεστώθη δρόμος
κτύπου κροτητῶν ἀρμάτων· κόνις δ' ἄνω
φορεῖθ'· ὁμοῦ δὲ πάντες ἀναμεμιγμένοι   715
φείδοντο κέντρων οὐδέν, ὡς ὑπερβάλοι
χνόας τις αὐτῶν καὶ φρυάγμαθ' ἱππικά.
ὁμοῦ γὰρ ἀμφὶ νῶτα καὶ τροχῶν βάσεις
ἤφριζον, εἰσέβαλλον ἱππικαὶ πνοαί.
κεῖνος δ' ὑπ' αὐτὴν ἐσχάτην στήλην ἔχων   720
ἔχριμπτ' ἀεὶ σύριγγα, δεξιὸν δ' ἀνεὶς
σειραῖον ἵππον εἶργε τὸν προσκείμενον.
καὶ πρὶν μὲν ὀρθοὶ πάντες ἔστασαν δίφροι·
ἔπειτα δ' Αἰνιᾶνος ἀνδρὸς ἄστομοι
πῶλοι βίᾳ φέρουσιν, ἐκ δ' ὑποστροφῆς,   725
τελοῦντες ἕκτον ἕβδομόν τ' ἤδη δρόμον,
μέτωπα συμπαίουσι Βαρκαίοις ὄχοις·
κἀντεῦθεν ἄλλος ἄλλον ἐξ ἑνὸς κακοῦ
ἔθραυε κἀνέπιπτε, πᾶν δ' ἐπίμπλατο
ναυαγίων Κρισαῖον ἱππικῶν πέδον.   730
γνοὺς δ' οὐξ Ἀθηνῶν δεινὸς ἡνιοστρόφος
ἔξω παρασπᾷ κἀνοκωχεύει παρεὶς
κλύδων' ἔφιππον ἐν μέσῳ κυκώμενον.
ἤλαυνε δ' ἔσχατος μὲν ὑστέρας ἔχων
πώλους Ὀρέστης, τῷ τέλει πίστιν φέρων·   735
ὅπως δ' ὁρᾷ μόνον νιν ἐλλελειμμένον,
ὀξὺν δι' ὤτων κέλαδον ἐνσείσας θοαῖς
πώλοις διώκει, κἀξισώσαντε ζυγὰ
ἠλαυνέτην, τότ' ἄλλος, ἄλλοθ' ἅτερος
κάρα προβάλλων ἱππικῶν ὀχημάτων.   740

721 δεξιόν τ' Triclinius.   732 κἀνακωχεύει MSS.: corr. Cobet.
734 ὑστέρας ἔχων L¹: ὑστέρας δ' ἔχων Lᶜ (a late hand), A, vulg.
736 ὅπως δ' L¹, Γ: ὁδ' ὡς ὁ' Lᶜ: ὁδ' ὡς or ὁ δ' ὡς r.   738 κἀξισώσαντε L: -ες A, vulg.

καὶ τοὺς μὲν ἄλλους πάντας ἀσφαλεῖς δρόμους
ὠρθοῦθ᾽ ὁ τλήμων ὀρθὸς ἐξ ὀρθῶν δίφρων·
ἔπειτα λύων ἡνίαν ἀριστερὰν
κάμπτοντος ἵππου λανθάνει στήλην ἄκραν
παίσας· ἔθραυσε δ᾽ ἄξονος μέσας χνόας,   745
κἀξ ἀντύγων ὤλισθε· σὺν δ᾽ ἑλίσσεται
τμητοῖς ἱμᾶσι τοῦ δὲ πίπτοντος πέδῳ
πῶλοι διεσπάρησαν εἰς μέσον δρόμον.
στρατὸς δ᾽ ὅπως ὁρᾷ νιν ἐκπεπτωκότα
δίφρων, ἀνωλόλυξε τὸν νεανίαν,   750
οἳ᾽ ἔργα δράσας οἷα λαγχάνει κακά,
φορούμενος πρὸς οὖδας, ἄλλοτ᾽ οὐρανῷ
σκέλη προφαίνων, ἔστε νιν διφρηλάται,
μόλις κατασχεθόντες ἱππικὸν δρόμον,
ἔλυσαν αἱματηρόν, ὥστε μηδένα   755
γνῶναι φίλων ἰδόντ᾽ ἂν ἄθλιον δέμας.
καί νιν πυρᾷ κέαντες εὐθὺς ἐν βραχεῖ
χαλκῷ μέγιστον σῶμα δειλαίας σποδοῦ
φέρουσιν ἄνδρες Φωκέων τεταγμένοι,
ὅπως πατρῴας τύμβον ἐκλάχῃ χθονός.   760
τοιαῦτά σοι ταῦτ᾽ ἐστίν, ὡς μὲν ἐν λόγῳ
ἀλγεινά, τοῖς δ᾽ ἰδοῦσιν, οἵπερ εἴδομεν,
μέγιστα πάντων ὧν ὄπωπ᾽ ἐγὼ κακῶν.
ΧΟ. φεῦ φεῦ· τὸ πᾶν δὴ δεσπόταισι τοῖς πάλαι
πρόρριζον, ὡς ἔοικεν, ἔφθαρται γένος.   765
ΚΛ. ὦ Ζεῦ, τί ταῦτα, πότερον εὐτυχῆ λέγω,
ἢ δεινὰ μέν, κέρδη δέ; λυπηρῶς δ᾽ ἔχει,
εἰ τοῖς ἐμαυτῆς τὸν βίον σῴζω κακοῖς.
ΠΑ. τί δ᾽ ὧδ᾽ ἀθυμεῖς, ὦ γύναι, τῷ νῦν λόγῳ;
ΚΛ. δεινὸν τὸ τίκτειν ἐστίν· οὐδὲ γὰρ κακῶς   770
πάσχοντι μῖσος ὧν τέκῃ προσγίγνεται.

757 κήαντες L (κείαντες Triclinius): corr. Brunck, Erfurdt.
760 ἐκλάχῃ r: ἐκλάχοι L, vulg.

ΠΑ.   μάτην ἄρ' ἡμεῖς, ὡς ἔοικεν, ἥκομεν.
ΚΛ.   οὔτοι μάτην γε· πῶς γὰρ ἂν μάτην λέγοις;
      εἴ μοι θανόντος πίστ' ἔχων τεκμήρια
      προσῆλθες, ὅστις τῆς ἐμῆς ψυχῆς γεγώς,   775
      μαστῶν ἀποστὰς καὶ τροφῆς ἐμῆς, φυγὰς
      ἀπεξενοῦτο· καί μ', ἐπεὶ τῆσδε χθονὸς
      ἐξῆλθεν, οὐκέτ' εἶδεν· ἐγκαλῶν δέ μοι
      φόνους πατρῴους δείν' ἐπηπείλει τελεῖν·
      ὥστ' οὔτε νυκτὸς ὕπνον οὔτ' ἐξ ἡμέρας   780
      ἐμὲ στεγάζειν ἡδύν, ἀλλ' ὁ προστατῶν
      χρόνος διῆγέ μ' αἰὲν ὡς θανουμένην.
      νῦν δ', ἡμέρᾳ γὰρ τῇδ' ἀπήλλαγμαι φόβου
      πρὸς τῆσδ' ἐκείνου θ'· ἥδε γὰρ μείζων βλάβη
      ξύνοικος ἦν μοι, τοὐμὸν ἐκπίνουσ' ἀεὶ   785
      ψυχῆς ἄκρατον αἷμα—νῦν δ' ἔκηλά που
      τῶν τῆσδ' ἀπειλῶν οὕνεχ' ἡμερεύσομεν.
ΗΛ.   οἴμοι τάλαινα· νῦν γὰρ οἰμῶξαι πάρα,
      Ὀρέστα, τὴν σὴν ξυμφοράν, ὅθ' ὧδ' ἔχων
      πρὸς τῆσδ' ὑβρίζει μητρός. ἆρ' ἔχει καλῶς;   790
ΚΛ.   οὔτοι σύ· κεῖνος δ' ὡς ἔχει καλῶς ἔχει.
ΗΛ.   ἄκουε, Νέμεσι τοῦ θανόντος ἀρτίως.
ΚΛ.   ἤκουσεν ὧν δεῖ κἀπεκύρωσεν καλῶς.
ΗΛ.   ὕβριζε· νῦν γὰρ εὐτυχοῦσα τυγχάνεις.
ΚΛ.   οὔκουν Ὀρέστης καὶ σὺ παύσετον τάδε;   795
ΗΛ.   πεπαύμεθ' ἡμεῖς, οὐχ ὅπως σε παύσομεν.
ΚΛ.   πολλῶν ἂν ἥκοις, ὦ ξέν', ἄξιος τυχεῖν,
      εἰ τήνδ' ἔπαυσας τῆς πολυγλώσσου βοῆς.
ΠΑ.   οὐκοῦν ἀποστείχοιμ' ἄν, εἰ τάδ' εὖ κυρεῖ.
ΚΛ.   ἥκιστ'· ἐπείπερ οὔτ' ἐμοῦ καταξίως   800
      πράξειας οὔτε τοῦ πορεύσαντος ξένου.

783   ἀπήλλαγμαι (sic) L, prob. made by the first hand from ἀπηλλάγην,
the reading of Γ and of Suidas (s. v. προστατῶν) : but A and most MSS.
have the perf.   797   τυχεῖν A, vulg. (made in L from φιλεῖν): φιλεῖν r
(φίλος l').

ἀλλ᾿ εἴσιθ᾿ εἴσω· τήνδε δ᾿ ἔκτοθεν βοᾶν
ἔα τά θ᾿ αὑτῆς καὶ τὰ τῶν φίλων κακά.

ΗΛ. ἆρ᾿ ὑμὶν ὡς ἀλγοῦσα κὠδυνωμένη
δεινῶς δακρῦσαι κἀπικωκῦσαι δοκεῖ   805
τὸν υἱὸν ἡ δύστηνος ὧδ᾿ ὀλωλότα;
ἀλλ᾿ ἐγγελῶσα φροῦδος. ὦ τάλαιν᾿ ἐγώ·
᾿Ορέστα φίλταθ᾿, ὥς μ᾿ ἀπώλεσας θανών.
ἀποσπάσας γὰρ τῆς ἐμῆς οἴχει φρενὸς
αἵ μοι μόναι παρῆσαν ἐλπίδων ἔτι,   810
σὲ πατρὸς ἥξειν ζῶντα τιμωρόν ποτε
κἀμοῦ ταλαίνης. νῦν δὲ ποῖ με χρὴ μολεῖν;
μόνη γάρ εἰμι, σοῦ τ᾿ ἀπεστερημένη
καὶ πατρός. ἤδη δεῖ με δουλεύειν πάλιν
ἐν τοῖσιν ἐχθίστοισιν ἀνθρώπων ἐμοὶ   815
φονεῦσι πατρός. ἆρά μοι καλῶς ἔχει;
ἀλλ᾿ οὔ τι μὴν ἔγωγε τοῦ λοιποῦ χρόνου
ξύνοικος εἴσειμ᾿, ἀλλὰ τῇδε πρὸς πύλῃ
παρεῖσ᾿ ἐμαυτὴν ἄφιλος αὐανῶ βίον.
πρὸς ταῦτα καινέτω τις, εἰ βαρύνεται,   820
τῶν ἔνδον ὄντων· ὡς χάρις μέν, ἢν κτάνῃ,
λύπη δ᾿, ἐὰν ζῶ· τοῦ βίου δ᾿ οὐδεὶς πόθος.

στρ. ά.   ΧΟ. ποῦ ποτε κεραυνοὶ Διός, ἢ ποῦ φαέθων
          2 ῞Αλιος, εἰ ταῦτ᾿ ἐφορῶντες κρύπτουσιν ἔκηλοι;   826
ΗΛ.   3 ἒ ἔ, αἰαῖ.
ΧΟ.   4 ὦ παῖ, τί δακρύεις;
ΗΛ.   5 φεῦ. ΧΟ. μηδὲν μέγ᾿ αὔσῃς. ΗΛ. ἀπολεῖς. ΧΟ.
          πῶς;   831
ΗΛ.   6 εἰ τῶν φανερῶς οἰχομένων
          7 εἰς ᾿Αίδαν ἐλπίδ᾿ ὑποίσεις, κατ᾿ ἐμοῦ τακομένας
          8 μᾶλλον ἐπεμβάσει.   835

ἀντ. ά.   ΧΟ. οἶδα γὰρ ἄνακτ᾿ ᾿Αμφιάρεων χρυσοδέτοις

818   εἴσειμ᾿ Hermann: ἔσσομ᾿ L, vulg.

2 ἔρκεσι κρυφθέντα γυναικῶν· καὶ νῦν ὑπὸ γαίας

ΗΛ. 3 ἒ ἔ· ἰώ.   840

ΧΟ. 4 πάμψυχος ἀνάσσει.

ΗΛ. 5 φεῦ. ΧΟ. φεῦ δῆτ'· ὀλοὰ γὰρ ΗΛ. ἐδάμη. ΧΟ. ναί.

ΗΛ. 6 οἶδ' οἶδ'· ἐφάνη γὰρ μελέτωρ   845
7 ἀμφὶ τὸν ἐν πένθει· ἐμοὶ δ' οὔτις ἔτ' ἔσθ'· ὃς γὰρ
ἔτ' ἦν,
8 φροῦδος ἀναρπασθείς.

στρ. β'. ΧΟ. δειλαία δειλαίων κυρεῖς.

ΗΛ. 2 κἀγὼ τοῦδ' ἴστωρ, ὑπερίστωρ,   850
3 πανσύρτῳ παμμήνῳ πολλῶν
4 δεινῶν στυγνῶν τ' αἰῶνι.

ΧΟ. 5 εἴδομεν ἀθρήνεις.

ΗΛ. 6 μή μέ νυν μηκέτι
7 παραγάγῃς, ἵν' οὐ ΧΟ. τί φής;   856

ΠΛ. 8 πάρεισιν ἐλπίδων ἔτι
9 κοινοτόκων
10 εὐπατριδᾶν ἀρωγαί.

ἀντ. β'. ΧΟ. πᾶσι θνατοῖς ἔφυ μόρος.   860

ΗΛ. 2 ἦ καὶ χαλαργοῖς ἐν ἀμίλλαις
3 οὕτως ὡς κείνῳ δυστάνῳ
4 τμητοῖς ὁλκοῖς ἐγκῦρσαι;

ΧΟ. 5 ἄσκοπος ἁ λώβα.

ΗΛ. 6 πῶς γὰρ οὔκ; εἰ ξένος   865
7 ἄτερ ἐμᾶν χερῶν ΧΟ. παπαῖ.

ΠΛ. 8 κέκευθεν, οὔτε του τάφου
9 ἀντιάσας
10 οὔτε γόων παρ' ἡμῶν.   870

838 After γυναικῶν the MSS. add ἀπάταις: del. Brunck.   852 αἰῶνι
Hermann: ἀχέων L, vulg.: ἀχαίων A.   853 ἀθρήνεις Dindorf: ἆ θροεῖς
MSS.   856 After τί φής, the MSS. add αὐδᾶς δὲ πυῖον; del. Triclinius.
859 εὐπατριδᾶν τ' MSS.: τ' om. Suidas s. v. παραγαγῃς.

ΧΡΥΣΟΘΕΜΙΣ.

ὑφ᾽ ἡδονῆς τοι, φιλτάτη, διώκομαι
τὸ κόσμιον μεθεῖσα σὺν τάχει μολεῖν.
φέρω γὰρ ἡδονάς τε κἀνάπαυλαν ὧν
πάροιθεν εἶχες καὶ κατέστενες κακῶν.

ΗΛ. πόθεν δ᾽ ἂν εὕροις τῶν ἐμῶν σὺ πημάτων   875
ἄρηξιν, οἷς ἴασιν οὐκ ἔνεστ᾽ ἰδεῖν;

ΧΡ. πάρεστ᾽ Ὀρέστης ἡμίν, ἴσθι τοῦτ᾽ ἐμοῦ
κλύουσ᾽, ἐναργῶς, ὥσπερ εἰσορᾷς ἐμέ.

ΗΛ. ἀλλ᾽ ἦ μέμηνας, ὦ τάλαινα, κἀπὶ τοῖς
σαυτῆς κακοῖσι κἀπὶ τοῖς ἐμοῖς γελᾷς;   880

ΧΡ. μὰ τὴν πατρῴαν ἑστίαν, ἀλλ᾽ οὐχ ὕβρει
λέγω τάδ᾽, ἀλλ᾽ ἐκεῖνον ὡς παρόντα νῷν.

ΗΛ. οἴμοι τάλαινα· καὶ τίνος βροτῶν λόγον
τόνδ᾽ εἰσακούσασ᾽ ὧδε πιστεύεις ἄγαν;

ΧΡ. ἐγὼ μὲν ἐξ ἐμοῦ τε κοὐκ ἄλλης σαφῆ   885
σημεῖ᾽ ἰδοῦσα τῷδε πιστεύω λόγῳ.

ΗΛ. τίν᾽, ὦ τάλαιν᾽, ἰδοῦσα πίστιν; εἰς τί μοι
βλέψασα θάλπει τῷδ᾽ ἀνηκέστῳ πυρί;

ΧΡ. πρός νυν θεῶν ἄκουσον, ὡς μαθοῦσά μου
τὸ λοιπὸν ἢ φρονοῦσαν ἢ μώραν λέγῃς.   890

ΗΛ. σὺ δ᾽ οὖν λέγ᾽, εἴ σοι τῷ λόγῳ τις ἡδονή.

ΧΡ. καὶ δὴ λέγω σοι πᾶν ὅσον κατειδόμην.
ἐπεὶ γὰρ ἦλθον πατρὸς ἀρχαῖον τάφον,
ὁρῶ κολώνης ἐξ ἄκρας νεορρύτους
πηγὰς γάλακτος, καὶ περιστεφῆ κύκλῳ   895
πάντων ὅσ᾽ ἔστιν ἀνθέων θήκην πατρός.
ἰδοῦσα δ᾽ ἔσχον θαῦμα, καὶ περισκοπῶ
μή πού τις ἡμῖν ἐγγὺς ἐγχρίμπτῃ βροτῶν.
ὡς δ᾽ ἐν γαλήνῃ πάντ᾽ ἐδερκόμην τόπον,

898 ἐγχρίμπτῃ Γ: ἐγχρίπτηι L, vulg.: ἐγχρίπτει Γ.

32 ΣΟΦΟΚΛΕΟΥΣ

τύμβου προσεῖρπον ἆσσον· ἐσχάτης δ' ὁρῶ 900
πυρᾶς νεώρη βόστρυχον τετμημένον·
κεὐθὺς τάλαιν' ὡς εἶδον, ἐμπαίει τί μοι
ψυχῇ σύνηθες ὄμμα, φιλτάτου βροτῶν
πάντων Ὀρέστου τοῦθ' ὁρᾶν τεκμήριον·
καὶ χερσὶ βαστάσασα δυσφημῶ μὲν οὔ, 905
χαρᾷ δὲ πίμπλημ' εὐθὺς ὄμμα δακρύων.
καὶ νῦν θ' ὁμοίως καὶ τότ' ἐξεπίσταμαι
μή του τόδ' ἀγλάϊσμα πλὴν κείνου μολεῖν.
τῷ γὰρ προσήκει πλήν γ' ἐμοῦ καὶ σοῦ τόδε;
κἀγὼ μὲν οὐκ ἔδρασα, τοῦτ' ἐπίσταμαι, 910
οὐδ' αὖ σύ· πῶς γάρ; ᾗ γε μηδὲ πρὸς θεοὺς
ἔξεστ' ἀκλαύστῳ τῆσδ' ἀποστῆναι στέγης.
ἀλλ' οὐδὲ μὲν δὴ μητρὸς οὔθ' ὁ νοῦς φιλεῖ
τοιαῦτα πράσσειν οὔτε δρῶσ' ἐλάνθαν' ἄν·
ἀλλ' ἔστ' Ὀρέστου ταῦτα τἀπιτύμβια. 915
ἀλλ', ὦ φίλη, θάρσυνε. τοῖς αὐτοῖσί τοι
οὐχ αὑτὸς ἀεὶ δαιμόνων παραστατεῖ.
νῷν ἦν τὰ πρόσθεν στυγνός· ἡ δὲ νῦν ἴσως
πολλῶν ὑπάρξει κῦρος ἡμέρα καλῶν.
ΗΛ. φεῦ τῆς ἀνοίας, ὥς σ' ἐποικτίρω πάλαι. 920
ΧΡ. τί δ' ἔστιν; οὐ πρὸς ἡδονὴν λέγω τάδε;
ΗΛ. οὐκ οἶσθ' ὅποι γῆς οὐδ' ὅποι γνώμης φέρει.
ΧΡ. πῶς δ' οὐκ ἐγὼ κάτοιδ' ἅ γ' εἶδον ἐμφανῶς;
ΗΛ. τέθνηκεν, ὦ τάλαινα· τἀκείνου δέ σοι
σωτήρι' ἔρρει· μηδὲν εἰς κεῖνόν γ' ὅρα. 925
ΧΡ. οἴμοι τάλαινα· τοῦ τάδ' ἤκουσας βροτῶν;
ΗΛ. τοῦ πλησίον παρόντος ἡνίκ' ὤλλυτο.
ΧΡ. καὶ ποῦ 'στιν οὗτος; θαῦμά τοί μ' ὑπέρχεται.
ΗΛ. κατ' οἶκον, ἡδὺς οὐδὲ μητρὶ δυσχερής.

914 ἐλάνθαν' ἄν Heath: ἐλάνθανεν MSS. (written ἐλάνθανι in L).
ἔληθεν ἄν conj. Meineke. 915 τἀπιτίμια MSS.: corr. Dindorf.

ΧΡ. οἴμοι τάλαινα· τοῦ γὰρ ἀνθρώπων ποτ' ἦν 930
τὰ πολλὰ πατρὸς πρὸς τάφον κτερίσματα;
ΗΛ. οἶμαι μάλιστ' ἔγωγε τοῦ τεθνηκότος
μνημεῖ' Ὀρέστου ταῦτα προσθεῖναί τινα.
ΧΡ. ὦ δυστυχής· ἐγὼ δὲ σὺν χαρᾷ λόγους
τοιούσδ' ἔχουσ' ἔσπευδον, οὐκ εἰδυῖ' ἄρα 935
ἵν' ἦμεν ἄτης· ἀλλὰ νῦν, ὅθ' ἱκόμην,
τά τ' ὄντα πρόσθεν ἄλλα θ' εὑρίσκω κακά.
ΗΛ. οὕτως ἔχει σοι ταῦτ'· ἐὰν δέ μοι πίθῃ,
τῆς νῦν παρούσης πημονῆς λύσεις βάρος.
ΧΡ. ἦ τοὺς θανόντας ἐξαναστήσω ποτέ ; 940
ΗΛ. οὐκ ἔσθ' ὅ γ' εἶπον· οὐ γὰρ ὧδ' ἄφρων ἔφυν.
ΧΡ. τί γὰρ κελεύεις ὧν ἐγὼ φερέγγυος ;
ΗΛ. τλῆναί σε δρῶσαν ἃν ἐγὼ παραινέσω.
ΧΡ. ἀλλ' εἴ τις ὠφέλειά γ', οὐκ ἀπώσομαι.
ΗΛ. ὅρα, πόνου τοι χωρὶς οὐδὲν εὐτυχεῖ. 945
ΧΡ. ὁρῶ. ξυνοίσω πᾶν ὅσονπερ ἂν σθένω.
ΗΛ. ἄκουε δή νυν ᾗ βεβούλευμαι ποεῖν.
παρουσίαν μὲν οἶσθα καὶ σύ που φίλων
ὡς οὔτις ἡμῖν ἐστιν, ἀλλ' Ἅιδης λαβὼν
ἀπεστέρηκε καὶ μόνα λελείμμεθον. 950
ἐγὼ δ' ἕως μὲν τὸν κασίγνητον βίῳ
θάλλοντ' ἔτ' εἰσήκουον, εἶχον ἐλπίδας
φόνου ποτ' αὐτὸν πράκτορ' ἵξεσθαι πατρός·
νῦν δ' ἡνίκ' οὐκέτ' ἔστιν, εἰς σὲ δὴ βλέπω,
ὅπως τὸν αὐτόχειρα πατρῴου φόνου 955
ξὺν τῇδ' ἀδελφῇ μὴ κατοκνήσεις κτανεῖν
Αἴγισθον· οὐδὲν γάρ σε δεῖ κρύπτειν μ' ἔτι.
ποῖ γὰρ μενεῖς ῥᾴθυμος, ἐς τίν' ἐλπίδων

941 ἔσθ' ὅ γ A, vulg. : ἔσθ' ὅδ' L (with γ superscr.): ἐς τόδ' r.
947 ποεῖν] τελεῖν A. 950 λελείμμεθον L, vulg.: λελείμμεθα r.
952 θάλλοντ' ἔτ' Reiske, Musgrave: θάλλοντά τ' L, vulg. (θάλλοντά γ' r.)
956 κατοκνήσεις r: κατοκνήσῃς L, vulg.

βλέψασ᾽ ἔτ᾽ ὀρθήν; ἢ πάρεστι μὲν στένειν
πλούτου πατρῴου κτῆσιν ἐστερημένη,   960
πάρεστι δ᾽ ἀλγεῖν ἐς τοσόνδε τοῦ χρόνου
ἄλεκτρα γηράσκουσαν ἀνυμέναιά τε.
καὶ τῶνδε μέντοι μηκέτ᾽ ἐλπίσῃς ὅπως
τεύξει ποτ᾽· οὐ γὰρ ὧδ᾽ ἄβουλός ἐστ᾽ ἀνὴρ
Αἴγισθος ὥστε σόν ποτ᾽ ἢ κἀμὸν γένος   965
βλαστεῖν ἐᾶσαι, πημονὴν αὑτῷ σαφῆ.
ἀλλ᾽ ἢν ἐπίσπῃ τοῖς ἐμοῖς βουλεύμασιν,
πρῶτον μὲν εὐσέβειαν ἐκ πατρὸς κάτω
θανόντος οἴσει τοῦ κασιγνήτου θ᾽ ἅμα·
ἔπειτα δ᾽, ὥσπερ ἐξέφυς, ἐλευθέρα   970
καλεῖ τὸ λοιπὸν καὶ γάμων ἐπαξίων
τεύξει· φιλεῖ γὰρ πρὸς τὰ χρηστὰ πᾶς ὁρᾶν.
λόγων γε μὴν εὔκλειαν οὐχ ὁρᾷς ὅσην
σαυτῇ τε κἀμοὶ προσβαλεῖς πεισθεῖσ᾽ ἐμοί;
τίς γάρ ποτ᾽ ἀστῶν ἢ ξένων ἡμᾶς ἰδὼν   975
τοιοῖσδ᾽ ἐπαίνοις οὐχὶ δεξιώσεται,
ἴδεσθε τώδε τὼ κασιγνήτω, φίλοι,
ὣ τὸν πατρῷον οἶκον ἐξεσωσάτην,
ὣ τοῖσιν ἐχθροῖς εὖ βεβηκόσιν ποτὲ
ψυχῆς ἀφειδήσαντε προὐστήτην φόνου·   980
τούτω φιλεῖν χρή, τώδε χρὴ πάντας σέβειν·
τώδ᾽ ἔν θ᾽ ἑορταῖς ἔν τε πανδήμῳ πόλει
τιμᾶν ἅπαντας οὕνεκ᾽ ἀνδρείας χρεών.
τοιαῦτά τοι νὼ πᾶς τις ἐξερεῖ βροτῶν,
ζώσαιν θανούσαιν θ᾽ ὥστε μὴ 'κλιπεῖν κλέος. 985
ἀλλ᾽, ὦ φίλη, πείσθητι, συμπόνει πατρί,
σύγκαμν᾽ ἀδελφῷ, παῦσον ἐκ κακῶν ἐμέ,
παῦσον δὲ σαυτήν, τοῦτο γιγνώσκουσ᾽, ὅτι
ζῆν αἰσχρὸν αἰσχρῶς τοῖς καλῶς πεφυκόσιν.
ΧΟ.   ἐν τοῖς τοιούτοις ἐστὶν ἡ προμηθία   990

---

973 λόγων Dobree, Bothe: λόγῳ MSS.

καὶ τῷ λέγοντι καὶ κλύοντι σύμμαχος.

ΧΡ. καὶ πρίν γε φωνεῖν, ὦ γυναῖκες, εἰ φρενῶν
ἐτύγχαν' αὕτη μὴ κακῶν, ἐσώζετ' ἂν
τὴν εὐλάβειαν, ὥσπερ οὐχὶ σώζεται.
ποῖ γάρ ποτ' ἐμβλέψασα τοιοῦτον θράσος   995
αὐτή θ' ὁπλίζει κἄμ' ὑπηρετεῖν καλεῖς;
οὐκ εἰσορᾷς; γυνὴ μὲν οὐδ' ἀνὴρ ἔφυς,
σθένεις δ' ἔλασσον τῶν ἐναντίων χερί.
δαίμων δὲ τοῖς μὲν εὐτυχὴς καθ' ἡμέραν,
ἡμῖν δ' ἀπορρεῖ κἀπὶ μηδὲν ἔρχεται.   1000
τίς οὖν τοιοῦτον ἄνδρα βουλεύων ἑλεῖν
ἄλυπος ἄτης ἐξαπαλλαχθήσεται;
ὅρα κακῶς πράσσοντε μὴ μείζω κακὰ
κτησώμεθ', εἴ τις τούσδ' ἀκούσεται λόγους.
λύει γὰρ ἡμᾶς οὐδὲν οὐδ' ἐπωφελεῖ   1005
βάξιν καλὴν λαβόντε δυσκλεῶς θανεῖν·
οὐ γὰρ θανεῖν ἔχθιστον, ἀλλ' ὅταν θανεῖν
χρῄζων τις εἶτα μηδὲ τοῦτ' ἔχῃ λαβεῖν.
ἀλλ' ἀντιάζω, πρὶν πανωλέθρους τὸ πᾶν
ἡμᾶς τ' ὀλέσθαι κἀξερημῶσαι γένος,   1010
κατάσχες ὀργήν. καὶ τὰ μὲν λελεγμένα
ἄρρητ' ἐγώ σοι κἀτελῆ φυλάξομαι,
αὐτὴ δὲ νοῦν σχὲς ἀλλὰ τῷ χρόνῳ ποτέ,
σθένουσα μηδὲν τοῖς κρατοῦσιν εἰκαθεῖν.

ΧΟ. πείθου· προνοίας οὐδὲν ἀνθρώποις ἔφυ   1015
κέρδος λαβεῖν ἄμεινον οὐδὲ νοῦ σοφοῦ.

ΗΛ. ἀπροσδόκητον οὐδὲν εἴρηκας· καλῶς δ'
ἤδη σ' ἀπορρίψουσαν ἀπηγγελλόμην.
ἀλλ' αὐτόχειρί μοι μόνῃ τε δραστέον
τοὔργον τόδ'· οὐ γὰρ δὴ κενόν γ' ἀφήσομεν.   1020

999 εὐτυχὴς A, vulg.: εὐτυχεῖ L (but with ἦς superscr. by the first
hand), r.   1015 πείθου L, A, vulg.: πιθοῦ r.   1019 αὐτόχειρί
μοι L, A: αὐτοχειρί μοι r.

36   ΣΟΦΟΚΛΕΟΥΣ

ΧΡ. φεῦ·
    εἴθ' ὤφελες τοιάδε τὴν γνώμην πατρὸς
    θνῄσκοντος εἶναι· πᾶν γὰρ ἂν κατειργάσω.
ΗΛ. ἀλλ' ἦ φύσιν γε, τὸν δὲ νοῦν ἥσσων τότε.
ΧΡ. ἄσκει τοιαύτη νοῦν δι' αἰῶνος μένειν.
ΗΛ. ὡς οὐχὶ συνδράσουσα νουθετεῖς τάδε.   1025
ΧΡ. εἰκὸς γὰρ ἐγχειροῦντα καὶ πράσσειν κακῶς.
ΗΛ. ζηλῶ σε τοῦ νοῦ, τῆς δὲ δειλίας στυγῶ.
ΧΡ. ἀνέξομαι κλύουσα χὤταν εὖ λέγῃς.
ΗΛ. ἀλλ' οὔ ποτ' ἐξ ἐμοῦ γε μὴ πάθῃς τόδε.
ΧΡ. μακρὸς τὸ κρῖναι ταῦτα χὠ λοιπὸς χρόνος.   1030
ΗΛ. ἄπελθε· σοὶ γὰρ ὠφέλησις οὐκ ἔνι.
ΧΡ. ἔνεστιν· ἀλλὰ σοὶ μάθησις οὐ πάρα.
ΗΛ. ἐλθοῦσα μητρὶ ταῦτα πάντ' ἔξειπε σῇ.
ΧΡ. οὐδ' αὖ τοσοῦτον ἔχθος ἐχθαίρω σ' ἐγω.
ΗΛ. ἀλλ' οὖν ἐπίστω γ' οἷ μ' ἀτιμίας ἄγεις.   1035
ΧΡ. ἀτιμίας μὲν οὔ, προμηθίας δὲ σοῦ.
ΗΛ. τῷ σῷ δικαίῳ δῆτ' ἐπισπέσθαι με δεῖ;
ΧΡ. ὅταν γὰρ εὖ φρονῇς, τόθ' ἡγήσει σὺ νῷν.
ΗΛ. ἦ δεινὸν εὖ λέγουσαν ἐξαμαρτάνειν.
ΧΡ. εἴρηκας ὀρθῶς ᾧ σὺ πρόσκεισαι κακῷ.   1040
ΗΛ. τί δ'; οὐ δοκῶ σοι ταῦτα σὺν δίκῃ λέγειν;
ΧΡ. ἀλλ' ἔστιν ἔνθα χἠ δίκη βλάβην φέρει.
ΗΛ. τούτοις ἐγὼ ζῆν τοῖς νόμοις οὐ βούλομαι.
ΧΡ. ἀλλ' εἰ ποήσεις ταῦτ', ἐπαινέσεις ἐμέ.
ΗΛ. καὶ μὴν ποήσω γ', οὐδὲν ἐκπλαγεῖσά σε.   1045
ΧΡ. καὶ τοῦτ' ἀληθές, οὐδὲ βουλεύσει πάλιν;
ΗΛ. βουλῆς γὰρ οὐδέν ἐστιν ἔχθιον κακῆς.
ΧΡ. φρονεῖν ἔοικας οὐδὲν ὧν ἐγὼ λέγω.
ΗΛ. πάλαι δέδοκται ταῦτα κοὐ νεωστί μοι.
ΧΡ. ἄπειμι τοίνυν· οὔτε γὰρ σὺ τἄμ' ἔπη   1050
    τολμᾷς ἐπαινεῖν οὔτ' ἐγὼ τοὺς σοὺς τρόπους.

1022 πάντα γὰρ ἂν L (ἂν partly erased): πάντα γὰρ r: corr. Dawes.

ΗΛ. ἀλλ' εἴσιθ'. οὔ σοι μὴ μεθέψομαί ποτε,
οὐδ' ἦν σφόδρ' ἱμείρουσα τυγχάνῃς· ἐπεὶ
πολλῆς ἀνοίας καὶ τὸ θηρᾶσθαι κενά.

ΧΡ. ἀλλ' εἰ σεαυτῇ τυγχάνεις δοκοῦσά τι   1055
φρονεῖν, φρόνει τοιαῦθ'· ὅταν γὰρ ἐν κακοῖς
ἤδη βεβήκῃς, τἄμ' ἐπαινέσεις ἔπη.

στρ. α΄. ΧΟ. τί τοὺς ἄνωθεν φρονιμωτάτους οἰων-
2 οὺς ἐσορώμενοι τροφᾶς
3 κηδομένους ἀφ' ὧν τε βλάστ-   1060
4 ωσιν ἀφ' ὧν τ' ὄνασιν εὕρ-
5 ωσι, τάδ' οὐκ ἐπ' ἴσας τελοῦμεν;
6 ἀλλ' οὐ τὰν Διὸς ἀστραπὰν
7 καὶ τὰν οὐρανίαν Θέμιν,
8 δαρὸν οὐκ ἀπόνητοι.   1065
9 ὦ χθονία βροτοῖσι φά-
10 μα, κατά μοι βόασον οἰκ-
11 τρὰν ὄπα τοῖς ἔνερθ' Ἀτρεί-
12 δαις, ἀχόρευτα φέρουσ' ὀνείδη·

ἀντ. α΄. ὅτι σφιν ἤδη τὰ μὲν ἐκ δόμων νοσεῖ   1070
2 δή, τὰ δὲ πρὸς τέκνων διπλῆ
3 φύλοπις οὐκέτ' ἐξισοῦ-
4 ται φιλοτασίῳ διαί-
5 τᾳ. πρόδοτος δὲ μόνα σαλεύει
6 Ἠλέκτρα, τὸν ἀεὶ πατρὸς   1075
7 δειλαία στενάχουσ', ὅπως
8 ἁ πάνδυρτος ἀηδών,
9 οὔτε τι τοῦ θανεῖν προμη-
10 θής, τό τε μὴ βλέπειν ἑτοί-

1063 ἀλλ' οὐ μὰ τὰν MSS.: corr. Turnebus.   1070 σφιν Schaefer:
σφίσιν L, vulg.   1071 δή add. Triclinius.   1075 Ἠλέκτρα, τὸν] ἁ
παῖς, οἶτον conj. Heath.   1077 πανόδυρτος MSS.: corr. Porson.
J. E.   7

11 μα, διδύμαν ἑλοῦσ' Ἐρι-   1080
12 νύν. τίς ἂν εὔπατρις ὧδε βλάστοι;

τρ. β'. οὐδεὶς τῶν ἀγαθῶν γὰρ
    2 ζῶν κακῶς εὔκλειαν αἰσχῦναι θέλει
    3 νώνυμος, ὦ παῖ παῖ·
    4 ὡς καὶ σὺ πάγκλαυτον αἰῶνα κοινὸν εἵλου,   1085
    5 τὸ μὴ καλὸν καθοπλίσασα δύο φέρειν ἐν ἑνὶ λόγῳ,
    6 σοφά τ' ἀρίστα τε παῖς κεκλῆσθαι.

ἀντ. β'. ζῴης μοι καθύπερθεν   1090
    2 χειρὶ καὶ πλούτῳ τεῶν ἐχθρῶν ὅσον
    3 νῦν ὑπόχειρ ναίεις·
    4 ἐπεί σ' ἐφεύρηκα μοίρᾳ μὲν οὐκ ἐν ἐσθλᾷ
    5 βεβῶσαν· ἃ δὲ μέγιστ' ἔβλαστε νόμιμα, τῶνδε
    φερομέναν   1095
    6 ἄριστα τᾷ Ζηνὸς εὐσεβείᾳ.

ΟΡΕΣΤΗΣ.

ἆρ', ὦ γυναῖκες, ὀρθά τ' εἰσηκούσαμεν,
ὀρθῶς θ' ὁδοιποροῦμεν ἔνθα χρήζομεν;
ΧΟ. τί δ' ἐξερευνᾷς καὶ τί βουληθεὶς πάρει;   1100
ΟΡ. Αἴγισθον ἔνθ' ᾤκηκεν ἱστορῶ πάλαι.
ΧΟ. ἀλλ' εὖ θ' ἱκάνεις χὠ φράσας ἀζήμιος.
ΟΡ. τίς οὖν ἂν ὑμῶν τοῖς ἔσω φράσειεν ἂν
    ἡμῶν ποθεινὴν κοινόπουν παρουσίαν;
ΧΟ. ἥδ', εἰ τὸν ἄγχιστόν γε κηρύσσειν χρεών.   1105
ΟΡ. ἴθ', ὦ γύναι, δήλωσον εἰσελθοῦσ' ὅτι
    Φωκῆς ματεύουσ' ἄνδρες Αἴγισθόν τινες.

1081 τίς ἂν οὖν L, vulg.: corr. Triclinius.   1082 γὰρ add.
Hermann.   1087 καθοπλίσασα] ἀπολακτίσασα conj. J. H. H.
Schmidt.   1088 ἐν ἑνί] ἐν add. Brunck.   1091 τεῶν
Hermann: τῶν MSS.   1092 ὑπόχειρ Musgrave: ὑπὸ χεῖρα MSS.
1097 Ζηνὸς Triclinius (from schol., γρ. ἀρίστα ταζηνός): Διὸς MSS.
1099 ὀρθῶς θ' 1: ὀρθῶς δ' A, vulg. (ὀρθῶς L¹: δ' add. S.)

ΗΛ. οἴμοι τάλαιν᾽, οὐ δή ποθ᾽ ἧς ἠκούσαμεν
φήμης φέροντες ἐμφανῆ τεκμήρια;

ΟΡ. οὐκ οἶδα τὴν σὴν κληδόν· ἀλλά μοι γέρων   1110
ἐφεῖτ᾽ Ὀρέστου Στρόφιος ἀγγεῖλαι πέρι.

ΗΛ. τί δ᾽ ἔστιν, ὦ ξέν᾽; ὥς μ᾽ ὑπέρχεται φόβος.

ΟΡ. φέροντες αὐτοῦ σμικρὰ λείψαν᾽ ἐν βραχεῖ
τεύχει θανόντος, ὡς ὁρᾷς, κομίζομεν.

ΗΛ. οἲ 'γὼ τάλαινα, τοῦτ᾽ ἐκεῖν᾽ ἤδη σαφὲς   1115
πρόχειρον ἄχθος, ὡς ἔοικε, δέρκομαι.

ΟΡ. εἴπερ τι κλαίεις τῶν Ὀρεστείων κακῶν,
τόδ᾽ ἄγγος ἴσθι σῶμα τοὐκείνου στέγον.

ΗΛ. ὦ ξεῖνε, δός νυν πρὸς θεῶν, εἴπερ τόδε
κέκευθεν αὐτὸν τεῦχος, εἰς χεῖρας λαβεῖν,   1120
ὅπως ἐμαυτὴν καὶ γένος τὸ πᾶν ὁμοῦ
ξὺν τῇδε κλαύσω κἀποδύρωμαι σποδῷ.

ΟΡ. δόθ᾽, ἥτις ἐστί, προσφέροντες· οὐ γὰρ ὡς
ἐν δυσμενείᾳ γ᾽ οὖσ᾽ ἐπαιτεῖται τάδε,
ἀλλ᾽ ἢ φίλων τις ἢ πρὸς αἵματος φύσιν.   1125

ΗΛ. ὦ φιλτάτου μνημεῖον ἀνθρώπων ἐμοὶ
ψυχῆς Ὀρέστου λοιπόν, ὥς σ᾽ ἀπ᾽ ἐλπίδων
οὐχ ὧνπερ ἐξέπεμπον εἰσεδεξάμην.
νῦν μὲν γὰρ οὐδὲν ὄντα βαστάζω χεροῖν·
δόμων δέ σ᾽, ὦ παῖ, λαμπρὸν ἐξέπεμψ᾽ ἐγώ.   1130
ὡς ὤφελον πάροιθεν ἐκλιπεῖν βίον,
πρὶν ἐς ξένην σε γαῖαν ἐκπέμψαι χεροῖν
κλέψασα τοῖνδε κἀνασώσασθαι φόνου,
ὅπως θανὼν ἔκεισο τῇ τόθ᾽ ἡμέρᾳ,
τύμβου πατρῴου κοινὸν εἰληχὼς μέρος.   1135
νῦν δ᾽ ἐκτὸς οἴκων κἀπὶ γῆς ἄλλης φυγὰς
κακῶς ἀπώλου, σῆς κασιγνήτης δίχα·
κοὔτ᾽ ἐν φίλαισι χερσὶν ἡ τάλαιν᾽ ἐγὼ

1127 ὥς σ᾽] σ᾽ add. Brunck.
1128 ὧνπερ L, vulg. (ὃνπερ Harl.): ὥσπερ r.

λουτροῖς σ' ἐκόσμησ' οὔτε παμφλέκτου πυρὸς
ἀνειλόμην, ὡς εἰκός, ἄθλιον βάρος.   1140
ἀλλ' ἐν ξέναισι χερσὶ κηδευθεὶς τάλας
σμικρὸς προσήκεις ὄγκος ἐν σμικρῷ κύτει.
οἴμοι τάλαινα τῆς ἐμῆς πάλαι τροφῆς
ἀνωφελήτου, τὴν ἐγὼ θάμ' ἀμφὶ σοὶ
πόνῳ γλυκεῖ παρέσχον. οὔτε γάρ ποτε   1145
μητρὸς σύ γ' ἦσθα μᾶλλον ἢ κἀμοῦ φίλος,
οὔθ' οἱ κατ' οἶκον ἦσαν, ἀλλ' ἐγὼ τροφός,
ἐγὼ δ' ἀδελφὴ σοὶ προσηυδώμην ἀεί.
νῦν δ' ἐκλέλοιπε ταῦτ' ἐν ἡμέρᾳ μιᾷ
θανόντι σὺν σοί. πάντα γὰρ συναρπάσας   1150
θύελλ' ὅπως βέβηκας. οἴχεται πατήρ·
τέθνηκ' ἐγὼ σοί· φροῦδος αὐτὸς εἶ θανών·
γελῶσι δ' ἐχθροί· μαίνεται δ' ὑφ' ἡδονῆς
μήτηρ ἀμήτωρ, ἧς ἐμοὶ σὺ πολλάκις
φήμας λάθρᾳ προὔπεμπες ὡς φανούμενος   1155
τιμωρὸς αὐτός. ἀλλὰ ταῦθ' ὁ δυστυχὴς
δαίμων ὁ σός τε κἀμὸς ἐξαφείλετο,
ὅς σ' ὧδέ μοι προὔπεμψεν ἀντὶ φιλτάτης
μορφῆς σποδόν τε καὶ σκιὰν ἀνωφελῆ.
οἴμοι μοι·   1160
ὦ δέμας οἰκτρόν, φεῦ φεῦ.
ὦ δεινοτάτας, οἴμοι μοι,
πεμφθεὶς κελεύθους, φίλταθ', ὥς μ' ἀπώλεσας·
ἀπώλεσας δῆτ', ὦ κασίγνητον κάρα.
τοιγὰρ σὺ δέξαι μ' ἐς τὸ σὸν τόδε στέγος,   1165
τὴν μηδὲν εἰς τὸ μηδέν, ὡς σὺν σοὶ κάτω
ναίω τὸ λοιπόν. καὶ γὰρ ἡνίκ' ἦσθ' ἄνω,
ξὺν σοὶ μετεῖχον τῶν ἴσων· καὶ νῦν ποθῶ
τοῦ σοῦ θανοῦσα μὴ ἀπολείπεσθαι τάφου.

1139 λουτροῖς σ' Γ: σ' om. L and most MSS.
1152 ἐγὼ σοί J.: ἐγώ σοι MSS. and edd.

    τοὺς γὰρ θανόντας οὐχ ὁρῶ λυπουμένους.   1170

ΧΟ. θνητοῦ πέφυκας πατρός, Ἠλέκτρα, φρόνει·
    θνητὸς δ' Ὀρέστης· ὥστε μὴ λίαν στένε.
    πᾶσιν γὰρ ἡμῖν τοῦτ' ὀφείλεται παθεῖν.

ΟΡ. φεῦ φεῦ, τί λέξω; ποῖ λόγων ἀμηχανῶν
    ἔλθω; κρατεῖν γὰρ οὐκέτι γλώσσης σθένω.   1175

ΗΛ. τί δ' ἔσχες ἄλγος; πρὸς τί τοῦτ' εἰπὼν κυρεῖς;

ΟΡ. ἦ σὸν τὸ κλεινὸν εἶδος Ἠλέκτρας τόδε;

ΗΛ. τόδ' ἔστ' ἐκεῖνο, καὶ μάλ' ἀθλίως ἔχον.

ΟΡ. οἴμοι ταλαίνης ἆρα τῆσδε συμφορᾶς.

ΗΛ. οὐ δή ποτ', ὦ ξέν', ἀμφ' ἐμοὶ στένεις τάδε;   1180

ΟΡ. ὦ σῶμ' ἀτίμως κἀθέως ἐφθαρμένον.

ΗΛ. οὔτοι ποτ' ἄλλην ἢ 'μὲ δυσφημεῖς, ξένε.

ΟΡ. φεῦ τῆς ἀνύμφου δυσμόρου τε σῆς τροφῆς.

ΗΛ. τί δή ποτ', ὦ ξέν', ὧδ' ἐπισκοπῶν στένεις;

ΟΡ. ὡς οὐκ ἄρ' ᾔδη τῶν ἐμῶν οὐδὲν κακῶν.   1185

ΗΛ. ἐν τῷ διέγνως τοῦτο τῶν εἰρημένων;

ΟΡ. ὁρῶν σὲ πολλοῖς ἐμπρέπουσαν ἄλγεσιν.

ΗΛ. καὶ μὴν ὁρᾷς γε παῦρα τῶν ἐμῶν κακῶν.

ΟΡ. καὶ πῶς γένοιτ' ἂν τῶνδ' ἔτ' ἐχθίω βλέπειν;

ΗΛ. ὁθούνεκ' εἰμὶ τοῖς φονεῦσι σύντροφος.   1190

ΟΡ. τοῖς τοῦ; πόθεν τοῦτ' ἐξεσήμηνας κακόν;

ΗΛ. τοῖς πατρός· εἶτα τοῖσδε δουλεύω βίᾳ.

ΟΡ. τίς γάρ σ' ἀνάγκῃ τῇδε προτρέπει βροτῶν;

ΗΛ. μήτηρ καλεῖται, μητρὶ δ' οὐδὲν ἐξισοῖ.

ΟΡ. τί δρῶσα; πότερα χερσίν, ἢ λύμῃ βίου;   1195

ΗΛ. καὶ χερσὶ καὶ λύμαισι καὶ πᾶσιν κακοῖς.

ΟΡ. οὐδ' οὑπαρήξων οὐδ' ὁ κωλύσων πάρα;

ΗΛ. οὐ δῆθ'· ὃς ἦν γάρ μοι σὺ προὔθηκας σποδόν.

ΟΡ. ὦ δύσποτμ', ὡς ὁρῶν σ' ἐποικτίρω πάλαι.

1174 ἀμηχανῶν r: ἀμηχάνων L, vulg.   1180 οὐ was read by the schol. in L (ἆρα οὐ περὶ ἐμοῦ τάδε;). τί L (with ·ου· superscr. by the first hand), vulg.   1187 σὲ J. (ed. 1867): σε MSS.   1193 ἀνάγκῃ r: ἀνάγκη L, A, vulg.

42 ΣΟΦΟΚΛΕΟΥΣ

ΗΛ. μόνος βροτῶν νυν ἴσθ' ἐποικτίρας ποτέ. 1200
ΟΡ. μόνος γὰρ ἥκω τοῖσι σοῖς ἀλγῶν κακοῖς.
ΗΛ. οὐ δή ποθ' ἡμῖν ξυγγενὴς ἥκεις ποθέν;
ΟΡ. ἐγὼ φράσαιμ' ἄν, εἰ τὸ τῶνδ' εὔνουν πάρα.
ΗΛ. ἀλλ' ἐστὶν εὔνουν, ὥστε πρὸς πιστὰς ἐρεῖς.
ΟΡ. μέθες τόδ' ἄγγος νυν, ὅπως τὸ πᾶν μάθῃς. 1205
ΗΛ. μὴ δῆτα πρὸς θεῶν τοῦτό μ' ἐργάσῃ, ξένε.
ΟΡ. πιθοῦ λέγοντι κοὐχ ἁμαρτήσει ποτέ.
ΗΛ. μή, πρὸς γενείου, μὴ 'ξέλῃ τὰ φίλτατα.
ΟΡ. οὐ φήμ' ἐάσειν. ΗΛ. ὦ τάλαιν' ἐγὼ σέθεν,
Ὀρέστα, τῆς σῆς εἰ στερήσομαι ταφῆς. 1210
ΟΡ. εὔφημα φώνει· πρὸς δίκης γὰρ οὐ στένεις.
ΗΛ. πῶς τὸν θανόντ' ἀδελφὸν οὐ δίκῃ στένω;
ΟΡ. οὔ σοι προσήκει τήνδε προσφωνεῖν φάτιν.
ΗΛ. οὕτως ἄτιμός εἰμι τοῦ τεθνηκότος;
ΟΡ. ἄτιμος οὐδενὸς σύ· τοῦτο δ' οὐχὶ σόν. 1215
ΗΛ. εἴπερ γ' Ὀρέστου σῶμα βαστάζω τόδε.
ΟΡ. ἀλλ' οὐκ Ὀρέστου, πλὴν λόγῳ γ' ἠσκημένον.
ΗΛ. ποῦ δ' ἔστ' ἐκείνου τοῦ ταλαιπώρου τάφος;
ΟΡ. οὐκ ἔστι· τοῦ γὰρ ζῶντος οὐκ ἔστιν τάφος.
ΗΛ. πῶς εἶπας, ὦ παῖ; ΟΡ. ψεῦδος οὐδὲν ὧν λέγω. 1220
ΗΛ. ἦ ζῇ γὰρ ἀνήρ; ΟΡ. εἴπερ ἔμψυχός γ' ἐγώ.
ΗΛ. ἦ γὰρ σὺ κεῖνος; ΟΡ. τήνδε προσβλέψασά μου
σφραγῖδα πατρὸς ἔκμαθ' εἰ σαφῆ λέγω.
ΗΛ. ὦ φίλτατον φῶς. ΟΡ. φίλτατον, συμμαρτυρῶ.
ΗΛ. ὦ φθέγμ', ἀφίκου; ΟΡ. μηκέτ' ἄλλοθεν πύθῃ. 1225
ΗΛ. ἔχω σε χερσίν; ΟΡ. ὡς τὰ λοίπ' ἔχοις ἀεί.
ΗΛ. ὦ φίλταται γυναῖκες, ὦ πολίτιδες,
ὁρᾶτ' Ὀρέστην τόνδε, μηχαναῖσι μὲν
θανόντα, νῦν δὲ μηχαναῖς σεσωσμένον.
ΧΟ. ὁρῶμεν, ὦ παῖ, κἀπὶ συμφοραῖσί μοι 1230
γεγηθὸς ἕρπει δάκρυον ὀμμάτων ἄπο.

1201 τοῖσι σοῖς Lᶜ, A, vulg.: τοῖς ἴσοις L¹.   1207 πιθοῦ r: πείθου L, vulg.
1226 ἔχοις L¹: ἔχεις Lᶜ, A, vulg.

στρ. ΗΛ. ἰὼ γοναί,
2 γοναὶ σωμάτων ἐμοὶ φιλτάτων,
3 ἐμόλετ' ἀρτίως,
4 ἐφηύρετ', ἤλθετ', εἴδεθ' οὓς ἐχρῄζετε. 1235
ΟΡ. 5 πάρεσμεν· ἀλλὰ σῖγ' ἔχουσα πρόσμενε.
ΗΛ. 6 τί δ' ἔστιν;
ΟΡ. 7 σιγᾶν ἄμεινον, μή τις ἔνδοθεν κλύῃ.
ΗΛ. 8 ἀλλ' οὐ μὰ τὴν ἄδμητον αἰὲν Ἄρτεμιν
9 τόδε μὲν οὔ ποτ' ἀξιώσω τρέσαι 1240
10 περισσὸν ἄχθος ἔνδον
11 γυναικῶν ὃν ἀεί.
ΟΡ. 12 ὅρα γε μὲν δὴ κἀν γυναιξὶν ὡς Ἄρης
13 ἔνεστιν· εὖ δ' ἔξοισθα πειραθεῖσά που.
ΗΛ. 14 ὀτοτοτοτοῖ τοτοῖ, 1245
15 ἀνέφελον ἐνέβαλες
16 οὔ ποτε καταλύσιμον,
17 οὐδέ ποτε λησόμενον
18 ἀμέτερον οἷον ἔφυ κακόν. 1250
ΟΡ. 19 ἔξοιδα καὶ ταῦτ'· ἀλλ' ὅταν παρουσία
20 φράζῃ, τότ' ἔργων τῶνδε μεμνῆσθαι χρεών.

ἀντ. ΗΛ. ὁ πᾶς ἐμοί,
2 ὁ πᾶς ἂν πρέποι παρὼν ἐννέπειν
3 τάδε δίκᾳ χρόνος· 1255
4 μόλις γὰρ ἔσχον νῦν ἐλεύθερον στόμα.
ΟΡ. 5 ξύμφημι κἀγώ· τοιγαροῦν σῴζου τόδε.
ΗΛ. 6 τί δρῶσα;
ΟΡ. 7 οὗ μή 'στι καιρὸς μὴ μακρὰν βούλου λέγειν.

1239 ἀλλ' οὐ τὰν Ἄρτεμιν τὰν αἰὲν ἀδμήταν MSS. (οὐ μὰ τὰν r): corr.
Fröhlich (but with τάν γ': τὴν Hermann). 1245 ὀτοτοτοῖ τοτοῖ
Hermann (= 1265): ὀτοττοῖ L, ὀττοτοῖ A. 1246 ἐνέβαλες· schol. in
L on 1245: ἐπέβαλες L, vulg.: ὑπέβαλες r. 1251 παροισία L, A,
vulg. (as the schol. in L also read): παρρησία r.

ΗΛ. 8 τίς οὖν ἂν ἀξίαν γε σοῦ πεφηνότος   1260
    9 μεταβάλοιτ' ἂν ὧδε σιγὰν λόγων;
    10 ἐπεί σε νῦν ἀφράστως
    11 ἀέλπτως τ' ἐσεῖδον.

ΟΡ. 12 τότ' εἶδες, εὖτε θεοί μ' ἐπώτρυναν μολεῖν
    ◡ ⏌ ◡ — ◡ ⏌ ◡ — ◡ ⏌ ◡ —

ΗΛ. 14 ἔφρασας ὑπερτέραν   1265
    15 τᾶς πάρος ἔτι χάριτος,
    16 εἴ σε θεὸς ἐπόρισεν
    17 ἁμέτερα πρὸς μέλαθρα·
    18 δαιμόνιον αὐτὸ τίθημ' ἐγώ.   1270

ΟΡ. 19 τὰ μέν σ' ὀκνῶ χαίρουσαν εἰργαθεῖν, τὰ δὲ
    20 δέδοικα λίαν ἡδονῇ νικωμένην.

ἐπ. ΗΛ. ἰὼ χρόνῳ μακρῷ φιλτάταν
    ὁδὸν ἐπαξιώσας ὧδέ μοι φανῆναι,
    μή τί με, πολύπονον ὧδ' ἰδὼν   1275

ΟΡ. τί μὴ ποήσω; ΗΛ. μή μ' ἀποστερήσῃς
    τῶν σῶν προσώπων ἁδονὰν μεθέσθαι.

ΟΡ. ἦ κάρτα κἂν ἄλλοισι θυμοίμην ἰδών.

ΗΛ. ξυναινεῖς;

ΟΡ. τί μὴν οὔ;   1280

ΗΛ. ὦ φίλαι, ἔκλυον ἂν ἐγὼ
    οὐδ' ἂν ἤλπισ' αὐδάν·
    οὐδ' ἂν ἔσχον ὁρμὰν
    ἄναυδον οὐδὲ σὺν βοᾷ κλύουσα.
    τάλαινα· νῦν δ' ἔχω σε· προὐφάνης δὲ   1285
    φιλτάταν ἔχων πρόσοψιν,
    ἃς ἐγὼ οὐδ' ἂν ἐν κακοῖς λαθοίμαν.

1260 ἂν ἀξίαν r: ἂν om. L¹, add. Lᶜ (above the line).   1264 εὖτε
J.: ὅτε MSS.—ἐπώτρυναν Reiske, Brunck: ὤτρυναν MSS.   1267 ἐπόρισεν
Dindorf, Fröhlich: ἐπῶρσεν L¹, A, vulg. (ἐπόρσεν Lᶜ.)   1275 πολύπονον
r: πολύστονον L, A, vulg.   1281 ἂν ἐγὼ r: ἂν ἐγὼ L.   1283 οὐδ' ἂν
before ἔσχον add. Arndt.—ὁρμὰν Blomfield: ὀργὰν MSS.

ΟΡ. τὰ μὲν περισσεύοντα τῶν λόγων ἄφες,
καὶ μήτε μήτηρ ὡς κακὴ δίδασκέ με,
μήθ᾽ ὡς πατρῴαν κτῆσιν Αἴγισθος δόμων   1290
ἀντλεῖ, τὰ δ᾽ ἐκχεῖ, τὰ δὲ διασπείρει μάτην·
χρόνου γὰρ ἄν σοι καιρὸν ἐξείργοι λόγος.
ἃ δ᾽ ἁρμόσει μοι τῷ παρόντι νῦν χρόνῳ
σήμαιν᾽, ὅπου φανέντες ἢ κεκρυμμένοι
γελῶντας ἐχθροὺς παύσομεν τῇ νῦν ὁδῷ.   1295
οὕτω δ᾽ ὅπως μήτηρ σε μὴ ᾽πιγνώσεται
φαιδρῷ προσώπῳ νῷν ἐπελθόντοιν δόμους·
ἀλλ᾽ ὡς ἐπ᾽ ἄτῃ τῇ μάτην λελεγμένῃ
στέναζ᾽· ὅταν γὰρ εὐτυχήσωμεν, τότε
χαίρειν παρέσται καὶ γελᾶν ἐλευθέρως.   1300
ΗΛ. ἀλλ᾽, ὦ κασίγνηθ᾽, ὧδ᾽ ὅπως καὶ σοὶ φίλον
καὶ τοὐμὸν ἔσται τῇδ᾽· ἐπεὶ τὰς ἡδονὰς
πρὸς σοῦ λαβοῦσα κοὐκ ἐμὰς ἐκτησάμην.
κοὐδ᾽ ἄν σε λυπήσασα δεξαίμην βραχὺ
αὐτὴ μέγ᾽ εὑρεῖν κέρδος· οὐ γὰρ ἂν καλῶς   1305
ὑπηρετοίην τῷ παρόντι δαίμονι.
ἀλλ᾽ οἶσθα μὲν τἀνθένδε, πῶς γὰρ οὔ: κλύων
ὁθούνεκ᾽ Αἴγισθος μὲν οὐ κατὰ στέγας,
μήτηρ δ᾽ ἐν οἴκοις· ἣν σὺ μὴ δείσῃς ποθ᾽ ὡς
γέλωτι τοὐμὸν φαιδρὸν ὄψεται κάρα·   1310
μῖσός τε γὰρ παλαιὸν ἐντέτηκέ μοι,
κἀπεί σ᾽ ἐσεῖδον, οὔ ποτ᾽ ἐκλήξω χαρᾷ
δακρυρροοῦσα. πῶς γὰρ ἂν λήξαιμ᾽ ἐγώ,
ἥτις μιᾷ σε τῇδ᾽ ὁδῷ θανόντα τε
καὶ ζῶντ᾽ ἐσεῖδον; εἴργασαι δέ μ᾽ ἄσκοπα·   1315
ὥστ᾽ εἰ πατήρ μοι ζῶν ἵκοιτο, μηκέτ᾽ ἂν

1297 ἐπελθόντοιν A: -ων L.   1298 λελεγμένῃ A, vulg.: δεδεγ-
μένηι L, with λ λ superscr. by an early hand.   1304 δεξαίμην r:
λεξαίμην L, with γρ. βουλοίμην βραχὺ in marg.: βουλοίμην A, vulg.
1306 ὑπηρετοίμην MSS.: corr. Musgrave, Elmsley.

τέρας νομίζειν αὐτό, πιστεύειν δ' ὁρᾶν.
ὅτ' οὖν τοιαύτην ἡμὶν ἐξήκεις ὁδόν,
ἄρχ' αὐτὸς ὥς σοι θυμός· ὡς ἐγὼ μόνη
οὐκ ἂν δυοῖν ἥμαρτον· ἢ γὰρ ἂν καλῶς   1320
ἔσωσ' ἐμαυτήν, ἢ καλῶς ἀπωλόμην.
ΟΡ.   σιγᾶν ἐπῄνεσ'· ὡς ἐπ' ἐξόδῳ κλύω
τῶν ἔνδοθεν χωροῦντος. ΗΛ. εἴσιτ', ὦ ξένοι,
ἄλλως τε καὶ φέροντες οἷ' ἂν οὔτε τις
δόμων ἀπώσαιτ' οὔτ' ἂν ἡσθείη λαβών.   1325
ΠΑ.   ὦ πλεῖστα μῶροι καὶ φρενῶν τητώμενοι,
πότερα παρ' οὐδὲν τοῦ βίου κήδεσθ' ἔτι,
ἢ νοῦς ἔνεστιν οὔτις ὑμὶν ἐγγενής,
ὅτ' οὐ παρ' αὐτοῖς ἀλλ' ἐν αὐτοῖσιν κακοῖς
τοῖσιν μεγίστοις ὄντες οὐ γιγνώσκετε;   1330
ἀλλ' εἰ σταθμοῖσι τοῖσδε μὴ 'κύρουν ἐγὼ
πάλαι φυλάσσων, ἦν ἂν ὑμὶν ἐν δόμοις
τὰ δρώμεν' ὑμῶν πρόσθεν ἢ τὰ σώματα·
νῦν δ' εὐλάβειαν τῶνδε προὐθέμην ἐγώ.
καὶ νῦν ἀπαλλαχθέντε τῶν μακρῶν λόγων   1335
καὶ τῆς ἀπλήστου τῆσδε σὺν χαρᾷ βοῆς
εἴσω παρέλθεθ', ὡς τὸ μὲν μέλλειν κακὸν
ἐν τοῖς τοιούτοις ἔστ', ἀπηλλάχθαι δ' ἀκμή.
ΟΡ.   πῶς οὖν ἔχει τἀντεῦθεν εἰσιόντι μοι;
ΠΑ.   καλῶς· ὑπάρχει γάρ σε μὴ γνῶναί τινα.   1340
ΟΡ.   ἤγγειλας, ὡς ἔοικεν, ὡς τεθνηκότα.
ΠΑ.   εἷς τῶν ἐν Ἅιδου μάνθαν' ἐνθάδ' ὢν ἀνήρ.
ΟΡ.   χαίρουσιν οὖν τούτοισιν; ἢ τίνες λόγοι;
ΠΑ.   τελουμένων εἴποιμ' ἄν· ὡς δὲ νῦν ἔχει,
καλῶς τὰ κείνων πάντα, καὶ τὰ μὴ καλῶς.   1345
ΗΛ.   τίς οὗτός ἐστ', ἀδελφέ; πρὸς θεῶν φράσον.
ΟΡ.   οὐχὶ ξυνίης; ΗΛ. οὐδέ γ' εἰς θυμὸν φέρω.
ΟΡ.   οὐκ οἶσθ' ὅτῳ μ' ἔδωκας εἰς χέρας ποτέ;

1343 χαίρουσιν οὖν A, vulg.: χαίρουσιν ἐν L.

ΗΛΕΚΤΡΑ 47

ΗΛ. ποίῳ; τί φωνεῖς; ΟΡ. οὐ τὸ Φωκέων πέδον
ὑπεξεπέμφθην σῇ προμηθίᾳ χεροῖν. 1350

ΗΛ. ἦ κεῖνος οὗτος ὅν ποτ᾽ ἐκ πολλῶν ἐγὼ
μόνον προσηῦρον πιστὸν ἐν πατρὸς φόνῳ;

ΟΡ. ὅδ᾽ ἐστί· μή μ᾽ ἔλεγχε πλείοσιν λόγοις.

ΗΛ. ὦ φίλτατον φῶς, ὦ μόνος σωτὴρ δόμων
Ἀγαμέμνονος, πῶς ἦλθες; ἦ σὺ κεῖνος εἶ 1355
ὃς τόνδε κἄμ᾽ ἔσωσας ἐκ πολλῶν πόνων;
ὦ φίλταται μὲν χεῖρες, ἥδιστον δ᾽ ἔχων
ποδῶν ὑπηρέτημα, πῶς οὕτω πάλαι
ξυνών μ᾽ ἔληθες οὐδ᾽ ἔφαινες, ἀλλά με
λόγοις ἀπώλλυς, ἔργ᾽ ἔχων ἥδιστ᾽ ἐμοί; 1360
χαῖρ᾽, ὦ πάτερ· πατέρα γὰρ εἰσορᾶν δοκῶ·
χαῖρ᾽· ἴσθι δ᾽ ὡς μάλιστά σ᾽ ἀνθρώπων ἐγὼ
ἤχθηρα κἀφίλησ᾽ ἐν ἡμέρᾳ μιᾷ.

ΠΑ. ἀρκεῖν δοκεῖ μοι· τοὺς γὰρ ἐν μέσῳ λόγους,
πολλαὶ κυκλοῦνται νύκτες ἡμέραι τ᾽ ἴσαι, 1365
αἳ ταῦτά σοι δείξουσιν, Ἠλέκτρα, σαφῆ.
σφῷν δ᾽ ἐννέπω γε τοῖν παρεστώτοιν ὅτι
νῦν καιρὸς ἔρδειν· νῦν Κλυταιμνήστρα μόνη·
νῦν οὔτις ἀνδρῶν ἔνδον· εἰ δ᾽ ἐφέξετον,
φροντίζεθ᾽ ὡς τούτοις τε καὶ σοφωτέροις 1370
ἄλλοισι τούτων πλείοσιν μαχούμενοι.

ΟΡ. οὐκ ἂν μακρῶν ἔθ᾽ ἡμὶν οὐδὲν ἂν λόγων,
Πυλάδη, τόδ᾽ εἴη τοὔργον, ἀλλ᾽ ὅσον τάχος
χωρεῖν ἔσω, πατρῷα προσκύσανθ᾽ ἔδη
θεῶν, ὅσοιπερ πρόπυλα ναίουσιν τάδε. 1375

ΗΛ. ἄναξ Ἄπολλον, ἵλεως αὐτοῖν κλύε,
ἐμοῦ τε πρὸς τούτοισιν, ἥ σε πολλὰ δὴ
ἀφ᾽ ὧν ἔχοιμι λιπαρεῖ προὔστην χερί.
νῦν δ᾽, ὦ Λύκει᾽ Ἄπολλον, ἐξ οἵων ἔχω

1365 κυκλοῦνται L¹ (changed to κυκλοῦσι by a later hand, but afterwards
restored, νται being written above the line), Γ : κυκλοῦσι A, vulg.

48 ΣΟΦΟΚΛΕΟΥΣ

αἰτῶ, προπίπτω, λίσσομαι, γενοῦ πρόφρων   1380
ἡμῖν ἀρωγὸς τῶνδε τῶν βουλευμάτων,
καὶ δεῖξον ἀνθρώποισι τἀπιτίμια
τῆς δυσσεβείας οἷα δωροῦνται θεοί.

στρ. ΧΟ. ἴδεθ᾽ ὅπου προνέμεται
2 τὸ δυσέριστον αἷμα φυσῶν Ἄρης.   1385
3 βεβᾶσιν ἄρτι δωμάτων ὑπόστεγοι
4 μετάδρομοι κακῶν πανουργημάτων
5 ἄφυκτοι κύνες,
6 ὥστ᾽ οὐ μακρὰν ἔτ᾽ ἀμμενεῖ
7 τοὐμὸν φρενῶν ὄνειρον αἰωρούμενον.   1390

ἀντ. παράγεται γὰρ ἐνέρων
2 δολιόπους ἀρωγὸς εἴσω στέγας,
3 ἀρχαιόπλουτα πατρὸς εἰς ἐδώλια,
4 νεακόνητον αἷμα χειροῖν ἔχων·
5 ὁ Μαίας δὲ παῖς   1395
6 Ἑρμῆς σφ᾽ ἄγει δόλον σκότῳ
7 κρύψας πρὸς αὐτὸ τέρμα, κοὐκέτ᾽ ἀμμένει.

στρ. ΗΛ. ὦ φίλταται γυναῖκες, ἄνδρες αὐτίκα
τελοῦσι τοὔργον· ἀλλὰ σῖγα πρόσμενε.
ΧΟ. πῶς δή; τί νῦν πράσσουσιν; ΗΛ. ἡ μὲν ἐς τάφον
λέβητα κοσμεῖ, τὼ δ᾽ ἐφέστατον πέλας.   1401
ΧΟ. σὺ δ᾽ ἐκτὸς ᾖξας πρὸς τί; ΗΛ. φρουρήσουσ᾽ ὅπως
Αἴγισθος ἡμᾶς μὴ λάθῃ μολὼν ἔσω.
ΚΛ. αἰαῖ· ἰὼ στέγαι

1380 προπίπτω J.: προ πιτνῶ (from προ πίτνω) L: προπιτνῶ A, vulg.
(προσπιτνῶ Γ.)   1389 ἀμμενεῖ Wunder: ἀμμένει L, vulg.   1394 νεακόνητον MSS.: νεοκόνητον Aldine ed. (1502 A.D.), and lemma of schol. on
v. 1394 as edited by J. A. Lascaris (Rome, 1518).   1396 σφ᾽ ἄγει Γ:
ἐ ἄγει (with an erasure after ἐ, rather larger than the space for one
letter) L: ἐπάγει A: ἐπεισάγει E.   1403 ἡμᾶς om. MSS. (superscr.
in cod. Ienensis, 14th cent.): add. Reiske.

φίλων ἔρημοι, τῶν δ' ἀπολλύντων πλέαι. 1405

ΗΛ. βοᾷ τις ἔνδον· οὐκ ἀκούετ', ὦ φίλαι;

ΧΟ. ἤκουσ' ἀνήκουστα δύστανος, ὥστε φρῖξαι.

ΚΛ. οἴμοι τάλαιν'· Αἴγισθε, ποῦ ποτ' ὢν κυρεῖς;

ΗΛ. ἰδοὺ μάλ' αὖ θροεῖ τις. ΚΛ. ὦ τέκνον τέκνον, 1410
οἴκτιρε τὴν τεκοῦσαν. ΗΛ. ἀλλ' οὐκ ἐκ σέθεν
ᾠκτίρεθ' οὗτος οὐδ' ὁ γεννήσας πατήρ.

ΧΟ. ὦ πόλις, ὦ γενεὰ τάλαινα, νῦν σοι
μοῖρα καθαμερία φθίνει φθίνει. 1414

ΚΛ. ὤμοι πέπληγμαι. ΗΛ. παῖσον, εἰ σθένεις, διπλῆν.

ΚΛ. ὤμοι μάλ' αὖθις. ΗΛ. εἰ γὰρ Αἰγίσθῳ γ' ὁμοῦ.

ΧΟ. τελοῦσ' ἀραί· ζῶσιν οἱ γᾶς ὑπαὶ κείμενοι.
παλίρρυτον γὰρ αἷμ' ὑπεξαιροῦσι τῶν κτανόντων
οἱ πάλαι θανόντες. 1421

ἀντ. καὶ μὴν πάρεισιν οἵδε· φοινία δὲ χεὶρ
στάζει θυηλῆς Ἄρεος, οὐδ' ἔχω ψέγειν.

ΗΛ. Ὀρέστα, πῶς κυρεῖτε; ΟΡ. τὰν δόμοισι μὲν
καλῶς, Ἀπόλλων εἰ καλῶς ἐθέσπισεν. 1425

ΗΛ. τέθνηκεν ἡ τάλαινα; ΟΡ. μηκέτ' ἐκφοβοῦ
μητρῷον ὥς σε λῆμ' ἀτιμάσει ποτέ.

ΧΟ. παύσασθε· λεύσσω γὰρ Αἴγισθον ἐκ προδήλου.

ΗΛ. ὦ παῖδες, οὐκ ἄψορρον; ΟΡ. εἰσορᾶτε ποῦ 1430
τὸν ἄνδρ'; ΗΛ. ἐφ' ἡμῖν οὗτος ἐκ προαστίου
χωρεῖ γεγηθώς ‒ ◡ ‒ ◡ ‒ ◡ ‒

1413 νῦν σοι R. Whitelaw (a conjecture made also by Hermann, who,
however, kept σε): σε MSS. 1414 φθίνει bis L: semel A. (φθίνειν
φθίνειν Hermann.) 1416 Αἰγίσθῳ γ'] γ' Hermann: θ' L, vulg.: δ' r.
1419 παλίρρυτον Bothe: πολύρρυτον MSS. 1422 f. The MSS. give
these two vv. to Electra: corr. Hermann. 1423 ψέγειν Erfurdt:
λέγειν MSS. 1424 κυρεῖτε Reisig, Elmsley: κυρεῖ L, vulg. (κυρεῖ γε
Triclinius: κυρεῖ δὲ Hermann.) 1431 L and most MSS. divide the
words thus: τὸν ἄνδρ' ἐφ' ἡμῖν; ΗΛ. οὗτος κ.τ.λ. 1432 After γεγηθώς
the rest of a trimeter is lost. Hermann conj. κάρτα σὺν σπουδῇ ποδός.

50 ΣΟΦΟΚΛΕΟΥΣ

ΧΟ. βᾶτε κατ' ἀντιθύρων ὅσον τάχιστα,
νῦν, τὰ πρὶν εὖ θέμενοι, τάδ' ὡς πάλιν.
ΟΡ. θάρσει· τελοῦμεν. ΗΛ. ᾗ νοεῖς ἔπειγέ νυν. 1435
ΟΡ. καὶ δὴ βέβηκα. ΗΛ. τἀνθάδ' ἂν μέλοιτ' ἐμοί.
ΧΟ. δι' ὠτὸς ἂν παῦρά γ' ὡς ἠπίως ἐννέπειν
πρὸς ἄνδρα τόνδε συμφέροι, λαθραῖον ὡς ὀρούσῃ
πρὸς δίκας ἀγῶνα. 1441

ΑΙΓΙΣΘΟΣ.

τίς οἶδεν ὑμῶν ποῦ ποθ' οἱ Φωκῆς ξένοι,
οὕς φασ' Ὀρέστην ἡμὶν ἀγγεῖλαι βίου
λελοιπόθ' ἱππικοῖσιν ἐν ναυαγίοις;
σέ τοι, σὲ κρίνω, ναὶ σέ, τὴν ἐν τῷ πάρος 1445
χρόνῳ θρασεῖαν· ὡς μάλιστα σοὶ μέλειν
οἶμαι, μάλιστα δ' ἂν κατειδυῖαν φράσαι.
ΗΛ. ἔξοιδα· πῶς γὰρ οὐχί; συμφορᾶς γὰρ ἂν
ἔξωθεν εἴην τῶν ἐμῶν τῆς φιλτάτης.
ΑΙ. ποῦ δῆτ' ἂν εἶεν οἱ ξένοι; δίδασκέ με. 1450
ΗΛ. ἔνδον· φίλης γὰρ προξένου κατήνυσαν.
ΑΙ. ἦ καὶ θανόντ' ἤγγειλαν ὡς ἐτητύμως;
ΗΛ. οὔκ, ἀλλὰ κἀπέδειξαν, οὐ λόγῳ μόνον.
ΑΙ. πάρεστ' ἄρ' ἡμῖν ὥστε κἀμφανῆ μαθεῖν;
ΗΛ. πάρεστι δῆτα, καὶ μάλ' ἄζηλος θέα. 1455
ΑΙ. ἦ πολλὰ χαίρειν μ' εἶπας οὐκ εἰωθότως.
ΗΛ. χαίροις ἄν, εἴ σοι χαρτὰ τυγχάνει τάδε.
ΑΙ. σιγᾶν ἄνωγα κἀναδεικνύναι πύλας
πᾶσιν Μυκηναίοισιν Ἀργείοις θ' ὁρᾶν,

1437—1441 δι' ὠτὸς...ἀγῶνα] These vv. are given by the MSS.
to Electra: corr. Triclinius.   1445 ναὶ σὲ Reiske: καὶ σὲ MSS.
1449 τῶν ἐμῶν τῆς φιλτάτης r, vulg.: τῶν ἐμῶν τε φιλτάτων L (but
with the read'ng τῆς φιλτάτης indicated by the first hand), A.   A few
MSS. have τῶν ἐμῶν τῶν φιλτάτων.   1457 τυγχάνει A, vulg.:
τυγχάνοι L.

ΗΛΕΚΤΡΑ 51

ὡς εἴ τις αὐτῶν ἐλπίσιν κεναῖς πάρος 1460
ἐξήρετ᾽ ἀνδρὸς τοῦδε, νῦν ὁρῶν νεκρὸν
στόμια δέχηται τἀμά, μηδὲ πρὸς βίαν
ἐμοῦ κολαστοῦ προστυχὼν φύσῃ φρένας.
ΗΛ. καὶ δὴ τελεῖται τἀπ᾽ ἐμοῦ· τῷ γὰρ χρόνῳ
νοῦν ἔσχον, ὥστε συμφέρειν τοῖς κρείσσοσιν. 1465
ΑΙ. ὦ Ζεῦ, δέδορκα φάσμ᾽ ἄνευ φθόνου μὲν οὐ
πεπτωκός· εἰ δ᾽ ἔπεστι νέμεσις, οὐ λέγω.
χαλᾶτε πᾶν κάλυμμ᾽ ἀπ᾽ ὀφθαλμῶν, ὅπως
τὸ συγγενές τοι κἀπ᾽ ἐμοῦ θρήνων τύχῃ.
ΟΡ. αὐτὸς σὺ βάσταζ᾽· οὐκ ἐμὸν τόδ᾽, ἀλλὰ σόν, 1470
τὸ ταῦθ᾽ ὁρᾶν τε καὶ προσηγορεῖν φίλως.
ΑΙ. ἀλλ᾽ εὖ παραινεῖς, κἀπιπείσομαι· σὺ δέ,
εἴ που κατ᾽ οἶκόν μοι Κλυταιμνήστρα, κάλει.
ΟΡ. αὕτη πέλας σοῦ· μηκέτ᾽ ἄλλοσε σκόπει.
ΑΙ. οἴμοι, τί λεύσσω; ΟΡ. τίνα φοβεῖ; τίν᾽ ἀγνοεῖς;
ΑΙ. τίνων ποτ᾽ ἀνδρῶν ἐν μέσοις ἀρκυστάτοις 1476
πέπτωχ᾽ ὁ τλήμων; ΟΡ. οὐ γὰρ αἰσθάνει πάλαι
ζῶντας θανοῦσιν οὕνεκ᾽ ἀνταυδᾷς ἴσα;
ΑΙ. οἴμοι, ξυνῆκα τοὔπος· οὐ γὰρ ἔσθ᾽ ὅπως
ὅδ᾽ οὐκ Ὀρέστης ἔσθ᾽ ὁ προσφωνῶν ἐμέ. 1480
ΟΡ. καὶ μάντις ὢν ἄριστος ἐσφάλλου πάλαι;
ΑΙ. ὄλωλα δὴ δείλαιος. ἀλλά μοι πάρες
κἂν σμικρὸν εἰπεῖν. ΗΛ. μὴ πέρα λέγειν ἔα
πρὸς θεῶν, ἀδελφέ, μηδὲ μηκύνειν λόγους.
τί γὰρ βροτῶν ἂν σὺν κακοῖς μεμιγμένων 1485
θνήσκειν ὁ μέλλων τοῦ χρόνου κέρδος φέροι;
ἀλλ᾽ ὡς τάχιστα κτεῖνε, καὶ κτανὼν πρόθες
ταφεῦσιν ὧν τόνδ᾽ εἰκός ἐστι τυγχάνειν,
ἄποπτον ἡμῶν· ὡς ἐμοὶ τόδ᾽ ἂν κακῶν
μόνον γένοιτο τῶν πάλαι λυτήριον. 1490

1466 φθόνου L², φόνου L¹.   1478 ζῶντας Tyrwhitt: ζῶν τοῖς MSS.

ΟΡ. χωροῖς ἂν εἴσω σὺν τάχει· λόγων γὰρ οὐ
νῦν ἐστιν ἀγών, ἀλλὰ σῆς ψυχῆς πέρι.

ΑΙ. τί δ᾽ ἐς δόμους ἄγεις με; πῶς, τόδ᾽ εἰ καλὸν
τοὔργον, σκότου δεῖ, κοὐ πρόχειρος εἶ κτανεῖν;

ΟΡ. μὴ τάσσε· χώρει δ᾽ ἔνθαπερ κατέκτανες 1495
πατέρα τὸν ἁμόν, ὡς ἂν ἐν ταὐτῷ θάνῃς.

ΑΙ. ἦ πᾶσ᾽ ἀνάγκη τήνδε τὴν στέγην ἰδεῖν
τά τ᾽ ὄντα καὶ μέλλοντα Πελοπιδῶν κακά;

ΟΡ. τὰ γοῦν σ᾽· ἐγώ σοι μάντις εἰμὶ τῶνδ᾽ ἄκρος.

ΑΙ. ἀλλ᾽ οὐ πατρῴαν τὴν τέχνην ἐκόμπασας. 1500

ΟΡ. πόλλ᾽ ἀντιφωνεῖς, ἡ δ᾽ ὁδὸς βραδύνεται.
ἀλλ᾽ ἔρφ᾽. ΑΙ. ὑφηγοῦ. ΟΡ. σοὶ βαδιστέον
πάρος.

ΑΙ. ἦ μὴ φύγω σε; ΟΡ. μὴ μὲν οὖν καθ᾽ ἡδονὴν
θάνῃς· φυλάξαι δεῖ με τοῦτό σοι πικρόν.
χρῆν δ᾽ εὐθὺς εἶναι τήνδε τοῖς πᾶσιν δίκην, 1505
ὅστις πέρα πράσσειν γε τῶν νόμων θέλει,
κτείνειν. τὸ γὰρ πανοῦργον οὐκ ἂν ἦν πολύ.

ΧΟ. ὦ σπέρμ᾽ Ἀτρέως, ὡς πολλὰ παθὸν
δι᾽ ἐλευθερίας μόλις ἐξῆλθες
τῇ νῦν ὁρμῇ τελεωθέν. 1510

1496 ὡς ἂν ἐν Triclinius: ὡς ἐν L, A, vulg.: ὡς ἂν (without ἐν) r.
1506 πέρα πράσσειν γε τῶν νόμων] πέρα τι τῶν νόμων πράσσειν Nicephorus
Vasilákes (circ. 1180 A.D.), Προγυμνάσματα c. 6, where he quotes 1505—1507
(Walz, Rhet. Gr. vol I. p. 461).—θέλει Lᶜ, A: θέλοι Lˡ, Γ. 1507
πανοῦργον] κακοῦργον Nicephorus l. c.

NOTES

Scene:—*At Mycenae, before the palace of the Pelopidae.*
The PAEDAGOGUS *enters on the left of the spectators, with*
ORESTES *and* PYLADES.
1—120   Prologue. Orestes explains his plan of action,
and then goes with Pylades to make offerings at Agamemnon's grave (1—85).—Electra's lament (86—120) properly
belongs to the πρόλογος, since it precedes the entrance of
the Chorus (121).

3   ὧν, since πρόθυμος ἦσθ' = ἐπεθύμεις.

4—8 Coming from Phocis, the travellers have reached
Mycenae by the road from Corinth, and are now standing
on the high ground of the Mycenaean citadel, in front of the
palace.

The old man, looking southward, points out the chief
features of the landscape. (1) The Argive plain, which lies
spread out before them to the south and west.   (2) The
agora and temple of Apollo Lyceios in the city of Argos,
distant about six miles to the south.   This temple was the
most conspicuous object in the town (Paus. 2. 19. 3); and
it may be supposed that a person standing at Mycenae
could see the building, or part of it.   (3) The Heraeum,
correctly described as being on the speaker's left hand.   Its
site was S.E. of Mycenae, at a distance of somewhat less
than two miles.

4 Ἄργος in prose usu. means the town only, the territory
being ἡ Ἀργεία or ἡ Ἀργολίς. But poetry retained the larger
sense which Homer had made familiar.

παλαιὸν refers not merely to the town, but to the associa-
tions of the land.   The oldest legends of intercourse between
Greece and Asia belonged to the shores of the Argive Gulf
(cp. Her. 1. 1).

5 τῆς οἰστροπλ...Ἰνάχου κόρης (*i.e.* Io).   The Inachus
(now the *Bonitza*) rises in the highlands between Arcadia

and Argolis; flows **N.E.**, and then **S.E.**, through the Argive plain; and enters the Gulf on the east side of the town. This river-god figured as the earliest king of Argos.

ἄλσος, the whole region, regarded as ground which her story has made sacred: ἔλεγον γὰρ πᾶν χωρίον ἀφιερωμένον θεῷ, κἂν ψιλὸν φυτῶν ᾖ, ἄλσος (schol. Pind. *O.* 3. 31).

6 f. The ἀγορὰ Λύκειος in Argos lay at the eastern foot of the Larisa, or citadel; as Livy (32. 25) describes it, *subiectum arci forum*. The temple of Apollo Λύκειος was probably on the north side of the agora, opposite to a temple of Zeus Νεμεαῖος.

Λύκειος must be ultimately traced to the root λυκ, *lux*, as designating the god of light. But it was popularly connected with λύκος. Sophocles here explains it by λυκοκτόνος, an attribute suitable to Apollo as protector of flocks and herds (νόμιος, *O. T.* 1103). The Λύκειος is invoked especially as a destroyer of foes.

8 Ἥρας...ναός. The site of the Heraeum, discovered by General Gordon in 1831, is about a mile and three quarters **S.E.** of Mycenae, and about five miles **N.E.** of Argos. It can be seen from Argos, but is hidden from Mycenae by a projecting spur of the hills.

9 φάσκειν (infin. as imperat.), = 'deem,' 'believe': *O.T.* 462. For the expression cp. Milton, *Paradise Regained*, 4. 44 f.: 'The city which thou seest no other *deem* | Than great and glorious Rome.'

Μυκήνας. This plural form (the prevalent one) occurs in *Il.* 2. 569, 4. 376; but elsewhere metrical convenience led the Homeric poet to prefer the sing. Μυκήνη, which allowed him to prefix εὐρυάγυια and πολυχρύσοιο.

The site of Mycenae is in a deep recess of the Argive plain, at its northern end,—μυχῷ Ἄργεος ἱπποβότοιο (*Od.* 3. 263). Between two peaks of Mount Euboea, a narrow glen runs out towards the plain, terminating in a rocky platform. This acropolis, naturally impregnable on three sides, was surrounded by Cyclopean walls, from 13 to 35 feet high, with an average thickness of 16 feet.

τὰς πολυχρύσους: the Homeric epithet (see above). It is illustrated by the number of golden cups, cylinders, diadems and other objects found in the graves at Mycenae by Schliemann; who estimated the amount of gold thus discovered at 'about 100 lbs. troy' (*Mycenae*, p. 379).

10 πολύφθορον, desolated by many deaths; so *Tr.* 477 ἡ πολύφθορος | ...Οἰχαλία. Atreus and Thyestes slew their brother Chrysippus; Atreus slew his own son Pleisthenes, and then two sons of Thyestes; Aegisthus, son of Thyestes, slew Atreus and Agamemnon.

11 πατρὸς ἐκ φόνων. For the plur. of φόνος, referring to one deed, cp. 779, *O. C.* 990: so θανάτους, 206.

ἐκ might be 'after': but is perhaps better taken as 'away from' the scene of slaughter. The boy's life, too, was in peril. Cp. 601: Pind. *P.* 11. 17 τὸν δὴ (Orestes) φονευομένου πατρὸς Ἀρσινόα Κλυταιμνήστρας | χειρῶν ὑπὸ κρατερᾶν κἀκ δόλου τροφὸς ἄνελε δυσπενθέος.

12 ὁμαίμου, 'kinswoman,' is here defined by κασιγνήτης: though Sophocles never uses ὅμαιμος or ὁμαίμων except of the fraternal tie (*O. C.* 330). The emphasis is like that of κοινὸν αὐτάδελφον (*Ant.* 1), or the Homeric κασίγνητος καὶ ὅπατρος (*Il.* 12. 371). Cp. 156.

13 f. ἤνεγκα is taken by the schol. to imply that Orestes was then a child in arms (οὗ τι βαδίσαι δυναμένου); but this is to press it overmuch. Orestes was born before his father went to Troy, and so must have been more than ten years old at the time of the murder.—κἀξεθρεψάμην. In poetry the midd. of τρέφω differs from the act. only as marking the interest felt by the τροφός.

τοσόνδ' ἐς ἥβης: cp. 961: *O. C.* 1138 ἐς τόδ' ἡμέρας: for the place of the prep., *O. T.* 178: for τοσόνδ', *Il.* 9. 485 (Phoenix to Achilles) καί σε τοσοῦτον ἔθηκα. Aegisthus reigned seven years, and was slain in the eighth (*Od.* 3. 303 ff.). Orestes, then, is about nineteen or twenty.

15 f. Pylades was the son of that Strophius, king of Phocis, in whose house the young Orestes had found a refuge. Thus Pindar speaks of a Pythian victory as won ἐν ἀφνεαῖς ἀρούραισι Πυλάδα (*P.* 11. 15).

17 f. ἡμῖν: cp. *O. C.* 25.—ἑῷα. The sights and sounds of early morning are in unison with the spirit of this play, in which the παννυχίδες (v. 92) of Electra's sorrow are turned to joy, and the god of light prevails.—κινεῖ...σαφῆ (proleptic): cp. 1366 ταῦτα...δείξουσιν σαφῆ.

19 ἄστρων εὐφρόνη = εὐφρόνη ἀστερόεσσα, the gen. of material or quality, like σῶμα...σποδοῦ (758), τόλμης πρόσωπον (*O. T.* 533), χιόνος πτέρυγι (*Ant.* 114).—ἐκλέλοιπεν, intrans. and absol., 'has failed': cp. 985, 1149.—Not, 'the dark night has lost its stars,' as one schol. construes, followed by Ellendt and others. In classical Greek ἐκλείπω never takes a gen., as ἐλλείπω does.

20 ἐξοδοιπορεῖν (a compound which occurs only here) has been needlessly suspected. ὁδοιπορεῖν in poetry is sometimes no more than ἔρχεσθαι or χωρεῖν. *e.g.*, *O. C.* 1251 ὦδ' ὁδοιπορεῖ: *Ai.* 1230 κἀπ' ἄκρων ὡδοιπόρεις.—They must concert their plans while there is yet no risk of their conversation being interrupted.

21 f. ξυνάπτετον, intrans., 'join,' as Eur. *Ph.* 702 ὡς ἐς λόγους ξυνῆψα Πολυνείκει. Here the modal dat. λόγοισιν takes the place of ἐς λόγους.

ἐμὲν as = ἐσμέν, found only in Callim. fr. 294, is undoubtedly corrupt. ἴμεν, the easiest correction, is excluded by its sense. It could not mean, 'we *are moving in* a place where...,' 'we are thereabouts' (Campbell). It would mean, 'we *are going to* a place where....' But he speaks of the present.

Supposing that ἐνταῦθ' is genuine—as seems most likely —no account of the passage is more probable than that the poet wrote ὡς ἐνταῦθ' ἵνα | οὐκ ἔστ' ἔτ' ὀκνεῖν καιρός, and that ἔστ' dropped out before ἔτ' precisely as in *Ph.* 23 the words τόνδ' ἔτ', εἴτ' have shrunk to τόνδ' ἦτ' in L. Then, v. 22 being defective, ἵνα was shifted to it from the end of v. 21, and the gap after ἐνταῦθ' was filled with ἐμέν,—a form which the later grammarians, at least, accepted.

ἔργων ἀκμή: cp. 1338: *Ph.* 12 ἀκμὴ γὰρ οὐ μακρῶν ἡμῖν λόγων: *Ai.* 811 οὐχ ἕδρας ἀκμή. Cp. Shakesp. *As You Like It*, act 2, sc. 3. 56 (Orlando to Adam): 'O good old man, how well in thee appears | The constant service of the antique world.'—σημεῖα φαίνεις (= δῆλος εἶ)...γεγώς: cp. Lycurg. § 50 φανερὸν πᾶσιν ἐποίησαν οὐκ ἰδίᾳ πολεμοῦντες.

25 ὥσπερ γὰρ ἵππος εὐγενὴς: Philostr. *Vit. Sophist.* 2. 23. 4 καὶ εἶδον ἄνδρα παραπλήσιον τῷ Σοφοκλείῳ ἵππῳ, νωθρὸς γὰρ ὑφ' ἡλικίας δοκῶν νεάζουσαν ὁρμὴν ἐν ταῖς σπουδαῖς ἀνεκτᾶτο.

26 f. ἐν τοῖσι δεινοῖς, in dangers: Thuc. 1. 70 ἐπὶ τοῖς δεινοῖς εὐέλπιδες; *ib.* 84 τῶν...ἐξοτρυνόντων ἡμᾶς ἐπὶ τὰ δεινά.— ἀπώλεσεν, gnomic aor., combined with pres. ἵστησιν: *Ai.* 674 ff. δεινῶν τ' ἄημα πνευμάτων ἐκοίμισε | στένοντα πόντον· ἐν δ' ὁ παγκρατὴς ὕπνος | λύει πεδήσας.

ὡσαύτως δὲ: here δὲ introduces the apodosis; so οὕτω δέ, *Ant.* 426.

Notes

57

28 ἐν πρώτοις ἔπει. The image is from the case of
leaders in battle, whose men follow them in several ranks;
this old man is in the front rank. Cp. *Il.* 8. 337 Ἕκτωρ δ᾽
ἐν πρώτοισι κίε.
31 εἰ μή τι. This adverbial τι is frequent in such ex-
pressions of diffidence: *Ph.* 1279 εἰ μή τι πρὸς καιρὸν λέγων |
κυρῶ: *Tr.* 586 εἰ τι μὴ δοκῶ | πράσσειν μάταιον. — καιροῦ
τυγχάνω: cp. Plat. *Legg.* 687 A πῶς...τοῦ καιροῦ ἀν...ἔτυχον;
Pind. *N.* 8. 4 καιροῦ μὴ πλαναθέντα. — μεθάρμοσον: ἐπανόρ-
θωσον schol.
32 ff. γάρ, merely prefatory (*O. T.* 277). — ἱκόμην,
followed by the historic pres. χρῆ: cp. 425.—μάθοιμ': the
elision gives quasi-caesura.—ἀροίμην, opt. of 2nd aor. ἠρόμην
(*Ant.* 907, *Ai.* 247). The direct deliberative form is τίνι τρόπῳ
ἄρωμαι; The indirect, (*a*) after a primary tense, ἱκνοῦμαι ὡς ἀν
μάθω ὅτῳ ἄρωμαι: (*b*) after a secondary tense, as above. Cp.
O. T. 71 f. ὡς πύθοιθ' ὅ τι | δρῶν...ρυσαίμην πόλιν.—For the
sense, 'win,' 'achieve,' cp. *Ai.* 193, *O. C.* 460.
35 χρῆ: the pres. of this χράω occurs also in Her. (1. 55
χρᾷ, etc.).—τοιαῦθ' (with οἴ, *Ant.* 691)...ὧν (instead of οἵων):
cp. *O. C.* 1353.—πεύσει. The gen. after this verb usu. denotes
the informant (as *O. T.* 333): but the thing heard is sometimes
put in the gen., instead of the regular acc.: thus *Od.* 2. 255
ἀγγελιάων | πεύσεται. So, too, with ἀκούω (*O. C.* 485, etc.),
and κλύω (*ib.* 1174).
36 f. αὐτὸν, alone; cp. *O. T.* 221, *O. C.* 1650.—ἄσκευον...
ἀσπίδων κ.τ.λ., 'unfurnished with' them: for the gen., cp. 1002:
O. T. 191 ἄχαλκος ἀσπίδων: *O. C.* 677 ἀνήνεμον...χειμώνων.
The adj. occurs also in *O. C.* 1029 οὐ ψιλὸν οὐδ᾽ ἄσκευον, 'not
without accomplice or resource.'—ἀσπίδων τε καὶ στρατοῦ = ὡπ-
λισμένου στρατοῦ, a rhetorical hendiadys, like 'without arms or
numbers.'—δόλοισι, in requital of the δόλος on the side of the
murderers (v. 197).—χειρὸς goes with σφαγάς (476 δίκαια χειροῖν
κράτη): the vengeance is to be won by his own right hand, not
by means of allies.—κλέψαι, to effect by stealth: *Ai.* 1137
κλέψειας κακά.
38 ff. ὅτε causal, = ἐπειδή: cp. 1318. *O. T.* 918: *Ant.*
170.—σὺ μὲν μολὼν κ.τ.λ.: for the absence of caesura, cp. *Ph.*
101, 1369, *Ant.* 1021.—καιρὸς is almost personified on p.
75: *Ph.* 466 καιρὸς γὰρ καλεῖ: *ib.* 837 καιρὸς...πάντων γνώμαν
ἴσχων.—ἴσθι, in the pregnant sense of 'take care to know,'
'acquaint thyself with.' Similarly in *O.C.* 1149 εἴσει = μαθήσει.

58   *Electra*

42 f. γήρᾳ refers to the change in his appearance; χρόνῳ μακρῷ, to the lapse of seven years (v. 14), which may have caused him to be forgotten.—οὐδ' ὑποπτεύσουσιν follows οὐ μὴ γνῶσι, as in *O. C.* 450 ff. οὐδ' ἥξει follows οὐ μὴ λάχωσι.

ὧδ' ἠνθισμένον, with grey hair: *O. T.* 742 λευκανθὲς κάρα: Erinna fr. 2 παυρολόγοι πολιαί, ταὶ γήραος ἄνθεα θνατοῖς.

45 Φωκεύς should not be changed to Φωκέως: it was desirable that the messenger himself should seem an alien.

ἀνδρὸς Φανοτέως. ἀνήρ, thus prefixed to a proper name, serves either: (*a*) to introduce a person not previously mentioned,—being more respectful than τις, as *Il.* 11 92 ἄνδρα Βιήνορα, Her. 8. 82 ἀνὴρ Παναίτιος: or (*b*) adds something of solemnity or pathos to the mention of a familiar name, as *O. C.* 109 ἀνδρὸς Οἰδίπου, *Ai.* 817 ἀνδρὸς Ἕκτορος.

Phanoteus was the eponymous hero of the town Phanoteus, or Panopeus, in Phocis, close to the Boeotian frontier,—about three miles west of Chaeroneia, and as many east of Daulis. He was the brother of Crisus, from whom the town of Crisa in Phocis (about two miles w. s. w. of Delphi) took its name. Between these brothers, said the legend, there was a deadly feud. Now Crisus was the father of Strophius, that king of Crisa who was the ally of Agamemnon, and with whom the young Orestes found a home. Hence Phanoteus, the foe of Crisus, is represented as the friend of Aegisthus and Clytaemnestra.

ὁ γάρ: other instances of the art., as demonstr. pron., immediately followed by γάρ (and not by μέν or δέ) are, *O. T.* 1082 (τῆς), 1102 (τῷ), *Ph.* 154 (τό). The art. ὁ, ἡ, when it stands as demonstr. pron., is sometimes written ὅ, ἥ: a practice which is recognised by Eustathius, but which seems to rest on no good ground.

46 μέγιστος, as in φίλος μέγιστος (*Ph.* 586, *Ai.* 1331) simply, 'greatest' friend; not, 'most powerful.'—τυγχάνει, without ὤν: cp. 313, 1457: *Ai.* 9 ἔνδον...τυγχάνει. Cp. Plat. *Hipp. Ma.* 300 A ἡ δι' ἀκοῆς ἡδονὴ...τυγχάνει καλή, *Tim.* 61 D τυγχάνει ...δυνατὰ ἱκανῶς λεχθῆναι.—δορυξένων: a word applied by the tragedians to a prince or chief who is in armed alliance with the head of another state.

47 ὅρκον, Reiske's correction of ὅρκῳ, seems right. With ὅρκῳ, the choice is between two explanations. (1) ἄγγελλε ὅρκῳ, προστιθεὶς (ὅρκον). This is exceedingly awkward, and ἀγγέλλειν ὅρκῳ would be a strange phrase. (2) ἄγγελλε ὅρκῳ προστιθείς (τὰ ἀγγελλόμενα): explained as an 'inversion' of προστιθείς ὅρκον τοῖς ἀγγελλομένοις. But it is hard to see how 'adding the report to an oath' could stand for 'adding an oath to the report.' Cp. fr. 431 ὅρκου δὲ προστεθέντος ἐπιμελεστέρα | ψυχὴ κατέστη.

48 ff. ἀναγκαίας τύχης, an accident ordained by ἀνάγκη, fate (*O. C.* 605).

ἄθλοισι (from ἆθλος) Πυθικοῖσιν. Here and at v. 682 the schol. notes the anachronism,—to which Attic Tragedy was wholly indifferent. From very early times there was an ἀγών at Delphi, but for music and poetry only. Athletic contests were first added when, on the conquest of Crisa by the Delphic Amphictyony, the festival was revived with a new splendour. The year Ol. 48. 3, 586 B.C. was that from which the Pythiads were dated.

τροχηλάτων implies 'rapid,' 'whirling': cp. Eur. *I. T.* 82 τροχηλάτου | μανίας.—ἱστάτω: be so 'constituted': *i.e.*, the whole story is to rest upon this basis. Cp. Plat. *Theaet.* 171 D ταύτῃ ἂν μάλιστα ἵστασθαι τὸν λόγον.

51 ff. ἐφίετο (*sc.* ὁ Φοῖβος, v. 35), like impf. ἐκέλευε.—λοιβαῖσι, a general word, which could mean either the χοαί poured to the νέρτεροι, or the σπονδαί to the ὕπατοι. In this case, milk (perhaps mixed with honey) was poured on the mound (894).—καρατόμοις χλιδαῖς, 'ornaments' (luxuriant locks) 'cut from the head.' (This adj. elsewhere = 'beheaded.') Cp. Eur. *Ph.* 223 ἐπιμένει με κόμας ἐμᾶς | δεῦσαι παρθένιον χλιδάν.—στέψαντες: cp. 441: *Ant.* 431 χοαῖσι τρισπόνδοισι τὸν νέκυν στέφει. Besides the offerings named here, flowers are mentioned below (896).

ἄψορρον...πάλιν: *O. T.* 430 οὐ πάλιν | ἄψορρος οἴκων τῶνδ᾽ ἀποστραφεὶς ἄπει;

54 τύπωμα, anything *formed* or *moulded*; Eur. *Ph.* 162 μορφῆς τύπωμα, 'the outline of his form.' The vague word is here defined by χαλκόπλευρον: which may be a reminiscence of the phrase used by Aesch. (*Ch.* 686) in the same context, λέβητος χαλκέοι πλευρώματα. The cinerary urn is described below as βραχὺς χαλκὸς (757), τεῦχος (1114), ἄγγος (1118), λέβης (1401).

ἠρμένοι, pass., = ἠρμένον ἔχοντες (schol.). Cp. Aeschin. or. 3 § 164 ἐπιστολὰς ἃς ἐξηρτημένος ἐκ τῶν δακτύλων περιῄεις. Others take ἠρμένοι as middle. This use of ἦρμαι is not unknown to later Greek, but there is no example of it in the classical period.

55 Join **που** with **καὶ σύ** ('thou, too, doubtless knowest'): cp. 948 παρουσίαν μὲν οἶσθα καὶ σύ που φίλων, κ.τ.λ. Since he has a definite spot in mind, που would less fitly be taken with θάμνοις, as = 'somewhere.'

56 f. λόγῳ κλέπτοντες: cp. *Il.* I. 131 μὴ... | κλέπτε νόῳ: Eur. *Ph.* 992 κλέψας λόγοισιν ὥσθ᾽ ἃ βούλομαι τυχεῖν.

φέρωμεν is clearly right: it depends on ἥξομεν κ.τ.λ. (53), and continues the exposition of the plan which he is about to execute. φέροιμεν could depend only upon κεκρυμμένον ('which *was hidden* in order that we *might* bring,' etc.).

ἔρρει = ἀπόλωλε: cp. 925: *O. T.* 560 ἄφαντος ἔρρει (Laïus). —**δέμας**, of a corpse, as 756, 1161: in Homer, always of the living (*Ant.* 205).

59 f. τί γάρ με λυπεῖ κ.τ.λ.: *i.e.*, 'It is true that it is ill-omened for the living to be described as dead; but why, in this case, need I care for the omen?' Cp. Eur. *Helen.* 1050 (Helen to Menelaüs): βούλει λέγεσθαι μὴ θανὼν τεθνηκέναι; He replies:—κακὸς μὲν ὄρνις· εἰ δὲ κερδανῶ λέγων, | ἕτοιμός εἰμι μὴ θανὼν λόγῳ θανεῖν.—**ἔργοισι**: the plur., as in *O. C.* 782.— **κἀξενέγκωμαι**, 'carry off' from the enterprise: *Tr.* 497 μέγα τι σθένος ἁ Κύπρις ἐκφέρεται νίκας ἀεί.

61 δοκῶ μέν: cp. 547: *O. C.* 995.—σὺν κέρδει (ὄν), when fraught with gain: cp. 899 ὡς δ᾽ ἐν γαλήνῃ (*sc.* ὄντα) πάντ᾽ ἐδερκόμην τόπον. For σύν, cp. 430 σὺν κακῷ.—κακόν, 'ill-omened'; *O. C.* 1433, *Ant.* 1001.

62 ff. πολλάκις. There were many such popular stories. Pythagoras was said to have hidden himself in a subterranean chamber, causing his death to be reported; and when he reappeared, he was supposed to have been born anew (schol.). Herodotus tells similar stories, *e.g.* of the Thracian Salmoxis, a slave and disciple of Pythagoras, who thus converted the Thracians to a doctrine of immortality.

λόγῳ μάτην θνῄσκοντας: for μάτην as = 'falsely,' cp. 1298, *Ph.* 345.

ἐκτετίμηνται. The emphatic perf. might denote either (1) permanence,—'they are in greater honour *thenceforth*'; or (2) the instantaneous result,—'*forthwith*.' Perhaps the usage of the perf. pass. of τιμάω rather favours (1).—The finite verb, instead of ἐκτετιμημένους, by a frequent idiom; cp. 192 (ἀμφίσταμαι).

65 f. ὡς, 'as,' seems better here than ὥς, 'thus.' It gives a smoother transition; and it is also more in accord with usage. Except in the phrases οὐδ' ὥς (*Ant.* 1042), καὶ ὥς, etc., Attic writers seldom use ὥς, 'thus.'

κἄμ' ἐπαυχῶ: for the accus. (though the pron. refers to the subject of the verb), cp. 470 f., *Tr.* 706.—ἄπο, not merely 'after' it, but as a result of it; cp. *Ant.* 695, *Ph.* 408.—δεδορκότ', = βλέποντα, living: Aesch. *Eum.* 322 ἀλαοῖσι καὶ δεδορκόσιν.—ἐχθροῖς is best taken with λάμψειν: 'alive, I shall shine as a star upon them,' *i.e.* to their terror.—ἄστρον: not specifically 'a *baleful* star.' It is simply an image of splendour; but to his foes, of course, he will prove an οὔλιος ἀστήρ.—Whitelaw: 'So living, doubt not, from this falsehood's cloud | I on my dazzled foes, starlike, shall break.'—ἔτι, menacing: cp. 471: *Tr.* 257.

67 f. πατρῷα γῆ κ.τ.λ.: cp. *Ph.* 1040 ἀλλ', ὦ πατρῷα γῆ θεοί τ' ἐπόψιοι.—εὐτυχοῦντα, proleptic: cp. 162 f.: *O. C.* 487 δέχεσθαι τὸν ἱκέτην σωτήριον.—ὁδοῖς, of a single journey: *O. C.* 553, *Ant.* 226.

70 καθαρτής: so in Aesch. *Ch.* 968 ff. the avenger is to drive the μύσος from the hearth, καθαρμοῖσιν ἀτᾶν ἐλατηρίοις.—πρὸς θεῶν ὡρμημένος: Aesch. *Ch.* 940 (of Orestes) ὁ πυθόχρηστος φυγὰς | θεόθεν εὖ φραδαῖσιν ὡρμημένος.

72 ἀλλ' ἀρχέπλουτον, *sc.* πέμψατε or the like, to be supplied from ἀποστείλητε, as αὐδῶ in *O. T.* 241 from ἀπαυδῶ, δεῖ in *O. C.* 1404 from οὐκ ἔξεστι, ἕκαστος in *Ant.* 263 from οὐδείς.

ἀρχέπλουτον, '*master of* my possessions'; cp. ἀρχέλαος, ἀρχέπολις (Pind. *P.* 9. 58). Others understand, 'having *ancient* wealth,' = ἀρχαιόπλουτον. If, however, the verbal part of the compound denoted 'beginning' rather than 'ruling,' analogy would suggest that ἀρχέπλουτος should mean, 'a *founder* of wealth'; cp. ἀρχέκακος (*Il.* 5. 63), ἀρχέχορος (ποῦς, Eur. *Tro.* 151), ἀρχέγονος, etc.

καταστάτην, as *restoring* its fortunes, ἀποκαθιστάντα.

74 f. εἴρηκα μέν νυν ταῦτα, one of those formulas which serve to close a speech, like πάντ' ἐπίστασαι, *Ant.* 402 f.

μελέσθω is probably impers. (as μέλεται in Theocr. 1. 53); though μέλεταί τί μοι is a less rare constr. for this midd. form (cp. 1436).

76 ἐπιστάτης, as controlling and regulating action; cp. 39 n.

77 ἰώ μοί μοι δύστηνος. An adj. is often added to such interjections: *Ant.* 850 ἰὼ δύστανος: *O. C.* 876 ἰὼ τάλας: *O. T.* 1307 αἰαῖ, φεῦ φεῦ, δύστανος. Electra speaks within.

78 f. καὶ μήν, announcing a new comer: 1422: *O. C.* 549.

θυρῶν is perhaps best taken as denoting *the quarter whence* the sound strikes the ear, so that it goes with αἰσθέσθαι ('hear *from* the doors'). The order of the words, and the rhythm, favour this. It might, however, be a local gen., '*at* the doors,' going wich ὑποστενούσης: cp. 900 n.

I should agree with the schol. in governing θυρῶν by ἔνδον, did not the wide separation of the words make this **so** awkward.

προσπόλων τινός: the old man conjectures that it is a slave, because a daughter of the house was not to be expected at the gates, especially at such an early hour: cp. 518 n. But Orestes fancies that he recognises the voice.

80 f. θέλεις | μείνωμεν...; Cp. *O. T.* 651 θέλεις...εἰκάθω; *Ph.* 761 βούλει λάβωμαι;

The reading of the MSS., κἀνακούσωμεν, was taken by some from ἀνακούω, and explained as 'listen further' (schol. in E). But no ἀνακούω is extant; nor does it seem probable. If the traditional reading is sound, it must be referred to ἐνακούω. The only authority for that word, in Greek of the classical age, is Hippocrates.

On the other hand Sophocles has ἐπακούω, 'to listen,' in *O. T.* 708, 794: *O. C.* 694: *Ph.* 1417. Nauck's correction, κἀπακούσωμεν, is thus highly plausible.

82 f. μηδὲν πρόσθεν, *sc.* ποιῶμεν: cp. *Ant.* 497.—τὰ Λοξίου, his commands, v. 51.—ἀρχηγετεῖν (a verb which occurs only here), not merely = ἄρχεσθαι, but rather 'to make an *auspicious* beginning' (Lat. *auspicari*), as ἀρχηγέτης denoted the god or hero to whom a city or family traced its origin (*O. C.* 60). This title was given especially to Apollo.

84 f. πατρός, possessive gen., as the offerings are due to him: cp. Eur. *Alc.* 613 νερτέρων ἀγάλματα.—λουτρά, the λοιβαί of v. 52, the πηγαὶ γάλακτος of 895, regarded as offerings demanded by purity. So in v. 434 λουτρά are the χοαί of v. 406.

φέρει...ἐφ ἡμῖν, *i.e.* brings (so as to place it) *in our power*; for this ἐπί, cp. *O. C.* 66, *Ph.* 1003. Not, 'brings *in our case*' (like ἐπ' ἀνδρὶ τῷδ', *O. T.* 829); nor, 'brings *upon* us' (*O. C.* 1472).

νίκην, the ultimate victory: κράτος τῶν δρωμένων, the upper hand, the mastery, in our course of action. For the com-

bination, cp. Plat. *Legg.* 962 A νίκην καὶ κράτος πολεμίων: Dem.
or. 19 § 130 κράτος καὶ νίκην πολέμου. For the pres. part.,
cp. 1333 τὰ δρώμεν', 'your plans'; *Tr.* 588. So *O. C.* 116 τῶν
ποιουμένων.
All three actors now leave the scene. Orestes and Pylades
go to Agamemnon's grave,—departing, probably, by the
entrance on the spectators' right. The Paedagogus leaves
by the entrance on the left,—to await the moment for seeking
admission to the house (v. 660). When they have gone,
Electra enters from the house.

86—120 A θρῆνος ἀπὸ σκηνῆς, or lyric lament delivered by
an actor alone, as dist. from the joint κομμός of actor and
Chorus (121 n.).

Verses 86—102 form a σύστημα, = vv. 103—120 (ἀντισύ-
στημα). If the text is sound, the correspondence is not exact,
since the dimeter in v. 99 answers to a monometer in v. 116.
These anapaests are, however, of the type usually known as
'free' or 'melic,' as having more of a lyric character than the
regular anapaests of the marching-songs (like those of the
Parodos in the *Ajax*).

86 f. ὦ φάος ἁγνὸν: the Sun-god abhors impurity (*O. T.*
1425 ff.). So too the αἰθήρ is ἁγνός (Aesch. *P. V.* 281).—These
opening words beautifully express the sense of relief with which
she passes from her sad vigil in the polluted house to the clear
sunlight and free air of morning.

γῆς ἰσόμοιρ' ἀήρ, 'air coextensive with earth,'—having a
μοῖρα, a domain in space, equal to that of earth. Cp. Hamlet's
phrase, 'this goodly frame, the earth...this most excellent
canopy, the air' (2. 2. 311). Hes. *Th.* 126 Γαῖα δέ τοι πρῶτον
μὲν ἐγείνατο ἶσον ἑαυτῇ | Οὐρανὸν ἀστερόενθ', ἵνα μιν περὶ πάντα
καλύπτοι.

ἰσόμοιρ' is a necessary correction of ἰσόμοιρος (cr. n.), which
would require ᾰ in ἀήρ,—a quantity found only in pseudo-
Phocylides 108, and an epigram quoted by Eustathius p. 17.
46.

88 f. πολλὰς μὲν...ᾖσθου. Each of these two verses is an
anapaestic dimeter lacking one long syllable ('catalectic'),
i.e., a 'paroemiac.' Two successive paroemiacs were admissible
only in anapaests of this 'free' or lyric character.

ἀντήρεις, lit. 'set opposite' (hence of an 'adversary,' Eur.
Ph. 754), here, 'dealt from opposite,' striking *full* on the
breast, like ἀνταία...πλαγά (195 f.). θρῆνος and κοπετός are

similarly combined in *Ai.* 631 ff. θρηνήσει, χερόπλακτοι δ' | ἐν
στέρνοισι πεσοῦνται | δοῦποι.

90 πληγὰς must be preferred to πλαγὰς here, unless we are
to write γᾶς (in 87), etc. As a rule, certainly, Doricism is
a mark of lyric (as dist. from marching) anapaests. But the
fact that these anapaests, though lyric in general character,
precede the first lyrics of the Chorus, may have led the poet to
prefer Attic forms.

91 ὑπολειφθῇ, lit., 'falls behind'; here = 'fails,' like the
intr. ἐκλέλοιπεν in 19. The subjunct. can follow ἦσθον, since
the thought is, 'hast heard' (and still hearest).

92 f. τὰ...παννυχίδων is best taken as acc. governed by
ξυνίσασ', rather than as a prefatory acc. of reference ('as to...'):
ὅσα...θρηνῶ (94) is epexegetic of it. τὰ παννυχίδων, a periphrasis
like τὰ τῶν πολέμων (Thuc. **2.** 11), τὰ τῆς τύχης (Eur. *Ph.*
1202), etc. The παννυχὶς (ἑορτή) was properly a joyous torch-
light festival, as at the Lenaea (Ar. *Ran.* 371), or the Bendideia
(Plat. *Rep.* 328 A).

ἤδη (which has been needlessly suspected) means merely,
'ere now,' implying the long duration of her grief.

95 κατὰ μὲν βάρβαρον αἶαν, *i.e.* at Troy. The whole form
of this passage (95—99) seems clearly to show a reminiscence
of *Od.* 11. 406—411, where the shade of Agamemnon says to
Odysseus,—οὔτ' ἐμέ γ' ἐν νήεσσι Ποσειδάων ἐδάμασσεν,... | οὔτε
μ' ἀνάρσιοι ἄνδρες ἐδηλήσαντ' ἐπὶ χέρσου, | ἀλλά μοι Αἴγισθος
τεύξας θάνατόν τε μόρον τε | ἔκτα σὺν οὐλομένῃ ἀλόχῳ, οἶκόνδε
καλέσσας, | δειπνίσσας, ὥς τίς τε κατέκτανε βοῦν ἐπὶ φάτνῃ.
Sophocles follows the Homeric version in conceiving Agamemnon as slain at a banquet (194, 203); and ἐξένισεν in v. 96
suggests a contrast with the entertainment which had been
prepared for him at home.

96 Ἄρης with ā (after Homeric precedent, *Il.* 5. 31 etc.),
as in *Ant.* 139, *Ai.* 254, 614.—ἐξένισεν. The ξένια with which
Ares welcomes his guests are wounds and death. Archilochus
fr. 7 ξείνια δυσμενέσιν λυγρὰ χαριζόμενοι.

97 κοινολεχὴς, 'paramour,' as in Aesch. *Ag.* 1441 Cassandra
is ἡ κοινόλεκτρος τοῦδε θεσφατηλόγος.

98 f. ὅπως δρῦν ὑλοτόμοι, *i.e.*, with as little pity. But in
Il. 13. 389 ff., ἤριπε δ', ὡς ὅτε τις δρῦς ἤριπεν, the point is the
crash with which the stately tree falls.—σχίζουσι, historic pres.,
following an aor. (*Tr.* 267, 702); as it often also precedes it
(*Ant.* 269, 406, 419).—κάρα, after ὅν (95), acc. defining the

part: *Ph.* 1301 μέθες με...χεῖρα.—πέλεκει : cp. *Il.* 23. 114
ὑλοτόμους πελέκεας ἐν χερσὶν ἔχοντες. It was a two-edged axe
(ἀμφάκης, 485), a πέλεκυς ἀμφίστομος or δίστομος, *bipennis*, as
dist. from the single-headed axe, πέλεκυς ἑτερόστομος.

100 f. ἄλλης, as in 885, instead of the more general
ἄλλου.—φέρεται must be more than merely '*proceeds* from':
it implies a passionate utterance. Cp. Pind. *P.* 1. 87, εἴ τι καὶ
φλαῦρον παραιθύσσει, μέγα τοι φέρεται | πὰρ σέθεν, where
Gildersleeve well remarks that the image is that of sparks
flying from an anvil (ἄκμονι v. 86), and renders φέρεται
'rushes.'

103 ἀλλ' οὐ μὲν δή : the combination ἀλλά...μὲν δή occurs
also in *O. T.* 523, *Tr.* 627.

105 f. ἄστρων | ῥιπάς. ῥιπή (ῥίπτω), 'swing,' 'vibration,'
is here applied to the *quivering* rays of starlight; as in *Ant.*
137, 930 to the *gusts* of fierce winds.—Instead of λεύσσω μὲν...
λεύσσω δὲ, we have the verb in the second clause only : cp.
Ant. 1105 μόλις μέν, καρδίας δ' ἐξίσταμαι. For the omission of
μέν in the first of two such clauses, cp. *Ant.* 806 f.

107 μὴ οὐ, after οὐ λήξω : *O. T.* 283.—τεκνολέτειρ', '*slayer*
of her child' (Itys, 148): as in Aesch. *Suppl.* 60 ff. 'the piteous
bride of Tereus' (Procne) sings of 'her child's fate, and how he
perished by her own hand.' Cp. [Eur.] *Rhes.* 550 παιδολέτωρ
μελοποιὸς ἀηδονίς.

108 f. ἐπὶ κωκυτῷ: the prep. is not merely = 'with,' but
implies, 'with *continual* wailing': cp. *Ant.* 759 ἐπὶ ψόγοισι.—
ἠχώ, a resounding cry (of grief); cp. Eur. *Hipp.* 790 ἴστε τίς
ποτ' ἐν δόμοις βοή; | ἠχὼ βαρεῖα προσπόλων μ' ἀφίκετο.

110—112 Electra invokes, (1) the house of Hades and
his bride Persephone, in which the spirit of Agamemnon now
dwells; (2) Hermes, who, as ψυχοπομπός, conducted him
thither,—and who will also guide the avengers on their way
(1395 f.); (3) Ἀρά, the imprecation uttered by the victim upon
his murderers,—the personified curse, here conceived as a
supernatural power (πότνια), which calls the Erinyes into action;
and (4) the Erinyes themselves.

110 Ἄϊδου gives a finer rhythm than Ἀΐδου here. In 137
Ἀΐδα has a similar recommendation; and in 833 Ἄϊδαν is
required by metre, as Ἀΐδᾳ is in *Ph.* 861.

111 ὦ χθόνι' Ἑρμῆ : *Ai.* 832 πομπαῖον Ἑρμῆν χθόνιον.—
Ἀρά. So in *O. C.* 1375 f. Oedipus invokes those ἀραί which
he had uttered, calling upon them to be his allies (ξυμμάχους)

66 *Electra*

against his sons; and afterwards separately invokes the Erinyes
(1391).—πότνια, as the Erinyes are πότνιαι δεινῶπες (*O. C.* 84).

112 σεμναί: *O. C.* 89 θεῶν | σεμνῶν ἕδραν (at Colonus):
Aesch. *Eum.* 1041 δεῦρ' ἴτε, σεμναί.—θεῶν παῖδες, in the general
sense that they are called into existence and activity by the
resolve of the gods to punish guilt: cp. *Ant.* 1075 Ἅιδου καὶ
θεῶν Ἐρινύες. Mythologically, the Erinyes are Γῆς τε καὶ
Σκότου κόραι.

114 αἳ τοὺς εὐνὰς ὑποκλεπτομένους: for the acc. with the
pass. verb, cp. Aesch. *P. V.* 171 σκῆπτρον τιμάς τ' ἀποσυλᾶται:
so ἀφαιροῦμαί τι, ἀποστεροῦμαί τι. Libanius has a reminiscence
of this verse in the phrase εὐνὴν κακῶς ὑποκλέπτειν (4. p. 598.
24).

These much-impugned words appear genuine. The murder
has been prompted by the guilty love: δόλος ἦν ὁ φράσας, ἔρος
ὁ κτείνας (197). In Electra's thought, they are inseparable.

116 f. ἡμετέρου (= 'my')...μοι: cp. *Ant.* 734 πόλις γὰρ
ἡμῖν (= ἐμοὶ) ἁμὲ χρὴ τάσσειν ἐρεῖ;—καί μοι should not be
changed to κἀμοί: cp. *Tr.* 684 καί μοι τάδ' ἦν πρόρρητα.

119 f. ἄγειν is said of a weight, in one scale of a balance,
which 'draws up' the weight in the opposite scale: Dem.
or. 22 § 76 (χρυσίδες, gold vessels) ἄγουσα ἑκάστη μνᾶν,
'weighing.' Here, Electra herself—*i.e.*, the power of en-
durance which she represents—is the weight in one scale,
and the load of grief is the weight in the other (ἀντίρροπον).
She can no longer 'outweigh' it,—*i.e.*, bear up against it. The
image is more forcible than the ordinary one of a burden, since
it expresses the strain of the effort to maintain an equipoise
between patience and suffering.

σωκῶ occurs only here and in Aesch. *Eum.* 36: σῶκος,
'strong,' only in *Il.* 20. 72 (as epithet of Hermes).

121—250 The Chorus has entered during Electra's delivery
of the last lines. Following the θρῆνος ἀπὸ σκηνῆς, the Parodos
takes the form of a κομμός, in which the lyric laments of the
Chorus are answered by those of the actor. It consists of
three strophes, three antistrophes, and an epode. Each of the
seven parts is divided between the Chorus and Electra. 1st
str., 121—136, = 1st antistr., 137—152. 2nd str., 153—172,
= 2nd antistr., 173—192. 3rd str., 193—212, = 3rd antistr.,
213—232. Epode, 233—250. For the metres, see Metrical
Analysis.

This lyric dialogue strikes the key-note of the play by

illustrating Electra's constancy. The Chorus, while sympathising with her, reminds her that grief is unavailing. Let her be calm, trusting in the gods, and hoping for the return of Orestes. Let her be more conciliatory towards Clytaemnestra and Aegisthus. She replies that such a change would be disloyalty towards the dead.

The general idea of this κομμός may have been suggested by that of the κομμός in the *Choephori* between the Chorus, Electra, and Orestes (306—478).

121 δυστανοτάτας, of guilt, as in 806: so 273 ταλαίνῃ, 275 τλήμων (and 439): *O. T.* 888 δύσποτμος: *Ant.* 1026 ἄνολβος.

123 ff. τάκεις...οἰμωγὰν = ποιεῖ τακερὰν οἰμωγάν, *makest* a *languishing* lament. Cp. *Tr.* 848 τέγγει δακρύων ἄχναν: *Ai.* 55 ἔκειρε...φόνον. For τήκομαι, said of pining in grief, cp. 283, Eur. *Med.* 158 μὴ λίαν τάκου δυρομένα σὸν εὐνάταν.—ἀκόρεστον: cp. Aesch. *Ag.* 1143 (of the nightingale) ἀκόρετος βοᾶς.—τὸν πάλαι κ.τ.λ., acc. depending on τάκεις οἰμωγάν as = οἰμώζεις: cp. 556, 710: *O. C.* 223 δέος ἴσχετε μηδὲν ὅσσ᾽ αὐδῶ.—πάλαι, some seven or eight years ago (13 f., n.).—ἐκ, here no more than ὑπό (*Ph.* 335 ἐκ Φοίβου δαμείς).—ἀθεώτατα: cp. 1181 (n.).—κακᾷ... χειρὶ πρόδοτον, betrayed (to death) by a dastardly hand. χειρὶ, following ἀπάταις, denotes the violent deed. Sophocles thinks of both Clytaemnestra and Aegisthus as active agents in the murder (99 σχίζουσι). This is against understanding, 'betrayed (by her) to (his) hand.'

ὡς is properly an exclamation ('how!'), as in ὡς ὤφελον: here it stands, like *utinam*, with the optat. There are Homeric examples, as *Il.* 18. 107 ὡς ἔρις...ἀπόλοιτο: *ib.* 22. 286 ὡς δή μιν σῷ ἐνὶ χροῒ πᾶν κομίσαιο. In Attic this ὡς with optat. is rare: Eur. *Hipp.* 407 ὡς ὄλοιτο παγκάκως.—ὁ τάδε πορὼν might refer to Clytaemnestra (for the masc., cp. *Ant.* 464), but is rather general, including both the authors of the crime.—εἴ μοι θέμις, like *Tr.* 809 εἰ θέμις δ᾽, ἐπεύχομαι: Aegisthus and Clytaemnestra are the rulers of Mycenae. And the Chorus might shrink from imprecations on the mother in her daughter's presence.

128 f. γενέθλα (fem. sing.), as 226: but γένεθλα (neut. pl.) *O. T.* 180.—γενναίων, in disposition (cp. *O. C.* 1636).—παραμύθιον might be nomin. in appos. with the subject of the verb, but is better taken as acc. in appos. with the sentence: cp. 564 (ποινὰς), 966 (πημονὴν): Eur. *Or.* 1105 Ἑλένην κτάνωμεν, Μενελέῳ λύπην πικράν.

131 ξυνίημι (ῐ): as Ar. *Av.* 946 begins a trimeter with ξυνίημ᾽ ὅτι βούλει. The initial ι of ἵημι is properly long in pres. (and impf.) indic., imper., infin., and partic. This is the regular quantity in Attic: cp. 596. The Tragedians, following epic precedent, sometimes shorten ι in the pres. and impf. of ἵημι: thus ἵησιν (ῐ) in lyrics, Aesch. *Th.* 310. But it is noteworthy that in tragic *dialogue* the examples of ῐ seem to be confined to the pres. part.

τάδ᾽: your kindly purpose.

132 οὐδ᾽ ἐθέλω = ἀλλ᾽ οὐκ ἐθέλω: cp. *Ai.* 222 ἀγγελίαν ἄτλατον οὐδὲ φευκτάν: *Il.* 24. 25 ἔνθ᾽ ἄλλοις μὲν πᾶσιν ἑήνδανεν, οὐδέ ποθ᾽ Ἥρῃ.

133 μὴ οὐ: 107 n.—τὸν ἐμὸν...πατέρ᾽ ἄθλιον: an adj., though not a predicate, is sometimes thus placed; cp. 1144: *Ph.* 393 τὸν μέγαν Πακτωλὸν εὔχρυσον: *O. T.* 1199 f. τὰν γαμψώνυχα παρθένον | χρησμῳδόν.

134 παντοίας, perh. a reminiscence of *Od.* 15. 245 ὃν περὶ κῆρι φίλει Ζεύς τ᾽ αἰγίοχος καὶ Ἀπόλλων | παντοίην φιλότητα. Literally: 'reciprocating the graciousness (kindliness) of friendship in every form,'—bound to me by a mutual friendship, which is sympathetic with every mood.

Electra's lyrics contain some Doricisms (129, 146 f., etc.): but it is best to retain φιλότητος, with the MSS. The form in η was so familiar through Homer that it may have been preferred to φιλότατος even in lyrics. Cp. 236.

135 ἀλύειν, to 'wander' in mind; to be wild with grief: cp. *Ph.* 1194 ἀλύοντα χειμερίῳ | λύπᾳ.

136 αἰαῖ, ἱκνοῦμαι = 152 αἰεὶ δακρύεις. The pause after αἰαῖ excuses the hiatus: cp. *Ant.* 1276 φεῦ φεῦ, ὦ πόνοι.

137 ff. τόν γ᾽ ἐξ Ἀίδα...λίμνας: cp. Dem. or. 9 § 42 τὸν χρυσὸν τὸν ἐκ Μήδων εἰς Πελοπόννησον ἤγαγεν.—παγκοίνου: so *Ai.* 1193 τὸν πολύκοινον Ἀίδαν: Aesch. *Th.* 860 πάνδοκον εἰς ἀφανῆ τε χέρσον.—ἀνστάσεις: for the apocopè of ἀνά, cp. *Tr.* 335.

139 οὔτε †γόοις οὔτε λιταῖσιν. The strophic verse (123) probably represents the true metre: τάκεις ὧδ᾽ ἀκόρεστον οἰμωγάν. On this point most modern critics are agreed, but the correction of v. 139 remains quite uncertain.

140 f. For the repetition of ἀλλά, so soon after the ἀλλά in 137, see 879—882.—ἀπὸ τῶν μετρίων: deserting moderation (τὰ μέτρια).—ἀμήχανον, admitting of no alleviation, like νόσων ἀμηχάνων *Ant.* 363.—διόλλυσαι here = προβαίνεις διολλυμένη:

cp. Dem. or. 21 § 139 φθείρεσθαι πρὸς τοὺς πλουσίους. With the help given by ἀπό and εἰς, such a sense for the verb is not forced.

142 f. ἐν οἶς, referring to the general sense of what precedes, 'in which course.'—ἀνάλυσις...κακῶν, properly, a 'dissolution,' a 'cancelling,' of troubles. They are not dissipated by grieving. The parallel sense of ἀναλύειν is common.— τί μοι κ.τ.λ. : the ethic dat. nearly = 'I pray thee' (887 : *O. C.* 1475).

145 f. νήπιος : for the general masc., cp. 771 : *Tr.* 151.— γονέων, meaning πατρός : for the plur., cp. 346, 498, 594.

147 ἐμέ γ'...ἄραρεν, suits, is congenial to, me. In this intrans. sense ἤραρον would naturally take a dat.; as in *Od.* 4. 777 μῦθον, ὃ δὴ καὶ πᾶσιν ἐνὶ φρεσὶν ἤραρεν ἡμῖν. For the acc. here, cp. *Ai.* 584 οὐ γάρ μ' ἀρέσκει. It may have been suggested by the acc. which follows this aor. when transitive ; ἤραρε θυμὸν ἐδωδῇ (*Od.* 5. 95), 'satisfied.'—φρένας, defining ἐμέ : cp. 99 κάρα, n.

148 αἰὲν Ἴτυν. The υ need not be explained by ictus, for it was originally long in these words, though in ordinary Attic usage it had become shortened. In *Od.* 5. 470 ἐς κλιτὺν ἀναβάς, and a few passages of Tragedy (as Eur. *H. F.* 5 στάχυς, *El.* 1214 γένυν), the υ remains. The reiterated Ἴτυν was heard in the nightingale's note; cp. Eur. fr. 773. 25 ὀρθρευομένα γόοις | Ἴτυν Ἴτυν πολύθρηνον.

149 ὄρνις with ῐ, as in *Ant.* 1021.θ ατυζομένα, bewildered, distraught with grief: cp. 135 ἀλύειν.—Διὸς ἄγγελος, as the harbinger of spring. The nightingale appears in Attica about the end of March, or early in April.

150 ff. Νιόβα, σὲ δ', κ.τ.λ. : for this δέ, cp. *O. T.* 1097 (Φοῖβε, σοὶ δὲ). By θεόν Electra means μακαρτάτην: cp. Sappho's φαίνεταί μοι κῆνος ἴσος θεοῖσιν. Niobe is happy in the highest, the divine, sense, because, by her perennial grief, she is true to the memory of those whom she has lost.—ἅτ', fem. of the epic relat. ὅς τε : so the neut. ὅ τε in *Tr.* 824.—ἐν τάφῳ πετραίῳ : the stone into which Niobe was turned on Mount Sipylus is her 'rocky tomb.'

154 οὔτοι σοὶ μούνᾳ : cp. 289. Cic. *Tusc.* 3. 33 § 79 *Ne illa quidem consolatio firmissima est, quanquam et usitata est et saepe prodest : Non tibi hoc soli.*

155 πρὸς ὅ τι, 'in respect to whatever (grief).'—τῶν ἔνδον εἰ περισσά, 'you are more excessive than those in the house,'—

i.e., less moderate in showing sorrow: the gen., as after περιγίγνομαι, περιεῖναι, περισσεύω (Xen. *An.* 4. 8. 11 περιττεύσουσιν ἡμῶν οἱ πολέμιοι). 'They are equally affected by every one of those troubles which you lament so much more vehemently than they do.'

156 οἷς, the masc. of general reference (145 n.), should be retained, though τῶν ἔνδον (also masc.) alludes to the two sisters only.—ὁμόθεν, of the same stock, is more closely defined by γονᾷ ξύναιμος, which denotes the fraternal tie. Cp. 12 n.

158 οἷα Χρ. ζώει. These words, explanatory of τῶν ἔνδον, seem to mean simply, 'such as Chrysothemis, who is living,' etc. (For οἷα Χρ. ζώει, = οἷα Χρ. ἐστίν, ἢ ζώει, cp. *O. T.* 1451.)

Acc. to the version followed by Sophocles, Agamemnon had four daughters, Iphigeneia, Electra, Chrysothemis, Iphianassa.—ζώει has more point when it is remembered that *one* sister had perished. The Ionic form occurs also in *O. C.* 1213.

καὶ Ἰφιάνασσα: so in *Il.* 9. 145 Χρυσόθεμις καὶ Λαοδίκη καὶ Ἰφιάνασσα, the name having the digamma.

159 ἀχέων is unquestionably the participle, familiar from the Homeric poems (*Il.* 2. 724, 5. 399, 18. 446: *Od.* 11. 195). Orestes is conceived as pining in exile for the moment when he shall return as an avenger.

160 ὄλβιος, ὃν κ.τ.λ. The respect in which he is 'happy' is defined by the following clause, according to a frequent poetical idiom. Hes. *Th.* 954 ὄλβιος, ὃς μέγα ἔργον ἐν ἀθανάτοισιν ἀνύσσας | ναίει ἀπήμαντος. *Od.* 11. 450 ὄλβιος· ἢ γὰρ τόν γε πατὴρ φίλος ὄψεται ἐλθών.

For the simple ὅς, instead of ὅς γε or ὅστις, with causal force, cp. below, 188, 261, 959.

162 f. δέξεται εὐπατρίδαν, *i.e.*, will receive him, so that he shall be once more a noble of the land, instead of an exile ; for the proleptic force, cp. 68 δέξασθέ μ' εὐτυχοῦντα (n.).

Διὸς εὔφρονι | βήματι, by the kindly guidance of Zeus ; βῆμα here having a sense parallel with that of the causal tenses, βήσω, ἔβησα. Schol. βήματι· ἀντὶ ὁδῷ, πομπῇ. This is certainly bold, though not too much so (I think) for Sophocles.— γᾶν, notwithstanding γᾶ in 161: cp. 375, 379 (γόων): 511, 515 (αἰκίαις, αἰκία): 871, 873 (ἡδονῆς, ἡδονὰς).

Ὀρέσταν, emphatically placed at the end, is drawn into the case of the relative ὅν: cp. *Od.* 1. 69 Κύκλωπος κεχόλωται, ὃν

Notes

ὀφθαλμοῦ ἀλάωσεν, | ἀντίθεον Πολύφημον. Aesch. *Th.* 553 τῷδ',
ὃν λέγεις τὸν Ἀρκάδα.

164 f. ἀκάματα with initial ᾰ: but in *Ant.* 339 ἀκαμάταν
with ᾱ. For the neut. plur. as adv., cp. 786 : *O. T.* 883 ὑπέ-
ροπτα.—ἀνύμφευτος is merely a rhetorical amplification of the
thought expressed by ἄτεκνος, and hence the poet is indifferent
to the order of the words; just as in 962 ἄλεκτρ᾿ι *precedes*
ἀνυμέναια, and as Oedipus forebodes the fate of his daughters,
χέρσους φθαρῆναι κἀγάμους (*O. T.* 1502).

οἰχνῶ, simply 'go about' (περιέρχομαι, schol.), here implying
her loneliness. Not = οἴχομαι ('I am lost'), as some take it.
οἰχνέω is, indeed, a poetical by-form of οἴχομαι, but does not
share this sense. Cp. 313, *Ai.* 564.

166 f. δάκρυσι μυδαλέα: as Hes. *Scut.* 270 (κόνις) δάκρυσι
μυδαλέη. The υ is properly short, as in μυδάω (*O. T.* 1278,
Ant. 410).—τὸν ἀνήνυτον: the art. means, '*that* endless doom
of mine'; cp. 176 τὸν ὑπεραλγῆ: *Ai.* 1187 τὰν ἄπαυστον... | ...
μόχθων ἄταν.—οἶτον ἔχουσα: *Il.* 9. 559 ἀλκυόνος πολυπενθέος
οἶτον ἔχουσα.

169 f. ὧν τ᾿ ἔπαθ᾿. The schol. understands, 'the benefits
which he has received' at Electra's hands, who saved him from
perishing with his father (12, 1128, 1350). But it seems
worthier of her heroic nature that she should mean,—'he
forgets *his wrongs*—those great wrongs which he is bound
to avenge.' This agrees, too, with ὧν τ᾿ ἐδάη, 'what he has
learned' by the messages which she has sent from Mycenae
to Phocis, as to the subsequent conduct of the partners in
crime. 'He forgets his father's murder, and his sister's
misery.'

τί γάρ...ἀγγελίας: cp. *Ant.* 1229 ἐν τῷ συμφορᾶς.—ἀπατώμενον, 'disappointed' by the result. The message is poetically
identified with the hope which it inspires. Cp. *Ant.* 630 ἀπάτας
λεχέων, a cheating (of his hope), a disappointment, concerning
marriage. The partic. here expresses the leading idea of the
sentence: 'what comforting message comes to me that is not
belied?' For τί...οὐκ as = πᾶν τι, cp. *O. T.* 1526.

171 f. ποθεῖ, ποθῶν δ᾿: cp. 319 φησίν γε· φάσκων δ᾿ οὐδὲν
ὧν λέγει ποεῖ. There, as here, there is a touch of mournful
bitterness, which οὐκ ἀξιοῖ brings out. As to the frequent
messages sent to Electra by Orestes, cp. 1154.

174 ἔτι μέγας οὐρανῷ = 154 ἄχος ἐφάνη βροτῶν. The simple
dat. of place seems warranted by such instances as 313 (ἀγροῖσι),

O. T. 1451 ναίειν ὄρεσιν, Pind. *N.* 10. 58 θεὸς ἔμμεναι οἰκεῖν τ᾽ οὐρανῷ.

176 τὸν ὑπεραλγῆ: for the art., cp. 166 n.—νέμουσα, 'assigning,' or 'committing,' it to Zeus. The verb is used as in νέμειν μοῖραν (*Tr.* 1238) or νέμειν γέρα (*O. C.* 1396) τινί. Wrath against evil-doers is an attribute and a prerogative of Zeus, to whom the injured should leave the task of inflicting retribution.

177 μήθ᾽ ὑπεράχθεο (τούτοις) οὓς ἐχθαίρεις μήτ᾽ ἐπιλάθου (αὐτῶν). For οἶς (by attraction, for οὕς), cp. Xen. *H.* 3. 5. 18 σὺν οἶς εἶχεν ᾔει. The clauses are co-ordinate, but the emphasis is upon μὴ ὑπεράχθεο. 'Without forgetting thy foes, refrain from excess of wrath against them.' The Chorus allow that Electra cannot forget the murder of her father. They only counsel moderation of behaviour.

179 εὐμαρὴς θεός, a god who brings ease,—soothing difficulties, and making burdens tolerable (cp. *O. C.* 7, 437). εὐμαρής has here an active sense: cp. *Ph.* 44 φύλλον...νώδυνον, a herb that soothes pain.

180 οὔτε γάρ, after χρόνος γάρ in 179: Sophocles often thus uses γάρ in two successive clauses (*Ai.* 20 f., 215 f., 514 f., 1262 f.; *Ph.* 1158 f.; *Ant.* 1255 f.). Here the second γάρ introduces a reason for thinking that, in this instance, Time will bring a remedy.

Crisa stood about two miles w.s.w. of Delphi, on a spur of Parnassus, at the lower outlet of the gorge through which the river Pleistus issues into the plain. The Homeric Hymn to the Pythian Apollo is the best witness to its ancient power. There, just as here, the name Κρῖσα includes the land which stretches southward from the town to its harbour on the 'wide gulf' (vv. 253—261).

181 βούνομον, 'grazed over by oxen,' seems fitter here than βουννόμον, 'giving pasture to oxen': but there is little to choose. Cp. Aesch. fr. 249 βούνομοί τ᾽ ἐπιστροφαί: and *O. T.* 26.— βούνομον ἀκτάν is in appos. with Κρῖσαν. When Crisa was humbled by the Delphians about 585 B.C., the Crisaean plain was devoted to Apollo and might not afterwards be violated with plough or spade.

182 ἀπερίτροπος, 'regardless.' The word occursonly here; and περιτρέπομαι does not occur in a corresponding sense. But the poet has followed the analogy of ἐντρέπομαι and the epic μετατρέπομαί τινος as = 'to regard.'

Notes 73

183 παρὰ τὸν Ἀχέροντα, because his realm extends along its banks. For the place of ἀνάσσων after θεὸς, cp. 695: *Ph.* 1316 τὰς...ἐκ θεῶν | τύχας δοθείσας. The 'god' is, of course, Hades; the King of the Dead is their avenger: cp. 110: *Ant.* 1075 Ἀιδου...Ἐρινύες.

185 f. μὲν merely emphasises ἐμέ: there is no corresponding clause with δέ: cp. *Ant.* 11 ἐμοὶ μέν.—ὁ πολὺς...βίοτος, the best part of it: see on 962, where she speaks of her sister as γηράσκουσαν. When ὁ πολύς thus means ὁ πλείων, the noun (with art.) usu. precedes it; as Her. 1. 102 ὁ στρατὸς...ὁ πολλός, Thuc. 1. 24 τῆς δυνάμεως τῆς πολλῆς.—ἀνέλπιστος, predic., has passed away from me without leaving me any hopes.

187 τεκέων. I am now satisfied that this is a true correction of τοκέων, for these reasons. (1) It would be inappropriate to justify ἀνέλπιστος (as the causal ἅτις does) by saying that she is pining away 'without *parents*,' or a husband's care, while the mention of *children* is perfectly in place. (2) The very order of the words, τεκέων...ἀνήρ, is confirmed by vv. 164 f., ἄτεκνος... ἀνύμφευτος. (3) If τοκέων be right, it means that, while Agamemnon is dead, the living Clytaemnestra is a μήτηρ ἀμήτωρ (1154): but this is forced.

189 ἀπερεί, like the common ὡσπερεί (*O. T.* 264).— ἔποικος..., an immigrant, an alien: cp. Plat. *Legg.* 742 A μισθωτοῖς, δούλοις καὶ ἐποίκοις, 'hirelings, slaves or immigrants.'

190 οἰκονομῶ θαλάμους: for the verb compounded with a noun similar in sense to θαλάμους, cp. *Tr.* 760 ταυροκτονεῖ... βοῦς: *Il.* 4. 3 νέκταρ ἐῳνοχόει. By οἰκονομῶ was meant properly the 'management' of a household, either by the master, or by a domestic of the higher grade, a ταμίας or οἰκονόμος, 'house-steward.' But here οἰκονομῶ θαλάμους denotes the discharge of humbler duties, in attending to the daily service of the house.

191 ἀεικεῖ σὺν στολᾷ: cp. the reference to her ζῶμα in 452; and the comments of Orestes on her whole appearance (1177, 1181).

192 κεναῖς δ' ἀμφίσταμαι τραπέζαις. κενὴ τράπεζα, a 'bare,' or scantily furnished, table, is opposed to τράπεζα πλήρης (Eur. *Hipp.* 110): it would be prosaic to insist that it must mean a table with nothing on it. While the docile Chrysothemis fares sumptuously (361), the rebel Electra is treated like a half-starved slave.—ἀμφίσταμαι, because to lie at meals on a κλίνη was a luxury refused to the δούλη: such food as she receives must be taken standing. The plur. τραπέζαις refers to her experience from day to day.

193—196 Hitherto the Chorus have offered consolation or counsel. At v. 213 they return to that strain. But here, moved by Electra's misery, they join with her in bewailing its cause.

οἰκτρὰ μὲν...πλαγά. At v. 95 it was noticed that verses 95—99 clearly show a reminiscence of *Od.* 11. 406—411,—the earlier part of the passage in which the departed Agamemnon relates his death to Odysseus. It seems that a later portion of the same passage was here present to the poet's mind,—viz., vv. 418—422:—ἀλλά κε κεῖνα μάλιστα ἰδὼν ὀλοφύραο θυμῷ, | ὡς ἀμφὶ κρητῆρα τραπέζας τε πληθούσας | κείμεθ᾽ ἐνὶ μεγάρῳ [cp. κοίταις here], δάπεδον δ᾽ ἅπαν αἵματι θῦεν. | οἰκτροτάτην δ᾽ ἤκουσα ὄπα [cp. οἰκτρὰ...αὐδά] Πριάμοιο θυγατρός, | Κασσάνδρης, τὴν κτεῖνε Κλυταιμνήστρη δολόμητις.

Sophocles, who follows the Homeric story as to the banquet, could not but remember the οἰκτροτάτην ὄπα of the dying Cassandra. And this might naturally suggest to him that other οἰκτρὰ αὐδή which she had uttered immediately after Agamemnon's return,—her presage of his fate, and her own.

The sense then is:—'There was a voice of lamentation at the return from Troy'; alluding especially to Cassandra's laments, but also, perhaps, to forebodings in the mouth of the people at Mycenae. 'And there was a voice of lamentation ἐν κοίταις πατρῴαις, when thy father lay on the couch at the fatal banquet.' The 'voice' at the banquet is, first, that of the dying Agamemnon; but Sophocles may have thought also of Cassandra's death-cry.

νόστοις might be governed by ἐν (cp. *O. T.* 734), but is more simply taken as a temporal dat., denoting the occasion, like τοῖς ἐπινικίοις (Plat. *Symp.* 174 A), etc. For the poet. plur., cp. *Ai.* 900 ὤμοι ἐμῶν νόστων.—**κοίταις,** 'couch,' here of feasting, as δείπνων (203) shows.—**ὅτε οἱ:** for the hiatus cp. *Tr.* 650 ἅ δέ οἱ. The MS. σοι is certainly wrong.—**ἀνταία,** striking full: cp. 8, ἀντήρεις (n.)—**γενύων,** the blades of the two-edged πέλεκυς (99 n.): cp. 485.

197 **δόλος...ἔρος:** guile planned the deed,—*i.e.*, devised the means of doing it: lust was 'the slayer,' as having supplied the motive.

198 f. **δεινὰν δεινῶς:** cp. 989.—The phrase δεινὰν...μορφάν

must be viewed in the light of the following words, εἴτ' οὖν
θεὸς εἴτε βροτῶν | ἦν ὁ ταῦτα πράσσων. The Chorus doubt
whether the agency in the terrible crime was merely human.
Perchance an evil δαίμων was there, working out the curse upon
the line of Pelops (504—515). The δεινὴ μορφή, offspring of
δόλος and ἔρος, is the act of murder, embodied in the image of
a supernatural ἀλάστωρ.

εἴτ' οὖν...εἴτε: cp. 560.—βροτῶν, partitive gen.: Xen. *M.* 1.
3. 9 εἶναι τῶν σωφρονικῶν ἀνθρώπων.—Cp. *O. T.* 1258 λυσσῶντι
δ' αὐτῷ δαιμόνων δείκνυσί τις· | οὐδεὶς γὰρ ἀνδρῶν.

201 f. πλέον...ἐχθίστα (instead of ἐχθρά), by redundant
emphasis: cp. *O. C.* 743 πλεῖστον ἀνθρώπων... | κάκιστος.—δὴ
with the superl., as *Ai.* 858 πανύστατον δή: Thuc. 1. 50 μεγίστη
δή.

203 νύξ, because the banquet was prolonged into the
night: cp. *Od.* 7. 102 φαίνοντες νύκτας κατὰ δώματα δαιτυμόνεσσι.
—δείπνων, a poet. plur. (*Tr.* 268 δείπνοις), like γάμοι (*Ant.* 575),
αὐλαί (*Tr.* 901).

204 ff. ἄχθη (a nomin., like νύξ) is defined by the following
words. But instead of saying ἄχθη, θάνατοι αἰκεῖς, τοὺς ἴδε κ.τ.λ.,
the poet has drawn θάνατοι αἰκεῖς into the relative clause. He
thus gains more prominence for τοὺς ἐμὸς ἴδε πατήρ. For the
tragic plur. θανάτους, cp. *Tr.* 1276 (Deianeira's death), *O. T.*
497 (that of Laïus): so below, 779 φόνους: *Ant.* 1313 μόρων:
Eur. *El.* 137 αἱμάτων.

διδύμαιν χειροῖν, the hand of Clytaemnestra and the hand of
Aegisthus. Cp. 1080 διδύμαν...Ἐρινύν.

207 f. εἷλον...πρόδοτον. The murderous hands 'took her
life captive,' since the crime placed her wholly in their power
(264); and this was done by treachery. πρόδοτον is predicative,
expressing the mode of capture; cp. Thuc. 6. 102 ἡγούμενοι
(τὸν κύκλον) ἐρῆμον αἱρήσειν.

209 οἷς, not αἷς, since χειροῖν (206) implies the persons;
cp. *O. C.* 730 τῆς ἐμῆς ἐπεισόδου· | ὃν μήτ' ὀκνεῖτε.—Ὀλύμπιος:
cp. 176 n.: *Ph.* 315 οἱ' Ὀλύμπιοι θεοὶ | δοῖέν ποτ' αὐτοῖς ἀντίποιν'
ἐμοῦ παθεῖν.

210 ποίνιμα κ.τ.λ.: the alliteration (παρήχησις) adds bitter
emphasis.

211 ἀγλαΐας, the external splendour of their life (cp. 268 f.,
280); as in *Od.* 17. 310 it is said of dogs whose value consists
only in their beauty, ἀγλαΐης δ' ἕνεκεν κομέουσιν ἄνακτες ('for
ornament'). The word is especially fitting here, as suggesting

triumph, for Ἀγλαΐα was especially the Grace of victory.—
ἀποναίατο: for the Ionic form, cp. *O. T.* 1274.

214 f. γνώμαν ἴσχεις = γιγνώσκεις (*Ph.* 837, 853).—ἐξ οἵων,
'by what kind of conduct.'

τὰ παρόντ', 'in respect to present circumstances,—'as
matters stand'; *i.e.*, already they are bad enough (217, 235).
Cp. Thuc. 4. 17 ἀεὶ γὰρ τοῦ πλέονος ἐλπίδι ὀρέγονται διὰ τὸ καὶ
τὰ παρόντα ἀδοκήτως εὐτυχῆσαι: where, as here, τὰ παρόντα is
acc. of respect, not subj. of the inf.

οἰκείας, 'caused by thyself': *Ai.* 260 οἰκεῖα πάθη, | μηδενὸς
ἄλλου παραπράξαντος.

217 πολύ...τι κακῶν, a large measure of trouble: cp. *Tr.* 497
μέγα τι σθένος.—ὑπερεκτήσω (a compound found only here),
above what was necessary.

219 f. τὰ δὲ, 'but those things' (referring to πολέμους), *i.e.*
'such contests,' οὐκ ἐριστὰ τοῖς δυνατοῖς, 'cannot be waged with
the powerful,' (ὥστε) πλάθειν (αὐτοῖς), 'so that one should come
into conflict with them.' The epexegetic inf. further explains
the meaning of ἐριστά. Such contentions must not be pushed
to an actual trial of force with those who are stronger than our-
selves. For the inf. thus defining an adj., cp. *Il.* 21. 482 χαλεπή
τοι ἐγὼ μένος ἀντιφέρεσθαι (for thee to encounter).—ἐριστά (only
here) = 'contested,' then, 'what can be contested.'—πλάθειν
(*Ph.* 728), in a hostile sense; cp. *Tr.* 1093 λέοντ', ἄπλατον
θρέμμα.

221 δεινοῖς ἠναγκάσθην: dread causes forced her (at the
first) to adopt this course; and they are still valid.

222 ὀργά alludes to δυσθύμῳ.. ψυχᾷ (218 f.). She knows
that her resentment is shown with passion.

223 f. ἀλλά...γὰρ is here elliptical; 'but (ye speak in vain),
for,' etc. Cp. *Ai.* 167. In 256 there is no ellipse.—ἐν...
δεινοῖς: cp. *Ph.* 185 ἔν τ' ὀδύναις.. | λιμῷ τ' οἰκτρός.—ταύτας
ἄτας, these infatuated laments.

225 ὄφρα is not elsewhere used by Sophocles: Aesch. has
it twice in lyrics (*Ch.* 360, *Eum.* 340): Eur. never. For the
omission of ἄν, cp. *Ph.* 764 ἕως ἀυῇ.—βίος ἔχῃ με is simply,
'while life is in me.'

226 ff. τίνι γάρ...τίνι φρονοῦντι καίρια, for *in the judgment of*
what person who thinks aright,' ἀκούσαιμ' ἂν πρόσφορον ἔπος,
'could I possibly hear a word of comfort suited to my case?'
That is: What reason for desisting from these lamentations
could possibly be suggested to me, which a right-minded person

would think satisfactory? For the ethic. dat. τίνι κ.τ.λ., cp. *O. C.* 1446 ἀνάξιαι γὰρ πᾶσίν ἐστε δυστυχεῖν. For πρόσφορον, 'suitable,' and hence 'suited to one's needs,' 'profitable,' cp. *O. C.* 1774 πρόσφορά θ᾽ ὑμῖν | καὶ τῷ κατὰ γῆς.

229 f. ἄνετε is more than ἐᾶτε, since it implies relaxing a strain; cp. 721 : *Ant.* 1101 ἄνες (κόρην), release her.—ἄλυτα, irremediable; cp. 939 : so λύσις, of a remedy (*Ant.* 598).— κεκλήσεται : they must be permanently accounted such : cp. *Ai.* 1368 σὸν ἄρα τοὔργον, οὐκ ἐμόν, κεκλήσεται.

231 f. For ἐκ, where the simple gen. would suffice, cp. 291, 987.—ἀνάριθμος has the second α short (as in Aesch. *Pers.* 40, etc.). For the form of the word, and also for the gen. θρήνων, cp. *Tr.* 247 ἡμερῶν ἀνήριθμον.

233 ἀλλ᾽ οὖν = 'well, at any rate (though I speak in vain)': γε emphasises εὐνοίᾳ : 'it is with *good-will* that I speak' : cp. 1035.

234 μάτηρ ὡσεί τις : these words have been taken as indicating that the Chorus was composed (in part, at least) of women older than Electra. Her own tone to them rather suggests ὁμήλικες (134).

235 μὴ τίκτειν, since a command is implied by αὐδῶ here, as elsewhere by λέγω, φωνῶ, ἐννέπω.—ἄταν ἄταις : the mere iteration suggests the notion of adding; but this is developed by the sense of the verb: cp. Eur. *Helen.* 195 δάκρυα δάκρυσί μοι φέρων.

236 f. καὶ τί μέτρον...; for this καί prefixed to an indignant question, cp. *O. C.* 263.—κακότατος is better attested than κακότητος here. In *O. C.* 521, too, the MSS. give κακότατ᾽. Cp. 134 n.—φέρε in the sense of φέρ᾽ εἰπέ : so Ar. *Ach.* 541 ff. φέρ᾽, εἰ Λακεδαιμονίων τις κ.τ.λ. | καθῆσθ᾽ ἂν ἐν δόμοισιν;—ἐπὶ τοῖς φθ., in their case.

238 ἔβλαστ᾽ : in what human being has such impiety ever been inborn? Cp. 440 : *Ant.* 563 οὐδ᾽ ὃς ἂν βλάστῃ μένει | νοῦς τοῖς κακῶς πράσσουσιν.

239 τούτοις, the persons who approve such forgetfulness of the dead.

240 εἴ τῳ πρόσκειμαι χρηστῷ : prosperity is here conceived as a *region* of comfort, close to which the person is securely established. 'When my lot is cast in pleasant places.' Cp. 1040 : Eur. fr. 418 κακοῖς γὰρ οὐ σὺ πρόσκεισαι μόνη.

241 ξυνναίοιμ᾽ : cp. *O. T.* 1205 τίς ἄταις...τίς ἐν πόνοις | ξύνοικος : Plat. *Rep.* 587 c ἡδοναῖς ξυνοικεῖ.

241 ff. γονέων | ἐκτίμους, not paying honour to parents: the gen. as with adjectives compounded with a privative (36). For this negative sense of ἐκ in composition, cp. ἔκδικος, ἐξαίσιος, ἔξωρος.—ἐκτίμους ἴσχουσα, restraining so that they shall not honour: for the proleptic adj., cp. Aesch. *Pers.* 298 ἄνανδρον τάξιν ἠρήμου θανών.—ὀξυτόνων, as *Ai.* 630 ὀξυτόνους...ᾠδὰς | θρηνήσει.

244 ff. εἰ γὰρ κ.τ.λ. She says:—'I will not cease to lament, and to invoke retribution on the murderers (209 f.). *For*, if they are *not* to pay with their blood for the blood which they have shed, there will be an end to regard for man and to fear of heaven.'

γᾶ here = σποδός, of the dead : Eur. fr. 522 κατθανὼν δὲ πᾶς ἀνὴρ | γῆ καὶ σκιά· τὸ μηδὲν εἰς οὐδὲν ῥέπει.—οὐδὲν (not μηδὲν) ὤν, though εἰ precedes: cp. *O. C.* 935 βίᾳ τε κοὐχ ἑκών (after εἰ μή): *Ai.* 1131 εἰ...οὐκ ἐᾷς. Here the parataxis affords a special excuse for οὐδέν,—viz., that this first clause, though formally dependent on εἰ, is not really hypothetical : he *is* dead. In the second clause (εἰ.. μὴ.. δώσουσ᾽), a real hypothesis, the negative is μή. Cp. Lys. or. 10 § 13 οὐκ οὖν δεινόν, εἰ ὅταν μὲν δέῃ σε.. τοὺς ἐχθροὺς τιμωρεῖσθαι, οὕτω τοὺς νόμους...λαμβάνεις, ὅταν δ' ἕτερον παρὰ τοὺς νόμους εἴπῃς κακῶς, οὐκ ἀξιοῖς δοῦναι δίκην;

Electra is contrasting her father, whose earthly life has been cut short, with his murderers, who survive. But she believes that his spirit lives in the world below, and will be active in aiding the vengeance (453 ff.).

πάλιν, in recompense : *O. T.* 100 φόνῳ φόνον πάλιν | λύοντας. —ἀντιφόνους δίκας, a penalty which exacts blood for blood : cp. *Ph.* 1156 ἀντίφονον...στόμα.

249 f. ἔρροι τ᾽: the τε should properly follow αἰδώς : cp. *O. T.* 258 κυρῶ τ᾽ ἐγὼ instead of ἐγώ τε κυρῶ.—αἰδώς is respect for those opinions and feelings of mankind which condemn wrong-doing ; as εὐσέβεια is reverence for the gods.

251—471 The first ἐπεισόδιον falls into two parts. In the earlier, Electra further justifies her behaviour, and the Chorus comforts her with the hope that Orestes will return. The second part (328—471) brings the character of Electra into contrast with that of Chrysothemis.

251 ἐγὼ μὲν : here μέν merely emphasises the pron.: cp. *Ant.* 11.—καὶ τὸ σὸν...καὶ τοὐμὸν : cp. *Ai.* 1313 ὅρα μὴ τοὐμὸν ἀλλὰ καὶ τὸ σόν. The chief stress is upon τὸ σόν : but the meaning is not merely that her interests are to them as their

Notes 79

own. These women, representing the people of Mycenae, desire the downfall of the usurper whose unpunished crime lays an ἄγος upon the land.

253 νίκα: cp. *Ai.* 1353 παῦσαι· κρατεῖς τοι τῶν φίλων νικώμενος.—ἅμα is best taken as an adv. (cp. *Ai.* 814 ἅμ' ἕψεται: *O. T.* 471 ἅμ' ἕπονται). It might, however, be a prep.; cp. *Tr.* 563 ξὺν Ἡρακλεῖ...ἑσπόμην.

255 πολλοῖσι θρήνοις, causal dat.; cp. 42 n.

256 ἀλλὰ...γὰρ: cp. 223 n.

257 ἥτις εὐγενὴς γυνή, *sc.* εἴη: cp. *Il.* 5. 481 τά τ' ἔλδεται, ὅς κ' ἐπιδευής (*sc.* ἔῃσι): and *id.* 14. 376. Here the adj. combines the ideas of birth and character: cp. 989: *Ph.* 874 ἀλλ' εὐγενὴς γὰρ ἡ φύσις κἀξ εὐγενῶν: *Ant.* 38 εἴτ' εὐγενὴς πέφυκας εἴτ' ἐσθλῶν κακή.

258 πατρῷα...πήματα, the woes arising from her father's murder; and so, here, the woes of her father's house. For this large sense of the adj., cp. *O. C.* 1196 πατρῷα καὶ μητρῷα πήμαθ' ἅπαθες.

259 f. κατ' εὐφρόνην is illustrated by 271 f.—θάλλοντα: cp. *Ph.* 258 ἡ δ' ἐμὴ νόσος | ἀεὶ τέθηλε. Shakesp. *Much Ado* 5. 1. 76, 'His May of youth and *bloom* of lustihood.'

261 f. ᾗ, causal: cp. 160 n.—πρῶτα μὲν...εἶτα...ἔπειτα (266). The influence of the relat. pronoun ᾗ is confined to the first clause.—τὰ μητρὸς is not a mere synonym for ἡ μήτηρ, but rather denotes her mother's relations with her.—ἔχθιστα συμβέβηκεν, have *come to be* such. This verb, though often joined with the participles of εἰμί and γίγνομαι, is rarely construed with a simple adj.: cp. however Plat. *Rep.* 329 D νεότης χαλεπὴ τῷ τοιούτῳ ξυμβαίνει.

264 κἀκ τῶνδ' ἄρχομαι. Cp. *Ant.* 63 ἀρχόμεσθ' ἐκ κρεισσόνων.

265 λαβεῖν...τὸ τητᾶσθαι. The aor. inf. expresses the act of receiving; the pres. inf., the state of privation. For λαβεῖν (without art.) as subject of πέλει, cp. *Tr.* 134 f. ἐπέρχεται | χαίρειν τε καὶ στέρεσθαι: for the use of the art. with τητᾶσθαι only, Eur. *Ph.* 495 καὶ σοφοῖς | καὶ τοῖσι φαύλοις.

266 ποίας...δοκεῖς κ.τ.λ.: cp. *Ph.* 276 σὺ δή, τέκνον, ποίαν μ' ἀνάστασιν δοκεῖς | αὐτῶν βεβώτων ἐξ ὕπνου στῆναι τότε;

267 ἴδω is followed by εἰσίδω δ' and ἴδω δὲ (271). For such change of the word in 'epanaphora,' cp. *Ant.* 898 f. φίλη μὲν.. προσφιλὴς δὲ.. φίλη δὲ.—μὲν is omitted in the first clause; cp. 105 n.

268 ff. ἐσθήματα, the royal robes. He carried Agamemnon's sceptre (420).—ἐκείνῳ = τῷ πατρί, implied in πατρῴοις.

παρεστίους...λοιβάς (52 n.). In v. 1495 the words ἔνθαπερ κατέκτανες denote the place *within* the palace where Agamemnon was slain at the banquet (203). The words ἔνθ' ἐκεῖνον ὤλεσεν here similarly denote the banqueting-hall. At the daily meals in the μέγαρον, Aegisthus, as master of the house, pours the libations to Hestia and other deities.

Acc. to *Homer. Hymn.* 29. 4 ff., feasts began and ended with libations to Hestia : οὐ γὰρ ἄτερ σοῦ | εἰλαπίναι θνητοῖσιν, ἵν' οὐ πρώτῃ πυμάτῃ τε | Ἱστίῃ ἀρχόμενος σπένδει μελιηδέα οἶνον.

271 τούτων (neut.), partitive gen.: 'the crowning outrage in all this.' Others make it fem., *sc.* τῶν ὕβρεων.

272 αὐτοέντην, the form in *O. T.* 107. αὐθέντης, used by Aesch. and Eur., does not occur in Sophocles. Brunck first adopted αὐτοέντην from the schol., in place of αὐτοφόντην, the reading of all the MSS. The latter word occurs only in Eur. *Med.* 1269.—ἡμῖν, ethic dat., expressing indignant horror.

273 ταλαίνῃ, like τλήμων (275), refers to infatuated guilt ; cp. 121 δυστανοτάτας (n.).

275 f. μιάστορι, one who defiles by bloodshed, as *O. T.* 353 : but below, 603, one who punishes the blood-guilty.

277 ἐγγελῶσα τοῖς ποιουμένοις, with mocking exultation in her course of conduct (cp. 85 τῶν δρωμένων, n.). So ἐγγελῶσα in 807. ἐγγελᾶν τινι properly = to laugh *at* a person or thing; and that is strictly the sense here, since Clytaemnestra's deeds are Electra's misfortunes.

278 εὑροῦσ', if sound, means simply, 'having ascertained.' We may suppose that at least some interval had elapsed between the murder and the institution of these rites. The usurper could not at first feel secure. Having resolved to institute such a festival, Clytaemnestra was careful to see that the day of the month chosen should be precisely that on which the crime was committed. The word τότε, implying some lapse of time, confirms this view : cp. *Ai.* 650.

280 f. χορούς ἵστησι, the regular phrase (Her. 3. 48, Dem. or. 21 § 51, etc.): whence Στησίχορος.—μηλοσφαγεῖ...ἱερά : cp. 190 οἰκονομῶ θαλάμους (n.).

ἔμμηνʼ ἱερά. Every month, on the date of Agamemnon's death, choruses sang paeans, victims were sacrificed to the saving gods, and a banquet (284) followed. Monthly celebrations were frequent in Greece.

Notes 81

τοῖς σωτηρίοις: especially to Zeus Σωτήρ, and to Apollo προστατήριος (637). Artemis, too, was often worshipped as σώτειρα or σωσίπολις: but indeed all the greater Olympian deities shared this attribute.

282 κατὰ στέγας goes with κλαίω rather than with ὁρῶσα. Seeing the festivities in front of the palace, she retires to weep in secret (285).

283 f. τέτηκα has the force of an intensive present, like γέγηθα, δέδοικα, κέκηδα (Tyrtaeus fr. 12. 38), μέμηνα, etc. So *Il.* 3. 176 τὸ καὶ κλαίουσα τέτηκα.

πατρὸς κ.τ.λ. The normal order would be, τὴν πατρὸς ἐπωνομασμένην δυστάλαιναν δαῖτα. (As the words stand, the partic. would properly be predicative; 'I lament that the feast has been called after him.') Cp. Thuc. 7. 23 αἱ πρὸ τοῦ στόματος νῆες ναυμαχοῦσαι. For the gen., Eur. *H. F.* 1329 (τεμένη) ἐπωνομασμένα σέθεν.

The δαίς is the feast which, in Homeric fashion (*Il.* 1. 467), would follow the sacrifice (281). The poet may mean that Clytaemnestra called the festival Ἀγαμεμνόνειος δαίς, in direct allusion to δεῖπνα ἄρρητα (203): and this would give a special point to ἐγγελῶσα (277). But the words do not necessarily imply more than that she called it Ἀγαμεμνόνεια.

285 f. αὐτὴ πρὸς αὑτήν. For αὑτήν (= ἐμαυτήν) cp. *Ai.* 1132, *O. T.* 138.—κλαῦσαι, rather than κλαίειν, since the thought is that she is not allowed to complete the indulgence of her grief. Cp. 788 οἴμοι τάλαινα· νῦν γὰρ οἰμῶξαι πάρα.—ἡδονὴν φέρει: lit., 'as much as my inclination makes it pleasant (to weep).' φέρειν ἡδ. = 'to afford pleasure' (but ἔχειν, 'to feel' it): *O. C.* 779 ὅτ' οὐδὲν ἡ χάρις χάριν φέροι.

287 ἡ λόγοισι γενναία, noble in her professions (though not in her deeds), inasmuch as she claimed to be the instrument of heaven in avenging her daughter: ἡ γὰρ Δίκη νιν εἷλεν, οὐκ ἐγὼ μόνη (528).

288 φωνοῦσα expresses the loud tone in which the taunts are uttered: cp. *Tr.* 267 (Eurytus taunting Heracles), φωνεῖ δέ, δοῦλος κ.τ.λ.

289 f. δύσθεον = ἄθεον, ἀσεβές: properly, 'having untoward gods,' as δυσδαίμων = 'having evil fortune.'—μίσημα, like στύγημα, δούλευμα, etc. Cp. *Ph.* 991 ὦ μῖσος.—σοὶ μόνῃ: cp. 154 n.—ἐν πένθει, as 847 τὸν ἐν πένθει: Plat. *Rep.* 605 D ἐν πένθει ὄντα.

291 f. ἐκ γόων, instead of the simple gen.; cp. 231, 987.—οἱ κάτω θεοί. Electra has invoked these deities as avengers (110).

The prayer is that they may leave her in her present wretchedness.

293 f. τάδ', instead of ταῦτ', referring to the words just quoted : cp. *Ph.* 1045 βαρύς τε καὶ βαρεῖαν ὁ ξένος φάτιν | τήνδ' εἶπ'.

ἥξοντ' Ὀρέστην. In vv. 778 ff. Clytaemnestra speaks as if this threat, which kept her in constant alarm, was made by Orestes himself. But his messages to Electra were secret (1155). The meaning is that rumours of his purpose reached her from friends in Phocis, such as Phanoteus (45).

295 παραστᾶσ', coming up to her in a threatening manner: cp. *O. C.* 992 εἴ τίς σε... | κτείνοι παραστάς.

296 f. ἥτις after σόν, as in *O. C.* 731 ὃν after τῆς ἐμῆς.— ὑπεξέθου, to Strophius at Crisa (180). Cp. 1350 ὑπεξεπέμφθην Thuc. 1. 89 διεκομίζοντο εὐθὺς ὅθεν ὑπεξέθεντο (from Aegina) παῖδας καὶ γυναῖκας.

299 f. ὑλακτεῖ, the word used of a dog's bark, here describes a yell of rage, as in Eur. *Alc.* 760 ἄμουσ' ὑλακτῶν is said of the drunken Heracles.—σὺν is here an adv. (and not, as in 746, a case of tmesis): cp. *Ai.* 1288 ὅδ' ἦν ὁ πράσσων ταῦτα, σὺν δ' ἐγὼ παρών.—πέλας is combined with παρών as in *Ai.* 83: so with παρέστατε, *ib.* 1183: and παραστατήσειν, *O. T.* 400.—παρών implies support and aid; cp. *Ph.* 373, 1405.

301 The adv. πάντα often thus strengthens an adj., as *Ai.* 911 ὁ πάντα κωφός, ὁ πάντ' ἄϊδρις.—ἄναλκις: *Od.* 3. 310 ἀνάλκιδος Αἰγίσθοιο.—ἡ πᾶσα βλάβῃ, equiv. in sense to ὁ πᾶς βλάβη ὤν: cp. *Ph.* 622, where this phrase is applied to Odysseus: *ib.* 927 ὦ πῦρ σὺ καὶ πᾶν δεῖμα.

302 σὺν γυναιξί, *i.e.* with Clytaemnestra for his ally.—τὰς μάχας, such fights as he wages: for the art., cp. *Ant.* 190 τοὺς φίλους ποιούμεθα.

304 ἐφήξειν: cp. *Ai.* 34 (Ajax to Athena) καιρὸν δ' ἐφήκεις (come to my aid).

305 f. μέλλων...δρᾶν τι, intending to do something great,— as his frequent messages promised (1155). For this sense of δρᾶν τι, cp. *Tr.* 160 ἀλλ' ὥς τι δράσων εἷρπε: for μέλλων with pres. inf., *O. T.* 967.—τὰς οὔσας τε...καὶ τὰς ἀπούσας, simply, 'all possible' hopes ; (not, 'present, or more distant':) cp. *Ant.* 1108 ἴτ' ἴτ' ὀπάονες, | οἵ τ' ὄντες οἵ τ' ἀπόντες.—διέφθορεν. The perf. διέφθορα has always this act. sense where it occurs in Attic writers (Eur., and the Comic poets).

307 f. σωφρονεῖν, to observe such moderation as the Chorus

Notes 83

recommend; **εὐσεβεῖν**, to abstain from the unfilial behaviour which Clytaemnestra resents (596), and which Electra herself deplores as a cruel necessity (616—621).

ἐν τοι κακοῖς: similarly τοι can separate the art. from its noun (*O. C.* 880, etc.). The vulg. **ἐν τοῖς κακοῖς** is not unmetrical (since not only τοῖς, but also **ἐν**, coheres with κακοῖς), but is weak.—**κἀπιτηδεύειν κακά**: *i.e.*, as her circumstances are evil, so, on her own part (καί, 1026), she is driven to an evil behaviour,—*i.e.*, to defying her mother: as she says in 621 αἰσχροῖς γὰρ αἰσχρὰ πράγματ' ἐκδιδάσκεται.

I place only a comma, not a colon, after **πάρεστιν**, as the context requires; for the opposition expressed by **ἀλλά** is merely to the negative form of the preceding clause, not to its sense.

310 f. ὄντος...βεβῶτος. The leading idea of the sentence is here expressed by the gen. absol., as so often by the participle in other cases (*O. C.* 1038).—It was necessary for the plot that the absence of Aegisthus should be notified to the spectators at some early moment; Clytaemnestra reminds them of it at v. 517.

312 f. ἢ κάρτα recurs below, 1278; *Tr.* 379; *Ai.* 1359: but only here as an independent affirmative, which is elsewhere καὶ κάρτα (*O. C.* 65, 301).—**θυραῖον**, fem., as is θυραῖος in *Tr.* 533.—**οἰχνεῖν**: 165 n.—**ἀγροῖσι**, like 174 οὐρανῷ n.—**τυγχάνει**, without ὤν, 46 n.

314 f. ἢ κἄν...ἱκοίμην..; The force of **ἢ καί**, which inquires with a certain eagerness (663, *O. T.* 368, 757), seems exactly in place here. The leader of the Chorus, not without trepidation, approaches the subject which is uppermost in their thoughts. —**ἐς λόγους τοὺς σοὺς ἱκοίμην** instead of ἐς λόγους ἱκοίμην σοι.

316 ὡς νῦν is better here than ὡς νυν.

ὑστέρει· τί σοι φίλον; This punctuation is necessary unless the text is to be altered. It has been called 'harsh.' But it is not more abrupt than εἰδέναι θέλω in 318, and it suits the slight surprise with which Electra hears the question.

317 f. καὶ δή, *i.e.*, without further preface : cp. 892 : *Ant.* 245 καὶ δὴ λέγω σοι.—**τοῦ κασιγνήτου τί φής**...; Cp. *Od.* 11. 174 εἰπὲ δέ μοι πατρός τε καὶ υἱέος : *Ph.* 439 ἀναξίου μὲν φωτὸς ἐξερήσομαι.

ἥξοντος, about to come (soon), **ἢ μέλλοντος**, or delaying? Do his messages indicate zeal, or do they not? The words could also mean, 'about to come soon, or (at least) *purposing* to do

so' (cp. *Tr.* 75 ἐπιστρατεύειν..ἢ μέλλειν ἔτι): but the antithesis recommends the former view.—The participles explain τί, being equiv. to ὅτι ἥξει, ἢ μέλλει; cp. Aesch. *Ag.* 271 εὖ γὰρ φρονοῦντος ὄμμα σοῦ κατηγορεῖ.

319 φησίν γε, *sc.* ἥξειν: cp. 171 f.

321 καὶ μὴν ἔγωγ'. It depends on the context in each case whether καὶ μήν signifies (1) 'and *indeed*,' as in 556; or (2) 'and *yet*,' as here, and in 1045, 1188. For the addition of γε, cp. 1045.—οὐκ ὄκνῳ, a dat. of manner (= οὐκ ὀκνοῦσα). The emphasis is upon this phrase.

322 ἀρκεῖν = ἐπαρκεῖν, as in *O. C.* 262.

323 ἐπεί, 'for *else*'; *i.e.*, εἰ μὴ ἐπεποίθη. So in *O. T.* 433 ἐπεί implies εἰ ἤδη.—μακρὰν means, 'so long as I actually have lived.' 'If I had not (hitherto) been confident, I should not have continued to live so long.'

324 Chrysothemis is seen coming from within. Here, as in 316, νῦν is better than νυν. The Chorus wish Electra to cease speaking of Orestes, because they regard Chrysothemis as a partisan of Clytaemnestra and Aegisthus.—δόμων, gen. of the place whence, with φέρουσαν: cp. *Ph.* 613 ἄγοιντο νήσου.

325 ὅμαιμον is further defined, as in 12: cp. 156. Lys. or. 32 § 4 ἀδελφοὶ...ὁμοπάτριοι καὶ ὁμομήτριοι.—φύσιν, adverbial acc., 'by birth': cp. 1125.

326 Χρυσόθεμιν: the name occurs nowhere else in the play, except in v. 158. For the place of the name in the sentence, cp. 695.—ἐντάφια, ἐναγίσματα, offerings for the grave of Agamemnon, viz., (1) libations, χοαί, and (2) some other articles, such as flowers, and perhaps cakes, described at v. 434 by the word κτερίσματα, as distinct from λουτρά. Cp. v. 405 ἔμπυρα(n.). Chrysothemis carries some, at least, of the gifts in her own hands: cp. 431 ὧν ἔχεις χεροῖν.—For the tribrach in the 5th foot, cp. *O. T.* 719.

327 οἷα is nom. to νομίζεται, not acc., as though φέρειν were understood: cp. 691.

328 πρὸς θυρῶνος ἐξόδοις, close to the thoroughfare of the θυρών or vestibule (*O. T.* 1242): cp. Aesch. *Th.* 33 πυλῶν ἐπ' ἐξόδοις. These words go with φωνεῖς, while ἐλθοῦσα emphasises her boldness in seeking such publicity. As αὖ implies, she has often done so before; cp. 517 ὅς σ' ἐπεῖχ' ἀεὶ | μή τοι θυραίαν γ' οὖσαν αἰσχύνειν φίλους.

330 For the absence of caesura, cp. *Ph.* 101.

332 καίτοι τοσοῦτόν γ' οἶδα, as in *O. T.* 1455: cp. *Ai.* 441

καίτοι τοσοῦτόν γ' ἐξεπίστασθαι δοκῶ.—κἀμαυτήν, ὅτι, instead of ὅτι κἀγώ: cp. 520 f.: *Ph.* 444 τοῦτον οἶσθ' εἰ ζῶν κυρεῖ;

333 f. For the repeated ἄν, cp. *O. T.* 339.—οἴ' αὑτοῖς φρονῶ: cp. Ar. *Ach.* 446 Τηλέφῳ δ' ἁγὼ φρονῶ.

335 ὑφειμένῃ, *submisse*: cp. Eur. *Alc.* 524 κατθανεῖν ὑφειμένην, 'resigned to die.' Here the figurative πλεῖν gives a special sense to the partic., viz., 'with lowered sail.' So Ar. *Ran.* 1220 ὑφέσθαι μοι δοκεῖ· | τὸ ληκύθιον γὰρ τοῦτο πνευσεῖται πολύ.

336 καὶ μὴ δοκεῖν κ.τ.λ. Her thought is, δοκεῖς μὲν δρᾶν τι, πημαίνεις δὲ οὔ: 'you have merely the semblance of being active against our foes, without really harming them. I will not imitate you.' The first μὴ affects all that follows it. Such a combination of independent negatives is especially frequent in denials of illogical conduct; since Greek idiom loved to bring out a want of consistency by a parataxis with μέν and δέ. Thus Plat. *Alcib.* I. p. 124 C ἐγὼ γάρ τοι οὐ περὶ μὲν σοῦ λέγω ὡς χρὴ παιδευθῆναι, περὶ δ' ἐμοῦ οὔ. Dem. or. 18 § 179 οὐκ εἶπον μὲν ταῦτα, οὐκ ἔγραψα δέ ('I did not say these things and then fail to propose them').

337 τοιαῦτα δ' ἄλλα. She wishes Electra's behaviour to be a faithful copy of her own. Cp. Her. I. 191 τά περ ἡ τῶν Βαβυλωνίων βασίλεια ἐποίησε..., ἐποίεε καὶ ὁ Κῦρος ἕτερα τοιαῦτα. —The MS. ἀλλὰ is impossible.

338 ff. καίτοι τὸ μὲν δίκαιον κ.τ.λ. Chrysothemis, like Ismene (*Ant.* 65), recognises the duty from which she shrinks. The poet's object is not to contrast a good with a base nature, but the heroic with the commonplace.—κρίνεις, decide, choose. The contrast is between the pronouns rather than between the verbs: thus the sense would be the same, if we had, οὐχ ᾗ ἐγὼ κρίνω, ἀλλ' ᾗ σύ. (Cp. *O. T.* 54.)—εἰ..με δεῖ = εἰ μέλλω: cp. *O. T.* 1110 εἰ χρή τι κἀμέ κ.τ.λ.: *Tr.* 749 εἰ χρὴ μαθεῖν σε.— ἐλευθέραν, whereas Electra is a slave (1192).

ζῆν. A monosyllable, followed by a pause, can begin the verse even when, as here, it is non-emphatic: so *O. T.* 1448 θοῦ. But more often it has emphasis, as *O. T.* 546 σοῦ, *ib.* 986 ζῇ.—πάντ', adv. (301).—ἀκουστέα: for the plur., cp. *Ant.* 677 f. ἀμυντέα...ἡσσητέα.

341 δεινόν γε. For this γε in comment, cp. *Ph.* 1225 δεινόν γε φωνεῖς.

342 τῆς...τικτούσης, as *O. T.* 1247, the pres. part. expressing the permanent relationship; cp. Eur. *Ion* 1560 ἥδε τίκτει σ' ('is thy mother').

J. E.   10

μέλαν: schol. φροντίζειν. The personal use of μέλειν was admitted by Aesch. (*Ag.* 370 θεοὺς βροτῶν ἀξιοῦσθαι μέλειν), and Eur. (*H. F.* 772 θεοὶ τῶν ἀδίκων | μέλουσι). We are not obliged to assume it here, but it gives the simplest construction.

343 f. τἀμὰ νουθετήματα: the possessive pron. = an objective gen., ἐμοῦ: cp. *O. T.* 969 τώμῷ πόθῳ: *O. C.* 332 σῇ...προμηθίᾳ. **—κείνης διδακτά**: cp. *Tr.* 934 ἐκδιδαχθεὶς τῶν κατ᾽ οἶκον: *O. T.* 1437 μηδενὸς προσήγορος.**—ἐκ σαυτῆς**: cp. 885.

345—351 The train of thought is somewhat obscured by compression.

'You forget your father, and care only for your mother. All your counsels to me come from her. Then (ἔπειτα),—that being so,—give up the attempt at a compromise. Make a *choice* (ἑλοῦ γε). You can be imprudent (φρονεῖν κακῶς),—as you say that I am,—and loyal to your dead father. Or you can be prudent (φρονοῦσα), and forgetful of him,—as you actually are; you who (ἥτις) say, indeed, that you would show your hatred of the murderers if you could; and yet, when I *do* resist them, you try to turn me from my purpose. You merely add the shame of cowardice to our woes.'

345 ἔπειθ᾽, 'then,' 'after that'; *i.e.*, 'such being the case,'—that you side with Clytaemnestra. This use of the word in logical inference is not rare (cp. *Il.* 5. 812, 10. 243).

ἑλοῦ γε. The effect of γε is merely to emphasise the verb,—opposing a definite *choice* to a compromise. Cp. 411 συγγένεσθέ γ᾽: 1035 ἐπίστω γ᾽.

φρονεῖν κακῶς, to be imprudent. The chief theme of the timid sister's speech (328—340) has been prudence; as in 994 she insists on τὴν εὐλάβειαν, and Electra says (1027) ζηλῶ σε τοῦ νοῦ, τῆς δὲ δειλίας στυγῶ.

346 τῶν φίλων, meaning esp. her father: cp. 241 γονέων: 652 φίλοισι.

347 f. ἥτις, causal, because v. 346 describes the course which she is actually taking. The words λέγεις μὲν...ἐκδείξειας ἄν correspond with φρονοῦσα, as illustrating her prudence; while 349 f. explain the sense in which she forgets her father.**—μῖσος**: Electra puts bluntly what Chrysothemis veiled by the euphemism οἶ᾽ αὐτοῖς φρονῶ (334).

349 πάντα, adv.**—τιμωρουμένης**: the midd., as in 399, where the active would be normal. 'To avenge one' is usu. τιμωρεῖν τινι (the accus., denoting the person chastised, being often

Notes 87

omitted), as *O. T.* 136 γῇ τῇδε τιμωροῦντα. 'To *punish* a person' is usu. τιμωρεῖσθαί τινα (to which a dat. of the person avenged can be added): *Ph.* 1258 ὅς σε τιμωρήσεται.

350 οὔτε...τε: cp. *O. C.* 1397: *Ph.* 1321 f., 1363.—τὴν τε δρῶσαν: more pointed here than ἐμέ τε δρῶσαν: '*her* who *does* act.'

351 πρὸς κακοῖσι, 'in addition to the miseries' of the family. —δειλίαν ἔχει, cp. Dem. or. 18 § 279 τὸ δὲ δὴ καὶ τοὺς πρὸς ἐμὲ αὐτὸν ἀγῶνας ἐάσαντα νῦν ἐπὶ τόνδ' ἥκειν καὶ πᾶσαν ἔχει κακίαν.

352 ἐπεί, *i.e.*, if there be indeed any good in such counsels. Cp. 323. For this controversial ἐπεί with the imperat., see *O. T.* 390, *O. C.* 969.—ἢ μάθ' ἐξ ἐμοῦ: cp. 565 ἢ 'γὼ φράσω. For the parenthesis, Schneid. cp. Eur. *Cycl.* 121 σπείρουσι δ', ἢ τῷ ζῶσι, Δήμητρος στάχυν;

354 ἐπαρκούντως occurs nowhere else in classical Greek. But the corresponding sense of ἐπαρκεῖν, though rare, is well-attested: Solon fr. 5, 1 τόσον κράτος, ὅσσον ἐπαρκεῖ.

356 προσάπτειν, render as a tribute: cp. *Il.* 24. 110 τόδε κῦδος Ἀχιλλῆι προτιάπτω. Pind. *N.* 8. 36 ὡς παισὶ κλέος | μὴ τὸ δύσφαμον προσάψω.

εἴ τις ἔστ' ἐκεῖ χάρις, if any gratification can be felt in the nether world,—ὅπου τὸ χαίρειν μηδαμοῦ νομίζεται (Aesch. *Eum.* 423). For ἐκεῖ = ἐν Ἅιδου, cp. *Ai.* 855, *Ant.* 76.

357 f. ἡμῖν, ethic dat., (thou, whom I am asked to regard as hating,) 272.—ξύνει, here = 'art their *ally*': whereas in 263 the same phrase, applied to Electra, means merely that she dwells in the same house.

359 f. τὰ σὰ...δῶρ', the privileges (in regard to soft living) which the rulers confer upon her.—ἐφ' οἷσι, as in 333, instead of the simple dat.—χλιδᾷς, *superbis*. Eur. fr. 986 πλούτῳ χλιδῶσα θνητὰ δή, γύναι, φρόνει.

361 f. πλουσία: in contrast with the κεναὶ τράπεζαι of 192. —περιρρείτω, be superabundant; a sense of περιρρεῖν not else-where found in Greek of this age; but cp. Plut. *Per.* 16 (referring to the domestic economy of Pericles), οὐδενὸς οἷον (as is usual) ἐν οἰκίᾳ μεγάλῃ καὶ πράγμασιν ἀφθόνοις περιρρέοντος.

363 f. τοὐμὲ μὴ λυπεῖν: 'For me, let it be food enough that I do not pain myself (by a base compliance with the murderers)': ἐμὲ for ἐμαυτήν, as ἐμοί for ἐμαυτῷ in *Ant.* 736 ἄλλῳ γὰρ ἢ 'μοὶ χρή με τῆσδ' ἄρχειν χθονός; For the figurative sense of βόσκημα, cp. Aesch. *Ch.* 26 δι' αἰῶνος δ' ἰυγμοῖσι βόσκεται κέαρ. The phrase λυπεῖν ἑαυτόν seems to have been familiar: Eur. *Cycl.*

88 *Electra*

336 ὡς τοὐμπιεῖν γε καὶ φαγεῖν τοῦφ' ἡμέραν, | Ζεὺς οὗτος ἀνθρώ-
ποισι τοῖσι σώφροσι, | λυπεῖν δὲ μηδὲν αὐτόν: Eur. (?) fr. 174
(Nauck) μὴ οὖν ἔθελε λυπεῖν σαυτόν. The tone of the phrase
here is explained by the context. In the preceding verses
Electra has fully set forth her view : now she is summing it up,
in words suited to a hearer of whose sympathy she despairs.
'Enough for me if I do not offend my own sense of right';
i.e., 'I must obey my own instincts,—as you follow yours.'

365 οὐδ' ἂν σὺ κ.τ.λ., *sc.* ἐρῴης (or ἤρας), as οὖσα = εἰ εἴης (or
ἦσθα) : for the ellipse of a verb after ἄν, cp. *Tr.* 462, *Ph.* 115.

366 παῖδα, where the dat. παιδὶ is also admissible: cp. *Ant.*
838.—κεκλῆσθαι: cp. fr. 83 καταρκεῖ τοῦδε κεκλῆσθαι πατρός.
By forgetting her duty to her father, she as it were repudiates
him, and will be known only as Clytaemnestra's daughter.
Here (as in 341 f.) it is implied that the paternal claim on filial
piety is naturally stronger than the maternal (Aesch. *Eum.*
658 ff.: Eur. *Or.* 552 f.).

369 μηδὲν, *sc.* εἴπῃς: πρὸς ὀργὴν, 'angrily'; like πρὸς βίαν,
πρὸς ἡδονήν, etc.: Ar. *Ran.* 856 σὺ δὲ μὴ πρὸς ὀργήν, Αἰσχύλ',
ἀλλὰ πραόνως | ἔλεγχ'.

370 ἀμφοῖν is best taken as dat. fem., 'for both of you,'
'on both your parts': though (notwithstanding its position) it
could be also gen. fem. The objection to taking it as dat.
masc. with τοῖς λόγοις is that the noun or pron. joined to ἀμφω
or ἀμφοτέρω is usu. dual.

371 τῆσδε...αὕτη, referring to the same person, as *Ph.* 841
τοῦδε...τοῦτον. Electra is in need of caution, and Chrysothemis
of loyalty. For πάλιν, cp. 1434.

372 f. ἐγὼ μὲν: 251 n.—πως, *fere*: *Ai.* 327 τοιαῦτα γάρ πως
καὶ λέγει κωδύρεται.—μύθων, in a disparaging sense, as Eur.
Andr. 744 τοὺς σοὺς δὲ μύθους ῥαδίως ἐγὼ φέρω.

374 f. ἰὸν: cp. *O. C.* 1771 ἰόντα φόνον | τοῖσιν ὁμαίμοις.—
σχήσει: 223.

376 τὸ δεινὸν: so Antigone to Ismene, *Ant.* 95 ἔα με... |
παθεῖν τὸ δεινὸν τοῦτο.—εἰ γὰρ τῶνδέ μοι. Elmsley proposed δὲ
instead of γάρ. But the spondee can stand in the 5th foot,
since εἰ coheres with the following words (the metrical effect
being as that of one word, *e.g.* ἐξαιρούμενον): so *O. C.* 115 ἐν
γὰρ τῷ μαθεῖν.

379 γὰρ, prefatory: 32.—γόων, though v. 375 ends with
the same word: cp. 161, 163 (γᾶ...γᾶν).

380 ff. ἐνταῦθα = ἐνταυθοῖ, as in *Tr.* 1193.—ἔνθα μή ποτε...

προσόψει: cp. 436: *O. T.* 1412 ἐκρίψατ', ἔνθα μήποτ' εἰσόψεσθ' ἔτι: *Tr.* 800, *Ai.* 659.—ζῶσα, implying that it will be a living death; cp. *Ant.* 888 ζῶσα τυμβεύειν.

κατηρεφεῖ, lit. 'roofed over'; the στέγη meant is a vault or dungeon, not a natural cavern (though the adj. would suit that also). So the sepulchral chamber of Antigone is a κατηρεφὴς τύμβος (*Ant.* 885).

χθονὸς τῆσδ' ἐκτὸς, because the usurpers might well fear the sympathy which disaffected Mycenaeans (like the women of the Chorus) would feel with Electra.

ὑμνήσεις, *decantabis*: cp. *Ant.* 658 πρὸς ταῦτ' ἐφυμνείτω Δία | ξύναιμον. *Ai.* 292 βαῖ, ἀεὶ δ' ὑμνούμενα.

383 f. πρὸς ταῦτα is often joined to the imperat. in warning or menace; cp. 820; *O. T.* 426.

ἐν καλῷ, εὔκαιρον schol.: Xen. *H.* 4. 3. 5 νομίσαντες οὐκ ἐν καλῷ εἶναι πρὸς τοὺς ὁπλίτας ἱππομαχεῖν.

385 ἢ ταῦτα δὴ κ.τ.λ. The formula ἢ...δὴ expresses lively surprise, just as in *Ph.* 565 ἢ ταῦτα δὴ Φοῖνίξ τε χοὶ ξυνναυβάται | . δρῶσιν ..;

καὶ βεβούλευνται: καί emphasises the verb: cp. *Ant.* 726 οἱ τηλικοίδε καὶ διδαξόμεσθα δή ..; *O. T.* 772. For the perf. pass. with middle force, cp. 947.

387 ἀλλ' ἐξίκοιτο : cp. *O. C.* 44 ἀλλ' ἵλεῳ...δεξαίατο.—τοῦδέ γ' οὕνεκ', 'for that matter,' 'if that is all'; cp. 605, 787.

388 τίνα...τόνδ' : cp. *Tr.* 184 τίν' εἶπας, ὦ γεραιέ, τόνδε μοι λόγον;—τάλαινα, 'misguided,' as Ismene says to Antigone, οἴμοι ταλαίνης (*Ant.* 82).

389 εἴ τι τῶνδε, with a shade of irony, 'anything of this kind': *O. C.* 1034 νοεῖς τι τούτων; *O. T.* 1140 λέγω τι τούτων κ.τ.λ.

390 ποῦ ποτ' εἶ φρενῶν; Cp. *Ant.* 42 ποῦ γνώμης ποτ' εἶ;

391 ὅπως without ἄν, as in 688.—ὑμῶν, bitterly identifying her sister with her foes, whom she has hitherto called '*them*' (348, 355, 361).—προσωτατ'. Several recent editions read προσωτάτω φύγω with L. Dindorf, on the ground that this was the correct form of the superl. adv. It is certainly the only form which elsewhere occurs in classical Attic. But it seems rash to assert that Sophocles could not possibly have used προσώτατα, especially when it is so decidedly commended by euphony.

392 βίου...τοῦ παρόντος, as compared with the life in the vault (381). Electra herself had said that it sufficed for her (354).

393 καλὸς γὰρ κ.τ.λ. For this use of γὰρ in a sarcastic retort, cp. Ar. *Ach.* 71, where the πρέσβυς has described himself and his colleagues as ἀπολλύμενοι, and Dicaeopolis rejoins, σφόδρα γὰρ ἐσῳζόμην ἐγώ κ.τ.λ.—θαυμάσαι: cp. Thuc. i. 138 ἄξιος θαυμάσαι.

395 τοῖς φίλοις, *i.e.* τῷ πατρί, as in 346.

397 ταῦτα, cogn. acc., ταύτην τὴν θωπείαν. For the verb, cp. *O. C.* 1336.—οὐκ ἐμοὺς κ.τ.λ.: ἐμοὺς is predicative, like τίν' in 388 (n.).

398 γε emphasises καλόν: μέντοι = 'however.'—μὴ 'ξ. The crasis of μή with ἐκ occurs also in *Ai.* 278, *O. T.* 1075, *Ph.* 467, *Tr.* 727, 1235.—πεσεῖν, to be ruined; as *O. T.* 50, 146, 376: *O. C.* 395.

399 A woman, speaking of herself in the plur., uses the masc.: *Ant.* 926 παθόντες ἂν ξυγγνοῖμεν ἡμαρτηκότες.

400 συγγνώμην. Ismene defends herself by a like excuse, —αἰτοῦσα τοὺς ὑπὸ χθονὸς | ξύγγνοιαν ἴσχειν (*Ant.* 65).

401 τἄπη, maxims, sentiments: cp. Aesch. *Th.* 717 οὐκ ἄνδρ' ὁπλίτην τοῦτο χρὴ στέργειν ἔπος.—πρὸς κακῶν, it befits them: for this use of πρός, cp. *Ai.* 319, 581, 1071.

403 μή πω, ironical; cp. Eur. *Hec.* 1278 μή πω μανείη Τυνδαρὶς τοσόνδε παῖς: id. *Med.* 365 ἀλλ' οὔ τι ταύτῃ ταῦτα· μὴ δοκεῖτέ πω.

404 οἷπερ...ὁδοῦ. The gen. is partitive, just as in 1035 οἷ...ἀτιμίας. The only peculiarity is that ὁδοῦ is used in an abstract sense,—'to that point of *journeying*';—as we might have οἷ πορείας, or οἷ πλανημάτων.

405 ἔμπυρα probably refers to some articles of food, perhaps cakes, which she (or a handmaid) was carrying to be burned at the grave (cp. 326 n.). Chrysothemis, in her reply, naturally speaks of the χοαί, since they formed the most characteristic part of the rite. But it seems impossible that the word ἔμπυρα should directly denote the libations, as was supposed by the schol. (τάδ' ἔμπυρα· ταύτας τὰς σπονδάς), and by Triclinius.

406 τυμβεῦσαι χοάς, to *offer* them *at* the tomb; cp. *Ai.* 1063 σῶμα τυμβεῦσαι τάφῳ.

407 βροτῶν, though referring to the dead; cp. 462: Aesch. *Ch.* 129 χέουσα τάσδε χέρνιβας βροτοῖς (to Agamemnon).

408 ὃν ἔκταν' αὐτή. Not ὃν γ': she is finishing Electra's sentence for her. Cp. *Ph.* 105, 985.

409 τῷ τοῦτ' ἤρεσεν; The spondee in the 5th foot is

correct, since τοῦτ' coheres with its verb, giving the effect of a single word. (Cp. 376.)

410 δείματος, a word often used of a terrifying dream: Aesch. *Ch.* 523 ἔκ τ' ὀνειράτων | καὶ νυκτιπλάγκτων δειμάτων πεπαλμένη | χοὰς ἔπεμψε τάσδε δύσθεος γυνή.

δοκεῖν ἐμοί: cp. *O. T.* 82 ἀλλ' εἰκάσαι μέν, ἡδύς. At v. 426 she speaks positively ; as if the recital of the dream had raised her surmise into certainty.

411 θεοὶ πατρῷοι, the gods of the Pelopid house : see on *O. C.* 756 πρὸς θεῶν πατρῴων : and for the synizesis in θεοί, also *ib.* 964.

συγγένεσθέ γ': cp. *O. T.* 275 εὖ ξυνεῖεν εἰσαεὶ θεοί: Aesch. *Ch.* 460 (the Chorus invoking Agamemnon) ξὺν δὲ γενοῦ πρὸς ἐχθρούς. For γε, cp. 345 n.

ἀλλὰ νῦν, 'now at least,'—though not sooner. Cp. *O. C.* 1276 πειράσατ' ἀλλ' ὑμεῖς γε. She hails the dream as a sign from the nether world that vengeance is imminent, and invokes the gods of her house to co-operate with the χθόνιοι.

413 εἴποιμ' ἂν τότε. When ἄν is the second syllable of the 5th foot, it is usually preceded by an elision ; as in Eur. *Andr.* 935, 1184.

414 ἐπὶ σμικρὸν, lit. 'to a small extent,' like ἐπὶ πολύ, ἐπὶ μέγα, ἐπὶ μακρόν, etc. Cp. Plat. *Soph.* 254 B κοινωνεῖν .. τὰ μὲν ἐπ' ὀλίγον, τὰ δ' ἐπὶ πολλά.—φράσαι is almost redundant, as in *O. C.* 35, 50, 1582.

415 σμικροὶ λόγοι, here in the sense of 'few,' 'brief,' rather than trivial. Cp. *O. T.* 120 ἐν γὰρ πόλλ' ἂν ἐξεύροι μαθεῖν. *O. C.* 443 ἔπους σμικροῦ χάριν.

417 ff. πατρὸς...δευτέραν ὁμιλίαν = πατέρα αὖθις ὁμιλοῦντα : cp. *Ai.* 872 ναὸς κοινόπλουν ὁμιλίαν : Eur. *Heracl.* 581 ὑμεῖς δ', ἀδελφῶν ἡ παροῦσ' ὁμιλία, | εὐδαιμονοῖτε.

ἐφέστιον (with σκῆπτρον, predicative) πῆξαι : cp. *O. T.* 1411 θαλάσσιον ἐκρίψατ'. The floor of the Homeric megaron was not of wood or stone, but merely of earth trodden hard ; πῆξαι, then, affords no reason against referring ἐφέστιον to the hearth in the megaron (270 n.). But the vision of the tree becomes more intelligible if we imagine the sceptre planted at the altar of Zeus Herkeios in the open αὐλή of the house.

This sceptre is described in the *Iliad* (2. 101 f.) as the work of Hephaestus, who gave it Zeus ; Hermes transmitted it to Pelops, from whom it passed to Atreus and Agamemnon.

421 ff. ἔκ τε may have been preferred by the poet to ἐκ δὲ

on account of τανῦν δ'.—βρύοντα, luxuriant (with foliage): cp. *Il.*
17. 56 (ἔρνος) βρύει ἄνθεϊ.—ᾧ...γενέσθαι: for the inf. in a relative
clause of oratio obliqua, cp. Her. 6. 117 ἄνδρα οἱ δοκέειν ὁπλίτην
ἀντιστῆναι μέγαν, τοῦ τὸ γένειον τὴν ἀσπίδα πᾶσαν σκιάζειν.
Thuc. 2. 102 λέγεται δὲ καὶ Ἀλκμαίωνι..., ὅτε δὴ ἀλᾶσθαι αὐτὸν...,
τὸν Ἀπόλλω...χρῆσαι κ.τ.λ.
The vision resembles that of Astyages, who dreamed that a
vine sprang from his daughter Mandanè, the wife of Cambyses,
τὴν δὲ ἄμπελον ἐπισχεῖν τὴν Ἀσίην πᾶσαν.

424 f. τοῦ παρόντος: the constr. is τοιαῦτα ἐξηγουμένου
ἔκλυόν του, παρόντος ἡνίκα ἡλίῳ δείκνυσι τὸ ὄναρ: and παρόντος
is properly predicative, = 'inasmuch as he was present' (and
therefore able to tell).

Ἡλίῳ δείκνυσι τοὔναρ. Cp. Eur. *I. T.* 42 ἃ καινὰ δ' ἥκει νὺξ
φέρουσα φάσματα, | λέξω πρὸς αἰθέρ', εἴ τι δὴ τόδ' ἔστ' ἄκος.
Schol.: τοῖς γὰρ παλαιοῖς ἔθος ἦν ἀποτροπιαζομένους (by way of
expiation) τῷ ἡλίῳ διηγεῖσθαι τὰ ὀνείρατα. The popular attri-
butes of Ἥλιος suggest more than one reason for such a custom.
1. He is the god of light and purity, ἁγνὸς θεός (Pind. *O.* 7. 60),
who dispels the terrors of darkness. 2. As the all-seeing god,
πανόπτης, he is especially the detector of guilt (*Od.* 8. 270), able
to reveal the lurking danger which an evil dream might fore-
shadow. 3. And, generally, he is a saving power (σωτήρ).

426 f. οὐ κάτοιδα, πλὴν κ.τ.λ.: cp. 410 n.

428—430 These three verses, which the MSS. give to
Electra, clearly belong to Chrysothemis. Electra's exclamation
of joy (411) caused Chrysothemis to ask if her sister had any
ground for hope (412). Electra replied that, when she had
heard the dream, she would say. This showed her sister that
Electra relied merely on the fact that Clytaemnestra had seen
some fearful vision. Now, therefore, instead of asking for
Electra's interpretation, she merely repeats her counsel (383 f.)
before proceeding on her errand. The words πρός νυν θεῶν
κ.τ.λ. (428 ff.) show the train of her thought. To Chrysothemis,
the dream is only a new reason why Electra should be cautious,
—not why she should hope.

428 τῶν ἐγγενῶν, 'the gods of our race': cp. *Ant.* 199 γῆν
πατρῴαν καὶ θεοὺς τοὺς ἐγγενεῖς. The phrase of Electra, θεοὶ
πατρῷοι (411),—recalling the memory of her father,—would be
less fitting for Chrysothemis.

429 f. ἀβουλίᾳ, causal dat.; cp. 398 ἐξ ἀβουλίας.—σὺν κακῷ,
= κακὸν παθοῦσα (383 f.). Cp. 61 σὺν κέρδει.—μέτει, *sc.* με, 'thou

Notes

93

wilt come in search of me,' to help thee : schol. αὐτὴ μετελεύσῃ
με καὶ ἀξιώσεις μετὰ σοῦ γενέσθαι.

431 ἀλλ', beginning the appeal : *O. T.* 14, *O. C.* 238 f.—
ὦ φίλη. The bitter feeling seen in vv. 391 and 403 has passed
away before the new hope, and she speaks with affectionate
earnestness.—τούτων μὲν, as opposed to the offerings recommended in 449.

432 ff. οὐ...θέμις, it is not sanctioned by usage, οὐδ' ὅσιον,
nor is it pious towards the gods : *ius fasque vetant.*

ἐχθρᾶς ἀπὸ γυναικὸς : for ἀπό, 'on the part of,' cp. 1469 :
O. C. 1289 καὶ ταῦτ' ἀφ' ὑμῶν...βουλήσομαι | .. κυρεῖν ἐμοί.
The prep., emphasising the quarter from which the offerings
come, is suitable here.

κτερίσματ', used at 931 as including libations (894), but here
distinguished from them. See on *O. C.* 1410 ἀλλ' ἐν τάφοισι
θέσθε κἀν κτερίσμασιν. The verb κτερίζειν occurs in *Ant.* 204.—
λουτρὰ = χοάς : 84 n.

435 f. ἀλλ' ἢ πνοαῖσιν κ.τ.λ., 'cast them to the winds—or
bury them deep in the earth.' The first thought is a passionate
utterance of scorn and loathing. Cp. Eur. *Bacch.* 350, where
Pentheus, in his rage against Teiresias, cries, καὶ στέμματ'
ἀνέμοις καὶ θυέλλαισιν μέθες. *Tro.* 418 'Αργεῖ' ὀνείδη καὶ Φρυγῶν
ἐπαινέσεις | ἀνέμοις φέρεσθαι | παραδίδωμ'.

κρύψον adapts the general notion (ἀφάνισον) to κόνει : with
πνοαῖσιν we supply παράδος, or the like. The zeugma is of a
common type : *Od.* 9. 166 ἐς γαῖαν ἐλεύσσομεν... | καπνόν τ'
αὐτῶν τε φθογγὴν ὀΐων τε καὶ αἰγῶν : Aesch. *P. V.* 21 ἵν' οὔτε
φωνὴν οὔτε του μορφὴν βροτῶν | ὄψει.

νιν here and in 624 = αὐτά : it stands for the masc. pl.
in *O. T.* 868, and for the fem. in *O. C.* 43.—ἔνθα μή ποτ', with
fut.: cp. 380 n. The meaning is, 'in a place *where* they will
have no access' to his tomb, *i.e.*, where they will be *remote*
from it.—εὐνὴν is peculiarly fitting here, since the offerings
are those of a false wife. Cp. Aesch. *Ch.* 318 ἔνθα σ' ἔχουσιν
εὐναί.

437 f. ἀλλ' ὅταν θάνῃ. If the offerings are buried deep in
the ground, they will thereby be committed to the care of the
νέρτεροι : cp. *Ai.* 658 ff. κρύψω τόδ' ἔγχος τοὐμόν, ἔχθιστον βελῶν, |
γαίας ὀρύξας ἔνθα μή τις ὄψεται, | ἀλλ' αὐτὸ νὺξ Ἅιδης τε σῳζόντων
κάτω. When Clytaemnestra passes to the nether world, let her
find these treasures laid up for her there. They will be witnesses
to her conscious guilt.

κειμήλι': cp. *Il.* 23. 618 (of a cup), τῇ νῦν, καὶ σοὶ τοῦτο, γέρον, κειμήλιον ἔστω.

439 ἀρχὴν, *omnino*, preceding the negative, as in *Ant.* 92, *Ph.* 1239.—**τλημονεστάτη**: cp. 275.

440 ἔβλαστε, with initial ἔ, as in 1095, *Ph.* 1311 ἐξ ἧς ἔβλαστες: but above, in 238, this ε is long.

441 ὅν γ'...τῷδ': for ὅδε after a relat., cp. *O. C.* 1332 οἷς ἂν σὺ προσθῇ, τοῖσδ' ἔφασκ' εἶναι κράτος: *Ph.* 86 f.: *Tr.* 23, 820.—**ἐπέστεφε**: 53 n.

442 f. The position of **αὐτῇ** shows that the dat. must be influenced by προσφιλῶς, though it would be sufficiently explained by δέξασθαι: cp. Eur. *Hec.* 535 δέξαι χοάς μοι τάσδε.

δέξεσθαι. Sophocles has joined δοκῶ (1) with the *future* infinitive in at least nine places. (2) With the infin. (*pres.* or *aor.*) and ἄν in six places. (3) With the simple aor. inf. in *El.* 805, and *Ph.* 276: in both of which places the reference is to past time.

It seems, then, a reasonable inference that here, where the reference is to future time, he would have written **δέξεσθαι** rather than **δέξασθαι**, or else would have added ἄν to the aor. inf. Indeed it seems most probable that the simple aor. infin. with δοκεῖ could never refer to the future.

444 ff. Join **θανὼν ἄτιμος**, ruthlessly slain: cp. 98: 1181: *Ant.* 1069 ψυχήν τ' ἀτίμως ἐν τάφῳ κατῴκισας.

ἐμασχαλίσθη. The verb occurs only here and in Aesch. *Ch.* 439 ἐμασχαλίσθη δέ γ', ὡς τόδ' εἰδῇς. Murderers used to cut off the extremities of their victim, and suspend these at his arm-pits (μασχάλαι) and from his neck. Hence μασχαλίζω is paraphrased by ἀκρωτηριάζω.

Two different motives are assigned by the Greek commentators; viz.:—(1) the desire to render the dead incapable of wreaking vengeance (ὥσπερ τὴν δύναμιν ἐκείνων ἀφαιρούμενοι): (2) the desire to make an atonement (ἐξιλάσασθαι τὴν δολοφονίαν —ἀφοσιοῦσθαι τὸν φόνον). There can be little doubt that the first of these motives was the primitive origin of the custom.

κἀπὶ λουτροῖσιν κ.τ.λ.: 'and, for ablution, she wiped off the blood-stains (from her sword) on his head.' ἐπὶ here = 'with a view to' (cp. *Ant.* 792 ἐπὶ λώβᾳ, *O. T.* 1457 ἐπὶ .κακῷ), and ἐπὶ λουτροῖς = ἐπὶ καθάρσει. The action was a symbolical way of saying, 'on thy head, not mine, be the guilt,'—as though the victim had provoked his own fate (thus Clytaemnestra claimed to be the avenger of Iphigeneia). This is better than to take

Notes 95

ἐπὶ λουτροῖς as = 'for washing (of the corpse),'—*i.e.*, in lieu of the λουτρά which it was the duty of relatives to give the dead.

ἐξέμαξεν, *sc.* ἡ Κλυταιμνήστρα: not ὁ νέκυς, which would require ἐξεμάξατ'. The change of subject is softened by the transition from a relative clause (ὑφ' ἧς κ.τ.λ.) to an independent sentence (cp. 188 ff., *O. C.* 424); and Greek idiom was tolerant in this matter.

ἆρα μὴ (*Ant.* 632), like μῶν ('can it be that..?').

448 οὐκ ἔστιν, finally rejecting the supposition, like οὐκ ἔστι ταῦτα (*Tr.* 449: *Ai.* 470).

ταῦτα μὲν μέθες· σὺ δὲ κ.τ.λ. Here σὺ δέ marks an antithesis, not of persons, but of clauses, and serves merely to emphasise the second clause. This is a peculiarly Ionic usage. *Il.* 9. 300 εἰ δέ τοι (= σοι) 'Ατρείδης μὲν ἀπήχθετο.. | .. σὺ δ' ἄλλους περ Παναχαιοὺς | τειρομένους ἐλέαιρε. The Attic poets took the idiom from the Ionians: Aesch. *Ag.* 1060 εἰ δ' ἀξυνήμων οὖσα μὴ δέχει λόγον, | σὺ δ' ἀντὶ φωνῆς φράζε καρβάνῳ χερί.

449 f. βοστρύχων ἄκρας φόβας, since the offering at the grave was to be merely a lock of hair (πλόκαμος πενθητήριος, Aesch. *Ch.* 8), in token of grief. The hair is not now to be cut short, as for a recent death.

κἀμοῦ ταλαίνης is a possessive genitive, going with τήνδ' ἀλιπ. τρίχα. It is so placed in the sentence as to heighten the pathos:—'give him a lock cut from (thine own head),—and (give) on *my* part .. this hair,' etc.

451 ἀλιπαρῆ. The schol.'s paraphrase αὐχμηράν gives the sense which we require. Cp. Eur. *El.* 183 σκέψαι μου πιναρὰν κόμαν | καὶ πέπλων τρύχη τάδ' ἐμῶν. But ἀλιπαρής, the negative of λιπαρής, could mean only, 'not earnest;' 'not persevering.'

(1) The words τήνδ' ἀλιπαρῆ τρίχα may conceal some corruption: τήνδ' ought possibly to be τήνδε τ' (which is preferable to τήνδε γ' here), followed by ἀλίπαρον (cr. n.), 'not sleek or glossy,' as with unguents. I incline to this view. The genuine word was in any case probably *negative*, parallel with οὐ χλιδαῖς ἠσκημένον in 452.

(2) Or else, if the text be sound, ἀλιπαρῆ may mean οὐ λιπαράν. There is no doubt that λιπ, 'fat,' is the root both of λιπαρός, 'shining,' and of λιπαρής, 'sticking.' It is barely possible that, in coining a new negative compound, the poet may have transferred the sense of λιπαρός to λιπαρής: but it seems improbable.

452 ζῶμα here = ζώνην, a sense which recurs only in later

Greek; as in *Anth Pal*. 6. 272 a woman dedicates her ζῶμα to
Artemis.—χλιδαῖς (cp. 52, 360), such as embroidery, or metal
work. ζῶναι were often elaborate and costly.—The ζῶμα is to
be laid on the grave, as ribands etc. sometimes were: cp.
schol. Ar. *Lys*. 603 τὰς ταινίας ἃς τοῖς νεκροῖς ἔπεμπον οἱ φίλοι.

453 f. προσπίτνουσα, at the tomb.—αὐτὸν, 'himself' (rather
than merely 'him'), as the next verse shows.

455 f. ἐξ ὑπερτέρας χερός : ἐκ expresses the condition : cp.
Tr. 875 ἐξ ἀκινήτου ποδός.—ζῶντ', instead of dying first, as his
foes hope. The thought is, 'may he live to do it.'

457 f. ἀφνεωτέραις. ἀφνεός is used by Pindar, Theognis,
and Aesch. (though only in lyrics, *Pers*. 3 and fr. 96): ἀφνειός
is the only Homeric form.—στέφωμεν : cp. 53, 441.

459 οἶμαι μὲν οὖν : 'Now (οὖν) I *think* (οἶμαι μὲν) that our
father is already aiding us of his own accord; but still (ὅμως δέ,
461) pray for his help.'   Here the particles μὲν οὖν have each
their separate force, as in *O. T*. 483, *O. C*. 664, *Ant*. 65 : not
their compound force, 'nay rather' (1503).

If μέλον be kept, we must supply ἦν, and take οἶμαι as
parenthetic. This is possible, but harsh. Probably μέλειν
(Nauck and Blaydes) was corrupted to μέλον through a mis-
understanding of the construction. The sense is, νομίζω ὅτι
καὶ ἐκείνῳ ἔμελέ τι (adv., 'in some degree') πέμψαι κ.τ.λ. She
means that, though the *gods* below are the primary authors of
the vision, the spirit of the dead was also in some measure
active.

461 σοί = σεαυτῇ : cp. 363 (ἐμέ = ἐμαυτήν), n.

462 βροτῶν : cp. 407 n.

464 πρὸς εὐσέβειαν = εὐσεβῶς : cp. 369 πρὸς ὀργὴν (n.).

466 f. δράσω. Chrysothemis here accepts the lock of hair
and the girdle which Electra offers to her.   We must suppose
that, after leaving the scene, she puts Clytaemnestra's gifts
somewhere out of sight.

τὸ γὰρ δίκαιον κ.τ.λ.   The sense is, 'When a duty has once
become clear, there is no more room for disputing,—one should
act forthwith.'   Two constructions are possible; I prefer the
first.

(1)   τὸ δίκαιον is an acc. of general reference, and οὐκ ἔχει
λόγον is impersonal.   'With regard to what is (clearly) right, it
is unreasonable for two persons to dispute ; rather both should
hasten on the doing (of it).'   With ἀλλ' ἐπισπεύδειν we supply
the notion δεῖ from the negative οὐκ ἔχει λόγον (as from οὐκ

ἔξεστι in *O. C.* 1402 ff.; cp. *O. T.* 817 ff.). For the form of the sentence, cp. Xen. *H.* 7. 3. 7 τοὺς περὶ Ἀρχίαν...οὐ ψῆφον ἀνεμείνατε, ἀλλὰ ὁπότε πρῶτον ἐδυνάσθητε ἐτιμωρήσασθε. So here the acc. τὸ δίκαιον, which represents the object of δρᾶν, is separated from it by the parenthesis οὐκ ἔχει λόγον δυοῖν ἐρίζειν.

(2) Or τὸ δίκαιον might be nom.: 'that which is clearly right does not *afford any ground* (οὐκ ἔχει λόγον) for two persons to dispute,' etc. So far as the verb ἔχει is concerned, this sense is quite admissible: cp. Thuc. 2. 41 οὔτε τῷ πολεμίῳ ἐπελθόντι ἀγανάκτησιν ἔχει (ἡ πόλις). The objection is that the phrases ἔχειν λόγον, οὐκ ἔχειν λόγον, which are very common, regularly mean, 'to be reasonable,' 'to be unreasonable.'

469 **παρ' ὑμῶν**, on your part: cp. *Tr.* 596 μόνον παρ' ὑμῶν εὖ στεγοίμεθ'.

470 f. **πικρὰν**, to my cost: Eur. *Bacch.* 356 ὡς ἂν λευσίμου δίκης τυχὼν | θάνῃ, πικρὰν βάκχευσιν ἐν Θήβαις ἰδών. *I. A.* 1315 πικράν, | πικρὰν ἰδοῦσα δυσελέναν.—For **δοκῶ με...τολμήσειν**, cp. *Tr.* 706 ὁρῶ δέ μ' ἔργον δεινὸν ἐξειργασμένην.—For **ἔτι**, cp. 66. Exit Chrysothemis.

472—515 First στάσιμον. Strophe, 472—487=antistrophe, 488—503: epode, 504—515. For the metres see Metrical Analysis.

Encouraged by the tidings of Clytaemnestra's dream, the Chorus predict an early retribution on the murderers.

473 **γνώμας λειπομένα**, *failing in* it: cp. *Tr.* 936 οὔτ' ὀδυρμάτων | ἐλείπετ' οὐδέν.

475 f. **ἁ πρόμαντις Δίκα**, because she has sent the dream, a presage of her own advent. The fact that μάντις has just preceded gives no ground for suspecting πρόμαντις: cp. 163 (γᾶν after γᾶ) n. For Δίκη as an avenging power, cp. 528: *Ai.* 1390 μνήμων τ' Ἐρινὺς καὶ τελεσφόρος Δίκη.

δίκαια φερομένα χεροῖν κράτη. The goddess Justice is here conceived as being in her person the victorious avenger. The words mean literally, 'bearing away just triumphs of prowess.' Cp. *Il.* 13. 486 αἶψά κεν ἠὲ φέροιτο μέγα κράτος ἠὲ φεροίμην: for the plur. κράτη, Aesch. *Suppl.* 951 εἴη δὲ νίκη καὶ κράτη τοῖς ἄρσεσι: and for χεροῖν κράτη, above, v. 37 χειρὸς ἐνδίκους σφαγάς.—Others render: 'carrying just victory *in her hands.*' But the picture thus given seems less clear and strong.

477 **μέτεισιν**, will come in pursuit (of the guilty): Aesch. *Cho.* 273 εἰ μὴ μέτειμι τοῦ πατρὸς τοὺς αἰτίους.—**οὐ μακροῦ χρόνου**: cp. *O. C.* 397 ἥξοντα βαιοῦ κοὐχὶ μυρίου χρόνου.

479 ff. ὕπεστί μοι θάρσος is followed by κλύουσαν as if ὑφέρπει or ὑπῆλθέ με had preceded. Cp. Aesch. *Pers.* 913 λέλυται γὰρ ἐμοὶ γυίων ῥώμη | τήνδ᾽ ἡλικίαν ἐσιδόντ᾽ ἀστῶν: *Cho.* 410 πέπαλται δ᾽ αὖτέ μοι φίλον κέαρ | τόνδε κλύουσαν οἶκτον.

ἀδυπνόων...ὀνειράτων: cp. the invocation of Sleep, *Ph.* 828, εὐαὲς ἡμῖν ἔλθοις.

482 ἀμναστεῖ γ᾽ ὁ φύσας σ᾽. The pronoun σε is indispensable here, and could have easily fallen out after φύσας. To add it there is better than to read ἀμναστεῖ σ᾽ ὁ φύσας: for the γε after the verb, marking assurance, is expressive.

484 f. χαλκόπλακτος, act., 'striking with bronze'; cp. *Ph.* 688 ἀμφιπλάκτων ῥοθίων, 'billows that beat around him.'—γένυς: cp. 159 γενύων (n.).

The very axe (φόνιος πέλεκυς, 99) with which the blow was dealt is imagined as nourishing a grudge against the murderers who had set it such a task.

487 ἐν αἰκίαις: ἐν denotes the manner; cp. *O. C.* 1682 ἐν ἀφανεῖ τινι μόρῳ φερόμενον. The penultimate of αἰκία is always long.

488 f. καὶ πολύπους καὶ πολύχειρ: as with the might of a resistless host. Cp. 36.

490 f. λόχοις: cp. *Ant.* 1074 τούτων σε λωβητῆρες ὑστερο-φθόροι | λοχῶσιν Ἅιδου καὶ θεῶν Ἐρινύες.—χαλκόπους: so *O. T.* 418 δεινόπους ἀρά.

492 ff. ἄλεκτρ᾽ ἄνυμφα: cp. 1154 ἀμήτωρ: *O. T.* 1214 ἄγαμον γάμον. The epithets, which properly describe the γάμοι, are given to the whole phrase: cp. 1290: 1390: *Ant.* 794 νεῖκος ἀνδρῶν ξύναιμον.—γάμων ἁμιλλήμαθ᾽, eager haste for marriage; the plur. is fitting, since both the partners in guilt were striving for that goal.—ἐπέβα, like ἐπέπεσε, suggesting the violence of the passion which seized them.—οἷσιν: constr. γάμους ἐκείνων (= πρὸς ἐκείνους) οἷσιν οὐ θέμις γάμους συνάπτειν.

495—498 πρὸ τῶνδέ τοι...συνδρῶσιν: 'therefore I am confident that we shall never see (ἡμῖν, ethic dat.) the portent draw near to the murderess and her accomplice without giving them cause to complain of it';—*i.e.*, 'we shall assuredly find that the dream has been an omen of their ruin.'

Verses 495—497 (πρὸ τῶνδέ τοι...τέρας) answer metrically to vv. 479—481 ὕπεστί μοι...ὀνειράτων, where the text is certain, save for the doubt whether θράσος or θάρσος should stand in 479. Here we must first decide two points.

(1) Are the words πρὸ τῶνδε sound? I think so. The sense is, '*for* (= on account of) these things.' This is a rare, but not unexampled, sense of πρό, in which the notions 'before' and 'by reason of' were associated, just as in Lat. *prae* and our own 'for.' See *Il.* 17. 666 μή μιν Ἀχαιοὶ | ἀργαλέου πρὸ φόβοιο ἕλωρ δηίοισι λίποιεν, = *prae timore*, '*for* fear.' *Tr.* 505 κατέβαν πρὸ γάμων, 'entered the contest *for* the marriage.'

(2) Could ἔχει με, μήποτε τέρας πελᾶν (etc.) mean, '*the belief* possesses me, that' etc.? Surely not. No real parallel for so strange a phrase has been produced. Either, then, the subject to ἔχει has dropped out, or the words μ' ἔχει conceal a corruption.

The following remedies are possible: I incline to the first, as involving least change. (1) Reading in 479 ὕπεστί μοι θράσος, we may read here πρὸ τῶνδέ τοί μ' ἔχει | < θάρσος τι >, μήποθ' ἡμῖν etc. (2) Or, reading in 479 ὕπεστί μοι θάρσος, we could read here πρὸ τῶνδέ τοι θάρσος ἴσχει με.

In those MSS. which have μή ποτε μή ποθ' ἡμῖν, the first μήποτε (absent from L) was probably an attempt to fill the gap.

497 ἀψεγές: schol. θαρρῶ ὅτι τοῖς δρῶσι ταῦτα τὰ ἄδικα καὶ συνδρῶσιν αὐτοῖς οὐκ ἔσται ἄψεκτος ὁ ὄνειρος· παθόντες γὰρ ψέξουσι τὸ ὀφθέν.

πελᾶν, 'Attic' fut. inf. of πελάζω: cp. *O. C.* 1060 πελῶσ': Aesch. *P. V.* 282 πελῶ.

498 τοῖς δρῶσι, Clytaemnestra, to whom the dream came: τοῖς συνδρῶσιν, Aegisthus (cp. 97 ff.): for the plur. cp. 146 (γονέων), n.

499 μαντεῖαι βροτῶν, means of divination for men.

503 εὖ κατασχήσει, come safely into harbour,—as a seafarer was said κατέχειν εἰς γῆν (*Ph.* 221). Cp. *Tr.* 826 (of oracles) καὶ τάδ' ὀρθῶς | ἔμπεδα κατουρίζει.

505 ἱππεία here = driving of horses, like ἱπποσύνη (*Il.* 4. 303 etc.); a word used by Eur. *H. F.* 374 with ref. to the raids of Centaurs (χθόνα Θεσσαλῶν ἱππείαις ἐδάμαζον).

Oenomaüs, king of Pisa in Elis, had promised the hand of his daughter Hippodameia to the suitor who should defeat him in a chariot-race; the penalty of failure being death. The young Pelops, son of Tantalus, offered himself as a competitor. Myrtilus, the charioteer of Oenomaüs, was persuaded (either by Hippodameia or by Pelops) to betray his master. So Pelops won the race, and the bride. But Oenomaüs was soon avenged on the traitor; for Myrtilus insulted Hippodameia, and was thrown into the sea by Pelops; upon whose house he invoked a curse, as he sank.

In the older and nobler form of the myth, Pelops won, not by a fraud, but by the grace of Poseidon, who gave him winged horses (Pindar *O.* 1. 87 ἔδωκεν δίφρον τε χρύσεον πτεροῖσίν τ' ἀκάμαντας ἵππους).

506 αἰανὴς suits the idea of *persistent* calamity. Whatever its real etymology, it was associated with ἀεί (Aesch. *Eum.* 572 ἐς τὸν αἰανῆ χρόνον, *ib.* 672 αἰανῶς μένοι), and was used to denote that which pains by wearying, or wearing (as Pind. *P.* 1. 82 κόρος...αἰανής: *I.* 1. 49 λιμὸν αἰανῆ).

The form αἰανὴς has the best authority, and some critics hold that αἰανὸς (Hesych.) was a Byzantine invention. But in Aesch. *Eum.* 416, ἡμεῖς γάρ ἐσμεν νυκτὸς αἰανῆς τέκνα, αἰανῆ is far less suitable.

508 f. εὖτε, 'since,'= ἐξ οὗ, like ὅτε (Thuc. 1. 13 ἔτη δ' ἐστὶ μάλιστα τριακόσια...ὅτε Ἀμεινοκλῆς Σαμίοις ἦλθε).

ὁ ποντισθεὶς Μυρτίλος. The legendary scene was at Geraestus (now Cape Mandelo), the s. promontory of Euboea.

ἐκοιμάθη: cp. *Ai.* 831 καλῶ θ' ἅμα | πομπαῖον Ἑρμῆν χθόνιον εὖ με κοιμίσαι.

510 ff. παγχρυσέων δίφρων, the golden chariot given to Pelops by Poseidon: see Pind. *O.* 1. 87, in n. on 505. This plur. (750), as denoting *one* chariot (like ὄχεα, ἅρματα), is not Homeric. παγχρυσέων (– – ᴗ –), the epic form, suits the metre here. Cp. *Tr.* 1099 χρυσέων (– ᴗ –).—**πρόρριζος** here = πανώλεθρος, as in Ar. *Ran.* 587 πρόρριζος αὐτός, ἡ γυνή, τὰ παιδία, | κάκιστ' ἀπολοίμην.

514 ἔλειπεν (cr. n.) is confirmed by metre, since every other v. of this epode has anacrusis, which ἔλιπεν would exclude. For the intrans. λείπω, cp. Eur. *H. F.* 133 τὸ δὲ κακοτυχὲς οὐ λέλοιπεν ἐκ τέκνων: *Helen.* 1156 οὔποτ' ἔρις | λείψει κατ' ἀνθρώπων πόλεις. And ἔλειπεν in turn confirms οἴκου as against οἴκους. For πω suits the imperf. in this sense ('was never yet absent from the house'), but would require the aor. if the sense were, 'has never yet left the house.' For the sing. οἴκου (=family), cp. 978.

516—1057 This second ἐπεισόδιον comprises four scenes. (1) 516—659. Electra and Clytaemnestra. (2) 660—803. The disguised Paedagogus enters, and relates to Clytaemnestra the death of Orestes. She presently goes with him into the house. (3) 804—870. Electra and the Chorus. (4) 871—

1057. Chrysothemis re-enters, and tells what she has seen at the grave. Electra speaks with her of a new resolve.

516 Clytaemnestra enters from within. ἀνειμένη is emphasised by μέν, which has no corresponding δέ: the implied antithesis is, ἐπέχειν δέ σε ἐγὼ μόνη οὐ δύναμαι (519 f.). Cp. *Ant.* 578 ἐκ δὲ τοῦδε χρὴ | γυναῖκας εἶναι τάσδε μηδ᾽ ἀνειμένας.— ὡς ἔοικας: *Tr.* 1241.

στρέφει, *versaris*, go about (instead of remaining in the seclusion of the γυναικωνῖτις): cp. Xen. *H.* 6. 4. 16 ἐν τῷ φανερῷ ἀναστρεφομένους. *Tr.* 907 ἄλλῃ δὲ κἄλλῃ δωμάτων στρωφωμένη. The simple στρέφομαι is very rarely so used; but cp. Solon fr. 4. 23 ταῦτα μὲν ἐν δήμῳ στρέφεται κακά.

Clytaemnestra begins in the same strain as Chrysothemis, who likewise emphasised her reproof by the word αὖ (328).

518 μή τοι θυραίαν γ᾽: τοι (Lat. *sane*) here limits with an ironical force, while γε lays stress on the adj.—αἰσχύνειν φίλους: said from an Athenian point of view. The Homeric maiden of noble birth, such as Nausicaa, has more freedom.

520 ff. καίτοι: you disregard my authority, *and yet* complain of it as oppressive.—δή goes with πολλούς: cp. 202 ἐχθίστα δή (n.).—ἐξεῖπάς με...ὡς: cp. 332 n.

θρασεῖα, 'insolent': cp. Plat. *Legg.* 630 B θρασεῖς καὶ ἄδικοι καὶ ὑβρισταί. Eur. *I. T.* 275 ἀνομίᾳ θρασύς.—ἄρχω, 'rule': it should not be taken with the partic., as = 'provoke with insult' (552). Cp. 264 κἀκ τῶνδ᾽ ἄρχομαι: 597 δεσπότιν.

523 f. ὕβριν...οὐκ ἔχω: cp. *Ant.* 300 πανουργίας...ἔχειν. In the next clause, κακῶς κλύουσα, etc., are the emphatic words: 'Insolent I am not; my words to you are only such as you address to me.'

525 f. πατὴρ γάρ κ.τ.λ. A comma should follow ἄλλο, since τέθνηκεν depends on πρόσχημά σοί (ἐστιν) ὡς: cp. Her. 7. 157 πρόσχημα μὲν ποιεύμενος ὡς ἐπ᾽ Ἀθήνας ἐλαύνει.—πρόσχημα here = σκῆψις, πρόφασις. Cp. 682.

528 ἡ γὰρ Δίκη. The γάρ is right. 'He certainly died, and by my hand; *for* Justice, whose instrument I was, required his death.' As to Δίκη the avenger, cp. 475 f. (n.).

529 ᾗ χρῆν σ᾽ ἀρήγειν κ.τ.λ. The in.. represents the apodosis; *i.e.*, 'It was your duty *to help*,' implies, 'you would have helped,' ἀρωγὸς ἂν ἦσθα. Cp. Eur. *Med.* 586 χρῆν σ᾽, εἴπερ ἦσθα μὴ κακός, πείσαντ᾽ ἐμὲ | γαμεῖν γάμον τόνδ᾽ (*i.e.*, πείσας ἂν ἐγάμεις). Lys. or. 32 § 23 εἰ ἐβούλετο δίκαιος εἶναι,... ἐξῆν αὐτῷ...μισθῶσαι τὸν οἶκον (*i.e.*, ἐμίσθωσεν ἄν).

530 The order of words in the MSS., ἐπεὶ πατὴρ οὗτος σός, is probably right; the words would then fall from her with a certain deliberate bitterness.

531 μοῦνος Ἑλλήνων. He of all men—the father of the maiden—was the one who resolved on sacrificing her. The sacrifice was, indeed, approved by the other chiefs (Aesch. *Ag.* 230 φιλόμαχοι βραβῆς); and several persons took part in the deed itself (*ib.* 240 ἕκαστον θυτήρων). But, in the first instance, when Calchas spoke, the decision rested with Agamemnon. Sophocles, like Aeschylus, ignores the legend used by Euripides, that Iphigeneia was not really slain at Aulis, but wafted by Artemis to the Tauric Chersonese.

532 f. The regular mode of expression would be, οὐκ ἴσον λύπης καμὼν ἐμοί, ὁ σπείρας τῇ τικτούσῃ. But, having written ὅτ᾽ ἔσπειρε, the poet explains ἐμοί by repeating the comparison in a new form, ὥσπερ ἡ τίκτουσ᾽ ἐγώ. (For ὡς or ὥσπερ after ἴσος, cp. Lys. or. 19 § 36 ἡγοῦντο...τὰ ἐκεῖ...εἶναι ἴσα ὥσπερ τὰ ἐνθάδε.)

534 τοῦ χάριν, τίνων: τοῦ (neut.) χάριν, 'wherefore?' (as in *Ph.* 1029, τί μ᾽ ἀπάγεσθε; τοῦ χάριν;): τίνων (masc.) χάριν; 'for the sake of what men?' 'Wherefore—to please *whom*—did he immolate her?' This is the only construction of the words which fits Ἀργείων in 535. The twofold question also suits the vehemence of the speaker, who is seeking to drive the point home.

The alternative, which most editors have preferred, is to take τίνων as the participle. But there is an insuperable objection to this. The words, τοῦ χάριν τίνων; could mean only, 'paying a debt of gratitude *for what?*' They could not mean, 'paying a debt of gratitude *to whom?*' The latter would be τῷ χάριν τίνων; Hence the question, τοῦ χάριν τίνων; could not possibly be answered by Ἀργείων.

536 ἀλλ᾽ οὐ μετῆν κ.τ.λ.: cp. *Ant.* 48 ἀλλ᾽ οὐδὲν αὐτῷ τῶν ἐμῶν μ᾽ εἴργειν μέτα (= μέτεστι).

537 f. ἀλλ᾽ ἀντ᾽ ἀδελφοῦ δῆτα. Here the first supposition is introduced by πότερον, and the second by ἀλλὰ δῆτα, as in *Ai.* 460—466. ἀλλά was regularly used in thus putting the imagined arguments of an adversary. In this verse, ἀλλά introduces both the supposed argument and the reply, since κτανών = εἰ ἔκτανεν (as = 'granting that he slew'). Cp. Andoc. or. 1. § 148 τίνα γὰρ καὶ ἀναβιβάσομαι δεησόμενον ὑπὲρ ἐμαυτοῦ; τὸν πατέρα; ἀλλὰ τέθνηκεν. ἀλλὰ τοὺς ἀδελφούς; ἀλλ᾽ οὐκ εἰσίν. ἀλλὰ τοὺς παῖδας; ἀλλ᾽ οὔπω γεγένηνται.

ἀντὶ ἀδελφοῦ here = 'in his stead,' *i.e.*, 'to save him from slaying *his* child ': not, 'for his sake.' Nor is it short for ἀντὶ [τῶν τοῦ] ἀδελφοῦ.—τάμ' : for the neut. referring to persons, cp. 972 : *O. T.* 1195.

539 παῖδες...διπλοῖ. The schol. observes that, according to Homer, Helen bore to Menelaüs only a daughter Hermionè (*Od.* 4. 14,—indicated, though not named, in *Il.* 3. 175); but that Hesiod mentioned also a son (fr. 131): ἣ τέκεθ' Ἑρμιόνην δουρικλειτῷ Μενελάῳ, | ὁπλότατον δ' ἔτεκεν Νικόστρατον, ὄζον Ἄρηος. Sophocles follows Hesiod, since Menelaüs could not have been expected to sacrifice an only child.

542 f. ἢ here introduces a third supposition (cp. 530), and in 544 a fourth.—ἢ τῶν ἐμῶν Ἅιδης: the absence of caesura gives a harsh emphasis to the words ; cp. 530.

δαίσασθαι, *sc.* αὐτά (fr. 731 ὠμόβρως ἐδαίσατο | τὸν Ἀστάκειον παῖδα): epexegetic inf.: cp. 1277 : Eur. *Med.* 1399 φιλίου χρῄζω στόματος | παίδων ὁ τάλας προσπτύξασθαι (*sc.* αὐτό, cp. *Phoen.* 1671): Plat. *Crito* 52 B οὐδ' ἐπιθυμία σε ἄλλης πόλεως οὐδ' ἄλλων νόμων ἔλαβεν εἰδέναι.—The destroying gods, such as Ares (*Il.* 5. 289) and Thanatos (Eur. *Alc.* 844), were supposed to rejoice, like the dead (*Od.* 11. 96, Eur. *Hec.* 536), in draughts of blood.

544 f. πανώλει expresses intense hatred, as in *Ph.* 1357 Odysseus is τῷ πανώλει παιδὶ τῷ Λαερτίου.—παρεῖτο, lit., 'had been neglected,'—allowed to pass out of his thoughts. This plpf. (identical in form with the 2nd aor.) is somewhat rare.

The sense does not absolutely require us to take Μενέλεω δ' as = τῶν δὲ Μενέλεω (παίδων); but that is clearly what is meant.

546 ἀβούλου, inconsiderate,—not taking proper thought for his children ; cp. *Tr.* 139 τίς ὧδε | τέκνοισι Ζῆν' ἄβουλον εἶδεν;—κακοῦ γνώμην, perverse,—in choosing to sacrifice his own offspring, rather than another's. There is a bitter irony in this mode of characterising what she regards as unnatural cruelty.

547 δοκῶ μέν : 61 n.—εἰ καί, though (as is the case): cp. *O. T.* 408 εἰ καὶ τυραννεῖς.

548 εἰ φωνὴν λάβοι: cp. Aesch. *Ag.* 37 (οἶκος) εἰ φθογγὴν λάβοι. In the *Odyssey* the departed spirits are conceived unable to recognise or to accost the living, until they have tasted the offerings of blood (11. 153).

549 τοῖς πεπραγμένοις, causal dat.; cp. Thuc. 3. 98 τοῖς πεπραγμένοις φοβούμενος τοὺς Ἀθηναίους : *Tr.* 1127.

551 γνώμην δικαίαν σχοῦσα κ.τ.λ. : first attain to a just view of the matter, and then, but not sooner, blame thy neighbours. Schol. : οἶον λογισμῷ χρησαμένη δικαίῳ τότε [= εἶτα] τοὺς πέλας ψέγε ἡμᾶς. The usual sense of the aor. ἔσχον ('came to have,' 'acquired') is a reason for taking the words thus, rather than as referring to the subject of δοκῶ, 'though I have held a just view'; in the latter case, we should have expected ἔχουσα.

552 f. ἐρεῖς μὲν οὐχὶ κ.τ.λ. The antithesis implied by μὲν is given by vv. 554 f. : 'I have not, indeed, provoked this discussion; still, I should like to speak.' For ἐρεῖς preceding the negative, cp. *Ant.* 223 ἄναξ, ἐρῶ μὲν οὐχ κ.τ.λ. For the constr., ἐρεῖς...μ' ὡς, cp. 520.

ἄρξασά τι λυπηρὸν : cp. fr. 339 ἄρξασι Φρυξὶ τὴν κατ' Ἀργείων ὕβριν.—τάδ' ἐξήκουσ', alluding to the reproaches in vv. 518, 529, etc. Cp. *Ph.* 378 δηχθεὶς πρὸς ἀξήκουσεν, 'stung by the abuse.'

554 f. τοῦ τεθνηκότος θ' ὕπερ. She will speak justly in the cause of both. The pathos of Iphigeneia's death is not diminished, but enhanced, if Agamemnon acted against his own will.

556 f. καὶ μὴν, lit., 'and verily,'—expressing assent to the request : cp. *Ant.* 221.—λόγους ἐξῆρχές με = προσεφώνεις με : cp. 123 ff. τάκεις...οἴμωγὰν...Ἀγαμέμνονα : *O. C.* 1120 τέκνα... μηκύνω λόγον (speak at length to my children). ἐξάρχω was said esp. of beginning a musical strain. Here it perhaps suggests the same idea, with a tinge of irony : 'if you always began in such a key,'—viz., of filial deference.

558—609 Clytaemnestra has argued that she was justified in slaying Agamemnon, because he had slain Iphigeneia. The topics of Electra's reply are as follows.

(1) 558—562. The wife who slew her husband would be a criminal, even if the motive had been just retribution; but the real motive was her love for Aegisthus. (2) 563—576. Agamemnon was not a free agent in slaying Iphigeneia; the act was forced upon him by Artemis. (3) 577—583. Suppose, however, that he was a free agent, and wished to please his brother; still she was not justified in taking his life. (4) 584—594. And in any case her plea does not excuse her for living with the man who helped to slay her husband.—The speech then closes in a strain of reproach and defiance (595—609).

558 f. καὶ δὴ λέγω σοι: the same formula as in 892 and *Ant.* 245,—καὶ δὴ expressing prompt compliance. The sense of πατέρα is relative to the speaker, and not (as would be more natural) to the subject of φῂς.—For the doubled ἄν, cp. 333 f.

560 εἴτ’ οὖν...εἴτε: cp. 199. We supply ἔκτεινας: cp. Aesch. *Eum.* 468 σὺ δ’, εἰ δικαίως εἴτε μή, κρῖνον δίκην, where ἔκτεινα is understood from v. 463.—λέξω: the fut. here implies the sense of a task from which the speaker will not shrink; ‘I have to tell thee.’

561 f. ὡς οὐ δίκη γ’: γε, emphasising δίκη, is suitable here, since δικαίως (560) expressed the first of two alternatives. For the omission of the object to ἔκτεινας, cp. *Ph.* 801 (ἔμπρησον).— ἔστασεν, a stronger word than εἷλκυσε: cp. *Ant.* 791 (of Erôs) σὺ καὶ δικαίων ἀδίκους φρένας παρασπᾷς ἐπὶ λώβᾳ.—πειθὼ: cp. *Od.* 3. 264 (Aegisthus) πόλλ’ Ἀγαμεμνονέην ἄλοχον θέλγεσκ’ ἐπέεσσιν.

563 f. κυναγὸν: the Doric form, as in λοχαγός, ὁδαγός, etc. (*Ant.* 715): but κυνηγετεῖν (*Ai.* 5), κυνηγία, κυνηγέτης.— ποινὰς, acc. in appos. with the sentence; cp. 129 n., Aesch. *P. V.* 563 τίνος ἀμπλακίας ποινὰς ὀλέκεις;

τὰ πολλὰ πνεύματ’ ἔσχ’, ‘she stayed those frequent winds,’ which ordinarily blow from the coast of Greece,—causing a calm of unusual length. For τὰ πολλά, cp. 931 : *O. C.* 87 τὰ πόλλ’ ἐκεῖν’ ὅτ’ ἐξέχρη κακά. For ἔσχε as = ‘stopped,’ cp. *O. C.* 888 βουθυτοῦντά μ’...ἔσχετ’.

Acc. to Aesch. (*Ag.* 149 f., 192), the Greeks were detained by *adverse winds*, blowing from the N.E.: and this seems to have been the account given in the *Cypria* (*c.* 776 B.C.). But other authorities speak of a *calm*.

It has been objected that vessels provided with oars need not have been detained by a calm. But the ships of the Greek fleet were not light craft, and it is intelligible that they should await the aid of wind before attempting the passage of the Aegaean. We must remember, too, the strong and shifting currents in the Euripus.

Αὐλίδι. Aulis was so named from the channel (αὐλός), as other towns were named from αὐλών ‘a valley.’ It stood on the Boeotian coast, in the territory of Tanagra, about three miles S. of the point where, at Chalcis in Euboea, the Euripus is narrowest.

565 ἢ ’γὼ φράσω, a self-correction, as in 352 ἢ μάθ’ ἐξ

ἐμοῦ. It is not θέμις for a mortal to cross-question a goddess face to face.—For the simple gen. κείνης, cp. 668: *Ph.* 370 μαθεῖν ἐμοῦ.

566 f. ὡς ἐγὼ κλύω : implying the possibility of other accounts. Aeschylus does not define the offence which had angered Artemis (*Ag.* 132). According to Euripides, Agamemnon had rashly vowed that he would sacrifice to her the fairest creature that the year should bring forth (*I. T.* 20).

θεᾶς...κατ' ἄλσος, a sacred precinct near the temple of Artemis at Aulis, mentioned in Eur. *I. A.* 1544, Ἀρτέμιδος ἄλσος λείμακάς τ' ἀνθεσφόρους, and called πολύθυτον, *ib.* 185. At many places on the eastern coasts of Greece Artemis was worshipped, esp. as λιμενοσκόπος.

παίζων, 'amusing himself,' 'taking his pleasure.' The allusion is to the pursuit of game, though παίζω had no definitely technical sense like that of our word 'sport.'

ποδοῖν : *i.e.*, by the sound of his feet ; not by their touch.

568 ἔλαφον, 'a stag.' The word can also mean 'a hind,' as in fr. 86 κερούσσα...ἔλαφος.—στικτὸν (*Ph.* 184) = βαλιόν : Eur. *Bacch.* 111 στικτῶν...νεβρίδων.—κεράστην: cp. the Homeric ἔλαφον κεραόν (*Il.* 3. 24, etc.).

οὗ κατὰ σφαγὰς, *concerning* the slaughter of it : cp. Her. 1. 31 τὰ κατὰ τὸν Τέλλον...εἴπας : *id.* 2. 3 κατὰ μὲν δὴ τὴν τροφὴν τῶν παιδίων τοσαῦτα ἔλεγον. Others understand (less well, I think), '*on the occasion of* the slaughter.'

569 ἐκκομπάσας ἔπος τι τυγχάνει, 'he chanced to utter a certain (irreverent) boast,' βαλών, 'after hitting' (with an arrow, or perh. with a javelin). ἔπος τι is euphemistic : cp. Hyginus *Fab.* 98 *superbiusque in Dianam locutus est.* The vaunt would naturally follow, not precede, the hit.

This is the reason against taking τυγχάνει with βαλών, as = 'he shoots and hits.'

Others take βαλὼν with ἔπος : 'he chanced to *let fall* some boastful word.' But (1) βάλλειν ἔπος does not seem to occur : (2) ἐκκομπάσας, combined with βαλών in this sense, would be awkwardly redundant.

570 ἐκ τοῦδε, *idcirco.*—μηνίσασα, of divine wrath, as in *O. C.* 965, *Tr.* 274 : and so μῆνις, *Ai.* 656, 757.—Λητῷα κόρη : cp. *O. T.* 267 τῷ Λαβδακείῳ παιδί.

571 f. ὡς : the will of the goddess was interpreted by Calchas.—ἀντίσταθμον, = ἀντίρροπον, 'in compensation for.'— ἐκθύσεις. The midd. ἐκθύεσθαι is to *expiate* (ἄγος), or to *propitiate* (θεόν). But the act. ἐκθύειν is merely a strengthened θύειν, 'to make a sacrifice of,' implying some cruelty or violence: Eur. *Cyc.* 371 ἐφεστίους ἱκτῆρας ἐκθύεις δόμων.

573 f. ὦδ' ἦν, instead of ὦδ' εἶχε or τοιαῦτα ἦν. When an adv. is joined with εἶναι, the verb is more often impers., as in εὖ γὰρ ἔσται (Eur. *Med.* 89).—τὰ...θύματ': for the poet. pl., cp. *Tr.* 627 τὰ τῆς ξένης... | προσδέγματ'.—λύσις, 'release' from the detention at Aulis.

πρὸς οἶκον. The weather, which stopped the voyage to Troy, would also hinder some of the islanders from going home; but most of the allies from the mainland could have reached their respective ports with less difficulty; and we can only suppose that Calchas threatened them with the wrath of Artemis.

575 πολλὰ goes with both participles.—ἀντιβὰς: cp. Her. 6. 73 (οὐκ) ἐδικαίευν ἔτι ἀντιβαίνειν. Verg. *Geo.* 4. 301 *Multa reluctanti.*—μόλις, *aegre*: *Ant.* 1105 μόλις μέν, καρδίας δ' ἐξίσταμαι.

577 εἰ δ' οὖν, ' but if it *was* with the wish,' etc.,—referring to Clytaemnestra's words in 537 ff. Cp. Aesch. *Ag.* 1042 εἰ δ' οὖν ἀνάγκη τῆσδ' ἐπιρρέποι τύχης ('but if the doom of slavery *should* befall ').—ἐρῶ γὰρ καὶ τὸ σόν, 'for I will state thy plea (537 ff.) also': cp. *Tr.* 479 δεῖ γὰρ καὶ τὸ πρὸς κείνου λέγειν.

578 f. τούτου...οὕνεκ': for the large interval between the case and this prep., cp. *O. T.* 857 f.—νόμῳ, ' rule,' ' principle '; *Ant.* 908, *Tr.* 616.

580 f. ὅρα...μὴ...τιθῆς. The subjunctive here is supported by our best MS., L, while in 584 it has τίθησ. In 584 τίθης is clearly right: 'see that you *are not* making a false excuse' (she is actually making it). Cp. Plat. *Theaet.* 145 C ὅρα μὴ παίζων ἔλεγεν.

Here, either τίθης or τιθῆς would be suitable. (1) With τίθης:—'See that, in making this rule, you *are not* making woe for yourself.' This means that to make the rule (as she is doing) is at once (logically) to make the woe. (2) With τιθῆς: —' See *lest*, in making this rule, you *make* woe for yourself': *i.e.*, the rule may have the woe as a consequence. The woe is a future contingency (583 εἰ δίκης γε τυγχάνοις), against which Electra warns her.

τιθεῖσα...νόμον: cp. Eur. *Alc.* 57 πρὸς τῶν ἐχόντων, Φοῖβε, τὸν νόμον τίθης.

582 f. **εἰ γὰρ κτενοῦμεν.** Note two points of syntax here. (1) We have two protases, not co-ordinate: the first of them, **εἰ κτενοῦμεν**, states the primary condition, on which everything else depends. '*If* that is to be the rule,—*then* (*if* you got your due) you would die.' Cp. *Ai.* 782 f. : Eur. *Suppl.* 1084 **εἰ δ' ἦμεν νέοι | δὶς καὶ γέροντες, εἴ τις ἐξημάρτανε, | διπλοῦ βίου λαχόντες ἐξωρθούμεθ' ἄν.** (2) The first protasis has the fut. indic. : the second protasis and the apodosis have the optat. with **ἄν**, not as a softened future, but in a potential sense. Cp. Thuc. I. 142 **φρούριον δ' εἰ ποιήσονται, τῆς μὲν γῆς βλάπτοιεν ἄν τι μέρος.**

πρώτη : *i.e.*, no one has more fully deserved the penalty.

584 f. **εἰσόρα**, instead of **ὅρα** : cp. 611, 997.—**οὐκ οὖσαν**, = **ψευδῆ**, unreal, false : cp. Ar. *Ran.* 1052 ΕΥ. **πότερον δ' οὐκ ὄντα λόγον τοῦτον περὶ τῆς Φαίδρας ξυνέθηκα; ΑΙΣ. μὰ Δί', ἀλλ' ὄντ'.** —**τίθης**: see on 580 f.—**εἰ . . θέλεις**, here merely a form of ironical courtesy.

587 f. **τῷ παλαμναίῳ**, more forcible than **φονεῖ**: cp. *Tr.* 1207 **φονέα γενέσθαι καὶ παλαμναῖον σέθεν.**—**πρόσθεν ἐξαπώλεσας.** The point of **πρόσθεν** is that, having *first* used his aid to slay her husband, she has put him in that husband's place.

589 f. **παιδοποιεῖς.** The active voice of this verb is rarer than the middle, but is proved by metre in Eur. *Heracl.* 524, Ar. *Eccl.* 615. In both forms it is usually said of the man.

Erigonè, daughter of Aegisthus and ͵Clytaemnestra, was mentioned by the early cyclic poet Cinaethon, and was the theme of Sophocles in his **Ἠριγόνη.**

εὐσεβεῖς: schol. rec. : **ἐννόμους, ἤγουν ἐξ ἐννόμου γάμου.** 'Stainless,' as being the legitimate offspring of a lawful marriage.—**κἀξ εὐσεβῶν** : **τουτέστιν ἐννόμῳ γάμῳ ἡρμοσμένων** (schol.). The reference is to both parents, not to Agam. only.

By **τοὺς...πρόσθεν εὐσεβεῖς** Electra means Orestes and herself. Both are 'cast out' of their just rights. Cp. *O. T.* 611 **φίλον...ἐσθλὸν ἐκβαλεῖν.**—**ἐκβαλοῦσ' ἔχεις**, an emphatic perfect, like **ἀτιμάσας ἔχει** (*Ant.* 22).

591 f. **πῶς ταῦτ' ἐπαινέσαιμ' ἄν;** Cp. *Ph.* 451 **ποῦ χρὴ τίθεσθαι ταῦτα, ποῦ δ' αἰνεῖν...;** **ἤ** is better here than **ἤ.** 'How can such an act be approved? *Or* will you plead that, though bad in itself, it is excused by the provocation?'—The constr. is :—**ἢ ἐρεῖς ὡς καὶ ταῦτα λαμβάνεις ἀντίποινα τῆς θυγατρός;** lit., 'that thou takest this also as compensation,' etc.

593 f. αἰσχρῶς δ', *sc.* ἐρεῖς. I leave the traditional δ': for, though it might well be absent, it adds a certain vivacity to the retort. 'Will that be your plea? Nay, it will be a shameful one.'—ἐάν περ καὶ λέγῃς, 'if you *do* allege it' (as it is scarcely conceivable that you should). Here καὶ goes closely with the verb: cp. *Ant.* 90 εἰ καὶ δυνήσει γ'.

ἐχθροῖς γαμεῖσθαι. Cp. *Tr.* 1236 f., where Hyllus demurs to marrying Iolè (whom he regards as indirectly the cause of his father's death): κρεῖσσον κἀμέ γ', ὦ πάτερ, θανεῖν | ἢ τοῖσιν ἐχθίστοισι συνναίειν ὁμοῦ. Aegisthus is, in Electra's view, an ἐχθρός, primarily as having helped to murder Agamemnon. As the son of Thyestes, and the murderer of Atreus, he is in a further sense the ἐχθρός of all Atreidae.

595 f. ἀλλ' οὐ γὰρ, elliptical: 'But (I will argue no more), for,' etc.: cp. 223 n.—πᾶσαν ἵης γλῶσσαν, poet. for πᾶσαν φωνὴν ἵης: cp. fr. 843. 3 πολλὴν γλῶσσαν ἐκχέας μάτην.

597 f. κακοστομοῦμεν: the verb occurs only here: cp. εὐστομεῖν (*O. C.* 18).

καί σ' ἔγωγε δεσπότιν. It is not easy to decide whether καί here means (1) 'and *indeed*,'—or (2) like καίτοι, 'and *yet*.' The latter would refer to τὴν μητέρα. 'You complain that I revile my mother. *And yet* you are no mother in my view, but a mistress.' But the other interpretation is simpler. καὶ will then refer to the instance of harshness already given (ἢ πᾶσαν ἵης γλῶσσαν). '*And indeed* I regard you as being (in all things) as much a mistress as a mother.'

εἰς ἡμᾶς is best taken as = εἰς ἐμέ, since Orestes (601) is beyond the reach of the domestic tyranny denoted by δεσπότιν. Cp. 116 ἡμετέρου. There is no awkwardness in ἢ (599), since it follows νέμω.

599 f. βίον μοχθηρόν: see vv. 189 ff.—ἐκ τε σοῦ = ἐκ σοῦ τε: cp. 249 f. (n.).—κακοῖς...ξυνοῦσα: cp. 241 (ξυνναίοιμ'): *O. T.* 303 νόσῳ σύνεστιν.—συννόμου: so *O. C.* 340 αἱ...σύννομοι.

601 f. ὁ δ' ἄλλος: not, 'the other' (of us two), which would be ὁ ἕτερος (though Theocr. 6. 45 has οὐδαλλος for οὐδέτερος): but, 'that other one,'—that other member of our family,—of whom she was thinking when she spoke of τοὺς πρόσθεν εὐσεβεῖς (589).—χεῖρα σὴν: see on 11.

τρίβει βίον, in weary exile: cp. 159 ἀχέων: Ar. *Pl.* 526 ὀδυνηρότερον τρίψεις βίοτον.

603 The reason for writing δή με σοὶ rather than δή μέ σοι is that σοί, placed thus, would almost necessarily receive a slight emphasis when the verse was spoken. But the chief emphasis is on μιάστορα, and an enclitic σοι would suffice. Whitelaw's version brings this out :—'Of whom I hear thee rate me that he lives | Reared up by me, for vengeance.'

μιάστορα, here, the avenger of a crime, like ἀλάστωρ: so Aesch. *Eum.* 176 ἕτερον ἐν κάρᾳ | μιάστορ' ἐκ κείνου πάσεται. —Cp. 275.

605 τοῦδέ γ' οὕνεκα: 387 n.

606 f. εἰς ἅπαντας: cp. *O. T.* 93 ἐς πάντας αὔδα.—**χρῆς.** For the form, cp. *Ant.* 887 εἴτε χρῇ θανεῖν | εἴτ' ἐν τοιαύτῃ ζῶσα τυμβεύειν στέγῃ.

στόμαργον. It is probable that στόμαργος was only another form of στόμαλγος, which is not found ; though στομαλγία was preferred to στομαργία, as γλωσσαλγία to γλωσσαργία.

608 f. τῶνδε τῶν ἔργων ἴδρις, ironical, as though these ἔργα were praiseworthy accomplishments.—**σχεδόν τι,** 'almost,' *i.e.*, 'it may perhaps be said that…'; cp. *Ant.* 470 σχεδόν τι μώρῳ μωρίαν ὀφλισκάνω.

οὐ καταισχύνω: commonly in a good sense: cp. *Ai.* 1304 f.: *Il.* 6. 209 μηδὲ γένος πατέρων αἰσχυνέμεν. Eur. *Or.* 1169 (Orestes speaking of his father), ὃν οὐ καταισχυνῶ.

610 f. ὁρῶ μένος πνέουσαν κ.τ.λ.: 'I see that she (Electra) is breathing anger; but whether she has justice on her side, of that I *no longer* see any regard (on her part).' Electra's speech, which began with temperate argument, has passed (at v. 595) into a strain of angry reproach—closing with the avowal that she would have wished to see Orestes take blood for blood (604 f.). The leader of the Chorus has once before reproved Electra's vehemence (213—220).—For **μένος πνέουσαν** cp. Aesch. *Ch.* 33 κότον | πνέων.

σὺν δίκῃ ξύνεστι is an unusual pleonasm, but analogous to ἐνεῖναι ἔν τινι (*O. C.* 116), παρεῖναι παρά τινι (*Ph.* 1056), προσθέσθαι πρός τινι (Aesch. *Pers.* 531), etc. It would be awkward (1) to understand τὸ μένος ξύνεστιν αὐτῇ (schol.); or (2) ἐκείνη ξύνεστι τῷ μένει (Herm.).

612 ποίας δ' ἐμοὶ δεῖ. The Chorus having said that Electra takes no φροντίς as to whether she is in the right, Clytaemnestra rejoins, 'And what manner of φροντίς do *I* need in regard to *her*?'—*i.e.*, 'Must I not indeed be on my guard against her, seeing that she is capable of anything?' (614 f.). Cp. Ar. *Nub.* 1032 δεινῶν δέ σοι βουλευμάτων ἔοικε δεῖν πρὸς αὐτόν. The sense recommends **ἐμοὶ** in preference to **μοι.** The order of words also favours it, since μοι would have been better placed after δεῖ.

614 f. καὶ ταῦτα, 'and that too': *O. T.* 37, *Ant.* 322.—
τηλικοῦτος, fem. only here and in *O. C.* 751. The sense is, 'so mature,'—old enough to know better.—ἆρα, when the expected answer is 'yes,' has an ironical tone; 'pray, are you satisfied that she would...?': cp. *O. T.* 822 ἆρ᾽ ἔφυν κακός;—followed by ἆρ᾽ οὐχὶ πᾶς ἄναγνος ;—χωρεῖν ἂν (= ὅτι χωροίη ἂν) εἰς πᾶν ἔργον : cp. Ar. *Lys.* 543 ἐθέλω δ᾽ ἐπὶ πᾶν ἰέναι. So *Ant.* 301 παντὸς ἔργου.

616 ff. εὖ νυν ἐπίστω, as in *O. T.* 658. νυν precedes a vowel also in *O. T.* 644, *Ant.* 705, *Ai.* 1129.

ἔξωρα, 'unseasonable,' from ὥρα in the sense of καιρός : not, 'unsuited to my age.'—προσεικότα : *Ph.* 902 f. τὴν αὐτοῦ φύσιν | ὅταν λιπών τις δρᾷ τὰ μὴ προσεικότα.

619 ff. ἀλλά...γὰρ, elliptical : 'but (I have excuse), for,' etc. : cp. 223, 595.—ἡ...ἐκ σοῦ δυσμένεια : cp. *Ant.* 95 τὴν ἐξ ἐμοῦ δυσβουλίαν : *Tr.* 631 τὸν πόθον τὸν ἐξ ἐμοῦ.—ἐξαναγκάζει : cp. 256.—αἰσχροῖς, sc. πράγμασι : cp. 308 f.

622 f. The word θρέμμα is not necessarily scornful (see *Ph.* 243 ὦ τοῦ γέροντος θρέμμα Λυκομήδους); but it is sometimes applied to monsters (*Tr.* 1093, etc.), or used, as here, in a disparaging tone, like our word 'creature'; cp. Aesch. *Th.* 182 (said to the Chorus), θρέμματ᾽ οὐκ ἀνασχετά.

ἣ σ᾽ ἐγὼ κ.τ.λ., a bitter echo of Electra's phrase (619 f.) : 'Yes, indeed,—they draw only too many words from thee.'

624 f. νιν = αὐτά, the πόλλ᾽ ἄγαν (ἔπη) : cp. 436.—εὑρίσκεται, 'find for themselves,'—hardly more than εὑρίσκει. Cp. Milton, *Apology for Smectymnuus* : 'I might also tell them [the prelates], what Electra in Sophocles, a wise virgin, answered her wicked mother, who thought herself too violently reproved by her the daughter : "*'Tis you that say it, not I ; you do the deeds, | And your ungodly deeds find me the words.*"'

626 f. οὐ μὰ is here followed by a second negative, as in 1239 f. : *Il.* 1. 86 : Ar. *Ran.* 1043, etc.

Ἄρτεμιν. Clytaemnestra calls upon the virgin-goddess to witness her threat, because she regards Electra as guilty of unmaidenly conduct (516 ff.). Electra has already appealed to Artemis (563), and again invokes her in 1238.

θράσους τοῦδ᾽ οὐκ ἀλύξεις, 'thou shalt not escape (punishment) *for* this boldness'; causal gen. : cp. *Ant.* 931 τούτων τοῖσιν ἄνουσιν | κλαύμαθ᾽ ὑπάρξει.—μόλῃ : cp. 313.

628 ὁρᾷς, in reproach; cp. *O. T.* 687, *Ant.* 735.—ἐκφέρει: Thuc. 3. 84 ἀπαιδευσίᾳ ὀργῆς πλεῖστον ἐκφερόμενοι.
630 f. οὐδὲ goes with θῦσαι. For the aor. inf., implying, 'to complete the sacrifice,' cp. 532, 285.—ὑπ' εὐφήμου βοῆς, 'with hushed clamour,' *i.e.*, in silence. For ὑπό, denoting the accompaniment, cp. 711, *Tr.* 419.

ἐπειδὴ σοί γ': γε necessarily emphasises σοί: thus arranged, the words could not mean, ἐπειδή γέ σοι. She means, 'after giving *you* leave to say what you would, am *I* to meet with no forbearance?'—πᾶν λέγειν: Plat. *Apol.* 39 A ἐάν τις τολμᾷ πᾶν ποιεῖν καὶ λέγειν.
632 f. κελεύω, not 'command,' but 'exhort,' 'beg'; cp. Xen. *Athen. Resp.* 2. 18 κωμῳδεῖν...τὸν μὲν δῆμον οὐκ ἐῶσιν, ἰδίᾳ δὲ κελεύουσιν ('encourage' it). For the asyndeton, cp. Aesch. *P. V.* 937 σέβου, προσεύχου, θῶπτε τὸν κρατοῦντ' ἀεί.—τοὐμὸν στόμ': *O. T.* 426 Κρέοντα καὶ τοὐμὸν στόμα | προπηλάκιζε.
634 f. An altar, and probably an image, of Apollo stand before the palace. The attendant of Clytaemnestra carries offerings of various fruits, which she is now commanded to *raise,* as with a gesture of solemn oblation (ἐπαιρε), and to place upon the altar.

ἡ παροῦσά μοι, said to the πρόσπολος. For the nom. with art., instead of a voc., cp. Plat. *Symp.* p. 218 B οἱ δὲ οἰκέται... πύλας...τοῖς ὠσὶν ἐπίθεσθε.

θύματα...πάγκαρπα, commonly called (ἡ) παγκαρπία, or, for metre's sake, παγκάρπεια: fr. 366 (from the Μάντεις, in a list of objects used for sacred rites), ἐνῆν δὲ παγκάρπεια συμμιγὴς ὀλαῖς (= οὐλαῖς).
635 f. λυτηρίους...δειμάτων (410 n.): cp. 447, 1490. So Iocasta asks Apollo for a λύσιν εὐαγῆ (*O. T.* 921).

ἀνάσχω has been much suspected. Yet cp. Eur. *El.* 592, where the Chorus are exhorting Electra to pray for a happy result: ἔνεχε χέρας, ἄνεχε λόγον ('uplift thy prayer'), | ἵει λιτὰς ἐς θεούς.
637 κλύοις ἄν, a reverent petition; cp. 1491.—προστα-τήριε: *Tr.* 208 f. τὸν εὐφαρέτραν | Ἀπόλλω προστάταν. Like Artemis (Aesch. *Th.* 449), Apollo was thus called as 'defender' of the house before which his image or altar stood. Here Clytaemnestra is invoking him more especially as ἀλεξίκακος, averter of evil.
638 κεκρυμμένην, here = αἰνιγματώδη, covert in meaning,

though spoken aloud,—because she merely alludes to her vision, without describing it, and without naming the persons to whom she refers (644—654). So Theogn. 681 ταῦτά μοι ἠνίχθω κεκρυμμένα τοῖς ἀγαθοῖσιν. The ancients associated evil with any prayer which could not be freely uttered.—οὐ γὰρ ἐν φίλοις, meaning Electra: for the plur., cp. 652.

640 πρὸς φῶς with ἀναπτύξαι: cp. *Ph.* 580 δεῖ δ' αὐτὸν λέγειν | εἰς φῶς ὃ λέξει.

641 f. πολυγλώσσῳ, 'garrulous,' agrees with Clytaemnestra's complaints of Electra in 520, 623.—σπείρῃ: cp. fr. 592 μὴ σπεῖρε πολλοῖς τὸν παρόντα δαίμονα ('spread it abroad').—ματαίαν seems here to mean 'rash,' 'reckless,' rather than 'false.' If Clytaemnestra openly avowed her fears or hopes, Electra would merely wish to publish them.

643 ὧδ' refers to 638: 'hear my prayer in this covert form, for I on my part (κἀγὼ) can use no other.' Cp. *Tr.* 554 τῇδ' ὑμῖν φράσω.

644 f. γὰρ, prefatory (32).—δισσῶν ὀνείρων (neut., cp. Eur. *H. F.* 518 ὄνειρα), 'ambiguous' dreams, ἀμφιβόλων. The ordinary sense of δισσὰ ὄνειρα would be (1) 'two dreams,' or (2) 'two sets of dreams.' But it can mean also, (3) 'dreams of two kinds': cp. Arist. *Rhet.* I. 15 § 13 μάρτυρές εἰσι διττοί (are of two kinds), οἱ μὲν παλαιοὶ οἱ δὲ πρόσφατοι. And 'dreams of two kinds' are here, 'dreams which admit of two interpretations,' —*i.e.*, which may be either good or bad.

Λύκει' ἄναξ: Iocasta, too, appeals to Apollo in this quality (*O. T.* 919). Both as a god of light, and as a destroyer of foes, the Λύκειος is fitly invoked here: see above on 6.

646 f. ἐσθλά...ἐχθρά. Since the sceptre which put forth the luxuriant growth was that which *Aegisthus* now carries (420 f.), Clytaemnestra might well regard the dream as so far susceptible of a good meaning. On the other hand, the apparition of Agamemnon (ὁ πανώλης, 544) must needs disquiet her. And so the import of the vision as a whole seemed doubtful.

ἔμπαλιν μέθες, *retro mitte*, 'allow to *recoil*' upon them: so στρέφειν ἔμπαλιν (Eur. *Med.* 923, etc.). ἔμπαλιν would be weak here if it meant merely, 'on the contrary.'

648 f. εἴ τινες, meaning Electra and Orestes. Even before the dream, this thought had haunted her (293 ff.).

650 ἀλλ' ὧδε κ.τ.λ., *sc.* δός: cp. 72 n.—ἀβλαβεῖ βίῳ: *Tr.* 168 ζῆν ἀλυπήτῳ βίῳ.

114   *Electra*

651 f. **δόμους**: as she says to Aegisthus in Aesch. *Ag.* 1672, ἐγὼ | καὶ σὺ θήσομεν κρατοῦντε τῶνδε δωμάτων καλῶς.—**ἀμφέπειν**, attend to, here, 'sway': Pind. *O.* 1. 12 θεμιστεῖον ὃς ἀμφέπει σκᾶπτον. Cp. *Ant.* 1118 ἀμφέπεις | Ἰταλίαν. **φίλοισι**, *i.e.*, Aegisthus: for the plur., cp. 346.

653 f. **εὐημεροῦσαν** goes adverbially with ξυνοῦσαν, 'consorting in prosperity.' The acc. is better than the nom., since it includes this condition in her prayer.

καὶ τέκνων (τούτοις) **ὅσων** κ.τ.λ.: 'and with (those) of my children, from whom,' etc.: τέκνων is partitive gen., the antecedent to ὅσων being understood. Cp. Plat. *Rep.* 387 E ὀρθῶς ἄρ' ἂν...θρήνους...γυναιξί...ἀποδιδοῖμεν, καὶ...ὅσοι κακοὶ τῶν ἀνδρῶν, *i.e.* (τούτοις) ὅσοι.

ἐμοὶ...πρόσεστιν, attends upon me; cp. *Tr.* 453 ἐλευθέρῳ | ψευδεῖ καλεῖσθαι κὴρ πρόσεστιν οὐ καλή.

656 **πᾶσιν ἡμῖν**: *i.e.*, to herself, Aegisthus, and the loyal children (652 ff.).

657 **τὰ δ' ἄλλα πάντα**,—her wishes concerning her *foes*. When the news from Phocis comes a moment later, it is as if the god had answered the unspoken prayer.

660 Following the directions given in vv. 39 ff., the Paedagogus now appears as a ξένος Φωκεύς.

πῶς ἂν εἰδείην, a courteous mode of inquiry; cp. 1103: *O. T.* 924 ἆρ' ἂν παρ' ὑμῶν, ὦ ξένοι, μάθοιμ' ὅπου | τὰ τοῦ τυράννου δώματ' ἐστὶν Οἰδίπου; For πῶς ἂν in wishes, cp. *Ph.* 531 f.

663 f. **ἢ καὶ**: cp. 314 n.—**ἐπεικάζων κυρῶ**: cp. *Ph.* 223 τύχοιμ' ἂν εἰπών: Aesch. *Suppl.* 588 καὶ τόδ' ἂν γένος λέγων | ἐξ Ἐπάφου κυρήσαις. (But below, in 1176, εἰπὼν κυρεῖς has not this sense.)

πρέπει γὰρ: cp. Eur. *Suppl.* 1056 ὡς οὐκ ἐπ' ἀνδρὶ πένθιμος πρέπεις ὁρᾶν.

665 **μάλιστα πάντων**, in reply, as Ar. *Av.* 1531, Plat. *Phaedr.* 262 C πάντων γέ που μάλιστα. So μάλιστά γε (*O. T.* 994), and καὶ μάλιστα.

ἥδε σοι κείνη πάρα, yonder (ἥδε) is she for whom you ask: *Ant.* 384 ἥδ' ἔστ' ἐκείνη: *O. C.* 138 ὅδ' ἐκεῖνος ἐγώ. Cp. 1115.

666 f. The ὦ prefixed to χαῖρε marks joyous excitement, as in *Ai.* 91, Eur. *El.* 1334, etc.

668 **ἐδεξάμην τὸ ῥηθέν**, 'I welcome the omen' (of λόγους ἡδεῖς). For the aor., cp. 1322, 1479: *Ant.* 1307 ἀνέπταν: *O. C.* 1466 ἔπτηξα: *Ai.* 693 ἔφριξα.

Notes 115

Instant recognition of an utterance as well-omened was a way of appropriating the omen. The proper formula was δέχομαι τὸν οἰωνόν or τὸν ὄρνιν (Her. 9. 91; Ar. *Pl.* 63). But δέχομαι alone was enough (Xen. *An.* 1. 8. 17: cp. Aesch. *Ag.* 1653 δεχομένοις λέγεις θανεῖν σε).

εἰδέναι...σου: cp. 565 n.

670 Φανοτεὺς: 45 n. — πρᾶγμα πορσύνων μέγα, lit., 'in furtherance of an important matter'; *i.e.*, for the purpose of acquainting you with important news. Cp. Eur. *Alc.* 1149 τὸν προκείμενον πόνον | ...πορσυνῶ μολών.

671 τὸ ποῖον; cp. *O. T.* 120.

673 ἐν βραχεῖ ξυνθεὶς: cp. Eur. fr. 362. 5 βραχεῖ δὲ μύθῳ πολλὰ συλλαβὼν ἐρῶ: Thuc. 2. 41 ξυνελών τε λέγω. It has been supposed that the spectators were intended to perceive a second meaning in ξυνθείς,—that of 'composing' a false story (see n. on 584); but this would surely be unfitting here.

675 τί φής, τί φής...; This lively phrase (Ar. *Nub.* 1444, *Lys.* 710) serves to show that her excitement is of a joyful kind. It is in a different tone from the πῶς εἶπας which greets similar announcements elsewhere (*O. T.* 943, *Ph.* 414).—ταύτης, scornful: cp. *O. T.* 429 ἦ ταῦτα δῆτ' ἀνεκτὰ πρὸς τούτου κλύειν;

676 νῦν τε καὶ πάλαι: cp. *Ant.* 181. πάλαι could refer to a recent moment.

677 οὐδέν εἰμ' ἔτι: *Ph.* 1217 ἔτ' οὐδέν εἰμι.

678 f. τὰ σαυτῆς πρᾶσσ': as 'to be over-busy' is περισσὰ πράσσειν (*Ant.* 68) or δρᾶν (*Tr.* 617). Plat. *Rep.* 433 A τὸ τὰ ἑαυτοῦ πράττειν καὶ μὴ πολυπραγμονεῖν.—διόλλυται, historic pres., as *O. T.* 560 ἔρρει, *Ant.* 1175 αἱμάσσεται.

680 κἀπεμπόμην...καὶ...φράσω: 'as...so': *Ant.* 1112 αὐτός τ' ἔδησα καὶ παρὼν ἐκλύσομαι.

681 f. γὰρ: 32 n.—πρόσχημ' ἀγῶνος (defining gen.) = πρόσχημ' ἀγωνιστικόν, while Ἑλλάδος is possessive gen.: 'the pride of Greece, (consisting in) a festival.' Cp. Aesch. *Ch.* 183 καρδίας κλυδώνιον | χολῆς (defining gen.): Eur. *H. F.* 449 δακρύων (defining gen.).. | .. ὄσσων πηγάς.

πρόσχημα, anything 'put forward' (cp. 525), here means, that which is put forward as an ornament or glory: cp. Her. 5. 28 ἡ Μίλητος.. μάλιστα δὴ τότε ἀκμάσασα καὶ δὴ καὶ τῆς Ἰωνίης ἦν πρόσχημα ('glory').

Δελφ. ἄθλων: cp. 48 n.

683 f. ὀρθίων: cp. Eur. *I. A.* 94 ὀρθίῳ κηρύγματι | Ταλθύβιον εἶπον πάντ' ἀφιέναι στρατόν.

δρόμον .. οὖ πρώτη κρίσις. There were three classes of ἀγῶνες at the Pythian festival; (1) the μουσικοί, in music, poetry, etc., which, as Plut. (*Quaest. Conv.* 2. 4) shows, came first; (2) the γυμνικοί, foot-races, and trials of skilled strength; and (3) the ἱππικοί, chariot-races and horse-races. This passage shows that at Delphi, as in the Greek games generally, (*a*) the γυμνικοὶ ἀγῶνες, or a large part of them, preceded the ἱππικοί: and (*b*) of the γυμνικοί, the foot-races came first.

685 εἰσῆλθε, came into the lists (like κατέβη): cp. 700: Dem. or. 18 § 319 (of an Olympian victor) τῶν εἰσελθόντων πρὸς αὐτὸν ἄριστα ἐμάχετο.

686 ἰσώσας *τἀφέσει: 'having made the end of his course even with the starting-place,'—*i.e.*, having run back again to that place in the stadion from which he started. Musgrave's conjecture, τἀφέσει for τῇ φύσει, affords the best solution here. If it be right, then the foot-race meant is either (*a*) the δίαυλος, in which the competitor rounded the καμπτήρ at the further end of the course, and returned to the starting-place (Aesch. *Ag.* 344 κάμψαι διαύλου θάτερον κῶλον πάλιν): or better, (*b*) the δόλιχος, in which he performed that double course several times. The race in which the course was traversed only once (properly called στάδιον) cannot be intended, since the verse could not mean, 'having finished the race *as swiftly as* he began it': still less, 'having made the end seem *simultaneous with* the start,'—by his marvellous speed.

Now there is evidence that the customary order for the foot-races was, (1) δόλιχος, (2) στάδιον, (3) δίαυλος. It would agree, then, with the words οὖ πρώτη κρίσις (684) if the δόλιχος were meant here.

For ἄφεσις as = 'starting-place,' cp. Suidas (*s.v.* ἀπὸ γραμμῆς): γραμμῆς, ἣν ἄφεσιν καὶ βαλβῖδα καλοῦσιν.

687 νίκης .. γέρας. In the Pythian games the prize was a wreath of laurel; hence Paus. says ἀνείλετο τὴν δάφνην of a Pythian victor (10. 7. 7), as τὸν κότινον ἀνείλετο of a victor at Olympia (6. 13. 3). A palm-branch was also given, the palm (φοῖνιξ) being sacred to Apollo.

688 f. χὤπως μὲν κ.τ.λ.: 'and, to speak briefly, where there is much that might be told (ἐν πολλοῖσι), I do not know the deeds and triumphs of such a man,'—*i.e.*, I have never seen, or heard of, his equal. Then, in 690, ἓν δ' ἴσθ' κ.τ.λ., δέ answers to the μέν in 688: *i.e.*: 'The *briefest* way, indeed (μέν), of describing his exploits, is simply to say that they were matchless. But (δέ) one particular you must be told,—viz., that he won in *all* the contests.'—For ὅπως, without ἄν, cp. 390.

690 ὅσων, by attraction for ὅσους.

βραβῆς, the form of the nom. plur. for εν stems which prevails in Attic inscrr. down to the middle of the 4th cent. B.C. —These are the judges who award the prizes and regulate the contests : εἰσεκήρυξαν, because they ordered the κῆρυξ to do so (cp. n. on 693 ff.). The ἀγωνοθέται of the Pythian games were the Amphictyons, the games being held in April, in the Delphic month Βουκάτιος (= the Attic Munychion), when the ἐαρινὴ πυλαία took place at Delphi. The Amphictyons appointed ἐπιμεληταί, like the Olympic Ἑλλανοδίκαι, to superintend the festival, and the βραβῆς here are these, or their subordinates.

691 δρόμων διαύλων. It seems most probable that v. 691 is an interpolation, arising perhaps from a marginal gloss, and intended to explain a general phrase in the text. Thus, if the poet had written simply, ὅσων γὰρ εἰσεκήρυξαν βραβῆς | ἄθλων ἐνεγκὼν etc., then the reference to the diaulos and the pentathlon in v. 691 might have been prompted by a wish to define ἄθλων. And the interpolation would itself account for the change of ἄθλων in 692 to τούτων.

On the whole, I should incline to delete 691, and alter τούτων in 692 to ἄθλων.

692 ἐνεγκὼν, in the sense of the midd. : cp. *O. T.* 590 φέρω.—τἀπινίκια here = τὰ νικητήρια (Plat. *Legg.* 833 c). The word usu. means either (1) songs of victory, or (2) with ἱερά understood, a sacrifice in honour of it.

693 ff. ἀλβίζετ᾽ : the impf. refers to the series of victories ; ἀνακαλ. = ὅτε ἀνεκαλεῖτο. The official proclamation would be merely, Ὀρέστης Ἀγαμέμνονος Ἀργεῖος. Cp. Pind. *Ol.* 5. 8 ὃν πατέρ᾽ Ἄκρων᾽ ἐκάρυξε (the victor *caused* to be proclaimed), καὶ τὰν νέοικον ἕδραν (Camarina).

Ἀγαμέμνονος is irregularly placed between τοῦ and ἀγείραντος : cp. 183 (θεὸς) : *O. T.* 1245 τὸν ἤδη Λάϊον πάλαι νεκρόν. —ἀγείραντος, as Thuc. 1. 9 (of Agam.) τὸν στόλον ἀγεῖραι.

696 f. καὶ ταῦτα μὲν τοιαῦθ᾽, a form of summary used in transitions : Plat. *Theaet.* 173 B καὶ οὗτοι μὲν δὴ τοιοῦτοι.— βλάπτῃ, disable, impede one in his career : *Ai.* 456 εἰ δέ τις θεῶν | βλάπτοι, φύγοι τἂν χὠ κακὸς τὸν κρείσσονα.

ἰσχύων, without τις,—a rare usage, which has, however, epic precedent ; *Il.* 13. 287 οὐδέ κεν ἔνθα τεόν κε μένος καὶ χεῖρας ὄνοιτο. So *O. T.* 517 φέρον, *Ant.* 687 καλῶς ἔχον, without τι. Cp. 1323.

698 ἄλλης ἡμέρας, 'on another day'; not, 'on the *next* day,' which would require τῆς. Cp. Xen. *An.* 3. 4. 1 μείναντες δὲ ταύτην τὴν ἡμέραν τῇ ἄλλῃ ἐπορεύοντο.

ἱππικῶν, prob. neut.: cp. Xen. *H.* 7. 4. 29 τὰ δρομικὰ τοῦ πεντάθλου.

699 ἡλίου τέλλοντος. The passage of Xen. just cited, referring to the Olympic festival of 364 B.C., shows that the chariot-races then preceded the pentathlon, on the same day,— and must therefore have begun in the early morning.

701 Ἀχαιός. If Sophocles were more careful in regard to details of the heroic age, 'Achaean,' as designating a man from a particular district, would naturally point to Phthiotis in southern Thessaly, where the subjects of Achilles 'were called Myrmidons, Hellenes, and *Achaeans*' (*Il.* 2. 684). But a poet who makes Orestes compete at the Pythian games against a Barcaean (727) was just as likely to use Ἀχαιός in the local sense which it acquired after the Dorian conquest of Peloponnesus,—a man from 'Achaia' on the Corinthian Gulf.

702 Λίβυες, in a geographical sense only: none but Hellenes could compete. These men are from the Greek Libya,—Κυρηναία or Κυρηναϊκή. In the seventh century B.C. this country was colonised by Dorians from Peloponnesus and the islands. Cyrene was founded near the coast in 631 B.C. by Battus and his followers from Thera. Barca (cp. v. 727), about 52 miles S.W. of it, and more inland, was founded about 550 B.C.

ζυγωτῶν is merely a general epithet. In a τέθριππον, only the two middle horses were under the yoke (721 f.).—ἐπιστάται, 'masters,' 'controllers,' of chariots; as a warrior is ὅπλων ἐπιστάτης (Aesch. *Pers.* 379), and an oarsman ἐρετμῶν ἐπιστάτης (Eur. *Helen.* 1267).

703 f. κἀκεῖνος, Orestes, who was living with Strophius, king of Crisa (180), close to the scene of the games.

ἐν τούτοισι. Nauck pronounces ἐν 'impossible,' and writes ἐπὶ ('in addition to'). There would be force in this objection, if the poet were enumerating the competitors as *drawn up in line*. But we cannot assume that the order of mention here is identical with the order fixed by lot for the start (709 f.); ἐν τούτοισι may well mean, '*among* these,'—the competitors being here imagined as a group.

Θεσσαλὰς...ἵππους. Thessaly owed its fame as a horse-breeding country to (1) its level plains, the best in Greece for that purpose; and (2) the reliance of the wealthy oligarchies upon cavalry.

705 ξανθαῖσι. This epithet for the *Aetolian* mares may have been suggested to the poet by a Homeric reminiscence. It is by a chestnut horse (φοῖνιξ, *Il.* 23. 454) that Idomeneus recognises from afar the team of Diomedes, Αἰτωλὸς γενεήν (*ib.* 471).

πώλοις. Throughout this passage, πῶλος is a mere synonym for ἵππος (725, 735, 738, 748). Yet special races for πῶλοι, as distinct from ἵπποι τέλειοι, had been established in the Pythian games before 500 B.C.—The Aetolian, like Orestes, drives *mares*, which were most generally used.

Μάγνης: from Magnesia, that mountainous tract which stretches southward along the east coast of Thessaly from the mouth of the Peneius to the Gulf of Pagasae.

706 λεύκιππος, or λευκόπωλος, is often an epithet of deities or heroes, as in Pind. *O.* 6. 95 (Persephonè); *P.* 1. 66 (the Dioscuri): Ibycus fr. 16 (the sons of Poseidon, the Μολίονε of *Il.* 11. 709), etc. And white horses are especially praised for swiftness. Yet Verg. *G.* 3. 82 says *color deterrimus albo.*

Αἰνιάν. The Αἰνιᾶνες (Ion. Ἐνιῆνες, *Il.* 2. 749, where the ι is short, and Her. 7. 132) were a tribe in the south of Thessaly, dwelling in the upper valley of the Spercheius, among the highlands of Oeta.

707 τῶν θεοδμήτων, an epithet bestowed on Athens by Eur. also (*I. T.* 1449, *Hipp.* 974), recalls the legends of Cecrops, Athena, Poseidon.

708 ἄλλος, 'besides': Aesch. *Th.* 424 γίγας ὅδ' ἄλλος.—ἐκπληρῶν, making up that number: Her. 7. 186 οὗτοι...ἐκπληροῦσι τὰς ἴσας μυριάδας ἐκείνοισι.

709 στάντες: so at the start of the Homeric chariot-race, *Il.* 23. 358, στὰν δὲ μεταστοιχί ('in line').—†ὅθ' αὐτούς. The traditional ὅθ' can hardly be right: we should perh. read τν'. The use of ὅθι in Tragedy is elsewhere confined to lyric passages, and even in these the ι is never elided. The simplest remedy would be ὅτ', which is not necessarily excluded by στάντες: the sense might be, 'having taken their stations, *when* these had been assigned.' But we should rather expect a word meaning 'where.'

βραβῆς: cp. 690. The phrase οἱ τεταγμένοι is illustrated by

Paus. **5. 9. 5.** At Olympia three Hellanodicae had charge of the ἵππων δρόμος, and three of the pentathlon ; while the rest supervised the other contests.

710 *κλήρους ἔπηλαν.* I should much prefer to read αὐτοῖς in 709 : but αὐτοὺς is defensible. Two views are possible ; the first is generally received, and is perhaps simplest. (1) αὐτοὺς depends on κλήρους ἔπηλαν as = ἐκλήρωσαν: cp. Ar. *Eccl.* 683 κληρώσω πάντας, 'I will place them all by lot.' See above on 123, 556. (2) κλήρους ἔπηλαν καὶ = κλήρους πήλαντες, a parenthetic construction (διὰ μέσου), so that αὐτοὺς is governed by κατέστησαν only, and δίφρους is a second acc., defining αὐτούς, as in μέθες με...χεῖρα (*Ph.* 1301). See on 466 f.

ἔπηλαν. Each competitor casts his κλῆρος, or lot,—usu. a potsherd (ὄστρακον), or a small stone,—into a helmet, which one of the βραβῆς shakes, and the places are settled by the order in which the lots jump out.

711 **χαλκῆς,** as χαλκοστόμου in *Ai.* 17.—ὑπαὶ (1419) is admitted in trimeters by Aesch. and Soph., *Ant.* 1035.—οἱ δ', though referring to the subject of ᾖξαν: cp. 448 (σὺ δὲ) n.

712 **ὁμοκλήσαντες.** Cp. *Il.* 23. 362 οἱ δ' ἅμα πάντες ἐφ' ἵπποιιν μάστιγας ἄειραν, | πέπληγόν θ' ἱμᾶσιν ὁμόκλησάν τ' ἐπέεσσιν | ἐσσυμένως·...ὑπὸ δὲ στέρνοισι κονίη | ἵστατ' ἀειρομένη κ.τ.λ.

713 f. **ἐν δὲ,** tmesis, as in *Ant.* 420 ἐν δ' ἐμεστώθη.—κροτητῶν is usually explained, and perhaps rightly, as 'rattling' (or more strictly, 'rattled' along by the horses): cp. *Il.* 15. 453 (ἵπποι) κείν' ὄχεα κροτέοντες: 11. 160 κείν' ὄχεα κροταλίζον. Sophocles has used κροτητὸς with ref. to sound in fr. 220 κροτητὰ πηκτίδων μέλη, 'songs resounding from the harp,' under the touch of the *plectrum.*

715 **φορεῖθ':** note the omission of the syllabic augment in ῥήσεις.

716 f. **κέντρων.** There is no allusion to a *whip* in this narrative. Leaf on *Il.* 23. 387, ἄνευ κέντροιο θέοντες, remarks that the κέντρον mentioned there is identical with the μάστιγα φαεινὴν v. 384, and refers to the Burgon amphora in the British Museum, where the chariot-driver wields a long pliant rod, with two points like arrow-heads at the end.

ὡς ὑπερβάλοι: '*in order that* each of them might pass the wheels...(of the others).' For τις as = ἕκαστός τις, cp. *Il* 2. 382 εὖ μέν τις δόρυ θηξάσθω: Thuc. 1. 40 τοὺς...ξυμμάχους αὐτόν τινα κολάζειν.

χνόας, the box at the centre of a wheel, in which the axle turns; the 'nave' (akin to navel), or 'hub': cp. Aesch. *Th.* 153 ἀξόνων...χνόαι. The Homeric word is πλήμνη: others are σῦριγξ (721 n.), and χοῖνιξ.

φρνάγμαθ' ἱππικά = ἵππους φρυασσομένους. This is the moment after the start, and no one has yet a clear lead. Each driver seeks, first, to bring his own wheels in front of his rival's wheels; next, to bring them past the heads of his rival's horses.

718 f. ὁμοῦ γὰρ ἀμφὶ νῶτα κ.τ.λ. The driver who has *just passed* his rival feels the breath of the pursuing horses on his back: cp. *Il.* 23. 380 (Eumelus, in the chariot-race, closely pursued by Diomedes) πνοιῇ δ' Εὐμήλοιο μετάφρενον εὑρέε τ' ὤμω | θέρμετ'. But the driver who is being *overtaken* sees his wheels flecked with foam from the mouths of his rival's horses. —τροχῶν βάσεις = τροχοὺς βαίνοντας.—εἰσέβαλλον, intrans. (as when it means 'to invade'), 'kept rushing in.' We cannot supply ἀφρόν, as object, from ἤφριζον.

720 ὑπ' αὐτήν, *close* under it.—ἐσχάτην στήλην, the stone pillar (νύσσα, καμπτήρ) which marked the turning-point *at each end* of the course.—ἔχων, sc. τοὺς ἵππους, directing his course: cp. *Il.* 23. 325 (the skilful driver does not force the pace at first), ἀλλ' ἔχει ἀσφαλέως καὶ τὸν προὔχοντα δοκεύει.

721 f. ἔχριμπτ' ἀεὶ σύριγγα, brought the nave of his (left) wheel close to the post at each successive turning. σῦριγξ ('pipe') is strictly the *opening* in the nave (ἡ ὀπὴ τοῦ τροχοῦ, schol. on 716) which forms the socket of the axle; Aesch. *Suppl.* 181 σύριγγες οὐ σιγῶσιν ἀξονήλατοι (the sockets of the whirling axles). Here it is a synonym for the χνόη (717) or nave itself. That part of the wheel is rightly named here, because it projects slightly. Thus in v. 745 it is the χνόη that strikes the post.

δεξιὸν δ' ἀνεὶς κ.τ.λ. In a τέθριππον the four horses were harnessed abreast. The two in the middle were under the yoke (ζύγιοι), which was affixed to the pole (ῥυμός), and drew by the yoke-collars (λέπαδνα) only, not being in traces. They were called respectively ὁ μέσος δεξιὸς and ὁ μέσος ἀριστερός (schol. Ar. *Nub.* 122). The two outside horses drew by traces (σειραί) only, attached to their collars, and fastened to the ἄντυξ of the car at its lower edge: hence σειραῖοι, σειραφόροι. In turning from right to left, the right-hand trace-horse had most work to do; hence δεξιόσειρος, fig., a strong helper at need (*Ant.* 140).

Sophocles has in mind the words of Nestor to Antilochus. *Il.* 23. 336 τὸν δεξιὸν ἵππον | κένσαι ὁμοκλήσας, εἶξαί τέ οἱ ἡνία χερσίν· | ἐν νύσσῃ δέ τοι ἵππος ἀριστερὸς ἐγχριμφθήτω, | ὡς ἄν τοι πλήμνη γε δοάσσεται ἄκρον ἱκέσθαι | κύκλου ποιητοῖο.

προσκείμενον, *sc.* τῇ στήλῃ, *i.e.* τὸν ἀριστερόν.

723 πρὶν μὲν is defined by ἔπειτα δ᾽ : up to the moment of the Aenian's disaster.— ἔστασαν, plpf., epic (*Il.* 2. 777 etc.), and also Attic (Thuc. 4. 56, etc.).

724 f. ἄστομοι, schol. σκληρόστομοι. The only extant example of the word in this sense.—βίᾳ φέρουσιν : Eur. *Hipp.* 1223 αἱ δ᾽ ἐνδακοῦσαι στόμια πυριγενῆ γνάθοις | βίᾳ φέρουσιν.

ἐκ δ᾽ ὑποστροφῆς = ὑποστρέψαντες, a phrase like ἐξ ὑπερτέρας χερός (455). Cp. Polyb. 2. 25. 3 ἐξ ὑποστροφῆς ἀπήντων, 'wheeling round, they went to meet the enemy.'

726 f. τελοῦντες κ.τ.λ., 'finishing the sixth and now (entering upon) the seventh round.' The more general sense of τελοῦντες ('doing') is evolved from the special; cp. on κρύψον in 436.

The Aenian, closely followed by the others, had just completed his sixth δίαυλος, or double course, in the hippodrome : *i.e.*, he had just passed, for the sixth time, round the goal nearest to the starting-place, and was on the point of beginning his seventh course. Just as he was passing the goal, his horses bolted. Hence he could not work them quite round into the track. They turned out of the left-ward curve (ἐξ ὑποστροφῆς), and ran straight on. Meanwhile, one of the two Libyan chariots had swept round the goal in a wider circle, on the Aenian's right. The Aenian's horses dashed head-foremost into the Libyan's team, striking it on the left side.

Βαρκαίοις ὄχοις: cp. 702 n.: for the pl. (like the Homeric ὄχεα), meaning one chariot, cp. fr. 611 ὄχοις Ἀκεσταίοισιν ἐμβεβὼς πόδα.

728 ff. ἐξ ἑνὸς κακοῦ. Other chariots were close upon the Aenian and the Barcaean. The foremost of these collided with each other in the effort to avoid the wreck, and meanwhile those which were in the rear ran into them. Thus the words ἔθραυε καὶ ἐνέπιπτε vividly describe the process.

ναυαγίων: cp. [Dem.] or. 61 § 29 ἐν τοῖς ἱππικοῖς ἀγῶσιν ἡδίστην θέαν παρέχεται τὰ ναυαγοῦντα.— Κρισαῖον...πέδον (not πεδίον), not the whole Crisaean plain, but the whole hippodrome.

731 ff. γνοὺς δ᾽ κ.τ.λ. At the moment when the Aenian

ran into the Barcaean, the Athenian was among the *foremost* drivers behind these two. On seeing the crash, he drew aside, reining in his horses, and allowed the chariots behind him to rush past in the middle of the course. They were all wrecked or disabled. He then resumed the race.

κἀνοκωχεύει: cp. Her. 9. 13 πρὶν μέν νυν ἢ πυθέσθαι ἀνεκώχευε ('he held his hand,' 'kept quiet'). It may have been a nautical term: *id.* 6. 116 ἀνοκωχεύσαντες τὰς νέας ('after *lying to*'). The verb is Ionic and poetical; but ἀνοκωχή, from which it comes, is used by Thuc. (1. 40 etc.).

κλύδων', a surging mass: cp. Plat. *Legg.* 758 A πόλις...ἐν κλύδωνι τῶν ἄλλων πόλεων διαγομένη.

734 f. ἔσχατος μὲν corresponds with ὅπως δ' (736): he was then last, indeed; *but*, when he saw that only one competitor was left, he pressed to the front.—ὑστέρας ἔχων explains *why* he was ἔσχατος: he was purposely keeping his horses behind; and φέρων, again, gives the motive of this; *because* he relied on the finish. For πίστιν φέρων as = πιστεύων, cp. *O. T.* 1445. [Cp. J. H. Newman, *Apologia*, p. 56: 'with the racer in the Tragedy, look forward steadily and hopefully to the event, τῷ τέλει πίστιν φέρων.']

736 ὅπως δ' ὁρᾷ: when Orestes sees the Athenian.

737 ἐνσείσας. ἐνσείειν is sometimes 'to drive in with force': cp. *Ant.* 1274 ἐν δ' ἔσεισεν ἀγρίαις ὁδοῖς ('hurled me' into them): here the notion is, 'sent vibrating through their ears.'

738 ff. κἀξισώσαντε ζυγά: Orestes, who had kept on the inside all through (720), would quickly gain when the Athenian paused (732).

τότ'...ἄλλοθ': cp. Plat. *Phaedr.* 237 E τοτὲ μὲν ἡ ἑτέρα, ἄλλοτε δὲ ἡ ἑτέρα κρατεῖ.—ἄλλος.. ἄτερος. Cp. *Il.* 9. 313 ὅς χ' ἕτερον μὲν κεύθῃ ἐνὶ φρεσίν, ἄλλο δὲ εἴπῃ: Her. 1. 32 ἄλλο μὲν ἔχει, ἑτέρου δὲ ἐπιδέεται. So here ἄλλος is loosely substituted for ἕτερος.

κάρα προβάλλων κ.τ.λ.: 'showing his head in front of the (two) chariots.' The neck-and-neck race is described as it would appear to a spectator at one side of the hippodrome, who saw the drivers in profile. Each charioteer is leaning forward in his car (as so often seen on vases). The head, now of one driver, now of the other, would be seen in front.—Not: 'bringing the head of his equipage in front (of the other team).'

For προβάλλων in partitive appos. with the subject of

ἠλαυνέτην, cp. Plat. *Phaedr.* 248 A (αἱ ψυχαὶ) ξυμπεριφέρονται,... ἑτέρα πρὸ τῆς ἑτέρας πειρωμένη γενέσθαι.

741 f. τοὺς μὲν ἄλλους πάντας. Six rounds still remained to be run when Orestes and the Athenian were left alone (see on 726). The word ἔπειτα is vague, but probably the disaster of Orestes is conceived as happening in the middle of the last (or twelfth) round.—ἀσφαλεῖς is proleptic, 'in safety.'—ὠρθοῦθ', 'had a prosperous course': cp. *Ant.* 675 τῶν δ' ὀρθουμένων, 'of those whose course is fair.' This is explained by ὀρθὸς ἐξ ὀρθῶν δίφρων, where the sense of the adj., varying from that of the verb, saves the language from seeming too redundant. The prep. ἐκ denotes the condition ('with his chariot safe'): cp. 455.

743 λύων ἡνίαν ἀριστεράν. He was turning sharply round the goal from right to left, and was therefore pulling the rein of the left trace-horse. He slackened this rein a moment too soon, thus letting the horse draw with more force. The effect was to create an angular velocity, which brought the left wheel into collision with the goal.

745 χνόας. The wooden nave (717), in which the axle turned, was broken across (μέσας) by striking the στήλη, and the left wheel came off. χνόας might also denote the end of the axle itself (ἀκραξόνιον): but it seems needless to assume this sense, which is less suited to μέσας.

746 f. ἀντύγων, the 'rim' or rail, surmounting a barrier or breastwork, often of osier trellis-work, which protected the front, and both sides, of the chariot; the plur., as in *Il.* 5. 728 δοιαὶ δὲ περίδρομοι ἄντυγές εἰσι. In going round the corner, Orestes would have been leaning a little to the left (like a bicyclist in a similar case). When the left wheel came off, he would be thrown over the left ἄντυξ.

σὺν δ' ἑλίσσεται, tmesis (*Ant.* 432). The charioteer sometimes passed the reins round his body.—τμητοῖς (863), a general epithet of reins or thongs (*Il.* 10. 567 ἐϋτμήτοισιν ἱμᾶσιν: Eur. *Hipp.* 1245 τμητῶν ἱμάντων), suggesting neat workmanship.—πέδῳ, as Aesch. *Eum.* 479 πέδῳ (πέδοι Dind.) πεσών, *Tr.* 789 χθονὶ | ῥίπτων ἑαυτόν.

748 διεσπάρησαν εἰς μέσον δρόμον, 'were scattered into the middle of the course'; *i.e.*, left the track in which the race was being run (the 'course' in the narrower sense), and rushed on to the open ground between this track and the spectators διεσπάρησαν cannot be satisfactorily explained on the as sumption that all four horses remained harnessed to the car.

749 ff. στρατὸs here = λεὼς (*Tr.* 795).—δίφρων: the plur., as in 510: cp. 727 ὄχοις. In the narrower sense, δίφρος is the platform of the car, usu. made of interlaced thongs (ἱμάντες), stretched on a framework of wood or iron (*Il.* 5. 727).—ἀνωλόλυξε, here of grief, as ὀλόλυξαν in Ap. Rh. 3. 1218: elsewhere, almost always a triumphant cry, esp. of women (*Tr.* 205).—οἳ' ...οἷα: *Ai.* 923 οἷος ὢν οἵως ἔχεις.

752 ff. φορούμενος πρὸς οὖδας, 'dashed to the ground': cp. Eur. *I. T.* 49 βεβλημένον πρὸς οὖδας. These words can be taken in two ways: I prefer the first. (1) With reference to his *fall from the chariot*. The people speak of his mishap as a whole, not merely of what he is suffering at the moment. (2) With reference to what occurs while he is being dragged; he is dashed earthwards (*after* being tossed upward). But this would be most awkward, when the mention of his being tossed upward follows.

ἄλλοτ': the first ἄλλοτε is omitted: Eur. *Hec.* 28 κεῖμαι δ' ἐπ' ἀκταῖς, ἄλλοτ' ἐν πόντου σάλῳ.—οὐρανῷ σκέλη προφαίνων, *i.e.*, tossed feet uppermost to the sky. Cp. Shakesp. *Hamlet* 3. 3. 93 'Then trip him, that his heels may kick at heaven.'

753 f. διφρηλάται: the drivers of the eight previously disabled chariots would be still on the ground.

757 f. κέαντες. This aor. part. of καίω, found in the Ionic prose of Hippocr. (7. 422 ἀποκέας), occurs also in two Attic inscrr. of 408 B.C. (ἐγκέαντι *bis*, Meisterhans, p. 86, n. 686). The epic form is ἔκηα (for ἔκηϝα), part. κήας.

ἐν βραχεῖ χαλκῷ: cp. 1113 φέροντες αὐτοῦ σμικρὰ λείψαν' ἐν βραχεῖ | τεύχει θανόντος: and 54 n.—μέγιστον. The heroes were conceived as transcending later mortals in strength; and so also in stature: Her. 1. 68 (the grave of Orestes at Sparta) ἐπέτυχον σορῷ ἑπταπήχεϊ· ὑπὸ δὲ ἀπιστίης μὴ μὲν γενέσθαι μηδαμὰ μέζονας ἀνθρώπους τῶν νῦν ἄνοιξα αὐτήν, καὶ εἶδον τὸν νεκρὸν μήκεϊ ἴσον ('proportionate') ἐόντα τῇ σορῷ.—σῶμα...σποδοῦ, a body now *consisting in* (reduced to) dust: see on 682 πρόσχημ' ἀγῶνος. (The gen. cannot be taken with χαλκῷ, as = 'an urn filled with dust.')

Cp. Aesch. *Ag.* 440 (Ares) πυρωθὲν ἐξ Ἰλίου | φίλοισι πέμπει βραχὺ | ψῆγμα δυσδάκρυτον, ἀντήνορος σποδοῦ γεμίζων λέβητας εὐθέτου.

759 f. ἄνδρες Φωκέων (partitive gen.): Thuc. 7. 43 § 3 ἄνδρας τῶν φυλάκων.—**ἐκλάχῃ**, depending on φέρουσιν, is more natural here than ἐκλάχοι, which would depend on τεταγμένοι, and refer to the purpose of the senders.

761 f. **τοιαῦτά σοι** (ethic dat.) **ταῦτ᾽ ἐστίν**, as in *O. C.* 62.— **ὡς μὲν ἐν λόγῳ**, *so far as* mere narrative can convey an impression. For the limiting sense of ὡς, cp. *O. C.* 76 ὡς ἰδόντι.—**τοῖς δ᾽ ἰδ.**, οἵπερ εἴδομεν, = ἡμῖν δὲ τοῖς ἰδοῦσιν. Cp. *O. T.* 1237 τῶν δὲ πραχθέντων τὰ μὲν | ἄλγιστ᾽ ἄπεστιν· ἡ γὰρ ὄψις οὐ πάρα.

764 f. The word **δεσπόταισι** would usu. imply that the speaker was a slave. The women of the Chorus are free (1227 πολίτιδες), but it is simple to suppose that, in poetry, δεσπότης could bear its primary sense, 'master of the house,' 'lord,' without necessary reference to the special relation of master and slave.

πρόρριζον: see on 512.

766 **ὦ Ζεῦ.** Clytaemnestra regretted her failure to destroy Orestes in childhood (296 f.). But the poet is true to nature in blending some touch of maternal grief with her sense of gain. —**λέγω**, pres. subjunct.: cp. *O. T.* 651.

769 **τῷ νῦν λόγῳ**: the same phrase occurs in *O. T.* 90, *O. C.* 801.

770 f. **δεινόν**, a mysterious power, a strangely potent tie; cp. Aesch. *P. V.* 39 τὸ συγγενές τοι δεινὸν ἥ θ᾽ ὁμιλία: Isaiah xlix. 15 'Can a woman forget her sucking child, that she should not have compassion on the son of her womb?' **πάσχοντι**: for the masc., cp. 145 n.—**ὧν τέκῃ**, without ἄν (*O. T.* 1231). The *v.l.* τέκοι is possible, but less natural.

772 **μάτην ἄρ᾽ ἡμεῖς κ.τ.λ.** The old man speaks as if disappointed and aggrieved. Thus a cue is skilfully given for the change in Clytaemnestra's tone. ἡμεῖς may include the bearers of the urn (759).

773 **μάτην λέγοις**, say the word 'μάτην': cp. *Ant.* 567 ἀλλ᾽ ἥδε μέντοι μὴ λέγ᾽.

775 **ψυχῆς**, 'life'; cp. *O. C.* 998 f. Here the phrase has a pathetic force; his very life was her gift.

776 f. **μαστῶν κ.τ.λ.**: *i.e.*, 'he deserted me who had suckled and reared him': the words do not imply that Orestes was still an infant when he left her (see on 13 f.).

ἀπεξενοῦτο, 'became estranged.' Cp. Eur. *Hipp.* 1084 f. οὐκ ἀκούετε | πάλαι ξενοῦσθαι τόνδε προὐννέποντά με; ('that he is no longer my son').

779 **φόνους**: for the plur., 206 θανάτους (n.).

780 ff. ὥστ' οὔτε…στεγάζειν. When ὥστε is followed by the infin., the negative is ordinarily μή. There are, however, many exceptions. Instances strictly like the above are these :—Eur. *Ph.* 1357 οἶσθ' οὐ μακρὰν γὰρ τειχέων περιπτυχαί, | ὥστ' οὐχ ἅπαντά σ' εἰδέναι τὰ δρώμενα : [Dem.] or. 53 § 1 οὐδ' αὖ οὕτως ἄπορος ἦν ὥστ' οὐκ ἂν ἐξευρεῖν. But most of the examples occur under special conditions.

ἐξ ἡμέρας, *interdiu*. The phrase ἐκ νυκτῶν, 'in the night-watches,' is frequent (*Od.* 12. 286, Theognis 460, Aesch. *Ch.* 287).—στεγάζειν, lit. 'cover,' *i.e.*, cover the eyes.

ὁ προστατῶν χρόνος, lit., 'the time which stands in front (of the present),' the 'imminent' or 'coming' time (schol. ὁ ἐπιγινόμενος). From moment to moment she looked for death.— As προστατεῖν usu. means 'to govern' or 'to protect,' some understand, (1) 'Time standing over me' like a jailor (Campbell), 'the tyrannous time' (Whitelaw): or (2) generally, 'Time that controls all events.'

διῆγε, kept me living: Dem. or. 18 § 89 ὁ γὰρ τότε ἐνστὰς πόλεμος…ἐν πᾶσι τοῖς κατὰ τὸν βίον ἀφθονωτέροις…διήγαγεν ὑμᾶς τῆς νῦν εἰρήνης ('caused you to live').

783 f. The perf. ἀπήλλαγμαι, expressing final deliverance, is better here than the aor. ἀπηλλάγην (cr. n.).—μείζων, worse than the distant Orestes, because ξύνοικος.

785 ff. τοὐμὸν, not τῆς ἐμῆς, since ψυχῆς αἷμα forms one notion : cp. 1390 : *Ant.* 794.—ἐκπίνουσ': cp. *Ant.* 531 σὺ δ', ἣ κατ' οἴκους ὡς ἔχιδν' ὑφειμένη | λήθουσά μ' ἐξέπινες.—ἄκρατον, 'sheer,' implies the pitiless cruelty of the vampire: so Aesch. *Ch.* 577 φόνου δ' Ἐρινὺς οὐχ ὑπεσπανισμένη | ἄκρατον αἷμα πίεται.

νῦν δ': repeated from 783, after the long parenthesis.— ἔκηλα, adv.: cp. 164.—οὕνεχ': cp. 387.—ἡμερεύσομεν: a word used in Attic prose (as = 'to pass the day').

790 ἆρ' ἔχει καλῶς; 'Is it not well?' Cp. 816; and for ἆρα, 614.

791 οὔτοι σὺ sc. καλῶς ἔχεις. The sense is not merely, 'you are in an evil case'; but rather, 'you are not as I could wish'—and as Orestes is.

792 Νέμεσι : this voc. occurs also in Eur. *Ph.* 183, where, as here, νέμεσις is a *v.l.* (Cp. Ar. *Ran.* 893 ξύνεσι.)—τοῦ θανόντος ἀρτίως : for the place of the adv., cp. *Ai.* 635 ὁ νοσῶν μάταν : Aesch. *P. V.* 216 τῶν παρεστώτων τότε.

Nemesis is the goddess who requires that each man should

128   *Electra*

receive his due. The 'Nemesis of the dead man' is the avenger of wrong done to him.

793 ἤκουσεν ὧν δεῖ. Clyt. turns her retort as though τοῦ θανόντος depended on ἄκουε. 'Nemesis (the goddess of retribution generally) has heard a mother who prayed for the punishment of an unnatural son.'—κἀπεκύρωσεν: cp. 919 κῦρος.

795 οὔκουν...τάδε; This verse should probably be interrogative, as Electra's answer suggests. And οὔκουν (*nonne ergo..?*) seems better than οὐκοῦν (*ergo..?*).

796 οὐχ ὅπως σε παύσομεν = οὐ λέγω ὅπως κ.τ.λ.: 'not to speak' of doing so; *i.e.*, 'so far from' doing so (Lat. *nedum*). So οὐχ ὅτι: and (with λέγε understood) μὴ ὅτι, or (more rarely) μὴ ὅπως. These phrases usu. stand in the first clause, followed by ἀλλὰ καί in a second clause.

797 f. πολλῶν ἂν ἥκοις. Clyt. refers to Electra's words, πεπαύμεθ' ἡμεῖς: '*If* you have *indeed* silenced her, then you would deserve much,' etc. A protasis formed by εἰ and a past tense of the indic. is sometimes thus combined with an apodosis formed by the optat. and ἄν. In such cases the past tense usu. denotes an actual fact, or what is assumed to be such.

πολλῶν goes with ἄξιος, and τυχεῖν is epexegetic: cp. *Ant.* 699 οὐχ ἥδε χρυσῆς ἀξία τιμῆς λαχεῖν;

799 εὖ κυρεῖ: alluding to her words in 791.

800 f. With πράξειας we supply ἄν from ἀποστείχοιμ' ἄν. G. Wolff compares Plat. *Lys.* p. 208 B εἰ βούλοιο λαβὼν τὴν μάστιγα τύπτειν, ἐῷεν ἄν. Πόθεν δ', ἦ δ' ὅς, ἐῷεν; τοῦ πορεύσ. ξένου: Phanoteus (670).

803 τῶν φίλων, Orestes; for the plur., cp. 346. It is no concern of Clytaemnestra's to mourn him (cp. 776).

Clytaemnestra and the Paedagogus enter the house.

804 ff. ἆρ' ὑμῖν κ.τ.λ.: 'does she *not* seem,' etc.,—with bitter irony: cp. 790, 816.—ὧδ', by a death so piteous; cp. 751.

808 ὥς μ' ἀπώλεσας θανών: as Antigone says of her brother (*Ant.* 871), θανὼν ἔτ' οὖσαν κατήναρές με.

809 ἀποσπάσας (ἐκείνας) αἳ κ.τ.λ.: conversely *O. 1.* 1432 ἐλπίδος μ' ἀπέσπασας.

812 μολεῖν: cp. *O. C.* 1747 ποῖ μόλωμεν, ὦ Ζεῦ; ('whither shall we turn?').

814 ff. δουλεύειν: cp. 1192 : 597 δεσπότιν. She was treated like a slave (190 ff.).—πάλιν. Her servitude had never ceased, and could not be said to recommence. But in imagination, so long as Orestes lived, she could behold a deliverer. From those bright dreams she must now go *back* to a slavery without hope.

816 ἀρά μοι καλῶς ἔχει; cp. 790.

817 τοῦ λοιποῦ χρόνου, a partitive gen. (478), instead of the more usual τὸν λ. χρόνον, or τὸ λοιπόν: so τοῦ λοιποῦ in Her. 1. 189, Ar. *Pax* 1084.

818 εἴσειμ᾽, Hermann's correction of ἔσσομ᾽, is made certain by ἀλλὰ τῇδε πρὸς πύλῃ. No dative is needed to explain ξύνοικος, since φονεῦσι πατρός so closely precedes.

819 παρεῖσ᾽ ἐμαυτήν, allowing myself to sink to the ground: cp. *Tr.* 938 πλευρόθεν | πλευρὰν παρεὶς ἔκειτο.

821 χάρις, gratification: cp. 1266.

823—870 Kommos. 1st strophe, 823—835, = 1st antistr., 836—848: 2nd str., 849—859, = 2nd antistr., 860—870. For metres see Metrical Analysis. Changes of person occur within a verse (as in 829 ff., ΗΛ. φεῦ. ΧΟ. μηδὲν μέγ᾽ αὔσῃς. ΗΛ. ἀπολεῖς. ΧΟ. πῶς;). This indicates that the Chorus is here represented by the coryphaeus; it is, in fact, a lyric duet between the leader and Electra.

These lyrics mark the climax of Electra's grief. The comforter vainly seeks to rouse her from despair.

823 ff. ποῦ ποτε κ.τ.λ. 'where are they?' means here, 'what are they doing,—if they see this, and do not punish?' It is the part of the Sun-god to reveal guilt (cp. n. on 424 f.), and of the thunderbolts to smite it.—ἐφορῶντες, passively viewing;—just as in *Tr.* 1269 (θεοὶ) τοιαῦτ᾽ ἐφορῶσι πάθη.—κρύπτουσιν: schol. οὐκ ἄγουσιν εἰς φῶς, do *not* brand by exposure and chastisement.

828 τί δακρύεις; A gentle remonstrance; 'why dost thou thus give way to grief?' (Not: 'what is the cause of thy grief?')

830 μηδὲν μέγ᾽ αὔσῃς. In saying φεῦ, Electra lifted her face and stretched forth her hands to heaven, as if accusing the gods; and the Chorus hasten to warn her against any irreverent utterance (schol.). Cp. *Ai.* 386 μηδὲν μέγ᾽ εἴπῃς.—αὔσῃς, a loud cry (*Tr.* 565 ἐκ δ᾽ ἤϋσ᾽ ἐγώ).

831 ἀπολεῖς, *enecabis.* She takes their remonstrance as implying a doubt whether Orestes is dead. For this verb in ref. to *mental* pain, cp. *Ph.* 1172 τί μ᾽ ὤλεσας; ('afflicted me'— by reviving a painful memory).

832 f. τῶν...οἰχομένων, Orestes (for the plur., cp. 145 f.): φανερῶς, because the mention of the ashes (757 ff.) has removed the last doubt from her mind.—ἐλπίδα with gen. of the object; cp. 1460 f.

834 f. κατ' ἐμοῦ τακομένας. This constr., instead of the simple dat. (456), is due to the peculiar sense of ἐπεμβάσει: cp. ἐγγελᾶν and ἐπεγγελᾶν κατά τινος (*O. C.* 1339, *Ai.* 969).

836 f. οἶδα γὰρ κ.τ.λ.: 'Nay, (I can still offer thee comfort;) *for* I know that Amphiaraüs, like Agamemnon, was betrayed to death by a false wife; and yet now he is a great spiritual force beneath the earth, and is revered among men.' Although Orestes is dead, Agamemnon may still be *honoured.* The Chorus do not directly hint a belief that he can still be *avenged,* —as Amphiaraüs was. Electra then seizes on this point of contrast, Amphiaraüs found an avenger; her father cannot now find one.

Ἀμφιάρεων, scanned – ∪ ∪ –, as in *O. C.* 1313: ἄνακτα, as the seer Teiresias is so called, *O. T.* 284. Amphiaraüs, the Argive seer and warrior, married Eriphylè, sister of Adrastus, king of Argos. When Polyneices sought Argive aid against Thebes, Amphiaraüs opposed the enterprise, foreseeing a fatal issue. Polyneices then bribed Eriphylè with a golden necklace, and she persuaded her husband to join the expedition. The Argives were routed by the Thebans. In the flight, Amphiaraüs was approaching the river Ismenus, near Thebes, when the earth, riven by a thunderbolt, swallowed him up, with his chariot.

837 f. χρυσοδέτοις ἕρκεσι, nets, or snares, of golden links; *i.e.,* the toils of fate into which he was drawn through the necklace with which his wife was bribed. The epithet marks the figurative sense of ἕρκεσι (as a ship is λινόπτερον ὄχημα, Aesch. *P. V.* 468). γυναικῶν, *i.e.* Ἐριφύλης, an allusive plur. (145 n.), perhaps suggested by *Od.* 15. 247 (of Amphiaraüs), ἀλλ' ὄλετ' ἐν Θήβῃσι γυναίων εἵνεκα δώρων.

κρυφθέντα (*i.e.* ἀφανισθέντα) is the word repeatedly used with ref. to the end of Amphiaraüs: cp. *e.g.* Pind. *N.* 9. 24 ὁ δ' Ἀμφιάρῃ σχίσσεν κεραυνῷ παμβίᾳ | Ζεὺς τὰν βαθύστερνον χθόνα, κρύψεν δ' ἅμ' ἵπποις.

840 ἔ ἔ· ἰώ. The words ὑπὸ γαίας remind Electra of her father and brother.

841 πάμψυχος = πᾶσαν τὴν ψυχὴν ἔχων (cp. ἄψυχος). The mind of Amphiaraüs acts upon men through his oracles as fully as if he were alive. In the popular belief, the ordinary shades of the departed had either no intelligence or a feeble one.

Thus Teiresias is an exception (*Od.* 10. 495): τῷ καὶ τεθνηῶτι νόον πόρε Περσεφόνεια | οἴῳ πεπνῦσθαι· τοὶ δὲ σκιαὶ ἀΐσσουσιν.

The cult of Amphiaraüs had its chief seat in Boeotia, but afterwards spread thence to Argos, and throughout Greece.

842 ff. φεῦ.—φεῦ δῆτ'. Electra's cry, φεῦ, is drawn from her by the thought that, while Amphiaraüs has honour, her father's spirit is unhonoured. The Chorus suppose her to mean, 'Alas for Eriphylè's wickedness,' and respond φεῦ δῆτ', 'alas indeed' (cp. *O. C.* 536 XO. ἰώ. OI. ἰὼ δῆτα). Then they say, ὀλοὰ γὰρ, 'for the murderess—' intending to add, 'betrayed her husband's life.' But Electra, still thinking of the difference and not of the likeness between the case of Amphiaraüs and that of Agamemnon, quickly gives a different turn to the unfinished sentence by interjecting ἐδάμη;—'was laid low' (by her son Alcmaeon: see on 846).

ἐδάμη: Electra is not asking a question; she is rejecting the consolation. The Chorus admit, by their ναί, the fact that Eriphylè was slain, and then Electra points the contrast (οἶδ' οἶδ', κ.τ.λ.).

846 μελέτωρ (only here): 'one who cared' for the dead,— an avenger (cp. 237 ἀμελεῖν). Suidas *s.v.*, ὁ ἐπιμελούμενος, ὁ τιμωρούμενος τῷ πατρί.

Amphiaraüs was avenged by his son Alcmaeon,—the counterpart, in this story, of Orestes. Before setting out for Thebes, the seer had charged him with this duty. Eriphylè, bribed once more, prevailed upon her son to lead the Epigoni against Thebes. After its fall, he returned to Argos, and slew her.

847 τὸν ἐν πένθει, 'the mourner' (cp. 290): not, 'the lamented one.' The shade of the dead Amphiaraüs mourned until avenged. Cp. Aesch. *Ch.* 39 μέμφεσθαι τοὺς γᾶς | νέρθεν περιθύμως.

848 ἀναρπασθείς, by death, as by a storm: cp. Lucian *De luctu* 13 τέθνηκας καὶ πρὸ ὥρας ἀνηρπάσθης.

849 δειλαία δειλαίων. This adj., usu. said of persons, is applied to things in *O. C.* 513, *Tr.* 1026. Cp. Eur. *Hec.* 84 ἥξει τι μέλος γοερὸν γοεραῖς. The antistrophic verse (860), πᾶσι θνατοῖς ἔφυ μόρος, indicates that the αι of δειλαία and of δειλαίων is short, as in *Ant.* 1310.

850 ἴστωρ, fem., as in Eur. *I. T.* 1431: so πράκτωρ, θέλκτωρ, σωτήρ, λωβητήρ (*Ant.* 1074 n.).

851 f. πανσύρτῳ...αἰῶνι. The traditional text is πανσύρτῳ παμμήνῳ πολλῶν | δεινῶν στυγνῶν τ' ἀχέων (or ἀχαίων). Hermann substitutes αἰῶνι for ἀχέων, regarding the latter as a gloss upon the adjectives.

The literal sense then is :—'(I know this) by a life which, through all the months, is a turbid torrent of many things dread and horrible.' πανσύρτῳ seems rightly explained in one scholium as πάντα σύροντι τὰ κακά: *i.e.*, it has an active sense, like χαλκόπλακτος (484 n.). The genitive, πολλῶν δεινῶν στυγνῶν τ', may depend upon it, as in *Ant.* 1184 f. θεᾶς...προσήγορος = θεὰν προσηγοροῦσα. But we might also join the genitive with αἰῶνι, as = 'a life *of*' (made up of) these things. παμμήνῳ has a special point. The literal χειμάρρους flows only in winter.

This view gives πανσύρτῳ a more forcible and more poetical sense than if it be taken as = 'swept together from every side.' The meaning then would be, 'a life, through all the months, of many dread horrors, *accumulated* from every quarter.'

853 ἀθρήνεις. The MS. reading, ἃ θροεῖς, conflicts with the metre of the antistrophe (864), where the corresponding words are ἁ λώβα. The reasons for preferring ἀθρήνεις to ἃ θρηνεῖς are two. (1) A lengthening of ᾰ before θρ, though not impossible in lyrics, would be unusual. (2) The context favours the imperfect. In 850—852 Electra refers to the woes which she has so long endured. The Chorus now reply, 'We have seen what *thou wast* mourning,'—'the course of thy sorrow,'—through all those years (cp. 140 f.).

854 f. μὴ μέ νυν. Here νυν, not νῦν, is clearly right : 'If ye so well know my griefs, *then* desist,' etc.—παραγάγῃς, by delusive comfort: cp. *O. T.* 974 τῷ φόβῳ παρηγόμην.—ἵν', in a case where (cp. 21 f.).

856 τί φής; Her words, ἵν' οὐ, already indicate her thought ; 'where there is no—hope': and the Chorus interrupt her with a remonstrance. She rejoins by repeating that *her brother* is no more. While they are vaguely consolatory, she dwells on the loss of the only avenger to whom she could look.

857 ff. πάρεισιν ἐλπίδων ἔτι κ.τ.λ. The choice is between two readings ; (1) εὐπατριδᾶν ἀρωγαί, and (2) Neue's correction, εὐπατρίδων τ' ἀρωγαί. The first is best. The constr. then is, ἐλπίδων ἀρωγαί, aids consisting in hopes, κοινοτόκων εὐπατριδᾶν, from princes born of the same parents ; *i.e.*, sustaining hopes from a princely brother. For the defining gen. ἐλπίδων, cp.

682: for the second gen., denoting the source of the hope, cp. 1460 f., εἴ τις ἐλπίσιν πάρος | ἐξῆρετ' ἀνδρὸς τοῦδε.

With εὐπατρίδων τ', both epithets belong to ἐλπίδων, and ἐλπίδες κοινότοκοι εὐπάτριδές τε mean, 'hopes from brothers and princes,'—*i.e.*, 'hopes from a princely brother': the sense is unchanged, but the phrase is more artificial.

860 ἔφυ, with ref. to a law of nature or fate: cp. 236: *Tr.* 440 χαίρειν πέφυκεν οὐχὶ τοῖς αὐτοῖς ἀεί: *O. C.* 1444 (φῦναι).

861 ἦ καί, sc. πᾶσι θνατοῖς ἔφυ.—χαλαργοῖς (=χηλῶν ἀργῶν), a vivid epithet, describing the tramp and rush of the horses' feet. Cp. *O. C.* 1062 ῥιμφαρμάτοις | ...ἁμίλλαις.

863 τμητοῖς, the epithet of reins (747 n.), serves here to define the sense of ὁλκοῖς. Ordinarily ὁλκός means (1) a sort of hauling machine, or (2) a furrow.—ἐγκῦρσαι, 'to meet with them,' as a mode of death. Cp. Her. 2. 82 ὁτέοισι ἐγκυρήσει (what fortunes he will have) καὶ ὅκως τελευτήσει.

864 ἄσκοπος, such as could not have been even imagined beforehand,—inconceivably dreadful. Cp. 1315: *Tr.* 246 τὸν ἄσκοπον | χρόνον...ἡμερῶν ἀνήριθμον.—ἃ λώβα, the cruel doom: *Tr.* 996 οἵαν μ' ἄρ' ἔθου λώβαν.

865 ξένος: schol. ἐπ' ἀλλοδαπῆς: cp. *Tr.* 65 ἐξενωμένου.

866 ἄτερ ἐμᾶν χερῶν: cp. 1138 n.

868 ff. κέκευθεν, lies buried: *Ant.* 911 ἐν Ἅιδου...κεκευθό-τοιν.—οὔτε του: here του is equivalent to an adv., 'at all': cp. *Ai.* 290 οὔτε του κλύων | σάλπιγγος.—ἀντιάσας = ἀντήσας (*O. C.* 1445), 'having obtained,'—a rare sense for ἀντιάζω, which in Sophocles elsewhere means 'to entreat' (1009).

871 Re-enter Chrysothemis.—ὑφ' ἡδονῆς τοι. Here τοι prefaces the explanation of her haste: cp. *Ph.* 245, *Tr.* 234.

872 τὸ κόσμιον. Hurried movement in public was contrary to Athenian notions of εὐκοσμία. Cp. Plat. *Charmides* p. 159 B εἶπεν ὅτι οἱ δοκοῖ σωφροσύνη εἶναι τὸ κοσμίως πάντα ποιεῖν καὶ ἡσυχῇ ἔν τε ταῖς ὁδοῖς βαδίζειν καὶ διαλέγεσθαι.

873 For the place of ὧν at the end of the v., cp. *O. T.* 298, *O. C.* 14, *Tr.* 819.

875 f. σύ, though emphatic, is not scornful, but rather compassionate.—ἴασιν οὐκ ἔνεστ' ἰδεῖν. The *v.l.* ἴασις might at first sight seem preferable; but the vulgate is stronger, through the weight thrown on the impersonal οὐκ ἔνεστι.

878 ἐναργῶς, in bodily presence: cp. *O. C.* 910 ἐναργεῖς.. στήσῃς.

879 ἀλλ' ἦ..; In this formula, ἦ asks the question, while ἀλλά marks surprise: cp. *Ph.* 414.—τοῖς at the end of the v.: *O. C.* 351, *Ant.* 409, *Ph.* 263.

881 f. μὰ τὴν πατρῴαν ἐστίαν is a fitting asseveration here, since the hearth symbolises the very existence of the family.— ἀλλ' οὐχ ὕβρει. Here ἀλλά ('nay') protests against Electra's words, and, as usual, follows the oath: cp. Ar. *Ran.* 173 ΝΕ. δύο δραχμὰς μισθὸν τελεῖς; | ΔΙ. μὰ Δί', ἀλλ' ἔλαττον.—ἀλλ' ἐκεῖνον. This second ἀλλά merely opposes its clause to the former: 'I do not say this in mockery, but report him as (really) present': cp. *Ai.* 852 f. ἀλλ' οὐδὲν ἔργον ταῦτα θρηνεῖσθαι μάτην, | ἀλλ' ἀρκτέον τὸ πρᾶγμα σὺν τάχει τινί. For the ὡς, which might be absent (as in 676), cp. 1341: *O. T.* 956 πατέρα τὸν σὸν ἀγγελῶν | ὡς οὐκέτ' ὄντα Πόλυβον.—For the triple ἀλλά in vv. 879—882, cp. *Ph.* 645—651: *O. C.* 238—248.

885 ἐξ ἐμοῦ, on my own authority: cp. 344 ἐκ σαυτῆς.— For the use of τε καί in coupling opposites, cp. *O. T.* 1275 πολλάκις τε κοὐχ ἅπαξ, *O. C.* 935 βίᾳ τε κοὐχ ἑκών.

887 f. ἰδοῦσα πίστιν. Nauck substitutes ἔχουσα for ἰδοῦσα, but the latter is right, since πίστιν = 'warranty,' 'proof.' Cp. *O. T.* 1420 τίς μοι φανεῖται πίστις ἔνδικος;—εἰς τί μοι: for the ethic dat., cp. 144.

ἀνηκέστῳ, 'fatal': *Ai.* 52 τῆς ἀνηκέστου χαρᾶς.—πυρί, a feverish hope; cp. *Ai.* 478 κεναῖσιν ἐλπίσιν θερμαίνεται.

891 σὺ δ' οὖν: cp. *Ai.* 114 σὺ δ' οὖν, ἐπειδὴ τέρψις ἥδε σοι τὸ δρᾶν, | χρῶ χειρί.—τῷ λόγῳ, causal dat., since εἰ σοί τις ἡδονή (ἐστιν) = εἴ τι ἥδει.

892 καὶ δή: 317 n.—κατειδόμην: for the midd., cp. 977: *Ph.* 351.

893 ἀρχαῖον τάφον. The poet is thinking of an ancestral tomb, like those πατρῷα μνήματα at Athens in which members of the same γένος were buried. He may have conceived that the ashes of Agamemnon, after his corpse was burned (901 πυρᾶς), were deposited in a stone vault, above or beside which the tumulus (κολώνη) was raised.

894 ff. κολώνης ἐξ ἄκρας with νεορρύτους,—'which had newly streamed from the top of the mound'; this suits πηγάς.

γάλακτος: cp. Eur. *Or.* 114 ἐλθοῦσα δ' ἀμφὶ τὸν Κλυται-μνήστρας τάφον | μελίκρατ' ἄφες γάλακτος οἰνωπόν τ' ἄχνην.

περιστεφῆ..ἀνθέων: cp. *O. T.* 83 πολυστεφὴς..δάφνης.— ἴστιν, not ἐστίν, as the sense is, 'exist.'—θήκην, here denoting the κολώνη, was a general term for a sepulchre, whatever its form might be; thus Plato says (*Legg.* 947 D) θήκην δὲ ὑπὸ γῆς αὐτοῖς εἰργασμένην εἶναι ψαλίδα (vault) προμήκη λίθων.

897 f. ἴσχον θαῦμα = ἐθαύμασα: cp. 214 γνώμαν ἴσχεις, 1176 ἔσχες ἄλγος.—ἐγχρίμπτῃ is here more fitting than ἐγχρίμπτει, since the sense is, 'in fear lest some one be close by,' rather than, 'to see whether some one is not close by': cp. 581 τιθῇς (n.).

899 ἐν γαλήνῃ sc. ὄντα: cp. 61: *O. C.* 29 πέλας γὰρ ἄνδρα τόνδε νῷν ὁρῶ.

900 f. ἐσχάτης . . πυρᾶς, 'on the edge of the mound,'—the local gen., developed out of the possessive ('belonging to,' and so 'in the region of'): cp. *Il.* 9. 219 (ἵζεν) τοίχου τοῦ ἑτέροιο. The word πυρὰ can mean, not only a funeral pyre, but also the place where a corpse was formerly burned (*bustum*), and is here a synonym for τύμβος, κολώνη. So Pind. *I.* 7. 57 πυρὰν τάφον θ' (of Achilles): Eur. *Hec.* 386 πυρὰν 'Αχιλλέως.

νεώρη (ὥρα), recent, fresh (*O. C.* 730 φόβον νεώρη); here equivalent to an adverb (νεωστί) qualifying τετμημένον.

902 ff. ἐμπαίει κ.τ.λ.: 'there strikes, rushes, upon my soul a familiar image, (suggesting) that in this I see a sure token of Orestes.' ὄμμα is the 'face' or 'form' of her brother,— σύνηθες, because she was accustomed to think of him. The inf. ὁρᾶν, explanatory of the first clause, depends on the idea of a conception or belief which is implied in the mental image of the face; *i.e.*, ἐμπαίει μοι ὄμμα implies παρίσταταί μοι δόξα. The intrans. ἐμπαίειν (a stronger ἐμπίπτειν) occurs only here.—ψυχῇ is best taken with ἐμπαίει, though it could also go with σύνηθες.

905 βαστάσασα. The aor. of this verb often denotes taking into the hand (*Ph.* 657, etc.), as the pres. (below, 1129) denotes holding.—δυσφημῶ μὲν οὔ: *i.e.*, she refrains from uttering any mournful or reproachful word, with reference to his long delay in coming.—For the place of οὔ, cp. *Ai.* 545 ταρβήσει γὰρ οὔ.

907 f. νῦν θ' ὁμοίως καὶ τότ': cp. 676.—μή του. After a verb denoting confident belief, μή, not οὐ, is usu. joined with the inf.: cp. *O. T.* 1455 τοσοῦτόν γ' οἶδα, μήτε μ' ἂν νόσον | μήτ' ἄλλο πέρσαι μηδέν.—ἀγλάϊσμα: the word used by the Electra of Aeschylus in the same context, *Cho.* 193, εἶναι τόδ' ἀγλάϊσμά μοι τοῦ φιλτάτου | βροτῶν 'Ορέστου.

911 f. The elliptical πῶς γὰρ (*sc.* ἔδρασας) is followed by the relat. pron. ἥ γε, with a causal force, as in *Ph.* 1386 πῶς (*sc.*

φίλος εἶ), ὅς γε τοῖς ἐχθροῖσί μ᾽ ἐκδοῦναι θέλεις; This causal force is further marked here by the use of μηδέ instead of οὐδέ, —'one who is not allowed' (cui ne ad deos quidem *liceat* egredi).—πρὸς θεούς, *i.e.*, to their shrines; cp. Aesch. *P. V.* 530 θεοὺς ὁσίαις | θοίναις ποτινισσομένα. The reference is to the neighbouring Heraeum (v. 8), and to the altars or images of gods in front of the palace itself (637, 1374).

ἀκλαύστῳ: so L here, though it supports ἄκλαυτος in the other places. Cp. γνωστός and γνωτός.—For the sense, *impune*, cp. *O. T.* 401 κλαίων.

913 ἀλλ᾽ οὐδὲ μὲν δή, rejecting an alternative, as *Tr.* 1128, *Ai.* 877.

914 οὔτε δρῶσ᾽ ἐλάνθαν᾽ ἄν. Attic poets seldom elide the ε of the 3rd pers. sing. before ἄν: *e.g.* ἔγραψ᾽ ἄν, *scripsissem*, is easier to find than ἔγραψ᾽ ἄν, *scripsisset*. In respect to the weak (or 'first') aorists there was a reason for it, viz., that ἔγραψ᾽ ἄν, when meant as the 3rd pers., was liable to be confused with the 1st, unless the context was decisive; a reason which did not apply to the strong aorists or imperfects, *e.g.* to ἔλαθ᾽ ἄν or ἐλάνθαν᾽ ἄν.

But is ἐλάνθανεν, the reading of the MSS., even tenable? Surely not. The sense required is: 'Nor, if she had done it, would she have escaped notice.' But the words οὔτε δρῶσ᾽ ἐλάνθανεν could mean only one of two things: (1) 'nor, when she did it, *was she escaping* (or *used she to escape*) notice': (2) 'nor, when she did it, *was she in the way to escape* notice.' That is: whichever shade of meaning were given to ἐλάνθανεν, still δρῶσα, in the absence of anything to mark conditionality, would imply, not εἰ ἕδρα, but ὅτε ἕδρα.

915 τἀπιτύμβια is Dindorf's certain correction of τἀπιτίμια, a word which elsewhere always means, 'the price set' upon a thing, and so, 'the penalty' of a deed: cp. 1382. It cannot be explained as denoting 'the dues' paid by Orestes at the grave. Cp. *Ant.* 901 κἀπιτυμβίους | χοὰς ἔδωκα.

916 f. θάρσυνε. The verb is not elsewhere intrans., but here follows the analogy of βραδύνω, κρατύνω, ταχύνω.—οὐχ αὐτὸς ἀεί: cp. *Tr.* 129 ἐπὶ πῆμα καὶ χαρὰ πᾶσι κυκλοῦσιν.

918 f. νῷν ἦν. The insertion after νῷν of δ᾽ (omitted in L) seems no gain here.—κῦρος: *O. C.* 1779.

920 φεῦ τῆς ἀνοίας, ὥς κ.τ.λ. This punctuation is recommended by the order of the words: cp. Eur. *Phoen.* 1425 φεῦ φεῦ κακῶν σῶν, Οἰδίπου, σ᾽ ὅσον στένω. Others place a comma

Notes

after φεῦ, and take τῆς ἀνοίας with ἐποικτίρω: but in the passages which might seem similar the verb *precedes* the gen., as Aesch. *P. V.* 397 στένω σε τᾶς οὐλομένας τύχας.

922 ὅποι γῆς...φέρει (cp. *O. T.* 1309 ποῖ γᾶς φέρομαι..;), in a figurative sense,—'you know not into what regions your thoughts are straying,'—*i.e.*, how far from realities: ὅποι γνώμης explains this. Cp. 390.

923 πῶς δ' οὐκ ἐγὼ κάτοιδ'; cp. *Ph.* 250, πῶς γὰρ κάτοιδ', where κάτοιδα answers to οἶσθα (as here) in the line before.

924 f. τἀκείνου.. σωτήρια, such means of deliverance as he could afford,—like ἐλπίδες τινός, hopes *from* one (857 f., n.).

928 καὶ ποῦ; for καί prefixed to the interrogative word, cp. 236: *O. C.* 263.—ὑπέρχεται: cp. 1112.

929 μητρὶ goes with both adjectives; for its place, cp. *O. C.* 1399 οἴμοι κελεύθου τῆς τ' ἐμῆς δυσπραξίας: *Ant.* 1155 Κάδμου πάροικοι καὶ δόμων Ἀμφίονος.

931 τὰ πολλά: for the art., cp. 564.—πρὸς τάφον, not πρὸς τάφῳ, since the thought is, τίς προσήνεγκε ταῦτα;

932 f. μάλιστ', as the most probable explanation: cp. *Ph.* 617 οἴοιτο μὲν μάλισθ' ἑκούσιον λαβών.—μνημεῖ', predicative.

934 f. ὦ δυστυχής: *sc.* ἐγώ: so *Tr.* 377 ὦ δύστηνος.—τοιούσδ', so joyful.

936 ἵν' ἦμεν ἄτης: cp. *O. T.* 367 ἵν' εἶ κακοῦ: *ib.* 1442 ἵν' ἕσταμεν | χρείας.

939 λύσεις, do away with, remove; cp. *O. C.* 1615 ἀλλ' ἐν γὰρ μόνον | τὰ πάντα λύει ταῦτ' ἔπος μοχθήματα.

941 οὐκ ἔσθ' ὅ γ' εἶπον, 'It is not quite what I meant';— said with a gentle and mournful irony, which the next words, οὐ γὰρ ὧδ' ἄφρων ἔφυν, further mark. Electra is very gradually leading up to a proposal which, as she well knows, will dismay her sister; whose question—ἦ τοὺς θανόντας κ.τ.λ.—shows how far she is from conceiving that the present situation leaves any possibilities of action.

942 φερέγγυος, 'able to give security,' and so 'competent' for a purpose, stands with a gen. only here, the usual constr. being the inf. (as Aesch. *Eum.* 87); but Thuc. 8. 68 has πρὸς τὰ δεινά...φερεγγυώτατος.

943 τλῆναι.. δρῶσαν: cp. Aesch. *Theb.* 754 σπείρας.. | .. ἔτλα: *Ag.* 1041 πραθέντα τλῆναι.

944 ὠφελειά γ': the particle implies her belief that these counsels will prove ἀνωφελῆ.

945 ὅρα, an impressive warning that the task about to be

138   *Electra*

mentioned is a great one; cp. *O. C.* 587 ὅρα γε μήν· οὐ σμικρός,
οὐχ, ἀγὼν ὅδε.—πόνου.. εὐτυχεῖ: cp. Eur. fr. 233 σοὶ δ᾽ εἶπον, ὦ
παῖ, τὰς τύχας ἐκ τῶν πόνων | θηρᾶν.

946 ξυνοίσω, share the burden, help; cp. *Ph.* 627.

947 ποεῖν. The *v.l.* τελεῖν is less fitting here than the
simpler word.

948 παρουσίαν here implies the notion of 'support,' 'aid,'
as παρεῖναι often does (*Ph.* 373).—καὶ σύ που: cp. 55.

950 λελείμμεθον is the only classical instance of a 1st pers.
dual except περιδώμεθον in *Il.* 23. 485, and ὁρμώμεθον in *Ph.*
1079.—Cp. *Ant.* 58 μόνα δὴ νὼ λελειμμένα.

952 θάλλοντ᾽ ἔτ᾽ is Reiske's certain correction of θάλλοντά τ᾽.
Hermann, retaining the latter, followed Triclinius in taking βίῳ
as = ἐν βίῳ ὄντα, 'alive,' which is clearly untenable; as is also
the conjecture βιοῦν.—Cp. *Tr.* 235 καὶ ζῶντα καὶ θάλλοντα.

953 πράκτορ᾽, one who exacts a penalty; an avenger: as
the Erinyes are πράκτορες αἵματος (Aesch. *Eum.* 319). At
Athens the πράκτορες were officials who collected fines and
penalties (ἐπιβολαί, τιμήματα) imposed by law. We have a
similar figurative use of a technical term in *Ai.* 508 μητέρα |
πολλῶν ἐτῶν κληροῦχον. There are Shakespearian parallels;
e.g., Lear (act 3, sc. 2, 59) calls the raging elements 'these
dreadful summoners' (officers who warned offenders to appear
in court).

954 εἰς σὲ δὴ βλέπω: here δή, after ἡνίκ᾽ οὐκέτ᾽ ἔστιν, marks
the next resource, just as in *Ant.* 173 ἐγὼ κ ἄτη δή .. ἔχω follows
ὅτ᾽ οὖν ἐκεῖνοι.. ὤλοντο. Thus it is here rather an equivalent
for ἤδη than merely a mode of emphasising σέ.

956 κατοκνήσεις. The clause ὅπως κατοκνήσεις denotes the
object of the appeal implied in εἰς σὲ δὴ βλέπω. Cp. Ar. *Eq.*
1255 καί σ᾽ αἰτῶ βραχύ, | ὅπως ἔσομαί σοι Φανός. This is the
normal construction. The *v.l.* κατοκνήσῃς is also correct, but is
less probable. Any verb can be followed by a 'final' clause in
the *subjunctive*, expressing the 'end' or purpose of the action,
as ἔρχεται ἵνα ἴδῃ. But a verb of endeavouring, praying, con-
triving, usually takes an 'object' clause, expressing the object
of the effort, with ὅπως (or ὡς) and *fut. indic.*: as πειρᾶται ὅπως
ὄψεται.

957 κρύπτειν: cp. *Ph.* 915 οὐδέν σε κρύψω.—The mention
of the murderer's name, which Electra has hitherto uttered
only in her solitary lament (98), is forcible here; and the
emphatic place given to it is in the manner of Sophocles. The

words οὐδὲν γάρ σε κ.τ.λ. refer, of course, to the purpose which Electra now discloses—not to the guilt of Aegisthus.

In this play the fate of Aegisthus forms the climax. Electra has already said that Clytaemnestra shared in the murderous deed (97 ff., 206), and has avowed that she would have wished Orestes to wreak vengeance on her (604). But she does not suggest that she herself or her sister should slay their mother; even the plur. ἐχθροῖς in 979 need not mean more than Aegisthus. Sophocles avoids everything that could qualify our sympathy with Electra; while it suits the different aim of Euripides to make her plan the matricide. See Introduction.

958 f. ποῖ.. μενεῖς. For ποῖ as = μέχρι τίνος, εἰς τίνα χρόνον, cp. Ar. *Lys.* 526 ποῖ γὰρ καὶ χρῆν ἀναμεῖναι; It is also possible to join ποῖ with βλέψασα: 'to what quarter—to what hope—can you look?' But the order of the words is certainly against that.—βλέψασ': cp. 888.

960 κτῆσιν, which could depend on στένειν, is perhaps best taken with ἐστερημένῃ. Though the simple στερεῖσθαι (as distinguished from ἀποστερεῖσθαι) is not usually joined with an acc., there is at least one instance, Eur. *Helen.* 95 πῶς; οὔ τί που σῷ φασγάνῳ βίον στερείς;

961 ἐς τοσόνδε τοῦ χρόνου: cp. 14 τοσόνδ' ἐς ἥβης. For ὁ χρόνος as = one's term of life, cp. *Ant.* 461 εἰ δὲ τοῦ χρόνου | πρόσθεν θανοῦμαι.

962 ἄλεκτρα...ἀνυμέναια, as *Ant.* 917 ἄλεκτρον, ἀνυμέναιον. The inverse order of words would be more natural, as the ὑμέναιος escorted the bride and bridegroom to their home. Cp. 164 f., and 187.

γηράσκουσαν, acc. with ἀλγεῖν, while ἐστερημένη (960) depends on πάρεστι. Cp. Eur. *Med.* 1236 δέδοκται τοὖργον ὡς τάχιστά μοι | παῖδας κτανούσῃ τῆσδ' ἀφορμᾶσθαι χθονός, | καὶ μὴ σχολὴν ἄγουσαν ἐκδοῦναι τέκνα. The word γηράσκουσαν, like Electra's phrase ὁ πολὺς .. βίοτος in 185 ff., must be taken relatively to the ordinary age for marriage. It would suit the data to suppose that Electra was about twenty-five, and her sister a little younger.

963 f. τῶνδε, *i.e.* λέκτρων καὶ ὑμεναίων: as in *Tr.* 260 τόνδε refers to the preceding phrase, πόλιν τὴν Εὐρυτείαν.—ὅπως: cp. Eur. *Heracl.* 1051 μὴ γὰρ ἐλπίσῃς ὅπως | αὖθις πατρῴας ζῶν ἔμ' ἐκβαλεῖς χθονός.

965 f. ἢ κἀμὸν, 'or mine either.'—πημονὴν, acc. in apposition with the sentence: cp. 130 παραμύθιον: 564 ποινάς.

967 ἐπίσπῃ: cp. 1052: *Ant.* 636 (γνώμας) αἷς ἔγωγ' ἐφέψομαι.

968 f. εὐσέβειαν.. οἶσα, 'win praise of piety': cp. *Ant.* 924 τὴν δυσσέβειαν εὐσεβοῦσ' ἐκτησάμην: and for οἶσει.. ἐκ, *Tr.* 461 κοὔπω τις αὐτῶν ἔκ γ' ἐμοῦ λόγον κακὸν | ἠνέγκατ' οὐδ' ὄνειδος.— As θανόντος here denotes the state of the dead, and not the act of dying, κάτω can be joined to it; though it would have been clearer if the art. had been added.

970 ff. The compound ἐξέφυς implies the stock from which she sprang, as in *O. T.* 1084 τοιόσδε δ' ἐκφύς, 'such being my lineage.' It is usu. joined with a genitive.—καλεῖ: this fut. midd. (used by Ar. *Nub.* 1221 and *Eccl.* 864) seems to occur only here in a pass. sense; the fut. pass. is usu. κεκλήσομαι, more rarely κληθήσομαι.—τὰ χρηστὰ = τὰς χρηστάς: cp. 1507: *Ph.* 448 τὰ μὲν πανοῦργα καὶ παλιντριβῆ...τὰ δὲ | δίκαια καὶ τὰ χρηστά. With ὁρᾶν πρός τι, cp. Plat. *Alcib.* 1. p. 134 D εἰς τὸ θεῖον καὶ λαμπρὸν ὁρῶντες.

973 λόγων γε μὴν εὔκλειαν, lit., 'as to fame, *however*,' γε μήν merely marking that the speaker turns to a new point. Cp. *O. C.* 587 ὅρα γε μήν,—the only other instance of γε μήν in Sophocles. λόγων implies a contrast with ἔργα,—*i.e.*, the substantial gains mentioned in 971 f.

975 f. ἀστῶν ἢ ξένων. As in *O. T.* 1489 ff., the poet is thinking of festivals or spectacles at which Athenian women could appear in public, when many visitors from other cities were present.—δεξιώσεται, properly, to give the right hand to one in welcome; Aeschin. or. 3 § 87 ὁ νυνὶ πάντας δεξιούμενος καὶ προσγελῶν: then, generally, 'to greet'; Paus. 2. 16. 2 ἰδεῖν ἤθελε τὸν γονέα τῆς μητρός, καὶ λόγοις τε χρηστοῖς καὶ ἔργοις δεξιώσασθαι.

979 f. εὖ βεβηκόσιν: cp. 1057: Her. 7. 164 τυραννίδα...εὖ βεβηκυῖαν.—ἀφειδήσαντε, fem. (cp. 1003, 1006). The properly feminine form of the dual in participles of the third declension is actually rare, though it was certainly in use (thus ἐχούσα occurs in an Attic inscr. of 398 B.C.).

προὐστήτην φόνου, lit., 'became ministers of bloodshed.' Here, the presence of the dat. ἐχθροῖς serves to blend the sense of 'administering' required by φόνου with that of 'standing forth' to confront an adversary; cp. *Ai.* 1133 ἦ σοὶ γὰρ Αἴας πολέμιος προὐστη ποτέ;

981 f. For τούτω...τώδε, cp. *Ph.* 841.—As dist. from ἑορταῖς, the phrase πανδήμῳ πόλει denotes any gathering of the citizens, as in the ordinary intercourse of the agora; cp. *O. T.* 1489 ποίας γὰρ ἀστῶν ἥξετ᾽ εἰς ὁμιλίας, | ποίας δ᾽ ἑορτάς ..; For τοι introducing the final comment, cp. *Ai.* 776.

986 f. συμπόνει and σύγκαμνε are here synonymous, though the idea of effort is more prominent in the former, and that of distress in the latter. Instead of repeating a word, the poet often thus uses a synonym; cp. 1308 f. στέγας...οἴκοις: *O. T.* 54 ἔρξεις...κρατεῖς: *Ant.* 669 καλῶς...εὖ: *Tr.* 457 δέδοικας...ταρβεῖς.

Electra has already declared her faith that Agamemnon, in the nether world, is the ally of his children (454 ἀρωγόν: cp. 459). Orestes also, as she believes, is now there, working in the same cause. She asks her sister to aid their efforts.

παῦσον ἐκ κακῶν: cp. 231 ἐκ καμάτων ἀποπαύσομαι. For the aor. imper. combined with the pres., cp. *Ai.* 507 αἴδεσαι, 510 οἴκτιρε.

989 In τοῖς καλῶς πεφυκόσιν both senses of 'noble' are involved, just as in *Tr.* 721 ζῆν γὰρ κακῶς κλύουσαν οὐκ ἀνασχετόν, | ἥτις προτιμᾷ μὴ κακὴ πεφυκέναι.

990 f. ἐν τοῖς τοιούτοις κ.τ.λ. These words of the Chorus, though neutral in tone (like their words at v. 369), imply that Electra's plan is over-bold, and Chrys. speaks as if sure of their approval; which, indeed, she receives at v. 1015.—καὶ κλύοντι: for the omission of the art., cp. 1498: Aesch. *Ag.* 324 τῶν ἁλόντων καὶ κρατησάντων.—σύμμαχος here merely = σύμφορος, helpful. The figurative sense of the word is usually closer to the literal; as in Antiphon or. 5 § 43 τὸ εἰκὸς σύμμαχόν μοί ἐστιν ('is on my side').

993 For the place of μὴ, cp. *Ph.* 66 εἰ δ᾽ ἐργάσει | μὴ ταῦτα. —ἐσώζετ᾽, 'remembered': *Tr.* 682.

995 f. ἐμβλέψασα is a slightly strengthened βλέψασα, implying a more intent gaze; cp. Plat. *Ion* 535 E δεινὸν ἐμβλέποντας, 'with stern countenances.'—θράσος .. ὁπλίζει: the acc. as with ἀμφιέννυσθαι, etc.: Schneidewin cp. *Anthol. Pal.* 5. 93 ὥπλισμαι πρὸς Ἔρωτα περὶ στέρνοισι λογισμόν.

997 f. εἰσορᾷς: cp. 584.—γυνὴ μὲν κ.τ.λ.: as Ismene, too, reminds her sister (*Ant.* 61).—σθένεις δ᾽ ἔλασσον .. χερί: this is not merely an amplification of γυνὴ μὲν κ.τ.λ., meaning that a woman's arm is weaker than a man's, but refers to the fighting forces at the disposal of the rulers.

1000 ἀπορρεῖ, like water that runs off; cp. *Ai.* 523 ἀπορρεῖ μνῆστις.—κἀπὶ μηδὲν ἔρχεται: so fr. 788. 8 (the waning moon) πάλιν διαρρεῖ κἀπὶ μηδὲν ἔρχεται.

1001 f. τοιοῦτον, so strong and so prosperous.—ἄλυπος ἄτης: cp. *O. C.* 786 κακῶν ἄνατος: *ib.* 1519 γήρως ἄλυπα.

1004 κτησώμεθ᾽: cp. 217 πολὺ γάρ τι κακῶν ὑπερεκτήσω.

1005 f. λύει here = 'set free,' 'extricate' from trouble, and therefore takes the acc.: cp. *Tr.* 181 ὄκνου σε λύσω.

δυσκλεῶς θανεῖν, a death of ignominy, *i.e.*, such as is appointed for malefactors. The βάξις καλὴ from admiring citizens and foreigners (975) will poorly compensate for the doom which Aegisthus can inflict.

1007 f. οὐ γὰρ θανεῖν κ.τ.λ.: here γὰρ refers to δυσκλεῶς in 1006: '(a death *of ignominy*, I say,) *for* mere death is not the worst that we have to fear; we shall suffer a lingering death, and shall long in vain to be put out of our misery.'

1010 κἀξερημῶσαι γένος: cp. Dem. or. 43 § 73 ἐπιμέλειαν ἐποιησάμην τοῦ οἴκου τοῦ Ἁγνίου ὅπως μὴ ἐξερημωθήσεται.

1012 ἄρρητα...κάτελῇ, she will not divulge them, nor act upon them; they will be ἀτελῆ, as finding no accomplishment, and therefore doing no harm. The dat. σοι implies that this is for Electra's own interest.

1013 ἀλλὰ τῷ χρόνῳ ποτέ: for ἀλλὰ cp. 411. The same phrase occurs in *Ph.* 1041: in *Tr.* 201, ἀλλὰ σὺν χρόνῳ.

1015 The difference between πείθου and πιθοῦ is simply that the pres. implies a mental process ('be persuaded,' 'allow the reasoning to weigh with thee'), while the aor. denotes an act ('obey,' 'comply,'—do the thing recommended). πείθου, as more suggestive of gentle entreaty, seems a little the better here; while πιθοῦ is more fitting in v. 1207.

1017 f. καλῶς δ᾽: for the elision at the end of the v., cp. *O. T.* 29.

1019 f. αὐτόχειρί μοι. The older editions have the adverb αὐτοχειρί. Porson restored the adj. here.—μόνη τε: contrast *Tr.* 1194 αὐτόχειρα καὶ ξὺν οἷς χρῄζεις φίλων.—οὐ γὰρ δὴ rejects the alternative which γε emphasises, as in *O. C.* 110, 265.—κενόν, 'void,' since τοὖργον τόδ᾽ refers to what is still only a project.

1021 f. εἴθ᾽ ὤφελες: cp. 1131 ὡς ὤφελον. The ironical wish is a way of expressing how insane she thinks Electra's present design: 'It is a pity that thy courage was not shown in preventing, rather than avenging, our father's murder.'—πᾶν γὰρ ἂν κατειργάσω, lit., 'thou wouldst have achieved anything'; nothing would have been too hard for thee,—even to defeat the murderous conspiracy.

1023 **φύσιν γε**, *i.e.*, in loyalty,—as she proved by saving her brother; though she had not then the ripe intelligence to grasp the whole situation, or to form a plan for averting the crime. The retort of Chrysothemis shows that she feels the reproach to herself implied by **τότε**.

1025 **ὡς οὐχὶ συνδράσουσα κ.τ.λ.**: 'You wish that I were still **ἥσσων νοῦν**, *i.e.*, incapable of forming such a plan as that on which I now propose to act. This is a hint that you will not act with me.'—**νουθετεῖς** has the same tone as **νουθετήματα** in 343.

1026 **εἰκὸς γὰρ κ.τ.λ.**: '(I will not act with thee), for it is likely that one who makes the attempt should e'en (**καὶ**) fare ill.' It is perhaps best to take **ἐγχειροῦντα** in this absolute sense, rather than to supply **κακοῖς** (or **κακά**) from **κακῶς**. The participle is in the masc., since the statement is general: cp. 145.— **πράσσειν**, not **πράξειν**. For the pres. inf., cp. 305 **μέλλων..δρᾶν**: *Ph.* 1398 f. **ᾔνεσας .. | πέμπειν**. In such cases the notion of fut. time is sufficiently expressed by the principal verb.

1027 **ζηλῶ**: cp. Eur. *I. A.* 1407 **ζηλῶ δὲ σοῦ μὲν Ἑλλάδ', Ἑλλάδος δὲ σέ**.

1028 **ἀνέξομαι κ.τ.λ.**: 'I will listen patiently *also* when you commend me (as I now listen to your taunts),'—*i.e.*, 'when, taught by bitter experience, you recognise the wisdom of my advice': cp. 1044. The point of **ἀνέξομαι** is that it will be a trial of patience to hear Electra's acknowledgments and regrets when her rash attempt has failed.

1029 **μὴ πάθῃς τόδε**, *i.e.*, **μὴ ἐπαινεθῇς**: as if the mere fact of being praised by Electra was the trial foreseen by her sister.

1030 **τὸ κρῖναι**, instead of the simple inf.: cp. 1079 **τό τε μὴ βλέπειν ἑτοίμα**: *Ant.* 78. Since **μακρὸς** here implies 'long *enough*,' an inf. can go with it as with **ἱκανός, δυνατός**, etc.: cp. Thuc. 2. 61 **ταπεινὴ** (*i.e.*, **ἀδύνατος**) **ὑμῶν ἡ διάνοια ἐγκαρτερεῖν ἃ ἔγνωτε**.

χὡ λοιπὸς χρόνος: *i.e.*, 'whether I am right or not, cannot be decided by the present moment alone; there is *also* the future to be considered.' That is what **καὶ** marks here, but marks so lightly that if we say, 'Time enough in the future to decide that,' the slight emphasis which naturally falls on the word 'future' will sufficiently express it.

1033 **μητρὶ..σῇ**: cp. 366 **καλοῦ | τῆς μητρός**.

1034 **οὐδ' αὖ κ.τ.λ.** 'I will not, indeed, act with thee;

but, on the other hand (αὖ), I do not hate thee so bitterly as to report thy words'; *i.e.*, if they were reported, the consequences would be direful. For οὐδ' as = ἀλλ' οὐ, cp. 132.

1035 ἀλλ' οὖν .. γ: cp. 233.—οἱ .. ἀτιμίας: cp. 404: Dem. or. 4 § 9 οἱ προελήλυθεν ἀσελγείας ἄνθρωπος. The ἀτιμία is the rejection (1018 ἀπορρίψουσαν) of Electra's earnest and solemn appeal. She means, 'you disclaim hatred of me; but at least do not conceal from yourself the cruelty of the slight which you inflict.'

1036 ἀτιμίας μὲν οὔ: for οὔ, cp. 905. The genitive is adapted to the form of the preceding verse; 'do not call it ἀτιμία: it is προμηθία.'

1037 τῷ σῷ δικαίῳ: *i.e.*, 'you dissuade me from this deed because, as you say, you are anxious for my welfare. Am I not, then (δῆτ'), to obey my own sense of duty? Must I obey yours instead?' The peculiarity of the phrase is that τῷ σῷ δικαίῳ means here, 'what is right according to you,' whereas it would normally mean, 'the right on which you rely,' 'your plea, or claim.' Cp. 1110 τὴν σὴν κληδόν'.

1039 ἢ δεινὸν: cp. *Ant.* 323 ἦ δεινόν, ᾧ δοκεῖ γε, καὶ ψευδῆ δοκεῖν.—εὖ λέγουσαν, because the sentiment expressed by Chrysothemis is sound in itself: ἐξαμαρτάνειν, because Chrysothemis assumes that true wisdom is *now* upon her own side, and not upon Electra's.

1040 ᾧ σὺ πρόσκεισαι κακῷ: cp. 240 n.—Chrysothemis means that Electra εὖ λέγει, as upholding a right principle, but ἐξαμαρτάνει, in proposing a desperate scheme.

1041 f. τί δ'; οὐ δοκῶ σοι κ.τ.λ.: 'You say that I am in error. How then? Do you deny that right is on my side?' Chrysothemis had already admitted that τὸ δίκαιον was with Electra (338): she does so here also, but argues, as before, from expediency alone.

1044 εἰ ποήσεις: for the fut. indic. ('if you are going to do this') cp. *Ai.* 1155 εἰ γὰρ ποήσεις, ἴσθι πημανούμενος.

1045 καὶ μήν: cp. 556 n.

1046 βουλεύσει πάλιν = μεταβουλεύσει. Cp. *Ph.* 961 εἰ καὶ πάλιν | γνώμην μετοίσεις ('change it back,'—not, 'change a second time').

1048 φρονεῖν: *i.e.*, 'you seem to share none of my sentiments'; cp. *Ant.* 370 f. ἐμοὶ .. | .. ἴσον φρονῶν.

1049 ταῦτα, her own rules of conduct, as distinguished from her sister's.

1051 τολμᾷς, 'bring thyself' to do it; cp. *O. C.* 184 τόλμα .. | .. ὅ τι καὶ πόλις | τέτροφεν ἄφιλον ἀποστυγεῖν.

1052 οὔ σοι μὴ μεθέψομαι. When οὐ μή stands with the fut. indic., it can express either (1) a prohibition, if joined with the 2nd pers.; or (2) a denial, as here, if joined with the 1st or 3rd pers. Cp. Ar. *Ran.* 508 οὐ μή σ' ἐγὼ | περιόψομἀπελθόντ'.

1054 καὶ τὸ θηρᾶσθαι κενά: cp. *Ant.* 92 ἀρχὴν δὲ θηρᾶν οὐ πρέπει τἀμήχανα: and for καὶ, Plat. *Prot.* p. 317 A πολλὴ μωρία καὶ τοῦ ἐπιχειρήματος ('the very attempt is ridiculous').—κενά, vain dreams that her sister could ever feel and act with her: cp. 1031 σοὶ γὰρ ὠφέλησις οὐκ ἔνι.

After 1057 Chrysothemis enters the house.

1058—1097 Second στάσιμον. 1st strophe, 1058—1069, = 1st antistr., 1070—1081: 2nd str., 1082—1089, = 2nd antistr., 1090—1097. For the metres see Metrical Analysis.

The contrast between the attitude of the two sisters suggests the theme of this ode. Why does not Chrysothemis follow the example of natural piety which the very birds of the air set before us? But impiety will not go unpunished. Let the spirit of Agamemnon hear that Electra now stands utterly alone. She has chosen to suffer, and is ready to die, in her righteous cause. May she yet prevail!

1058 f. ἄνωθεν here = ἄνω: so 1449 ἔξωθεν: *Tr.* 601 ἔσωθεν: *Ant.* 521 κάτωθεν.—οἰωνοὺς with οἷ (the only example in this word): cp. 1001 τοιοῦτον: fr. 881 τὸν Βοιώτιον νόμον.—The stork was especially a type of parental and filial piety: Ar. *Av.* 1355 ἐπὴν ὁ πατὴρ ὁ πελαργὸς ἐκπετησίμους | πάντας ποήσῃ τοὺς πελαργιδῆς τρέφων, | δεῖ τοὺς νεοττοὺς τὸν πατέρα πάλιν τρέφειν.

1059 f. ἐσορώμενοι: for the midd., cp. *Tr.* 909 εἰσορωμένη. —(τούτων) ἀφ' ὧν: cp. *O. C.* 1388 κτανεῖν θ' ὑφ' οὗπερ ἐξελήλασαι.

1061 f. εὕρωσι, where εὕρωνται would be more usual: cp. 1305 μέγ' εὑρεῖν κέρδος.—ἐπ' ἴσας, *sc.* μοίρας: cp. Her. 1. 74 διαφέρουσί σφι ἐπὶ ἴσης τὸν πόλεμον.

1063 ἀλλ' οὐ τὰν κ.τ.λ. Although the text in the antistrophic v., 1075, is uncertain, it seems probable that the words Ἠλέκτρα, τὸν ἀεὶ πατρὸς there represent the true metre, and that therefore Turnebus was right in deleting μὰ before τὰν here. μὰ is similarly omitted in *O. T.* 660, 1088, *Ant.* 758.

1064 τὰν οὐρανίαν Θέμιν. There is a twofold fitness in the mention of her here. She is the goddess of just counsel, enthroned beside Zeus (Διὸς .. πάρεδρος .. Θέμις, Pind. *Ol.* 8. 21);

and her faithful daughters (the Ὧραι) will bring the time of vengeance.

1065 ἀπόνητοι = ἄπονοι, free from trouble or suffering; a form found elsewhere only in the adv. ἀπονητότατα (Her. 2. 14). The reference is explained by the words, τάδ' οὐκ ἐπ' ἴσας τελοῦμεν; 'Those of us mortals who neglect these duties do not long escape suffering.' A reflection suggested by the conduct of Chrysothemis is softened by being put in a general form.

1066 χθονία, preceding βροτοῖσι, serves to indicate that the dead are meant (cp. 462 βροτῶν n.): the dat. is ethic, denoting those who perceive the φάμα.

φάμα: cp. Pind. *O.* 8. 81, where the news of an athlete's victory is brought to his dead father in the under-world by Ἀγγελία, daughter of Hermes.

Some write Φάμα. Aeschines mentions Φήμης θεοῦ μεγίστης βωμόν at Athens (or. 1. § 291: cp. Hes. *Op.* 761 f.). But here, I think, φάμα rather hovers on the verge of personification than is actually personified, just as in Her. 9. 100 φήμη .. ἐσέπτατο ἐς τὸ στρατόπεδον.

1067 κατά .. βόασον: for the tmesis, cp. *O. T.* 1198 κατὰ μὲν φθίσας: *Ant.* 977 κατὰ δὲ τακόμενοι.—μοι: cp. 144.

1068 f. Ἀτρείδαις. As τέκνων in 1071 shows, the ref. is to Agamemnon only; for the plur., cp. 1419 οἱ γᾶς ὑπαὶ κείμενοι: Aesch. *Cho.* 49 τοὺς γᾶς | νέρθεν.

ἀχόρευτα: cp. *O. C.* 1222 f. (death) ἀνυμέναιος | ἄλυρος ἄχορος: Aesch. *Suppl.* 681 (war) ἄχορον ἀκίθαριν.—The ὀνείδη are the dishonours of the house,—not reproaches to the spirit of Agamemnon for inactivity; though it is implied, of course, that now more than ever his aid is needed.

1070 νοσεῖ answers to οἰωνοὺς (∪--) in 1058: it is certain, therefore, that a syllable has dropped out after it. δή (supplied by Triclinius) is at least tolerable, and is not precluded by ἤδη: cp. Eur. *Tro.* 233 δοῦλαι γὰρ δή ('*very* slaves') | Δωρίδος ἐσμὲν χθονὸς ἤδη. So here δή will emphasise νοσεῖ.

1071 ff. τὰ δὲ πρὸς τέκνων, acc.: lit., 'as to the relations between their children.'—διπλῆ φύλοπις, 'strife between two,' 'strife of sister with sister.' The use of the word in ref. to a private quarrel is like that of πολέμους in 219.

οὐκέτ' ἐξισοῦται, 'is no longer equalised'; *i.e.*, cannot be resolved into harmony, does not permit unity of feeling, φιλοτασίῳ διαίτᾳ, in a friendly home-life; for the dat. seems to be

modal rather than instrumental. The boldness of the phrase
resides in the fact that διπλῆ φύλοπις, 'strife between two,' is
treated as = 'two who are at strife,' and so ἐξισοῦται expresses
what would more properly be said of the sisters' minds.

1074 σαλεύει: *O. T.* 22 πόλις.. | ἤδη σαλεύει. Plato
similarly applies the word to persons, ἐν νόσοις ἢ γήρᾳ σαλεύ-
οντας (*Legg.* 923 B).

1075 Ἠλέκτρα, †τὸν ἀεὶ πατρὸς. The traditional interpretation, preserved in the scholia, took πατρὸς with στενάχουσ',
as = 'mourning for her sire,' and τὸν ἀεὶ as = τὸν ἀεὶ χρόνον. The
gen. in this sense is quite tenable, but there is nothing to show
that τὸν ἀεὶ could be used, without χρόνον, as = 'for ever.'
Hence it is now generally held that this verse is corrupt.

Far the best conjecture is Heath's, ἁ παῖς, οἶτον ἀεὶ πατρὸς.
A marginal gloss on ἁ παῖς, namely Ἠλέκτρα, would easily
cause the corruption, especially since the words τὸν ἀεὶ so often
stand together.

1078 f. οὔτε.. τε: cp. 350.—τὸ.. μὴ βλέπειν, instead of the
simple inf.: for the art., cp. 1030 (n.).

1080 διδύμαν..Ἐρινύν, Aegisthus and Clytaemnestra. So
the word is applied to Helen (Aesch. *Ag.* 749, Verg. *Aen.* 2.
573) and to Medea (Eur. *Med.* 1260).—ἐλοῦσα, 'when she has
slain,' *i.e.*, 'if she can but slay.'

1081 τίς ἂν εὔπατρις κ.τ.λ.: 'what woman so truly noble is
likely ever to be born?' Will the world see again a maiden so
worthy of her descent? εὔπατρις is chosen so as to suggest
the *father* to whom she was so loyal.

1082 οὐδεὶς τῶν ἀγαθῶν <γὰρ>. This is a comment on
Electra's devotion, as just described. The train of thought
is;—'Yet such devotion might be expected in one who is truly
noble (in nature as well as in race); *for* no generous soul will
stoop to baseness.' By τῶν ἀγαθῶν here are meant οἱ καλῶς
πεφυκότες in the full sense (989 n.). The quality of Electra's
heroism is such as belongs to them generally; though in the
degree of it she is unique.

1083 f. ζῶν κακῶς, by an unworthy, a base life (cp. 989
ζῆν.. αἰσχρῶς).—νώνυμος, proleptic; cp. 18 (σαφῆ), 242 (ἐκτίμους).

1085 πάγκλαυτον αἰῶνα κοινὸν, 'a life of mourning, shared
with thy friends,' *i.e.*, with the unavenged father whose spirit is
mourning in the world below (cp. 847 n.). For this sense of
κοινὸν, cp. *Ai.* 265 ff.: πότερα δ' ἂν, εἰ νέμοι τις αἵρεσιν, λάβοις, |

φίλους ἀνιῶν αὐτὸς ἡδονὰς ἔχειν, | ἢ κοινὸς ἐν κοινοῖσι λυπεῖσθαι ξυνών; 'to pain thy friends, and have delights thyself, or to share the grief of friends who grieve?'

εἷλου: the 'choice' is illustrated by Electra's replies to the Chorus in the Parodos (121—250), and it is to these more especially that they allude.

1087 τὸ μὴ καλὸν καθοπλίσασα. I believe that καθοπλίσασα is corrupt, and has supplanted some word which meant 'having rejected' or 'spurned.' In the antistrophic verse (1095), βεβῶσαν, ἃ δὲ μέγιστ' ἔβλαστε κ.τ.λ., two short syllables (ἃ δὲ) correspond with the (now) long final of καλόν. The best conjecture is J. H. Heinrich Schmidt's ἀπολακτίσασα. Cp. Aesch. *P. V.* 651 σὺ δ', ὦ παῖ, μὴ ἀπολακτίσῃς λέχος | τὸ Ζηνός: *Eum.* 141 κἀπολακτίσασ' ὕπνον.

If καθοπλίσασα be retained, the choice is between two explanations, of which I prefer the first.

(1) 'Having vanquished dishonour' (schol. καταπολεμήσασα τὸ αἰσχρόν), *i.e.*, having overcome the temptation of ignoble ease and security. καθοπλίζω elsewhere means to 'arm' or 'equip,' never 'to subdue by arms.'

(2) 'Having made ready an unlovely deed': *i.e.*, the vengeance on the murderers.

1088 φέρειν, *so as* to win (cp. 872 μολεῖν), = φέρεσθαι, as *O. T.* 590. Cp. *Ph.* 117 ὡς τοῦτό γ' ἔρξας δύο φέρει δωρήματα.— ἐν ἑνὶ λόγῳ, 'in,' or as we say, 'on,' one account.

1090 f. καθύπερθεν, an epic word not elsewhere used in Tragedy: this figurative sense of it is not Homeric, but is frequent in Herodotus (as 8. 60 τῶν ἐχθρῶν κατύπερθε γενέσθαι. —τεῶν, for the MSS. τῶν, is a simpler and far more probable correction than τοσόνδ'. The epic and Ionic τεός is used in lyrics by Aesch. (*P. V.* 162, *Th.* 105, 108): in *Ant.* 604 (lyr.) the MSS. give τεὰν, which seems right.

1092 ὑπόχειρ (Musgrave's correction of ὑπὸ χεῖρα) is not elsewhere extant, but is correctly formed (cp. ἐπίχειρ, ἀντίχειρ), and is placed beyond reasonable doubt by the metre. ὑποχείριος is frequent in this sense.

1094 f. μοίρᾳ .. οὐκ ἐν ἐσθλᾷ βεβῶσαν : cp. 1056 f. ἐν κακοῖς | βεβήκης.

1095 ff. μέγιστα .. νόμιμα, those 'unwritten and unfailing' laws of the gods which prescribe natural piety in human relationships.—ἔβλαστε: they are the greatest that have ever 'come into existence,' being of divine origin, and antecedent to any human law: ἀεί ποτε | ζῇ ταῦτα, κοὐδεὶς οἶδεν ἐξ ὅτου 'φάνη (*Ant.* 456).

τῶνδε φερομέναν ἄριστα: 'on account of these,—*i.e.*, for observance of them, — winning excellent things,' 'winning an excellent reward,'—viz., praise of the noblest kind. τῶνδε is then a causal gen.: cp. *O. T.* 48 σωτῆρα κλῄζει τῆς πάρος προθυμίας. That this is the sense of φερομέναν here, is strongly suggested by other passages; cp. 968 f. εὐσέβειαν .. | .. οἴσει, and esp. *O. T.* 863 ff. εἴ μοι ξυνείη φέροντι (= φερομένῳ) | μοῖρα τὰν εὔσεπτον ἁγνείαν λόγων | ἔργων τε πάντων, ὧν νόμοι πρόκεινται | ὑψίποδες ('winning the praise of reverent purity,' etc.).

1097 τᾷ Ζηνὸς εὐσεβείᾳ, 'by thy piety towards Zeus': ior the objective gen., cp. *O. T.* 239 θεῶν εὐχαῖσι. The MSS. have Διὸς, against metre, just as in *Tr.* 956 they have τὸν Διὸς ἄλκιμον γόνον. In both places, Ζηνὸς, the correction of Triclinius, seems the best.

1098—1383 Third ἐπεισόδιον. Orestes and Pylades present themselves as Phocians, followed by two attendants (1213), one of whom carries a bronze urn.

Orestes reveals himself to Electra, who gives utterance to her joy (1098—1287).

He then speaks of his plans. The Paedagogus enters (1326), and urges them to lose no more time. Orestes and Pylades, with their attendants and the Paedagogus, enter the house (1375).

Electra, after a brief prayer, follows them in (1383).

1098 f. εἰσηκούσαμεν, *i.e.*, from some one in the neighbourhood. These envoys from Strophius (1111) are not supposed to have travelled with the messenger from Phanoteus (670). The poet has skilfully varied the dialogue from the similar one in 660 ff.

ὀρθῶς θ'. The *v.l.* δ' for θ', though it has the better authority, is improbable here.—ἔνθα here = 'whither': *Ph.* 1466.

1101 Αἴγισθον: for the constr., cp. *Ph.* 444 τοῦτον οἶσθ' εἰ ζῶν κυρεῖ;—ᾤκηκεν, 'has fixed his abode,'—a light touch of dramatic irony, since his tenure of it is so nearly at an end. Plat. *Legg.* 666 E οὐκ ἐν ἄστεσι κατῳκηκότων (but nomads).

1102 ἀλλ', 'well': cp. *Tr.* 229 ἀλλ' εὖ μὲν ἵγμεθ'.—χὠ φράσας: cp. Pind. *P.* 4. 117 δόμους πατέρων... | φράσσατέ μοι. —ἀζήμιος, *i.e.*, οὐκ ἔνοχος ζημίᾳ: schol. ἄμεμπτος.

1103 f. τίς .. φράσειεν ἄν; For the form of the request, cp.

660 (n.); *O. C.* 70 ἆρ' ἄν τις αὐτῷ πομπὸς ἐξ ὑμῶν μόλοι; For the doubled ἄν, 333 (n.).

ποθεινὴν, passive, 'desired,' as in *Ph.* 1445 (the only other place where Soph. has the word). The Chorus are meant to understand that the arrival of the new comers has been expected, and will prove welcome, as confirming the news from Phocis. To the ear of the spectator ποθεινὴν suggests the longing of Electra for her brother's return.

1105 τὸν ἄγχιστον : *i.e.*, nearest of kin to Clyt. and Aegisthus; the Chorus do not surmise her relationship to the young Phocian. For the general masc., cp. 145, 1026.

1106 ἴθ', ὦ γύναι. As ἴθι was used in entreaty (*O. T.* 46), it is not, in itself, abrupt ; but the tone of the direction implies ignorance of Electra's rank, and is thus in keeping with the part of the Phocian ξένος. Orestes,—who thought that he recognised her voice when it was heard from within (v. 80),— can, of course, be in no doubt as to her identity. But he pretends not to know who she is until he hears her name pronounced by the Chorus (1171).

1108 οὐ δή ποθ' : cp. *Tr.* 876 οὐ δή ποθ' ὡς θανοῦσα;

1110 f. τὴν σὴν κληδόν' : cp. *Ph.* 1251 τὸν σὸν οὐ ταρβῶ φόβον.—Στρόφιος : see on 45. The name occurs nowhere else in the play.

1113 f. φέροντες, 'carrying' (in the urn), refers simply to the mode of conveyance ; κομίζομεν, 'we bring,' expresses the care with which they perform their mission. In κομίζω, 'care' is indeed the primary notion (cp. κομιδή) : that of 'taking a thing to a place' is secondary.

1115 f. τοῦτ' ἐκεῖν' κ.τ.λ. Three modes of punctuation are possible ; the first is perhaps the best, though the second is also satisfactory. (1) To place no point either after ἐκεῖν' or after σαφές. 'There, it seems, I clearly see that sorrow (= the sorrow which I foreboded) in your hands.' σαφὲς is then equiv. to an adv. with δέρκομαι. (2) To place a point after σαφές. 'This is what I feared (ἐκεῖνο), now placed beyond a doubt ; I see,' etc. The only objection to this is that the words πρόχειρον κ.τ.λ. then become a little abrupt and obscure. (3) To place a point after ἐκεῖν', and none after σαφές. 'That is it ; I now see clearly,' etc. But this colloquialism seems too homely for the style of Sophocles.

πρόχειρον, 'ready in the hand': *Ph.* 747 πρόχειρον εἴ τί σοι, τέκνον, πάρα | ξίφος χεροῖν.—ἄχθος, *i.e.*, the urn, but with ref. to the figurative sense, 'woe' (cp. 120, 204): *Ant.* 1172 τί δ' αὖ τόδ' ἄχθος βασιλέων ἥκεις φέρων;

1120 κέκευθεν, trans., as in *Il.* 22. 118 ὅσσα πτόλις ἥδε κέκευθε. In Attic it is elsewhere intrans.

1122 Cp. Aesch. *P.V.* 637 ὡς τἀποκλαῦσαι κἀποδύρασθαι τύχας.

1123 ff. δότε (αὐτῇ), ἥτις ἐστί: cp. *Ant.* 35 ὃς ἂν τούτων τι δρᾷ, | φόνον προκεῖσθαι.—ἐπαιτεῖται: the only instance of the midd.—πρὸς αἵματος: cp. *Ai.* 1305 τοὺς πρὸς αἵματος: Arist. *Pol.* 2. 3, § 7 (συγγένειαν) ἢ πρὸς αἵματος ἢ κατ' οἰκειότητα καὶ κηδείαν. —φύσιν: cp. 325 n.

1127 f. ψυχῆς Ὀρέστου λοιπόν, lit., 'remaining from the life of Orestes.'—ἀπ' ἐλπίδων, far away from my hopes, contrary to them: cp. Apoll. Rh. 2. 863 μάλα πολλὸν ἀπ' ἐλπίδος ἔπλετο νόστος.

οὐχ ὦνπερ (if sound) is best explained as standing, by attraction to ἐλπίδων, for οὐχ αἷσπερ: and the sense is:—'In a manner how contrary to my hopes—not with those hopes wherewith I sent thee forth—have I received thee back.' The notion of contrariety is thus expressed twice over; first by ἀπό, then by οὐχ. If this is awkward in grammar, yet it has a certain pathetic emphasis.

I retain the traditional reading, though not without a suspicion that either ἀπ' or ὦνπερ is unsound. Schaefer proposed ὑπ' for ἀπ'.

1129 f. νῦν μὲν γὰρ κ.τ.λ. The schol. on 1126 quotes *Il.* 19. 288 (Briseïs mourning Patroclus): ζωὸν μέν σε ἔλειπον ἐγὼ κλισίηθεν ἰοῦσα, | νῦν δέ σε τεθνηῶτα κιχάνομαι.—οὐδὲν ὄντα: cp. 1166 τὸ μηδέν.—βαστάζω: cp. 905 n.—λαμπρὸν refers to the bright light of life in the young face. Cp. *O. T.* 81 λαμπρὸς ὥσπερ ὄμματι: Eur. *Ion* 475 τέκνων οἷς ἂν...λάμπωσιν ἐν θαλάμοις | ...νεανίδες ἥβαι.

1131 ff. ὡς ὤφελον: cp. *Il.* 3. 428 ὡς ὤφελες αὐτόθ' ὀλέσθαι. Electra's self-reproach is that her action, without ultimately saving his life, deprived him of funeral rites at home. She goes on to lament that she herself had not rendered those rites (1138 ff.).

τοῖνδε, the fem. form in Attic inscriptions.—κἀνασώσασθαι, 'rescue': so the act. in *O. T.* 1351 ἀπό τε φόνου | ἔρρυτο κἀνέσωσε. The word means esp. to 'recover' what has been lost. —φόνου: cp. 11.

1134 f. ὅπως .. ἴκεισο, lit., 'in order that thou mightest have lain': cp. *O. T.* 1389 ἵν' ἦ τυφλός τε καὶ κλύων μηδέν, and *ib.* 1392 ὡς ἔδειξα μήποτε κ.τ.λ.—τύμβου πατρῴου: cp. n. on 893.

1136 φυγὰς: as Clyt. says (776 f.), φυγὰς | ἀπεξενοῦτο: and Electra (865 ff.), ξένος | ἄτερ ἐμᾶν χερῶν | ...κέκευθεν.

1138 ἐν, instrumental (*Ant.* 764).—φίλαισι, as opp. to ξέναισι (1141). Cp. Pope's *Elegy*, vv. 47 ff.: 'What can atone, oh ever-injured shade! | Thy fate unpity'd, and thy rites unpaid? | No friend's complaint, no kind domestic tear | Pleas'd thy pale ghost, or grac'd thy mournful bier. | By foreign hands thy dying eyes were clos'd, | By foreign hands thy decent limbs compos'd, | By foreign hands thy humble grave adorn'd, | By strangers honour'd, and by strangers mourn'd!'

1139 λουτροῖς σ' ἐκόσμησ': not merely, 'honoured with washings,' but rather, 'washed and *dressed*' for the πρόθεσις. The sense is thus the same as in *Ant.* 900 f. θανόντας αὐτόχειρ ὑμᾶς ἐγὼ | ἔλουσα κἀκόσμησα.

1140 ἄθλιον βάρος, the calcined bones. So in *Il.* 24. 793 (at Hector's funeral), when the body had been burned and the pyre quenched with wine, ὀστέα λευκὰ λέγοντο κασίγνητοί θ' ἔταροί τε. They then place them in a λάρναξ or urn, which is laid in a grave (κάπετος), and over this a mound (σῆμα) is raised.

1141 f. ἐν ξέναισι χερσὶ κηδευθείς: cp. Demades ὑπὲρ τῆς δωδεκαετίας § 9 (in Baiter and Sauppe's *Oratores Attici*, vol. II. p. 314) χιλίων ταφῇ Ἀθηναίων μαρτυρεῖ μοι, κηδευθεῖσα ταῖς τῶν ἐναντίων χερσίν (a reminiscence of this verse?).—σμικρὸς.. ὄγκος: cp. 758 n.

1143 ff. τῆς ἐμῆς.. τρ. ἀνωφελήτου: for the order of words, cp. 133 n.—παρέσχον, not παρεῖχον, because she is looking back on a closed chapter of her life.

1146 ἦ κἀμοῦ: for the redundant καί, see on *O. C.* 53 ὅσ' οἶδα κἀγώ.—μητρὸς.. φίλος, her 'dear one,' 'darling.'

1147 οἱ κατ' οἶκον, here = οἱ οἰκέται, as in *Tr.* 934 τῶν κατ' οἶκον. In Aesch. *Cho.* 749 ff. it is a domestic, the τροφός, who dwells on her care for the infancy of Orestes. ἦσαν, sc. τροφοί. —ἀλλ' ἐγὼ τροφός, sc. ἦ.

1148 ἀδελφὴ σοί, rather than ἀδελφή σοι, since a slight emphasis on the pron. better marks the reciprocity of affection; ' I was thy nurse; and by thee I was ever called "sister."' He had other sisters, but it was she who stood in the child's mind for all that ' sister' means.—προσηυδώμην: cp. 274.

1149 ff. ἐκλέλοιπε: 19 n.—θανόντι, in its simple pathos, is

better than the *v.l.* θανόντα, for which Brunck quotes Eur. *H.F.*
69 καὶ νῦν ἐκεῖνα μὲν θανόντ' ἀνέπτατο.—συναρπάσας, like the
more homely συλλαβὼν in *O. T.* 971.

1152 τέθνηκ' ἐγὼ σοί: 'I am dead in relation to thee.' For
Electra, this is another way of saying, 'I am dead, so far as
any aim or joy in life is concerned'; since the only hopes which
made life tolerable to her were centred in her brother. For
the dat. σοί, cp. *Ph.* 1030 τέθνηχ' ὑμῖν πάλαι. These words are
usu. written τέθνηκ' ἐγώ σοι: but the enclitic σοι destroys the point.

1154 ff. μήτηρ ἀμήτωρ: cp. *O. T.* 1214 τὸν ἄγαμον γάμον:
Ai. 665 ἄδωρα δῶρα: Aesch. *P.V.* 544 ἄχαρις χάρις.—ῆς, 'concerning whom,' depends primarily on φήμας προὔπεμπες (cp.
317 n.), but also denotes the object of τιμωρός. It must not be
taken with λάθρᾳ: the messages were of course secret; the
point here is their tenor and their frequency.

1163 f. κελεύθους, from Crisa to Mycenae: δεινοτάτας, since
the expected avenger returns as dust. For the poetical plur.,
cp. 68 ταῖσδε ταῖς ὁδοῖς.—ἀπώλεσας: cp. 808.—δῆτ': 842 n.

1165 f. τοιγὰρ σὺ δέξαι μ' κ.τ.λ.: cp. *Romeo and Juliet*, act 5,
sc. 3, 106:...'I still will stay with thee, | And never from this
palace of dim night | Depart again: here, here will I remain |
With worms that are thy chamber-maids; O, here | Will I set
up my everlasting rest'...

τὴν μηδὲν, as in *Ai.* 1231 τοῦ μηδὲν = τοῦ θανόντος.—τὸ μηδὲν
also can be said of a person who is dead or doomed to death:
but here, following τὴν μηδὲν, it rather suggests the state, 'thy
nothingness.'

1168 f. μετεῖχον τῶν ἴσων: cp. Dem. or. 21 § 96 τῶν ἴσων
μετεῖχε τοῖς ἄλλοις ἡμῖν.—μὴ ἀπολείπεσθαι: this mode of writing,
which implies synizesis, is now more usual than μάπο- (crasis),
or μὴ 'πο- (prodelision). ἀπολείπεσθαι = 'to be left behind by,'
and so, 'to be parted from,' 'deprived of': Eur. *Med.* 35 πατρῴας
μὴ ἀπολείπεσθαι χθονός.

1171 f. θνητοῦ κ.τ.λ.: 'as thy father was a mortal, so his son,
thy brother, was but mortal also': with θνητὸς supply ἦν.—φρόνει,
'bethink thee' (not, 'be patient').

1174 φεῦ φεῦ, τί λέξω; Orestes, deeply moved, speaks to
himself, though loud enough for Electra to hear.

λόγων goes with ποῖ, not with ἀμηχανῶν. Cp. *O.C.* 310 ὦ
Ζεῦ, τί λέξω; ποῖ φρενῶν ἔλθω, πάτερ;

1176—1226 It is well to observe the delicately gradual
process which leads up to the recognition.

(i) 1176—1187. She is surprised that *her* woes should affect the stranger, and he hints that they are his own. (ii) 1188—1198. She is thus led to speak more in detail of her sorrows, and of her despair,—caused by her brother's death. (iii) 1199—1204. He once more expresses his pity,—and this time in words which cause her to ask whether he can be a *kinsman*. He does not give a direct answer, but inquires whether the Chorus are friendly, and is assured that they are so.

The preparation is now complete: the actual disclosure follows. (i) 1205—1210. He asks her to give him the urn which is in her hands: she entreats that she may be allowed to keep it, and to pay it the last honours. (ii) 1211—1217. He tells her that she ought not to mourn for her brother. 'Why,' she asks: 'if these are his ashes?' 'They are not so,' he replies, —taking the urn from her hands. (iii) 1218—1221. 'Where, then,' she asks, 'is his grave?' 'The living have no grave.' 'He lives?' 'Yes,—as surely as I live.'

1176 ἴσχες ἄλγος: cp. 897 ἔσχον θαῦμα: and for the sense of the aor., 1256, 1465.

1177 κλεινὸν, as a daughter of the great Agamemnon, the names of whose children were widely known.—Though joined with εἶδος, κλεινὸν should not be taken as referring to the fame of her beauty; it is equivalent to κλεινῆς, by the common idiom (785).

1178 καὶ μάλ': here, as in 1455, the καὶ = 'and.'

1179 ταλαίνης is better taken with συμφορᾶς than with σοῦ understood. Cp. Aesch. *Th.* 695 τάλαιν' ἀρά: *Ai.* 980 ὤμοι βαρείας ἆρα τῆς ἐμῆς τύχης: where, as here, and in *O.T.* 1395, *O.C.* 409, ἆρα = simply ἄρα.

1180 οὐ δή ποτ', the reading of the scholiast, is clearly better than that which prevails in our MSS., τί δήποτ'. It expresses her first feeling of surprise: she can hardly believe that his pity is for her. In 1184, on the other hand, τί δή ποτ' is fitting: she has recognised the fact, and asks the cause. Cp. 1108.

1181 ἀτίμως, ruthlessly: cp. 444 n.—κἀθέως, in the act. sense of ἄθεος, 'disregarding the gods,' 'impious.' Kinsfolk have wronged their kinswoman. Cp. 124 ἀθεώτατα: Antiphon or. 1 § 21 ἀθέως καὶ ἀκλεῶς πρὸ τῆς εἱμαρμένης ὑφ' ὧν ἥκιστ' ἐχρῆν τὸν βίον ἐκλιπών.

1182 ἦ 'μέ: *Ant.* 83 μὴ 'μοῦ προτάρβει: ib. 736 ἦ 'μοί.— δυσφημεῖς: cp. 905 n. The schol. gives the sense rightly, τὰ δύσφημα ταῦτα ἃ λέγεις ἐμοὶ καὶ οὐκ ἄλλῳ τινὶ ἁρμόζει. For the fem. ἄλλην, cp. 100. The words express, courteously, yet with a certain reserve and dignity, her surprise that a stranger should make the comment; ξένε is significant.

1183 ἀνύμφου, as her forlorn appearance shows (cp. 188 φίλος οὔτις ἀνὴρ ὑπερίσταται: also 165, 962).—τροφῆς, way of life: *Ai.* 499 δουλίαν ἕξειν τροφήν.

1184 τί δή ποτ'. δή, which the scribe of L appears to have regarded as the true reading, is slightly better here than μοι, which would be an ethic dat. ('I pray thee': cp. 144). The partic. is absolute ('with this steadfast gaze'); it does not govern τί (as = 'with what meaning?').

1186 ἐν τῷ.. τῶν εἰρημένων, 'by means of what that has been said?': cp. Plat. *Prot.* p. 324 E ἐν τούτῳ.. λύεται ἡ ἀπορία.

1187 ὁρῶν σὲ κ.τ.λ. 'What,' she asks, 'has quickened this sense of *thy* woes?' 'The sight of *thine*,' he answers. Clearly we must write σέ, not σε: the antithesis with τῶν ἐμῶν (1185) requires it, and otherwise the point is lost.

ἐμπρέπουσαν. Cp. Aesch. *Ch.* 17 (Electra) πένθει λυγρῷ | πρέπουσαν: which refers to all the outward signs of grief, and not merely to dress.

1191 πόθεν, predicate: πόθεν ἐστὶ τοῦτο τὸ κακὸν ὃ ἐξεσήμηνας; Cp. *Ph.* 26 τοὔργον οὐ μακρὰν λέγεις.

1192 εἶτα marks a further aggravation of her lot. His murderers though they are, she is their slave.

1193 ἀνάγκη.. προτρέπει. Cp. *Il.* 6. 336 ἤμην ἐν θαλάμῳ, ἔθελον δ' ἄχεϊ προτραπέσθαι, 'to turn forwards towards' grief, and so, 'to *yield* myself up to it.' It seems possible that this Homeric use of the middle was that on which Sophocles modelled his use of the act. here. 'Who *causes* thee to *yield* to this necessity,'—'subjects thee' to it? No dative occurs with this verb elsewhere; nor is any emendation probable.

1194 ἐξισοῖ, trans., as in 738 and elsewhere in Sophocles: schol. οὐκ ἴσα πράττει τῷ τῆς μητρὸς ὀνόματι. Cp. *Tr.* 818 μηδὲν ὡς τεκοῦσα δρᾷ.

1195 χερσίν, personal violence, hinted at in 627, 912: λύμη βίου, in respect of food, lodging, dress, etc.; 189 ff. Cp. *Tr.* 793 λυμαντὴν βίου.

1198 προύθηκας, set before me, presented: cp. *Ai.* 1294 προθέντ' ἀδελφῷ δεῖπνον.

1201 τοῖσι σοῖς was the prevalent reading here, while τοῖς ἴσοις can claim to be the original reading of L: but, in a case where confusion was so easy, the authority of our MSS. is not great.

The word ξυγγενὴς in 1202 is the point which inclines me to prefer τοῖσι σοῖς. If he had said τοῖς ἴσοις,—'equal,' or 'equivalent,' woes,—that would have explained, indeed, why he should feel sympathy; but it would not have warranted the surmise that he was a kinsman.

1203 τὸ τῶνδε = αἴδε. Cp. Plat. *Legg.* p. 657 D οἱ μὲν νέοι... τὸ δὲ τῶν πρεσβυτέρων.

1205 νῦν refers to the assurance just given, πρὸς πιστὰς ἐρεῖς: it is clearly better than νῦν.

1207 πιθοῦ: cp. *Tr.* 470 πιθοῦ λεγούσῃ. L, with most MSS., has πείθου: see on 1015.

1208 πρὸς γενείου: a formula of solemn appeal, accompanied, perhaps, by the gesture of raising her right hand towards his face. In *Il.* 1. 500 f. Thetis clasps the knees of Zeus with her left hand, and places her right under his chin.

The reading of the MSS., μὴ 'ξέλῃ, is stronger and more pathetic than μ' ἐξέλῃ: and με is easily understood. For the reiterated μή, cp. *O.C.* 210 μή, μή μ' ἀνέρῃ.—ἐξέλῃ, properly, 'take out of my keeping,' while ἀφέλῃ would be simply 'take away from me.' So Her. 3. 137 ἐξαιρεθέντες τε τὸν Δημοκήδεα καὶ τὸν γαῦλον.. ἀπαιρεθέντες.—τὰ φίλτατα: cp. *O.C.* 1110 ἔχω τὰ φίλτατ' (his daughters).

1209 οὐ φήμ' ἐάσειν. Cp. *Ph.* 816 f. ΦΙ. μέθες, μέθες με... | ΝΕ. οὐ φήμ' ἐάσειν. He approaches her; she clings to the urn, and at v. 1216 is still holding it; then his words, ἀλλ' οὐκ 'Ορέστου (1217), reconcile her to parting with it, and he gently takes it from her hands.

The division of the trimeter (ἀντιλαβή) marks agitation, as again in 1220—1226, 1323, etc.

τάλαιν' ἐγὼ σέθεν: cp. *Tr.* 972 οἴμοι ἐγὼ σοῦ μέλεος.

1210 εἰ στερήσομαι. For εἰ with fut. ind., expressing a matter of grief or indignation, cp. *Ph.* 988 εἴ μ' οὗτος ἐκ τῶν σῶν ἀπάξεται βίᾳ.—ταφῆς, 'sepulture' (not 'sepulchre,' τάφου, 1169), —*i.e.*, the privilege of depositing the urn in a tomb: see 1140 n. At v. 760 it is said that the ashes are sent, ὅπως πατρῴας τύμβον ἐκλάχῃ χθονός.

1211 εὔφημα φώνει. He means that it is δύσφημον to speak of the living as if they were dead (59 n.). This is the earliest hint of the truth,—a hint which she, of course, cannot yet seize. She interprets his first phrase by the second, πρὸς δίκης γὰρ οὐ στένεις, as meaning that for *her* it is not right to lament.

1213 οὔ σοι προσήκει: not οὐ σοὶ: the stress is on the verb: 'it is not meet for thee (or for any one) to speak thus.' The pron. can be enclitic, though in a place which would usu. give emphasis: cp. *O. T.* 800 καί σοι, γύναι, τἀληθὲς ἐξερῶ.—τήνδε προσφωνεῖν φάτιν (αὐτόν), to apply this epithet to him, viz. θανόντα.

1214 ἄτιμος .. τοῦ τεθνηκότος: cp. Aesch. *Ch.* 295 πάντων δ᾽ ἄτιμον κἄφιλον θνῄσκειν χρόνῳ. 'Am I so contemned by the spirit of my dead brother,' she asks, 'that my lament would be displeasing to him?' Cp. 442 ff.

1215 By οὐδενὸς he avoids either accepting or correcting τεθνηκότος.—τοῦτο δ᾽ οὐχὶ σόν, 'but this (τὸ στένειν) is not thy part,'—not the thing which it is right for thee to do. Cp. 1470 οὐκ ἐμὸν τόδ᾽, ἀλλὰ σόν, κ.τ.λ.

1216 βαστάζω: cp. 905 n.

1217 πλὴν λόγῳ γ᾽ ἠσκημένον, lit., 'except so far as it has been dressed up in fiction.' ἠσκημένον is a metaphor from dress and ornament: cp. 452: Aesch. *Pers.* 182 πέπλοισι Περσικοῖς ἠσκημένη. For πλήν .. γε, cp. *Ph.* 441 ποίου δὲ τούτου πλήν γ᾽ Ὀδυσσέως ἐρεῖς;

1218 τοῦ ταλαιπώρου. She infers that his true ashes rest elsewhere,—among strangers; and that she has missed even the consolation of placing them in a tomb (1210 n.). Thus her former thought (1138 ff.) returns with increased bitterness.

1220 ὦ παῖ. The change from ὦ ξένε (1180, 1182, 1184, 1206) to this less formal mode of address marks her first flash of hope. For παῖς applied to a young man, cp. 455: 1430 (where Electra addresses Orestes and Pylades as ὦ παῖδες). It might perhaps be thought that the word is scarcely fitting in the mouth of a maiden who is only a few years older than the youth to whom she speaks. But it seems natural. A sister who has had the care of a younger brother is apt to feel the interval of age between herself and his contemporaries as greater than it really is.

1221 ἀνήρ, following ὦ παῖ, beautifully suggests how, in Electra's yearning imagination, the youthful brother, the hope of their house, had long been invested with heroic might.

1222 f. τήνδε...σφραγῖδα. There is no hint that Electra's memory had been awakened by anything in his appearance, or by his voice; and the mere possession of the ring was no proof. It is remarkable how swiftly Sophocles glides over the incident, as if conscious that the σημεῖον was little more than conventional. The σημεῖα of Aeschylus are of a like order,— the lock of hair, like Electra's own; the foot-prints, symmetrical with hers,—and the early work of her hand at the loom: but Aeschylus at least treats them in a thorough and deliberate manner (*Cho.* 168—234). It is Euripides, the innovator on the myths in form and spirit, who invents something more plausible,—the scar over one eyebrow of Orestes, caused by a fall in childhood (Eur. *El.* 513—573).

1224 ὦ φίλτατον φῶς. Cp. *Ph.* 530 ὦ φίλτατον μὲν ἦμαρ, ἥδιστος δ' ἀνήρ.

1225 ὦ φθέγμ'. A beautifully natural expression of her new joy in his living presence. So the solitary Philoctetes welcomes the sound of Greek speech,—ὦ φίλτατον φώνημα (*Ph.* 234).— μηκέτ' ἄλλοθεν πύθῃ. Cp. 1474: *O.C.* 1266 τἀμὰ μὴ 'ξ ἄλλων πύθῃ. For μηκέτ', cp. Pind. *O.* 1. 114 μηκέτι πάπταινε πόρσιον.

1226 ἔχω...ἔχοις ἀεί. Cp. Eur. *El.* 578 ὦ χρόνῳ φανείς, | ἔχω σ' ἀέλπτως. OR. κἀξ ἐμοῦ γ' ἔχει χρόνῳ.

1228 f. μηχαναῖσι: as Hamlet (3. 4. 188) is 'mad in craft.' —σεσωσμένον: cp. 60. Here the word implies, 'brought safely home' (*Tr.* 610 ἐς δόμους | .. σωθέντ').

1230 f. συμφοραῖσι. Eustathius p. 647. 37: καὶ ἡ συμφορὰ δὲ οὐ μόνον ἀποτρόπαιος ἀλλὰ καὶ ἀγαθή, ὡς δηλοῖ σὺν ἄλλοις καὶ ὁ εἰπὼν ἐπ' ἀγαθῷ τὸ ἐπὶ συμφοραῖς γεγηθὸς...ἄπο.—γεγηθὸς .. δάκρυον: cp. *Ant.* 527 φιλάδελφα κάτω δάκρυ' εἰβομένη.

1232—1287 A μέλος ἀπὸ σκηνῆς between Electra and Orestes. Strophe, 1232—1352, = antistr. 1253—1272 (a verse being lost after 1264). Epode, 1273—1287. For metres see Metrical Analysis.

1233 γοναὶ σωμάτων κ.τ.λ. This phrase seems to gain in fulness and force if taken as meaning, 'son of the father whom I so loved,' rather than as a mere periphrasis for σώματα φίλτατα, 'dearest of all men ever born.' In either case the use of the plur. σωμάτων instead of σώματος (schol. ἀντὶ τοῦ ἐνικοῦ) is very bold, and seemingly unique.

1234 f. ἀρτίως marks her sense of the sudden change from the despair which she was feeling but a few moments before.— οὓς, meaning herself: for the plur., cp. *O.T.* 1184 ξὺν οἷς τ' | οὐ χρῆν ὁμιλῶν, οὕς τέ μ' οὐκ ἔδει κτανών.—ἐχρῆζετε: cp. 171.

1236 σῖγ' ἔχουσα: so *Ph.* 258 σῖγ' ἔχοντες.

1239 τὴν ἄδμητον: cp. the prayer of the Danaïdes to Artemis,

Notes 159

Aesch. *Suppl.* 149 ἀδμάτας ἀδμάτα | ῥύσιος γενέσθω.—Ἄρτεμιν: 626 n.

1240 ff. τόδε μὲν.. ὂν ἀεί. These words express her new exultation in the sense that she has a brother for her champion. —περισσὸν ἄχθος, vainly burdening the ground: cp. fr. 859 ὡς οὐδέν ἐσμεν πλὴν σκιαῖς ἐοικότες, | βάρος περισσὸν γῆς ἀναστρωφώμενοι.—ἔνδον.. ὂν ἀεί. Cp. Eur. *Or.* 928 τἄνδον οἰκουρήμαθ'. The phrase is equivalent to γυναῖκας τάσδε, περισσὸν ἄχθος οὔσας, ἀεὶ ἔνδον οὔσας.

1243 f. γε μὲν δή: cp. *Tr.* 484 ἐπεί γε μὲν δή.—Ἄρης, the warlike spirit: cp. Aesch. *Ag.* 78 Ἄρης δ' οὐκ ἐνὶ χώρᾳ: id. *Suppl.* 749 γυνὴ μονωθεῖσ' οὐδέν· οὐκ ἔνεστ' Ἄρης.

1246 ff. ἀνέφελον.. κακόν. Her sorrow—the long and bitter strife with her mother—is one over which, from its nature (οἶον ἔφυ), no veil can be drawn; it is manifest to all, and fierce, like the sun in a cloudless summer sky. It is a sorrow which can never be done away with, οὔ ποτε καταλύσιμον, because no reconciliation is possible. And it is one of which no time can efface the memory (οὐδέ ποτε λησόμενον).

The author of the scholium on 1245 read ἐνέβαλες. This yields a good sense; 'thou hast mentioned' (*mentionem iniecisti*). Cp. Plat. *Rep.* 344 D οἷον ἐμβαλὼν λόγον ἐν νῷ ἔχεις ἀπιέναι. The traditional ἐπέβαλες has been explained in two ways. (1) 'You have *mentioned*.' For this sense there is no parallel. (2) 'You have *laid* the burden of the woe *upon* me,'—*i.e.*, 'brought it to my recollection.' This is perhaps just possible: but it is so artificial as to seem improbable.

καταλύσιμον, fitting here, as suggestive of καταλύεσθαι ἔχθραν, πόλεμον, κ.τ.λ.—λησόμενον: 'that never its own burden *can forget*,' as Whitelaw renders. The κακόν is half-personified here, though not in the preceding clauses.

The usual explanation is, 'that cannot *be forgotten*'; but λήσομαι is nowhere passive.

1251 f. ἔξοιδα καὶ ταῦτ': 'these things *also*,' *i.e.*, the sufferings to which she has just alluded. The change of καὶ to παῖ (rightly made in *Ph.* 79) is needless here.

παρουσία may be freely rendered 'occasion'; it seems to be a purposely vague word, intended to suggest 'the presence' of the murderers; a dark hint of the coming vengeance. When their presence admonishes (φράζῃ),—gives the signal for action, —then will be the time to recall their crimes; which are indicated, with a similar reserve, by ἔργων τῶνδε.

The *v.l.* παρρησία, doubtless a conjecture, would enfeeble the passage, and would further require us to alter φράξῃ.

1253 ff. ὁ πᾶς.. χρόνος, 'all time' to come: cp. Isocr. or. 1 § 11 ἐπιλίποι δ' ἂν ἡμᾶς ὁ πᾶς χρόνος, εἰ πάσας τὰς ἐκείνου πράξεις καταριθμησαίμεθα. παρὼν, 'when present,' *i.e.*, 'as it comes.' There can be no moment at which she might not fitly make her just complaints. δίκᾳ goes with ἐννέπειν, not with πρέποι.

μόλις γὰρ κ.τ.λ.: *i.e.*, having waited so long for freedom of utterance, she should not now be required to keep silence.— ἔσχον, 'have obtained': cp. 1176 n.

1257 σώζου τόδε, *i.e.*, the ἐλεύθερον στόμα. If she is over-heard in the house, she may yet lose the newly-gained freedom. Except in the sense of 'remembering' (993 n.), the midd. of the simple σώζω is somewhat rare.

1259 μακρὰν.. λέγειν: Ar. *Th.* 382 μακρὰν ἔοικε λέξειν.

1260 ff. τίς οὖν, a remonstrance, in which οὖν may be rendered by 'Nay.' ἀξίαν is predicative, and equiv. to an adverb, 'worthily,' 'fitly'; cp. the schol., τίς ἄν, φησί, σοῦ φανέντος δικαίως ἕλοιτο ἀντὶ λόγων σιωπήν; I agree with the schol. also in taking σοῦ πεφηνότος as a gen. absol., rather than as depending on ἀξίαν. For the absolute use of the latter, cp. 298 ἀξίαν δίκην: *O. T.* 1004 χάριν.. ἀξίαν: *ib.* 133 ἀξίως. Join λόγων with μεταβάλοιτ', not with σιγὰν: cp. Antiphon or. 5 § 79 ἠλλάξαντο.. εὐδαιμονίας.. κακοδαιμονίαν.—ὧδε, as thou biddest.

1264 After τότ' εἶδες, the MSS. have ὅτε: but the tribrach in the second foot, while there is no caesura in the third, makes an intolerably lame verse. Read εὖτε instead of ὅτε, and scan θεοὶ as a monosyllable by synizesis. ὅτε arose from τότ'.

ἐπώτρυναν, by the oracle (35): an answer to the reproach unconsciously conveyed by ἀέλπτως (1263). He came as soon as Apollo gave the word. After this verse, a trimeter has been lost, as the strophe shows, where v. 1244 (ἔνεστιν κ.τ.λ.) is certainly genuine.

1266 f. χάριτος, a grace shown to her, a matter for thank-fulness.— ἐπόρισεν is the best correction of the corrupt ἐπόρσεν or ἐπῶρσεν. It is true that πορίζω has not elsewhere the special sense of πορεύω, 'to convey,' 'bring': but a poet might easily transfer that sense to it.

1269 f. δαιμόνιον: cp. Xen. *Mem.* 1. 3. § 5 εἰ μή τι δαιμόνιον εἴη.—τίθημ' = τίθεμαι: *Ant.* 1166 οὐ τίθημ' ἐγὼ | ζῆν τοῦτον.

Electra remembers the warning dream (417 ff.), in which she had already surmised a supernatural agency (411: 459). It is indeed δαιμόνιον that Orestes, sent by Apollo, should arrive at this moment.

1271 τὰ μὲν.. τὰ δὲ (adverbial), 'on the one hand,' 'on the other.'

1274 ὁδόν.. φανῆναι: cp. 1318 ἐξήκεις ὁδόν. Here, too, the acc. is 'cognate,' since the verb implies ἐλθεῖν.

1276 τί μὴ ποήσω; He interrupts her entreaty, μή τί με—, by asking, 'what am I not to do?' (the negative form of the delib. subjunct.).

1277 f. μή μ᾽ ἀποστερήσῃς.. ἁδονάν: the double acc. with ἀποστερεῖν, though less frequent than acc. of person and gen. of thing, is not rare: cp. Antiphon *Tetral.* B. γ. § 2 τὸ ἥμισυ τῆς κατηγορίας ἐμαυτὸν ἂν ἀπεστέρησα.—μεθέσθαι, sc. αὐτῆς, epexegetic inf. (lit. 'so as for me to forego it'): see on 543 δαίσασθαι. Cp. Eur. *Med.* 736 ἄγουσιν οὐ μεθεῖ᾽ ἂν ἐκ γαίας ἐμέ, where the acc. depends on the part., and ἐμοῦ is to be supplied with the verb. —ἰδών, sc. ἀποστεροῦντά τινα.

1279 f. ξυναινεῖς, as in 402, *Ph.* 122.—τί μὴν οὔ; 'why should I not?' = 'of course I do.' Cp. [Eur.] *Rhes.* 706 HM. A. δοκεῖς γάρ; HM. B. τί μὴν οὔ;

1281 f. ὦ φίλαι. It seems fitting that, towards the close of these lyrics, Electra should address some words to the sympathetic Chorus,—as she did before, just after the discovery (1227); though at v. 1285 she again speaks to Orestes.

αὐδάν is unquestionably the living voice of Orestes, which 'she could never have hoped to hear,' after the apparent proofs of his death. Cp. 1225 ὦ φθέγμ᾽, ἀφίκου: and with οὐδ᾽ ἂν ἤλπισ᾽, cp. 1263 ἀέλπτως: 832 f. εἰ τῶν φανερῶς οἰχομένων | εἰς Ἀΐδαν ἐλπίδ᾽ ὑποίσεις: and 858 f.

1283 f. There can be no doubt that something has been lost before ἔσχον. Arndt supplies οὐδ᾽ ἂν, which might easily have been omitted, either through its likeness to αὐδάν just before it, or through the οὐδ᾽ ἂν above it. ὁρμᾶν, for the traditional ὀργὰν, is due to Blomfield (*Mus. Crit.* I. 214).

ὀργή in Sophocles means either (1) 'anger,' or (2) 'disposition': *Ant.* 875 αὐτόγνωτος.. ὀργά: *ib.* 355 ἀστυνόμους ὀργάς: *Ai.* 639 συντρόφοις ὀργαῖς. Neither sense can be fitted into any probable interpretation.

The context is the best guide to the sense which should be restored. Throughout these lyrics, Orestes has been endeavouring to repress Electra's cries, lest she should be overheard (1236, 1238, 1251 f., 1257, 1259, 1271 f.). The corrupt words probably referred to this. ὁρμὰν is the 'impulse' or 'emotion' which compelled her to utter her new joy. She turns to these sympathetic women, and excuses her incaution by her happiness.

οὐδ' ἂν ἔσχον is the potential indicative. ἄναυδον, proleptic: Aesch. *Ag.* 1247 εὔφημον...κοίμησον στόμα.

1285 τάλαινα is a comment on her own joyous emotion, precisely as in 902 κεὐθὺς τάλαιν' ὡς εἶδον κ.τ.λ.

1288—1383 The first part of the third ἐπεισόδιον began at 1098, with the entrance of Orestes. Now, after the μέλος ἀπὸ σκηνῆς (1232—1287), comes the second part, going down to the point at which the avengers pass into the house, followed by Electra.

1288 τὰ...περισσ. τῶν λόγων: cp. *Ph.* 24 τἀπίλοιπα τῶν λόγων.

1289 ff. καὶ μήτε μήτηρ κ.τ.λ. These verses plainly intimate the poet's opinion that it would be a fault in art to retard the action at this point by a long narrative.

1290 f. πατρῷαν, properly the epithet of δόμων (492 n.): cp. 960.—(τὰ μὲν) ἀντλεῖ, τὰ δ' ἐκχεῖ: cp. *O.T.* 1228 ὅσα | κεύθει, τὰ δ' αὐτίκ' εἰς τὸ φῶς φανεῖ κακά: *Tr.* 117 στρέφει, τὸ δ' αὔξει.

ἐκχεῖ, *effundit:* Aesch. *Pers.* 826 ὄλβον ἐκχέῃ μέγαν: *Anth. Pal.* 9. 367 τὸν πατρικὸν πλοῦτον... | αἰσχρῶς εἰς ἀκρατεῖς ἐξέχεεν δαπάνας. As dist. from ἐκχεῖ (profuse outlay on luxury), διασπείρει μάτην expresses *aimless* waste, which obtains no return. ἀντλεῖ, *exhaurit,* is properly the general term, while the other two verbs denote special modes of it. But, since τὰ μὲν is implied in τὰ δέ, the sentence is in form a rhetorical climax,— 'spends,' 'spends profusely,' 'spends aimlessly.'

1292 χρόνου.. καιρὸν, *temporis modum,* due limit or measure of time. Cp. Pind. *N.* 7. 58 τὶν δ' ἐοικότα καιρὸν ὄλβου | δίδωσι (Μοῖρα): Aesch. *Ag.* 785 πῶς σε σεβίζω, | μήθ' ὑπεράρας μήθ' ὑποκάμψας | καιρὸν χάριτος; ('the due measure of courtesy').— ἐξείργοι, 'shut out,' 'preclude.'

1294 f. φανέντες, if it be safe for them to enter the house (as it is, cp. 1308): κεκρυμμένοι, if it be necessary to wait in concealment until they can safely enter.—γελῶντας: cp. 1153.

1296 f. οὕτω δὲ (σκόπει) ὅπως: cp. Ar. *Ran.* 905 ἀλλ' ὡς τάχιστα χρὴ λέγειν· οὕτω δ' ὅπως ἐρεῖτον | ἀστεῖα.—ἐπιγνώσεται, 'detect': the dat. is instrumental.—νῷν, Orestes and Pylades: cp. 1372 f.—ἐπελθόντοιν δόμους: cp. *Ant.* 152 f. ναοὺς χοροῖς | .. ἐπέλθωμεν.

Notes 163

1298 f. μάτην, falsely: 63 n.—εὐτυχήσωμεν is strictly the 'ingressive' aorist, 'when we shall have become prosperous.'
1301 f. καὶ σοί, 'to thee, on thy part' (cp. 1146 n.): followed by καὶ τοὐμόν, as in *O. T.* 165 f. εἴ ποτε καὶ προτέρας ἄτας is followed by ἔλθετε καὶ νῦν.
ὧδ'.. τῇδε: cp. 643. τῇδε is here redundant, repeating the sense of ὧδε for emphasis.—τοὐμὸν = 'my conduct': cp. *Tr.* 53 φράσαι τὸ σόν.—For φίλον, cp. *O. C.* 1205 ἔστω δ' οὖν ὅπως ὑμῖν φίλον.
1303 κοὐκ ἐμάς, lit., 'and not as my own,'—*i.e.*, as the fruit of my own efforts. He has a right to restrict the joys which he has bestowed.
1304 κοὐδ'. The adverbial οὐδὲ goes with βραχὺ, though separated from it; cp. *Il.* 1. 354 νῦν δ' οὐδέ με τυτθὸν ἔτισεν. καὶ precedes it as in Xen. *An.* 3. 2. 4 καὶ οὐδὲ Δία Ξένιον ᾐδέσθη. —The part. λυπήσασα expresses the condition of δεξαίμην: cp. Andoc. or. 1 § 3 πάντα τὰ ἀγαθὰ ἔχειν στερόμενος τῆς πατρίδος οὐκ ἂν δεξαίμην.
1306 ὑπηρετοίην is a certain correction of the MS. ὑπηρετοίμην. The midd. is not found in classical writers, though it was frequent later.—δαίμονι, the god who has brought him home (cp. 1266 ff.). Her brother is the καθαρτὴς πρὸς θεῶν ὡρμημένος (70).
1307 τἀνθένδε = τὰ ἐνθάδε: cp. Eur. *Bacch.* 48 εἰς δ' ἄλλην χθόνα, | τἀνθένδε θέμενος εὖ, μεταστήσω πόδα.—Not, 'what should be done next.' That was, indeed, the regular sense of the sing. τοὐνθένδε (*Ph.* 895).
1308 ff. στέγας and οἴκοις are synonyms; cp. 986 f. συμπόνει .. σύγκαμν' (n.).—Electra here gives the information which was to have been brought by the old man (41). He, however, has been in the house since v. 803. At v. 1368 he repeats these facts.
δείσῃς .. ὡς .. ὄψεται: cp. 1426 f.: Xen. *Cyr.* 5. 2. 12 ἀνδρὸς μὴ φοβοῦ ὡς ἀπορήσεις ἀξίου.
1311 ἐντέτηκε: cp. Plat. *Menex.* p. 245 D ὅθεν καθαρὸν τὸ μῖσος ἐντέτηκε τῇ πόλει τῆς ἀλλοτρίας φύσεως. Lucian *Peregr.* 22 τοσοῦτος ἔρως τῆς δόξης ἐντέτηκεν αὐτῷ.
1314 f. ἥτις, with causal force: cp. 187.—ἐσεῖδον suits θανόντα no less than ζῶντα, since she had seen the urn: cp. 1129 νῦν μὲν γὰρ οὐδὲν ὄντα βαστάζω χεροῖν.—ἄσκοπα, in a way which she could not have imagined beforehand; cp. 864. As the next verses show, the meaning is not merely, 'thou hast given me

an unlooked-for joy,' but rather, 'thou hast wrought upon my mind with a bewildering effect of joy,—so that, if the dead returned, I should scarcely marvel.'

1318 f. ὅτι, causal: cp. 38.—τοιαύτην, so wondrous; prompted and conducted by a god (1266 ff.).—ὥς σοι is better than ὡς σοί, because, after the emphatic αὐτός, the next stress should fall rather on θυμός than on σοι ('rule me thyself, as thou *wilt*').

1320 f. οὐκ ἂν δυοῖν ἥμαρτον, *i.e.*, would have secured one of the two things. Classical Greek idiom preferred this negative form to a positive (such as δυοῖν θατέρου ἂν ἔτυχον). The modes of stating the dilemma vary; thus we find: (1) ἢ γὰρ .. ἢ, as here; Andoc. or. 1 § 4 δυοῖν .. οὐκ ἦν αὐτῷ ἁμαρτεῖν· ἢ γὰρ .. μηνῦσαι .. ἢ ἀποκτεῖναι: so Dem. or. 19 § 151, etc. (2) ἤ..ἤ, as Thuc. 1. 33 § 3 μηδὲ δυοῖν φθάσαι ἁμάρτωσιν (not fail to be beforehand with us in one of two things), ἢ κακῶσαι .. ἢ βεβαιώσασθαι. (3) εἰ μὲν γὰρ .. εἰ δέ, as Isocr. or. 11 § 43.

1322 f. σιγᾶν .. χωροῦντος. Although it is usually the Chorus that announces a new comer, it is best to follow the MSS. in ascribing these words to Orestes, who has already so often enjoined silence (1236, etc.). The ἀντιλαβή in 1323 confirms the MSS., since a trimeter is seldom divided between the Chorus and another speaker.—ἐπήνεσ': for the aor., cp. 668.

ἐπ' ἐξόδῳ: cp. *Tr.* 532 ὡς ἐπ' ἐξόδῳ.—τῶν ἔνδοθεν, *sc.* τινός: cp. 697 (n.).

1324 f. ἄλλως τε καὶ φέροντες: *i.e.*, besides the general claim of ξένοι, they have this special claim.

οἵ' ἄν .. ἀπώσαιτ': *i.e.*, ostensibly, the relics of a kinsman; in her secret meaning, retribution.

1326 f. The Paedagogus re-enters from the house.

τητώμενοι: 265 n. The faithful old servant scolds them as if he was still their παιδαγωγός.

παρ' οὐδὲν, 'of no account,' is usu. joined with εἶναι (as *O. T.* 983), or with verbs of 'esteeming,' such as ἄγειν (*Ant.* 35). The phrase here may be compared with *Ant.* 466 παρ' οὐδὲν ἄλγος (ἐστί).

1329 f. οὐ παρ' αὐτοῖς κ.τ.λ. Here παρὰ has its simple locative sense, 'beside.' παρὰ κακοῖς differs from ἐν κακοῖς just as παρὰ πυρί (*Od.* 7. 154) from ἐν πυρί. They stand, not 'just on the verge,' but 'just in the midst,' of deadly perils. αὐτοῖς is repeated, because it intensifies each of the prepositions. (Cp. 720 ὑπ' αὐτὴν .. στήλην, n.)

Notes 165

1331 σταθμοῖσι, the door-posts. Cp. *Od.* 22. 181 (with ref. to the watchers at the door of the armoury), τὼ δ᾽ ἔσταν ἑκάτερθε παρὰ σταθμοῖσι μένοντε. For the dat. of place, see 174 n. He stood there to intercept any inmate whom the sound of voices outside might have brought to the doors.

1332 f. ὑμῖν.. ὑμῶν: the repeated pron. has a certain sarcastic force; 'ye would have had your plans in the house,' etc. If any change were needed, ἡμῖν for ὑμῖν would be the best.—τὰ δρώμεν': 85 n. A listener at the doors must quickly have discovered that Orestes had returned; and Clyt. would have been warned. τὰ σώματα is a hint that the lives of the avengers would then have paid the penalty.

1334 f. νῦν δ᾽.. καὶ νῦν. Cp. *Tr.* 88 νῦν δ᾽ (= 'but as it was'), followed in 90 by νῦν δ᾽ (= 'but now').

1338 ἀπηλλάχθαι: for the perf. (implying 'at once'), cp. 64 n.: *Ai.* 479 ἀλλ᾽ ἢ καλῶς ζῆν ἢ καλῶς τεθνηκέναι | τὸν εὐγενῆ χρή. In 1335 we had ἀπαλλαχθέντε: cp. 163, n. on γᾶν.

1339 τἀντεῦθεν, 'the next things,' *i.e.*, the conditions with which he will have to deal as soon as he enters. Cp. 728 κἀντεῦθεν, and 1307 n. on τἀνθένδε.

1340 ὑπάρχει κ.τ.λ., 'it is secured that no one shall recognise thee': cp. Eur. *Heracl.* 181 ἄναξ, ὑπάρχει μὲν τόδ᾽ ἐν ᾗ σῇ χθονί, | εἰπεῖν ἀκοῦσαί τ᾽ ἐν μέρει πάρεστί μοι.—For the verbal ambiguity of σε.. τινά, cp. *Ant.* 288.

1341 ὡς ἔοικεν, ὡς τεθν.: for the double ὡς, cp. *Ant.* 735 ὁρᾷς τόδ᾽ ὡς εἴρηκας ὡς ἄγαν νέος; The pron. με is easily understood; cp. 1200.

1342 εἷς τῶν ἐν Ἅιδου.. ἀνήρ, 'one of the dead': for this indefinite use of εἷς, cp. Isocr. or. 20 § 11 ὧν οὗτος εἷς ὢν τυγχάνει. More often τις is added, as Ar. fr. 418. 2 τῶν ἀδολεσχῶν εἷς γέ τις. Here ἀνήρ virtually = τις.

1343 χαίρουσιν οὖν τούτοισιν..; Though ἐν has L's support, οὖν, the prevalent reading, is far better. With ἐν, the sense would be, 'rejoice under these circumstances' (not, '*in* these things').

1344 f. τελουμένων cannot mean 'when the *deed of vengeance* is being done.' Rather it is a purposely vague phrase; 'when our task is being finished'; 'towards the end': *i.e.*, when, the vengeance having been taken, that work is being crowned by re-establishing a rightful rule in the house.—For the neut. plur. part. in the gen. abs., without subject, cp. Aesch. *Th.* 274 εὖ ξυντυχόντων: Eur. *I.A.* 1022 καλῶς δὲ κρανθέντων.

J. E.   15

ὡς δὲ νῦν ἔχει, but, as things stand now, τὰ κείνων πάντα καλῶς
(ἔχει), all the conditions on their part (that of Clyt. and Aeg.)
are good (for us), καὶ τὰ μὴ καλῶς (ἔχοντα), even those which are
not morally good,—viz., Clytaemnestra's joy at the death of her
son, and those insults which expressed her new sense of
security (773—803).

1347 οὐχὶ ξυνίης; The ἀντιλαβή marks the interest of the
moment: cp. 1209 n.—οὐδέ γ' εἰς θυμὸν φέρω: lit., 'No, I cannot
even bring (a conjecture) into my mind'; 'I cannot form an
idea.' The phrase occurs nowhere else, and is not really like
O.T. 975, μή νυν ἔτ' αὐτῶν μηδὲν ἐς θυμὸν βάλῃς ('lay to heart').

1349 f. ποίῳ is conformed to ὅτῳ in 1348, since the acc. for
οἶσθα is suppressed; the practice being that, in a curt question
such as this, ποῖος takes the case of the word to which it refers
(*e.g.*, *O.T.* 1176 ποίων; *Ai.* 1322 ποίους;). It implies that, for
the moment, she fails not only to recognise the man but to
recall the occasion.

οὗ...χεροῖν: the long space between the words is noteworthy;
cp. *Ph.* 598 f. (τίνος .. χάριν).—πέδον: cp. *O.C.* 643 δόμους στεί-
χειν.—ὑπεξεπέμφθην: cp. 297 ὑπεξέθου (n.).—σῇ προμηθίᾳ: cp. 12,
1132 f.

1352 προσηῦρον πιστόν, '*found* a true *ally*': πρὸς denoting
the acquisition. Cp. Polyb. 1. 59. 6 προσηγυρέθη ἡ πρὸς τὴν
συντέλειαν (χορηγία), 'the funds for the completion of the
enterprise were made up.' Classical prose preferred προσεξ-
ευρίσκω (Isocr.), or προσεπεξευρίσκω (Thuc.).

1354 φῶς, day, as in 1224.

1356 τόνδε κἄμ': he saved Orestes from murder, and Electra
from that bereavement.—ἔσωσας, not ἔσωσεν, in spite of κεῖνος.
Cp. Eur. *Heracl.* 945 ff. ἐκεῖνος εἰ σύ, followed by ὅς .. ἠξίωσας.
So, when a speaker has referred to himself in the 3rd person,
he quickly reverts to the first, as in *O.C.* 6 ἐμοί follows Οἰδίπουν
in v. 3.

1357 f. ὦ .. χεῖρες: she takes his hands in her own. This
explains why the poet has not written φιλτάτας .. χεῖρας: we see,
too, how natural is the transition to ἔχων, as she is looking in
her old friend's face. The sense is, ἔχων πόδας οἳ τὰ ἥδιστα
ὑπηρέτησαν, viz., in the journeys to and from Phocis.

1359 οὐδ' ἔφαινες, 'and didst not give any light.' This
absolute use of the word is sufficiently interpreted by the
context; it is scarcely needful to supply (*e.g.*) τὴν ἀλήθειαν, or
συνόντα σεαυτόν.—For ἀλλά με cp. *Ai.* 361.

1360 ἔργ᾽ ἔχων, 'possessed of them,' 'knowing them': ἔργα being 'facts,' as opp. to λόγοι (59 f. ὅταν λόγῳ θανὼν | ἔργοισι σωθῶ). Cp. *Ant.* 9 ἔχεις τι κεἰσήκουσας ;—For ἐμοί, after με, cp. *O.C.* 811 μηδέ με | φύλασσ᾽ ἐφορμῶν ἔνθα χρὴ ναίειν ἐμέ.

1361 πατέρα. This is the only tragic trimeter in which the third foot is formed by a single word of three short syllables. When the third foot is a tribrach there is usu. a caesura both in the third and in the fourth foot (as *O.T.* 248 κακὸν κακῶς νιν ἄμορον ἐκτρῖψαι βίον: cp. Eur. *Tro.* 497): or at least in the third foot (as *Ant.* 31). But it should be observed that the pause after χαῖρ᾽, ὦ πάτερ makes a vital difference. The movement of the verse begins afresh at πατέρα, and the effect of that word to the ear is like that of a tribrach in the first, rather than in the third, place of a trimeter.

1364 ff. τοὺς .. ἐν μέσῳ λόγους, the story of the brother's and sister's experiences in the interval since Orestes left Mycenae. Cp. Eur. *Med.* 819 περισσοὶ πάντες οὖν μέσῳ λόγοι (between the present moment, and her deed).

The acc. τοὺς .. λόγους is resumed in 1366 by ταῦτα, because the sentence πολλαὶ κ.τ.λ. has intervened. Cp. Thuc. 2. 62 τὸν δὲ πόνον...ἀρκείτω μὲν ὑμῖν καὶ ἐκεῖνα ἐν οἷς ἄλλοτε.. ἀπέδειξα οὐκ ὀρθῶς αὐτὸν ὑποπτευόμενον.

κυκλοῦνται, the form originally written by the scribe of L, is confirmed by usage, though the other reading, κυκλοῦσι, displaced it in most MSS. *Tr.* 129 κυκλοῦσιν is the only instance of κυκλεῖν used intransitively which occurs in Greek before Aristotle.

1367 σφῷν δ᾽ ἐννέπω γε: 'And further' (γε, *i.e.*, besides counselling Electra), 'I tell *you*,' etc.: cp. *Ai.* 1150 ἐγὼ δέ γ᾽ ἄνδρ᾽ ὄπωπα κ.τ.λ.

1370 f. τούτοις refers to ἀνδρῶν in 1369, the male domestics, who are supposed to be now busied out of doors. ἄλλοισι are the body-guards, δορυφόροι, of Aegisthus, who may be expected to return ere long from the country (313); σοφωτέροις (μάχεσθαι), as being trained to arms. Since the two comparatives, σοφωτέροις and πλείοσιν, are not linked by a conjunction, τούτων cannot be construed with both; it is perhaps best taken with πλείοσιν. 'Ye will have to fight both with these men (the οἰκέται), and with others of greater skill, more numerous than these.'

1372 f. οὐδὲν is adv.: lit., 'this task would no longer seem to be in any way (οὐδὲν) a case for many words, but for entering,' etc. The two constructions of ἔργον ἐστίν, as = *opus est*, are here combined. (1) For the gen., cp. Ar. *Plut.* 1154 οὐκ ἔργον ἔστ' οὐδὲν στροφῶν: (2) for the inf., *Ai.* 11 καί σ' οὐδὲν εἴσω τῆσδε παπταίνειν πύλης | ἔτ' ἔργον ἐστίν. The peculiarity here is that, instead of the simple ἔργον, we have τόδε τοὖργον, from which ἔργον has to be supplied with the gen. and with the inf. Cp. Eur. *Andr.* 551 οὐ γάρ, ὡς ἔοικέ μοι, | σχολῆς τόδ' ἔργον.

1374 f. πατρῷα, instead of πατρῴων: cp. 1290 n.—**ἔδη,** images of the gods (*O. T.* 886 δαιμόνων ἔδη), placed in the **πρόπυλα,** here a statelier term for πρόθυρον, the porch or vestibule of the house. The gods of the entrance were esp. Apollo Agyieus (cp. 637 προστατήριε), and Hermes.

προσκύσαντε: the worshipper stretched forth his right arm towards the image, presenting to it the flat of his hand, by bending back the wrist; then kissed his hand, and wafted a salute to the god. Orestes and Pylades perform this act of reverence before each ἔδος in the vestibule. Meanwhile, turning towards the statue of Apollo Lykeios which stands in front of the palace (645), Electra makes her prayer.

Orestes and Pylades, with their attendants and the Paedagogus, enter the house.

1378 ἔχοιμι: optat. of indefinite frequency in past time; cp. *Tr.* 905 κλαῖε δ' ὀργάνων ὅτου | ψαύσειεν.

λιπαρεῖ, earnest, devout: cp. 451 n.—**προὔστην σε,** presented myself (as a suppliant) at thy shrine. Similarly προστάτης is 'one who presents himself before a god,' 'a suppliant,' *O. C.* 1171, 1278. The only other trace of προστῆναι as = 'to approach,' with an acc., is in a fragment from the Τυρώ of Sophocles: προστῆναι μέσην | τράπεζαν ἀμφὶ σίτια καὶ καρχήσια.

1379 ἐξ οἵων ἔχω | αἰτῶ: lit., 'I make the prayer with such means as I have'; *i.e.*, no longer with offerings—since none are at hand—but with heartfelt vows. Schol. ὡς δυνάμεως ἔχω, λόγοις ἀξιοῦν, οὐ θύειν.

1380 I read προπίπτω, as metre requires, not προπίτνω. The first syllable of πίτνω is never long.

1382 τἀπιτίμια. Eur. *Hec.* 1086 δράσαντι δ' αἰσχρὰ δεινὰ τἀπιτίμια.

Electra enters the house.

1384—1397 Third stasimon. Strophe, 1384—1390 = antistr., 1391—1397. For metres see Metrical Analysis.

This short ode fills the interval of suspense. The Chorus

imagine the avengers, who have just passed within, as guided by divine powers to their goal.

1384 **ὥεθ'**, like *Tr.* 821 ἴδ' οἷον, ὦ παῖδες κ.τ.λ. **προνέμεται** expresses a gradual and regular advance. προνέμεσθαι is lit. 'to go forward in grazing.' The midd. occurs only here; nor is the act. found in a strictly parallel sense.

1385 τὸ **δυσέριστον** αἷμα, bloodshed, deadly vengeance, against which the guilty will strive in vain. δυσέριστον = δύσμαχον: cp. 220 οὐκ ἐριστά.—φυσῶν: cp. Eur. *I. A.* 125 οὐ μέγα φυσῶν θυμὸν ἐπαρεῖ | σοί..; *I. T.* 288 (the Erinys) πῦρ πνέουσα καὶ φόνου.

1386 **δωμάτων** **ὑπόστεγοι**: cp. *Ai.* 796 σκηνῆς ὕπαυλον: Aesch. *Eum.* 669 σῶν δόμων ἐφέστιον.

1387 f. **μετάδρομοι..κύνες**, the Erinyes. Cp. Aesch. *Ch.* 1054 σαφῶς γὰρ αἴδε μητρὸς ἔγκοτοι κύνες.

1389 **ἀμμενεῖ** was in the schol.'s text (see cr. n.), and is clearly better than ἀμμένει. For the apocopè of ἀνά in comp., cp. *Ant.* 1275.

1390 **τοὐμὸν φρενῶν ὄνειρον**: cp. 492 n.—**αἰωρούμενον**. Cp. Her. 8. 100 (of Mardonius) ὑπὲρ μεγάλων αἰωρηθέντα, 'in suspense concerning great issues' (victory or death).

1391 f. **ἐνέρων..ἀρωγός.** Orestes is the champion, not only of his father's spirit, but also of Hades, who is 'not regardless' (184), and of the other powers invoked by Electra from the nether world (110 ff.). Cp. *O. T.* 126 Λαΐου δ' ὀλωλότος | οὐδεὶς ἀρωγὸς ἐν κακοῖς ἐγίγνετο.

1393 **ἀρχαιόπλουτα.** He is to eject the usurper, and to recover his inheritance (cp. 72: 162: 1290).

1394 **νεακόνητον αἷμα χειροῖν ἔχων.** The words, if sound, mean, 'bearing keen-edged death in his hands.' αἷμα is the deed of blood by which vengeance is to be taken. νεακόνητον refers primarily to the keen edge of the weapon (sword or dagger) with which the blow is to be dealt; but may suggest also the keen edge of the avengers' resolve (Aesch. *Th.* 715 τεθηγμένον τοί μ' οὐκ ἀπαμβλυνεῖς λόγῳ).

The bold use of αἷμα may be illustrated by Aesch. *Ch.* 932 πολλῶν αἱμάτων, 'many deeds of blood'; Eur. *Or.* 284 εἴργασται δ' ἐμοὶ | μητρῷον αἷμα, 'the murder of a mother.'

If **νεάκονητον** is right, the α must be short.

1395 f. ὁ **Μαίας δὲ παῖς.** Hermes χθόνιος, whom Electra had already invoked (111), acts here in his twofold quality as πομπαῖος and δόλιος. Cp. *Ph.* 133 Ἑρμῆς δ' ὁ πέμπων δόλιος ἡγήσαιτο νῷν.

Ἑρμῆς σφ' ἄγει is the most probable reading. If the σ of σφ' had been lost after Ἑρμῆς, φ'ἄγει might have led to ἐπάγει, and this to mistaken remedies, such as ἐπεισάγει (cr. n.).

1398—1510 Exodos: the vengeance.

1398—1441 A kommos. It falls into two principal parts. (1) 1398—1421; the death of Clytaemnestra. (2) 1422—1441; Orestes and Pylades re-enter; Aegisthus approaches; and they prepare to receive him.

The general structure of this kommos is clearly strophic; but critics differ on details. The simplest view is that of Dindorf and others, that vv. 1398—1421 form a single strophe, = antistr. 1422—1441. The lyric verses 1407, 1413—4, and 1419—1421, correspond respectively with 1428, 1433—4, and 1439—1441: for these, see Metrical Analysis.

1398 Electra hastens out of the house. She performs the part of an ἐξάγγελος, so far as to describe the situation at this moment in the house: then Clytaemnestra's cry is heard, like that of the dying king in Aesch. *Ag.* 1343 ff.

1399 τελοῦσι, fut.

1400 f. τάφον: cp. 1140 n.—λέβητα, the urn: cp. Aesch. *Ag.* 444 σποδοῦ γεμίζων λέβητας εὐθέτου.—κοσμεῖ. In *Il.* 23. 253 f. the golden urn containing the bones of Patroclus is 'covered with a linen veil.' In *Il.* 24. 796 the urn with Hector's ashes is 'shrouded in soft purple robes.' Some such 'dressing' is denoted by κοσμεῖ here; but wreaths of flowers may also be meant.

1404 Clytaemnestra's voice is heard from within.

αἰαῖ· ἰὼ στέγαι. Dindorf (*Metra* p. 106) reads these words as a dochmiac (◡◡◡–◡–): Nauck and Wecklein take them as an iambic tripody (––◡–◡–). The latter view seems correct. The hiatus after αἰαῖ is excused by the pause.

1407 ἀνήκουστα, lit., 'not to be heard': then, 'dreadful to hear'; cp. ἄρρητα. So Eur. *Hipp.* 362 ἔκλυες, ὦ, | ἀνήκουστα τᾶς | τυράννου πάθη μέλεα θρεομένας.

1410 ἰδού, referring to *sound* (as we could say, 'there!'): so *Ai.* 870 ἰδού, | δοῦπον αὖ κλύω τινά.—μάλ' αὖ: *O. C.* 1477 ἔα, ἰδοὺ μάλ' αὖθις ἀμφίσταται | διαπρύσιος ὄτοβος.

1411 f. ἐκ σέθεν: for ἐκ, cp. *O. C.* 51 κοὐκ ἄτιμος ἔκ γ' ἐμοῦ φανεῖ.—ὁ γεννήσας πατήρ: cp. 261: *Tr.* 311 ὁ φιτύσας πατήρ.

1413 f. The traditional reading φθίνει φθίνει is vindicated, and all difficulty is removed, by the slight change of σε to σοι. The μοῖρα καθαμερία is the fate which has afflicted the house day by day. In the only other place where καθαμέριος occurs (Eur.

Ph. 229), it has this sense, 'daily'; nor is any other, indeed, tenable. (Cp. 259 κατ' ἦμαρ.) This fate is now being extinguished (φθίνει) by the righteous act of vengeance, which, according to the poet's view in this play, closes the misfortunes of the race (cp. 1510 τῇ νῦν ὁρμῇ τελεωθέν). For φθίνειν said of an *evil* which wanes or dies out, cp. fr. 718 (ὕβρις).. ἀνθεῖ τε καὶ φθίνει πάλιν.

1415 f. Cp. Aesch. *Ag.* 1343 ΑΓ. ὤμοι, πέπληγμαι καιρίαν πληγὴν ἔσω ... 1345 ὤμοι μάλ' αὖθις, δευτέραν πεπληγμένος.— διπλῆν: cp. *O. C.* 544 δευτέραν ἔπαισας.

εἰ γὰρ Αἰγίσθῳ γ' ὁμοῦ (adv.). The dat., suggested by ὤμοι, depends on the notion which that exclamation implies; as if (*e.g.*) κακὸν ἥκει μοι were followed by εἰ γὰρ Αἰγίσθῳ γ' ὁμοῦ ἦκεν.—The reading Αἰγίσθῳ θ' ὁμοῦ, though not impossible, is very awkward. The sense would be: 'Oh that thou wert crying,—"and woe to Aegisthus also"!'

1417 f. τελοῦσ' ἀραί, 'are doing their work.' τελοῦσι is transitive, though the object (τὸ ἔργον) is not expressed.—οἱ.. κείμενοι, Agamemnon: for the plur. (like οἱ.. θανόντες, 1421), cp. 146 γονέων, n.—ὑπαί: 711 n.

1419 f. παλίρρυτον: cp. 246 πάλιν | δώσουσ' ἀντιφόνους δίκας: *Od.* 1. 379 παλίντιτα ἔργα, deeds of retribution.—ὑπεξαιροῦσι: cp. Eur. *Hipp.* 633 ὄλβον δωμάτων ὑπεξελών.

1422 f. Enter Orestes and Pylades from the house.

καὶ μήν: 78 n.—στάζει θυηλῆς: the gen. depends on the notion of fulness; cp. *O. C.* 16 βρύων | δάφνης: fr. 264 ἀραχνᾶν βρίθει.— The θυηλή is φόνος. Cp. Shakesp. *H. IV.*, pt. 1, act 4, sc. 1, 113, 'They come like sacrifices in their trim, | And to the fire-eyed maid of smoky war | All hot and bleeding will we offer them.'

ψέγειν, Erfurdt's correction of λέγειν, deserves the favour which it has found with almost all editors from Hermann onwards. If λέγειν be sound, the sense must be, 'utterance fails me,'—at a moment so terrible. But οὐδ' ἔχω λέγειν is not equivalent to οὐδ' ἔχω φωνεῖν, nor, again, to οὐδ' ἔχω τί λέγω (or τί φῶ).

1424 κυρεῖτε is a certain correction of κυρεῖ. With Hermann's conjecture, κυρεῖ δὲ, the sense would be, 'now, how goes it?'—δέ giving animation to the question.

1425 ἐθέσπισεν: cp. 36 f. Contrast the calm confidence of Orestes with his words of anguish in Aesch. *Ch.* 1016 f., ἀλγῶ μὲν ἔργα καὶ πάθος γένος τε πᾶν, | ἄζηλα νίκης τῆσδ' ἔχων μιάσματα.

1426 f. ἐκφοβοῦ.. ὥς: 1309 n. The sense of λῆμα is not necessarily either good or bad; thus Pind. *P.* 8. 44 τὸ γενναῖον .. | .. λῆμα: *O. C.* 960 λῆμ᾽ ἀναιδές: though it generally implies at least a *strong* spirit.

1429 ἐκ προδήλου, like ἐκ τοῦ ἐμφανέος (Her. 4. 120), ἐκ τοῦ προφανοῦς (Thuc. 3. 43 § 3): ἐκ being used as above in 455, 725. In this adverbial phrase the adj. is merely a stronger δῆλος, as in *Ai.* 1311 θανεῖν προδήλως ('before all eyes').

1430 ὦ παῖδες: cp. 1220 ὦ παῖ, n.—οὐκ ἄψορρον, sc. εἴσιτε, into the house. Cp. *Ai.* 369 οὐκ ἐκτὸς ἄψορρον ἐκνεμεῖ πόδα;

1431 ἐφ᾽ ἡμῖν, 'in our power'; cp. *O. C.* 66 ἢ 'πὶ τῷ πλήθει λόγος; *Ph.* 1003 μὴ 'πὶ τῷδ᾽ ἔστω τάδε. The sense of ἐφ᾽ ἡμῖν is the reason for giving the words to Electra, and not, as L does (cr. n.), to Orestes.

1433 βᾶτε κατ᾽ ἀντιθύρων, 'make for the vestibule.' If the words are sound, κατά, lit., 'down upon,' denotes *the point on which* the rapid movement is directed. The peculiarity here is that, while the movement is literal, the descent is figurative. I do not know any real parallel for this use of κατά. It seems to justify some suspicion of the text.

Here, τὰ ἀντίθυρα seems to mean, as in the *Odyssey*, a place close to the doors; probably just *inside* of them, and (from that point of view) 'over against them'; a *vestibule*, or entrance-hall. Cp. 328 πρὸς θυρῶνος ἐξόδοις. As προθυρών was a collateral form of πρόθυρον (*Etym. Magn.* 806. 4, etc.), ἀντιθυρών may have been such a form of ἀντίθυρον. If so, the desirable accus. for κατά could be at once obtained by κατ᾽ ἀντιθυρών'.

1434 εὖ θέμενοι: cp. *O. T.* 633 νεῖκος εὖ θέσθαι: fr. 324 ἦν παρὸν θέσθαι καλῶς | αὐτός τις αὐτῷ τὴν βλάβην προσθῇ φέρων.—τάδ᾽ ὡς πάλιν, sc. εὖ θῆσθε. For πάλιν as = 'in their turn,' cp. 371.

1435 ᾗ νοεῖς, lit., hasten 'on the path that thou hast in view,'—*i.e.*, to the execution of the plan within the house. Cp. *Ai.* 868 πᾷ γὰρ οὐκ ἔβαν ἐγώ;

The ground for giving the words ᾗ νοεῖς to Electra, rather than to Orestes, is not merely that her share in this verse then becomes the same as in v. 1415. The better reasons are these: (1) the simple τελοῦμεν is thus far more forcible. (2) ᾗ νοεῖς, if said by Orestes, would be a feeble reference to the wish of the Chorus; as said by Electra, it is a natural comment on τελοῦμεν.

1436 καὶ δὴ βέβηκα: cp. 558 n.: *Tr.* 345 καὶ δὴ βεβᾶσι. Exeunt Orestes and Pylades.

1437—1441 These verses are antistrophic to 1417—1421. δι' ὠτός implies gentle, whispering tones; cp. Theocr. 14. 27 χἀμῖν τοῦτο δι' ὠτὸς ἔγεντο πόχ' ἄσυχον οὕτως.—ὡς ἠπίως, '*as if* kindly,' 'with seeming gentleness': not like ὡς ἐτητύμως in 1452.—λαθραῖον, as epith. of ἀγῶνα, has a predicative force,— 'that he may rush upon his doom without foreseeing it'; it may thus be represented by an adv., 'blindly.'—δίκας ἀγῶνα. δίκη is the just retribution which awaits him. δίκης ἀγών is the struggle which this retribution brings upon him,—his conflict with the avenging power.

After 1441 Aegisthus enters.

1444 ναυαγίοις: cp. 730, where, however, it refers to the general wreck of chariots. Here it ought to denote the later and independent disaster, which affected the chariot of Orestes only.

1445 σέ τοι: cp. *Ant.* 441.—κρίνω = ἀνακρίνω, 'question': *Tr.* 314 τί δ' ἄν με καὶ κρίνοις;

1448 f. συμφορᾶς, which can denote either good fortune (1230) or evil, suits the purposed ambiguity. For the ear of Aegisthus, her reply means: 'Of course I know; else I should be a stranger to the fortune of my nearest *kinswoman*,'—viz., her mother. She leaves him to decide whether she means that Clytaemnestra is afflicted or rejoiced by the news. And meanwhile ἡ συμφορὰ τῆς φιλάτης has a further meaning—Clytaemnestra's death—which he cannot yet surmise.

Possibly this is the only ambiguity intended. But τῆς συμφορᾶς.. τῶν ἐμῶν τῆς φιλάτης might be genitive of ἡ συμφορὰ τῶν ἐμῶν ἡ φιλάτη, '*the most welcome fortune* of my kindred,'—*i.e.*, 'my brother's return.' Cp. 1273 φιλάταν | ὁδόν. To intend this as an inner meaning would certainly be quite in the manner of Sophocles.

1451 φίλης γὰρ προξένου κατήνυσαν. The ostensible meaning is that they have *reached her house*, οἶκον being understood. Cp. *Ai.* 607 ἀνύσειν | .. Ἀιδαν: *Ant.* 804 τὸν παγκοίτην .. θάλαμον | .. ἀνύτουσαν. *O. C.* 1562 ἐξανύσαι | .. τὰν .. | νεκρῶν πλάκα. The hidden meaning is, φίλης προξένου κατήνυσαν φόνον: they have *accomplished her murder*. To the ear of the audience, the nature of the ellipse would be plain enough. Whitelaw's rendering is, 'To the heart of their hostess they have found their way.'

1452 ἦ καί: 314 n.—ὡς ἐτητύμως, like ὡς ἀληθῶς, etc. This emphasising use of ὡς with adverbs of the positive degree was probably developed out of its use with superlatives, as ὡς μάλιστα.

1453 οὔκ, ἀλλὰ κἀπέδειξαν. The added words, οὐ λόγῳ μόνον, represent the sense of the clause suppressed after οὔκ: οὐ μόνον ἤγγειλαν, ἀλλὰ κ.τ.λ. Cp. Ar. *Ran.* 103 HP. σὲ δὲ ταῦτ' ἀρέσκει; ΔΙ. μὴ ἀλλὰ πλεῖν ἢ μαίνομαι: *i.e.*, μὴ (λέξῃς ὅτι) ἀρέσκει, ἀλλὰ κ.τ.λ.

1454 πάρεστ' is meant by Aegisthus to be impersonal; but suggests to the spectators another meaning ('is he here?'). —ὥστε: cp. *Ph.* 656 ἆρ' ἔστιν ὥστε κἀγγύθεν θέαν λαβεῖν;— κἀμφανῆ μαθεῖν, *sc.* αὐτόν, Orestes. The ambiguous gender of ἐμφανῆ suits the situation.

1455 πάρεστι δῆτα. The nom. ἄζηλος θέα renders it better to understand ὁ νεκρός with πάρεστι than to take the verb impersonally. For δῆτα, cp. 843 : καὶ μάλ', 1178.

1456 ἡ πολλὰ χαίρειν μ' εἶπας, lit., 'thou hast bidden me rejoice much,' *i.e.*, greeted me with most joyful news. The words would more usually mean 'a long farewell,' as in Eur. *Hipp.* 113 τὴν σὴν δὲ Κύπριν πόλλ' ἐγὼ χαίρειν λέγω.

1457 While τυγχάνοι has the support of L, the more prevalent reading τυγχάνει is the better here. She means, 'Rejoice, if this *is* matter for joy,' rather than, 'You might (or would) rejoice, if it *were*' such.

1458 κἀναδεικνύναι πύλας, if right, is a pregnant phrase, 'open the gates and show the interior.' Ar. *Nub.* 302 ἵνα | μυστοδόκος δόμος | ἐν τελέταις ἁγίαις ἀναδείκνυται. Bold as it is, I incline to believe that it is sound. No probable emendation has yet been made.

1459 Μυκηναίοισιν, the townsfolk : Ἀργείοις, the people of the neighbouring district : see 4 n., and cp. 160 ἁ κλεινὰ | γᾶ.. Μυκηναίων.—πᾶσιν: cp. *O. T.* 1287 βοᾷ διοίγειν κλῆθρα καὶ δηλοῦν τινα | τοῖς πᾶσι Καδμείοισι τὸν πατροκτόνον.

1460 f. ἐλπίσιν.. ἀνδρὸς: for the gen., cp. 857 n.

1462 f. στόμια, poet. plur.; so Aesch. *Ag.* 237 χαλινῶν. Cp. Plut. *Compar. Pericl. et Fabii* 1 σπαργῶντι τῷ δήμῳ χαλινὸν ἐμβαλεῖν ὕβρεως.—φύσῃ φρένας: *O. C.* 804 οὐδὲ τῷ χρόνῳ φύσας φανεῖ | φρένας ποτ'.

1464 f. καὶ δὴ κ.τ.λ.: lit., 'already my part is being performed.' For τἀπ' ἐμοῦ cp. *O. C.* 1682 τἀπὸ σοῦ βραδύνεται. She refers ostensibly to what he has just said : 'I, at least, am already resolved to be loyal and docile.' Her secret meaning is, 'My part in the plan of vengeance is being accomplished.'

She is luring him to his fate : cp. 1438 τἀνθάδ' ἂν μέλοιτ' ἐμοί.—τελεῖται is pres. There is no certain instance in Attic of τελοῦμαι as fut. pass.—τῷ.. χρόνῳ : for the art., cp. 1013.—συμφέρειν τοῖς κρείσσοσιν, to agree with them, to live in concord with them. Cp. Eur. *Med.* 13 αὐτή τε πάντα συμφέρουσ' Ἰάσονι. Ar. *Lys.* 166 ἀνήρ, ἐὰν μὴ τῇ γυναικὶ συμφέρῃ. This sense comes from that of 'sharing a burden' (946), so that it resembles our phrase, 'pull together.' Here it suits her inner meaning,—that she is working with those who now are the stronger (*i.e.*, the avengers).

As Electra utters these words, the central doors are opened, and the eccyclema is pushed forward. This was a small and low stage. A corpse is seen upon it, the face and outlines concealed by a covering. Near it stand Orestes and Pylades— the 'Phocians' whom Aegisthus seeks. The eccyclema remains displayed to the end, and at v. 1507 Orestes and Pylades go out behind it.

The corpse here is an effigy, like that of Haemon in *Ant.* 1261 ff. The deuteragonist, who had played Clytaemnestra, is now playing Orestes.

1466 f. δέδορκα φάσμ' κ.τ.λ.: 'I behold that which has not fallen without the jealousy of the gods.' Aegisthus is not openly exulting here ; he veils his joy in specious language, for he is in public, and speaks before hearers whom he distrusts. He affects to think that the gods have struck down his enemy. The meaning implied by φθόνου is that Orestes had incurred the divine displeasure by unnatural threats against his mother and his step-father (779 δεῖν' ἐπηπείλει τελεῖν).

The invocation, ὦ Ζεῦ, at once indicates the sense of φθόνου as = the *divine* jealousy. For that sense, see on *Ph.* 776 τὸν φθόνον δὲ πρόσκυσον.—The word φάσμα is chosen on account of δέδορκα, in place of a word like σῶμα, or πτῶμα, adapted to πεπτωκός.

ἔπεστι : cp. Aesch. *Eum.* 542 ποινὰ γὰρ ἐπέσται : Xen. *Cyr.* 6. 2. 33 ἔπεστι γάρ τις αἰσχύνη.—νέμεσις, the divine resentment; *O.C.* 1753 πενθεῖν οὐ χρή· νέμεσις γάρ. Nemesis is not here so definitely a person as above in 792.—οὐ λέγω, *indictum volo.* Aesch. *Eum.* 866 ἐνοικίου δ' ὄρνιθος οὐ λέγω μάχην.

Aegisthus corrects himself with hypocritical piety ; it is as if he said, 'but it is not for me to judge my fellow-mortal.'

1469 τὸ συγγενές : the neuter gender suits the intended ambiguity.—τοι emphasises τὸ συγγενές, as γε or γοῦν could do, but has also a sententious force, implying that such a tribute to kinship is a duty. Thus it suits the pious tone of the speaker: 'If he was my enemy, still he was my kinsman.'

κἀπ' ἐμοῦ = καὶ ἀπ' ἐμοῦ, from my side, on my part: cp. 433: *O. C.* 1289 f. καὶ ταῦτ' ἀφ' ὑμῶν .. βουλήσομαι | .. κυρεῖν ἐμοί.
—θρήνων τύχῃ: *Ai.* 924 ὡς καὶ παρ' ἐχθροῖς ἄξιος θρήνων τυχεῖν.

1470 f. βάσταζ', *sc.* τὸ κάλυμμα, 'handle it,' *i.e.*, 'lift it': cp. 905 n.—οὐκ ἐμὸν, since Orestes is supposed to be a Phocian stranger.—ταῦθ', 'these relics'; he avoids saying either τήνδ' or τόνδ'.

1472 f. σὺ δέ, Electra.—εἴ που κατ' οἶκόν μοι. The words mean properly, 'if she is anywhere in the house *for* me,' *i.e.*, 'so that I can see her.' The enclitic μοι, thus placed, could not go with κάλει.

1474 μηκέτ' ἄλλοσε σκόπει: cp. 1225 n.
Aegisthus removes the face-cloth from the corpse.

1475 τίνα φοβεῖ κ.τ.λ. As Aegisthus gazes in terror and horror on Clytaemnestra's face, Orestes says, 'Whom dost thou fear? Who is it that thou dost not know?' *i.e.*, 'Why should *that* face terrify thee? Is it not familiar?'

1476 f. ἀρκυστάτοις. The ἄρκυς (*cassis*) was a hunting tunnel-net, ending in a pouch (κεκρύφαλος, Xen. *Cyneg.* 6 § 7). It was meant to receive the game when driven to the extremity of the enclosed ground. ἀρκύστατα (ἄρκυς, ἵστημι) meant properly such nets *when set up*; and ἀρκυστάσιον, or ἀρκυστασία, is the enclosure formed by them (Xen. *Cyneg.* 6 § 6). Cp. Aesch. *Ag.* 1374 πῶς γάρ τις ἐχθροῖς ἐχθρὰ πορσύνων, φίλοις | δοκοῦσιν εἶναι, πημονῆς ἀρκύστατ' ἂν | φράξειεν ὕψος κρεῖσσον ἐκπηδήματος;

For μέσοις, cp. Aesch. *Eum.* 112 ἐκ μέσων ἀρκυστάτων | ὤρουσεν: Eur. *El.* 965 καλῶς ἄρ' ἄρκυν ἐς μέσην πορεύεται.— πέπτωκα with ἐν (instead of εἰς with acc.), as Eur. *H.F.* 1091 ὡς ἐν κλύδωνι καὶ φρενῶν ταράγματι | πέπτωκα δεινῷ.

1477 πάλαι goes with αἰσθάνει (lit., 'hast thou not long since been aware?'): not with ἀνταυδᾷς. For πάλαι referring to a recent moment, cp. 676.

1478 In ἀνταυδᾷς, a compound found only here, ἀντί has the same force as in ἀντονομάζω, Thuc. 6. 4. § 6 τὴν πόλιν (Rhegium) .. οἰκίσας Μεσσήνην...ἀντωνόμασε, 'changed its name' to Messene. Aegisthus 'changes the designation' of living men, and speaks of them ἴσα τοῖς θανοῦσιν, in the same terms which would properly be applied to the dead. Thus the strict

Notes 177

sense of the words is, 'Thou perversely (ἀντ-) speakest of the living as if they were dead.' The acc. ζῶντας stands with ἀνταυδᾷς as with the simple αὐδᾶν (e.g., Eur. *Hipp.* 582 αὐδῶν δεινὰ πρόσπολον κακά). If ἀνταυδᾷς meant 'reply to,' or 'speak face to face with,' it would require the dative.

Editors from Brunck onwards have been nearly unanimous in accepting ζῶντας, Tyrwhitt's correction of the MS. ζῶν τοῖς.

1479 f. ξυνῆκα: for the aor., cp. 668 n.—Cp. Aesch. *Ch.* 886 OI. τὸν ζῶντα καίνειν τοὺς τεθνηκότας λέγω. | ΚΛ. οἶ 'γώ, ξυνῆκα τοὔπος ἐξ αἰνιγμάτων.—οὐ γὰρ ἔσθ' ὅπως .. οὐκ: cp. *O. C.* 97: *O. T.* 1058.

1481 καὶ μάντις: 'and, though so good a prophet, (yet) thou wast deceived so long?' The interrogative καί (928, 1046) is here nearly = κᾆτα.

1482 f. πάρες κἂν σμικρὸν εἰπεῖν. Here κἂν is most simply explained as καὶ ἐάν, sc. παρῇς. Cp. Ar. *Ach.* 1021 μέτρησον εἰρήνης τί μοι, κἂν πέντ' ἔτη, sc. μετρήσῃς.

1485 f. βροτῶν is a partitive gen., on which θνήσκειν ὁ μέλλων depends (cp. Thuc. 4. 102 τῶν ἄλλων τὸν βουλόμενον, etc.); though the sense is not affected in a translation if it be rendered as a gen. absol.

σὺν κακοῖς μεμιγμένων, 'involved in miseries,' implying here, 'crimes, and their consequences.' Cp. *Od.* 20. 203 (ἄνδρας) μισγέμεναι κακότητι. For σὺν (which need not be taken as a case of tmesis), cp. Pind. *N.* 3. 77 μεμιγμένον μέλι λευκῷ | σὺν γάλακτι. So Pind. *I.* 3. 3 ἄξιος εὐλογίας ἀστῶν μεμῖχθαι.

θνήσκειν: for the pres. inf. with μέλλω, cp. 305.—τοῦ χρόνου, the time implied in μηκύνειν—to be taken with τί κέρδος ('what profit from the delay?').

Aegisthus has appealed to mercy, asking for a brief respite. Electra fears that her brother may relent. What gain, she asks, would such a respite be, even to the doomed wretch himself? And her own feeling requires his instant death.

1488 f. ταφεῦσιν, birds and dogs: Aesch. *Th.* 1020 ὑπ' οἰωνῶν... | ταφέντ' ἀτίμως.—ἄποπτον ἡμῶν, far from our sight; the gen. as after words of 'distance from' (*O. T.* 762). Cp. *Od.* 3. 258, where Nestor says that, if Menelaüs on his return had found Aegisthus still living,—τῷ κέ οἱ οὐδὲ θανόντι χυτὴν ἐπὶ γαῖαν ἔχευαν, | ἀλλ' ἄρα τόν γε κύνες τε καὶ οἰωνοὶ κατέδαψαν | κείμενον ἐν πεδίῳ ἑκὰς ἄστεος. Pausan. 2. 16 § 7 Κλυταιμνήστρα δὲ ἐτάφη καὶ Αἴγισθος ὀλίγον ἀπωτέρω τοῦ τείχους,

178 *Electra*

ἐντὸς δὲ ἀπηξιώθησαν, ἔνθα Ἀγαμέμνων τε αὐτὸς ἔκειτο καὶ οἱ σὺν
αὐτῷ φονευθέντες.

1492 ἀγών, *discrimen*, the issue: cp. *O. C.* 587 : Eur. *Ph.*
588 μῆτερ, οὐ λόγων ἔθ᾽ ἀγών.

1494 πρόχειρος.. κτανεῖν. In its primary and usual sense,
πρόχειρος denotes what is ready in the hand (1116). Here it
passes into a wholly different sense, applied to a person whose
hand is 'forward' or ready, as πρόθυμος is one whose spirit is
forward. Cp. Eur. *H. F.* 161 τῇ φυγῇ πρόχειρος ἦν, 'prompt
for flight' (= φεύγειν).

1495 μὴ τάσσε: cp. *Ant.* 664 τοὐπιτάσσειν τοῖς κρατύνου-
σιν.—ἔνθαπερ, *i.e.* (ἐκεῖσε) ἔνθαπερ : cp. 1099. The place meant
is the μέγαρον of the house : see on 268 f.

1497 f. πᾶσ᾽ ἀνάγκη, as *O. T.* 986, Her. **2**. 22, Plat. *Phaedo*
p. 67 A, etc.—τά τ᾽ ὄντα καὶ μέλλοντα: for the omission of the
art. with the second partic., cp. 991 n.

Aegisthus means : 'Must this house witness, not only those
sorrows of our family which exist already, but those others
which are to come, if I am slain?' He speaks of his impending
doom as if it were due, not to his own crimes, but to the
working of the hereditary ἀρά, and implies that it will be
followed by other deeds of bloodshed. In saying Πελοπιδῶν,
he appeals, as a last hope, to family sympathies.

1499 τὰ γοῦν σ᾽: σά, though emphatic, is elided; see on
O. T. 64 πόλιν τε κἀμὲ καὶ σ᾽ ὁμοῦ στένει.—ἄκρος: cp. Aesch.
Ag. 1130 οὐ κομπάσαιμ᾽ ἂν θεσφάτων γνώμων ἄκρος | εἶναι.

1500 τὴν τέχνην, *i.e.*, τὴν μαντικήν. Agamemnon fell into
the snare laid for him : *Ag.* 911 ἐς δῶμ᾽ ἄελπτον ὡς ἂν ἡγῆται
Δίκη.—Cp. *Ai.* 1121 οὐ γὰρ βάναυσον τὴν τέχνην ἐκτησάμην.

1501 Cp. *O. C.* 1628 πάλαι δὴ τἀπὸ σοῦ βραδύνεται.

1502 The double change of person within the verse (Or.
—Aeg.—Or.) is rare. As G. Wolff observes, there is no
instance of it in Aesch.; in Soph. the only other examples
occur in the two latest plays, *O. C.* 832, *Ph.* 810, 814, 816, at
moments of high excitement.

ἔρφ᾽. The word is always so written here, as if Orestes could
foresee that Aegisthus would utter an aspirated word. Similar
instances occur elsewhere. In the theatre, we must suppose, the
actor said ἕρπε at full length : and possibly the poet so wrote it.

1503 f. ἦ μὴ φύγῃ σε; '(dost thou do this), lest..?' Cp.
O. T. 1012 ἦ μὴ μίασμα τῶν φυτευσάντων λάβῃς;—μὲν οὖν :
O. T. 705.—καθ᾽ ἡδονὴν θάνῃς; *i.e.*, with such comfort as would

be given by permission to choose the place or mode of death. Cp. 1493.

1505—1507 The imperf. χρῆν, with εἶναι, implies that, though it ought to be so, it is not. The sense is, in substance, what might be expressed by a conditional sentence, ἥδε δίκη ἦν ἂν τοῖς πᾶσιν, εἰ τὸ εἰκὸς ἔπαθον.—εὐθὺς, immediately after the crime in each case; Aegisthus has enjoyed too long an impunity. Cp. 13 f. n.—θέλει is better here than θέλοι, since it suggests more clearly the reference to the actual case of Aegisthus.—τοῖς πᾶσιν...ὅστις: cp. *Ai.* 760, where ὅστις refers to σώματα in 758: *Ant.* 709, where οὗτοι follows ὅστις in 707.

πράσσειν γε: γε emphasises, not πράσσειν, but rather the whole sentence, and might have immediately followed ὅστις, if metre had allowed.

κτείνειν, rather than θνῄσκειν, because the speaker is himself the executioner. For the emphatic place of the word, cp. 957 Αἴγισθον.—τὸ πανοῦργον, equiv. in sense to οἱ πανοῦργοι: cp. 972 n.: Thuc. 1. 13 τὸ ληστικὸν καθῄρουν.—Shakesp. *Meas. for Meas.* act 2, sc. 2, 91: 'Those many had not dared to do that evil, | If the first that did the edict infringe | Had answer'd for his deed.'

Orestes drives Aegisthus into the house.

1508 ὦ σπέρμ' Ἀτρέως. The dynasty of the Atreidae (δεσπόται οἱ πάλαι, 764) is about to be restored in the person of the rightful heir, Orestes (162), who displaces the usurper Aegisthus, the representative of the Thyestidae.

1509 δι' ἐλευθερίας.. ἐξῆλθες, come forth *in* freedom. For διά denoting the state, cp. Thuc. 6. 34 § 2 ἀεὶ διὰ φόβου εἰσί. The phrase here is in one respect peculiar. When the verb denotes *motion*, διά in this idiom usu. denotes a course of action, and not a state; *e.g.*, Thuc. 6. 60 § 3 διὰ δίκης ἐλθεῖν, Her. 6. 9 διὰ μάχης ἐλεύσονται.

1510 ὁρμῇ, the enterprise of the avengers against the tyrants. Cp. Xen. *An.* 3. 1. 10 οὐ γὰρ ᾔδει τὴν ἐπὶ βασιλέα ὁρμήν ('the purpose to attack him').—τελεωθέν, 'consummated,' 'perfected'; *i.e.*, 'made completely prosperous.' The word is applied to those who attain maturity in body and mind; Plat. *Rep.* 487 A τελειωθεῖσι.. παιδείᾳ τε καὶ ἡλικίᾳ.

This play contains no presage of trouble to come, and fitly ends with the word τελεωθέν. Contrast the closing words of the *Choephori* (1075 f.): ποῖ δῆτα κρανεῖ, ποῖ καταλήξει | μετακοιμισθὲν μένος ἄτης;

INDEXES.

I. GREEK.

The number denotes the verse, in the note on which the word or matter is illustrated. When the reference is to a *page*, p. is prefixed to the number.)(means, 'as distinguished from.'

186 *Indexes*

λέβης, 1401
λείπεσθαι γνώμης, 474 : λείπω, intrans., 514 : λελείμμεθον, form of, 950
λεύκιππος, 706
λῆμα, 1427
λήσομαι not passive, 1248
Λίβυες, Cyrenaic Greeks, 702
λιπαρής, devout, 1378
λουτρά = χοαί, 84
λόχοι of the Erinys, 490
λύειν, to remove (a trouble), 939 : to release from trouble, 1005
Λύκειος, 7
λυπεῖν ἑαυτόν, 363

μά, οὐ, with a second negative, 626 : μὰ followed by ἀλλά, 881 : omitted, 1063
μακρὰν λέγειν, 1259
μάλ' αὖ, 1410
μάλιστα πάντων, in reply, 665 : μάλιστα with οἶμαι, 932
μανθάνειν with simple gen., 565
μασχαλίζω, 445
μάτην, 'falsely,' 63
μέγα εἰπεῖν, etc., of irreverent speech, 830
μέγιστος φίλος, 46
μέλειν, pers. use of, 342 : μελέσθω, impers., 75
μελέτωρ, 846
μέλλω with pres. inf., 305, 1486
μέλος ἀπὸ σκηνῆς, 1232
μεμιγμένος σὺν κακοῖς, 1485
μέν omitted, 105, 267 : emphasises pron., 185, 251 : μὲν οὖν, where each word has its separate force, 459 : as = 'nay rather,' 1503
μεταβάλλεσθαί τί τινος, 1261
μετέχειν τῶν ἴσων, 1168
μετιέναι, to pursue, 477
μή, crasis of, with ἐκ, 398 : generic, with fut. indic., after ἔνθα, 380 : after ὅς γε (causal), 911 : placed after verb with εἰ, 993 : reiterated, 1208 : with inf. after verb of believing, etc., 908 : μή πω, ironical, 403 : μή τοί γε, 518
μηδέν, ἔρχεσθαι ἐπί, 1000 : μηδέν, ὁ, of the dead, combined with τὸ μηδέν, 1166

μηνίω of divine anger, 570
μάστωρ, 275, 603
μοι, ethic, 143 : with καί, at beginning of clause, 117
μόλις, *aegre*, 575
μυδαλέος, ῦ in, 166
Μυκῆναι and Μυκήνη, 9

ναυάγια, fig., 730
νεακόνητον αἷμα, 1394
νέμειν, to assign as due (Διΐ), 176
Νέμεσις, 792 : not distinctly personified, 1467
νεώρης, 901
νικᾶν in argument, 253
νίκη)(κράτος, 85
νιν as acc. neut. plur., 436
νομίζεσθαι, pass., of ritual, 327
νῦν = 'as it was,' followed by νῦν = 'now,' 1334 : νυν (ῠ) before a vowel, 616 : νῦν δέ, repeated after parenthesis, 786 : νῦν τε καὶ πάλαι, 676 : νῦν τε καὶ τότε, 907
νύσσα, in hippodrome, 720

ξενίζω said of Ares, 96
ξένος = 'in a foreign land,' 865

ὁ as demonstr. pron., followed by γάρ, 45
ὅδε after a relat. pron., 441 : with ref. to what precedes, 293 : with κεῖνος, 665
ὁδοί of a single journey, 68 : ὁδόν as cogn. acc. (with φανῆναι), 1273
ὅθι in Tragedy, 709
οἱ (dat.) with hiatus before it, 195 : οἱ κατ' οἶκον = οἱ οἰκέται, 1147
οἰκεῖος, caused by one's self, 215
οἰκονομῶ, 190
οἶος doubled (in a contrast), 751
οἰχνῶ, 165
οἰωνός, οἶ in, 1058
ὄλβιος defined by relat. clause, 160
ὁλκοί, sense of, 863
ὀλολυγμός, usu. joyous, 750
ὀλοός in act. sense, 843
ὅμαιμος with a further definition, 12, 325
ὁμιλία in periphrasis, 418
ὄμμα, 'face' or 'form,' 903
ὁμοκλήσας, 712

ὄντα τε, τά, καὶ τὰ ἀπόντα, 305
ὅποι γῆς (φέρει), fig., 922
ὅπως, final, with past tenses, 1134:
   ὅπως with (1) fut. indic., (2) aor.
   or pres. subjunct., 956
ὅρα in warning, 945: ὅρα μὴ τιθῇς
   and τίθης, 580: ὁρᾶν πρός τι, of
   an admiring gaze, 972: ὁρᾷς; in
   reproach, 628
ὀργή, meanings of, 1283
ὀρθοῦσθαι of a prosperous course,
   742
ὅρκον προστιθέναι, 47
ὁρμὴ of an enterprise, 1510
ὄρνις with ῑ, 149
ὅς as rel. to τοιοῦτος, 35: with
   causal force, 160, 261
ὅσιον, τὸ, and θέμις, 432
ὅστις with verb understood (εἴη), 257
ὅτε, causal, 38
οὐ after ὥστε with inf., 780: in
   dependence on εἰ, 244: after verb,
   905: after noun, 1036: οὐ γὰρ
   δή...γε, 1020: οὐ δή ποτε...; 1108,
   1180: οὐ λέγω, *indictum volo*,
   1467: οὐ μά, followed by a second
   negative, 626: οὐ μὴ and aor.,com-
   bined with fut. ind., 42: with fut.
   indic., 1052: οὐ φήμ' ἐάσειν, 1209:
   οὐκ, ἀλλὰ κ.τ.λ., 1453: οὐκ ἔσθ'
   ὅπως οὐ, 1479: οὐκ ἔστιν, in rejecting an idea, 448: οὐκ ἔχει λόγον,
   impers., 466: οὐκ ὤν=ψευδής,
   584
οὐδέ=ἀλλ' οὐ, 132, 1034
οὐδέν εἰμι, 677: οὐδὲν ὤν, of the
   dead, 244, 1129
οὔκουν, interrogative, 795
οὕνεκα at an interval after its case,
   579: ='so far as concerns,' 387
οὔτε...τε, 350, 1078
οὕτω δ' ὅπως, elliptical, 1296
οὐχ ὅπως, 796
ὄφρα, 225
ὄχοι of one chariot, 727

πάγκαρπα θύματα, 634
πάγκοινος, epith. of Hades, 138
παγχρύσεος, 510
παιδοποιεῖν, 589
παίζειν ref. to hunting, 567
παῖς, usage of, 1220

πάλαι of a recent moment, 676,
   1477
παλαμναῖος, 587
πάλιν βουλεύομαι = μεταβ., 1046:
   πάλιν='in recompense,' 245
παλίρρυτος, 1420
πάμψυχος, 841
πᾶν, 'anything,' 1022: πᾶν ἔργον,
   in bad sense, 615: πᾶν λέγειν,
   631
πάνδημος πόλις, 982
παννυχίς, 92
πάνσυρτος, 851
πάντα, adv., with adj., 301
πανώλης, 544
παρ' αὐτοῖς opposed to ἐν αὐτοῖς,
   1329: παρ' οὐδὲν κήδεσθαι τοῦ
   βίου, 1327: παρὰ with acc., denoting extent, 183: παρά τινος,
   on one's part, 469
παράγειν, to delude, 855
παραστάς (partic.), 295
παρείμην (plpf. pass.), 545
παρήχησις, 210
παριέναι ἑαυτόν, 819
παρουσία, 'support,' 948: a peculiar
   use of, 1251
πᾶσ' ἀνάγκη, 1497: πᾶσα βλάβη,
   ἡ, 301
πατήρ, ὁ γεννήσας, etc., 1412
πατρῷα πήματα, sense of, 258:
   πατρῷοι θεοί, 411
πείθου)(πιθοῦ, 1015
πελᾶν, fut. of πελάζειν, 497
πέλας with παρών, 299
πέλεκυς, 99
πένθει, εἶναι ἐν, 290
περιρρεῖν, to abound, 362
περισσός with gen., 155: 'un-
   profitable,' 1241
περιστεφής with gen., 895
πικρός='to one's cost,' 470
πίπτειν ἐν τινι, 1476: πέδῳ, 747
πίστιν φέρειν, 735: πίστις='proof,'
   887
πλάθειν of conflict, 220
πλέον with ἔχθιστος (instead of
   ἐχθρός), 201
πλήν...γε, 1217
πνεῖν μένος, 610
πνοαῖς παραδιδόναι, etc., 435
ποθεινός in passive sense, 1104

πόθεν, predicative, 1191
ποῖ; = εἰς τίνα χρόνον; 958: with
  λόγων, 1174
ποῖος in a curt question, 1349
πολλά with adj. or partic. as
  = 'very,' 575
πολύς, ὁ, = ὁ πλείων, 185
πορίζω = πορεύω, 1267
πορσύνειν, 670
πότερον followed by (1) ἀλλὰ δῆτα,
  (2) ἤ..., (3) ἤ..., 537
ποῦ φρενῶν εἶ; 390
πράκτωρ, an avenger, 953
πράσσειν τὰ ἑαυτοῦ, 678
πρέπει...ὡς, 'looks like'..., 664
πρὸ τῶνδε, 'therefore,' 495
πρόθυμος with gen., 3
προνέμεσθαι, 1384
πρόξενος (ἡ), = 'hostess,' 1451
προπίπτω and προπίτνω, 1380
πρόπυλα, 1375
πρόρριζος, 511
πρὸς with acc., where a noun implies motion (τὰ...πρὸς τάφον
  κτερίσματα), 931: πρὸς αἵματος,
  1125: πρὸς εὐσέβειαν = εὐσεβῶς,
  464: πρὸς ταῦτα with imperat.,
  383
προσάπτειν of a tribute, 356
προσεῖναι of attendant circumstance,
  654
προσευρίσκω, 1352
πρόσκειμαι κακοῖς, etc., 240
προσκύσαντε (ἕδη), 1374
προστατήριος, title of Apollo, 637
προστατῶν χρόνος, ὁ, 781
προστῆναι θεόν, to approach his
  shrine, 1378: φόνου, 980
πρόσφορος, 227
πρόσχημα = σκῆψις, 525: 'glory' or
  'pride,' 682
προσώτατα and προσωτάτω, 391
προτιθέναι, present to one, 1198
προτρέπειν ἀνάγκῃ τινά, 1193
πρόχειρος, 1116, 1494
πρῶτα...εἶτα...ἔπειτα, 261
πυνθάνομαι with gen. of thing
  heard, 35
πυρά, funeral mound, 901
πω, ironical, 403
πῶλος as merely = ἵππος, 705 : special
  races for πῶλοι, *ib.*

πῶς ἄν with optat., in courteous
  inquiry, 660: πῶς γάρ (elliptical),
  before ὅς γε, 911
πως = *fere*, 372

ῥιπαὶ ἄστρων, 105

σά, elided, though emphatic, 1499
σαλεύειν of persons, 1074
σειραῖοι ἵπποι, 721
σεμναί, the Erinyes, 112
σεσωσμένος, brought safely home,
  1229
σημεῖα φαίνειν with partic., 24
σῖγα ἔχειν, 1236
σκέλη προφαίνων οὐρανῷ, 752
σμικροὶ λόγοι, 415
σοί, as = σεαυτῇ, 461
σόν, 'thy proper part,' 1215: σόν,
  τό, 'thy interest,' 251 : 'thy plea,'
  577 : σός, ὁ, = 'of which you
  speak,' 1110
σπᾶν said of passion, 561
σπείρειν, to spread a rumour, 642
στάδιον, 686
στάζειν with gen., 1423
στεροῦμαι with acc., 960
στέφειν, with offerings, 53
στήλη of the hippodrome, 720
στικτός, 'dappled,' 568
στόμαργος, 607
στόμια, fig., 1462
στρατός = λεώς, 749
στρέφεσθαι, *versari*, 516
σὺ δέ (etc.) after a vocative, 150:
  emphasising a second clause,
  though there is no contrast of
  persons, 448
συγγίγνεσθαι said of an ally, 411
συμβαίνειν, 'come to be,' with adj.,
  262
συμφέρειν, to share a burden, 946:
  τινί, to agree with, 1465
συμφορά of good fortune, 1230:
  ambiguous, 1448
σύν, pleonastic, with ξυνεῖναι, 610:
  σὺν κακῷ, 430: σύν τινι with
  μίγνυσθαι, 1485
συνάπτω intrans., 21
συνεῖναι κακοῖς (neut.), 600: τινί
  (masc.), to be one's ally, 358
συνθεὶς ἐν βραχεῖ, 673

II. ENGLISH.